Best Wishes,

Edward M. Nevins

Forces of the British Empire
1914

Also by Edward Nevins

World Without Time: The Bedouin
(with Theon Wright, Foreword by Sir John Bagot Glubb)

FORCES OF THE BRITISH EMPIRE 1914

By Edward M. Nevins

Introduction By
David G. Chandler

VANDAMERE PRESS
a division of AB Associates

Published by
Vandamere Press
A Division of AB Associates
P.O. Box 5243
Arlington, Virginia 22205
USA

Copyright © 1992 Vandamere Press

ISBN 0-918339-18-9

Library of Congress Cataloging-in-Publication Data

Nevins, Edward M., 1938-
    Forces of the British Empire—1914 / by Edward M. Nevins :
introduction by David G. Chandler.
        p. cm.
    Includes bibliographical references and index.
    ISBN 0-918339-18-9 : $65.00
    1. Great Britain—Armed Forces—Organization—History—20th
century. 2. Great Britain—Armed Forces—Uniforms—History—20th
century. 3. Great Gritain—Armed Forces—Insignia—History—20th
century. I. Title
UA647.N52 1992   92-15109
355'.00941'09041—dc20   CIP

Manufactured in the United States of America. This book is set in ITC Garamond by Scott Photographics of Riverdale, Maryland.

All rights reserved, which includes the right to reproduce this book or any portion thereof in any form whatsoever, except as provided by U.S. Copyright Law. For information contact Vandamere Press.

DEDICATION

This book is dedicated to those alumni of the Virginia Military Institute who served voluntarily in the forces of the British Empire during World War I. The rank indicated after each name is the highest attained in British or Canadian service. Of the twenty alumni who served, two were killed in action, one died of his wounds, and seven others were wounded. Decorations awarded to this group included three Military Crosses, one Military Medal, and one Distinguished Conduct Medal.

WESLEY R. ALLISON
2nd Lieutenant. Royal Flying Corps.

JOSEPH FAVRE BALDWIN
Lieutenant. Royal Army Medical Corps, attached Royal Fusiliers (City of London Regiment). Killed in action, 7 August 1918.

ARTHUR P. BARRY
Private. (Overseas service; 176th Battalion, 12th Reserve Battalion, 164th Battalion, 125th Battalion, 102nd Battalion, Canadian Expeditionary Force).

ALEXANDER J. CONVERSE
Colour Sergeant. 107th East Kootenay Regiment, Canadian Militia. (Overseas service; 48th Battalion, Military Police, Railway Troops, Canadian Expeditionary Force).

WALTER ELLIS DENNY
Sergeant. British Army (Regiment or Corps unknown). Wounded, 15 September 1916.

JAMES H. DRAKE, JR. Lieutenant. 24th (County of London) Battalion (The Queens') The London Regiment). Died of wounds, 23 September 1918.

GUSTAVE R. GERSON
Lieutenant. Royal Army Medical Corps, attached Royal Field Artillery.

HERBERT R. HORDERN
2nd Lieutenant. Irish Guards. Wounded, 3 August 1916.

RICHARD J. HOWARD
2nd Lieutenant. Enlisted in the Seaforth Highlanders (Ross-shire Buffs, the Duke of Albany's. Commissioned and transferred to the Black Watch, Royal Highland Regiment). Killed in action, 17 March 1916.

NORMAN D. JONES
Lieutenant. Royal Flying Corps.

WILLIAM JEFFERSON LOTH, JR.
Temporary Sergeant Major. Army Service Corps (Mechanical Transport) attached Indian Cavalry Corps, 37th Infantry Division, 11th Infantry Division, 24th Siege Battery, 10th Corps Artillery, 7th Infantry Division; British Expeditionary Force.

SIDNEY A. LOUGHRIDGE
Captain. Royal Field Artillery. Wounded, 15 August 1915.

ALEXANDER McCLINTOCK, DCM
Sergeant. 1st Regiment (Grenadier Guards of Canada), Canadian Militia. (Overseas service; 87th Battalion, Canadian Expeditionary Force). Wounded, September 1916. Decoration: Distinguished Conduct Medal.

DONALD M. McRAE, MC
Lieutenant. 13th Royal Regiment, Canadian Militia. (Overseas service; 14th Battalion, Canadian Expeditionary Force). Wounded, 9 April 1917. Decoration: Military Cross.

B. BERTRAM OWENS, MM
Lance Corporal. Princess Victoria's (Royal Irish Fusiliers). Transferred to Machine Gun Corps. Wounded. Decoration: Military Medal.

ROBERT BARNWELL RHETT, MC
Lieutenant. U.S. Medical Corps Reserve. Volunteered for service in the British Army. Attached 16th (County of London) Battalion (Queen's Westminster Rifles) The London Regiment. Decoration: Military Cross.

VERNON SHAW-KENNEDY
Captain. Commissioned as Temporary 2nd Lieutenant Royal Scots Fusiliers. Transferred and gazetted 2nd Lieutenant Coldstream Guards.

GEORGE A SPEER, JR., MC
Captain. 59th Stormont and Glengarry Regiment, Canadian Militia. (Overseas service; 38th Battalion, 21st Battalion, 46th Battalion, 15th Reserve Battalion, Canadian Expeditionary Force). Decoration: Military Cross.

WALTER P. TALTAVALL
2nd Lieutenant. Royal Flying Corps.

EDWARD W. THOMSON
2nd Lieutenant. Royal Flying Corps.

ACKNOWLEDGMENTS

The following individuals, institutions, and government agencies provided invaluable help in locating material and answering questions. Others named here helped in technical matters in the preparation of this book.

A. Wahab Ajan (Johore, Malaysia), J.C. Andrews (U.K.), William T. Arnold (U.S.A.), Pat Berger (U.S.A), Lt. Col. F.R. Beringer (U.K.), Juliette Bourque (Canada), Aubrey Bowden (U.K.), Peter B. Boyden (U.K.), Frederick G. Brems (U.S.A.) Arthur F. Brown (U.S.A), Peter J. Burness (Australia), Prof. David G. Chandler (U.K.), Phillip Chaplin (Canada), Michael Chapman (U.K.) Rene Chartrand (Canada), Lucas Chin (Sarawak, Malaysia), F.W. Coles (U.K.), Karen Collett (Canada), W.A.B. Douglas (Canada), A.J. Francis (U.K.), Mary Gammage (U.K.), Russell Gammage, M.S.I.A. (U.K.), Phillip and Linda Gibson (U.S.A.), Capt. B.J.L. Hewitt (New Zealand), S.K. Hopkins (U.K.), Maj. Gen. B.P. Hughes (U.K.), CSM G. Jeffrey Jackson (U.S.A.), John Kasprzak (U.S.A.), Lt. Col. Thursa M. Kennedy (New Zealand), Lt. Col. Leonid Kondratiuk (U.S.A.), Lt. Col. R.I. Launder (New Zealand), John E. Listman, Jr. (U.S.A.), Maj. Gen James Lunt, C.B.E. (U.K.), Richard C. McWilliams, Jr. (U.S.A.), Boris Mollo, (U.K.), James E. Morrison, Sr. (U.S.A.), Maurice Mutowo (Zimbabwe), Michael E. Nevins (U.S.A), Col. Neville Colin Parkins (South Africa), Jane Peek (Australia), Lt. Col. Kenneth Powers (U.S.A.), Col. Frederick Rindel (South Africa), Charles H. Stewart (Canada), Elizabeth Talbot Rice (U.K.), Brig. K.A. Timbers (U.K.) Capt. R.J. Taylor (New Zealand), Lt. Col and Mrs. Gregory Tsoucalas (U.S.A.), Larry E. Turner (U.S.A.), Maj. G.E. Visser (South Africa), Robert Wentz, Jr. (U.S.A.), Maj. M.R. Wicksteed (New Zealand)

National Army Museum, London; Naval Historical Library and Air Historical Branch, Ministry of Defence, United Kingdom; Royal Artillery Institution; Royal Marines Historical Society; Public Archives of Canada; Directorate of History, National Defence Headquarters, Canada; Canadian War Museum; The Ministry of Defence, Australia; Australian War Memorial; Ministry of Defence, New Zealand; Queen Elizabeth II Army Memorial Museum, New Zealand; Office of Information, South African Defence Force; South African National Museum of Military History; Sarawak Museum, Malaysia; National Library of Singapore; National Library of Jamaica; National Archives of Zimbabwe

Mrs. June Cunningham and Mr. Keith Gibson were responsible for the Virginia Military Institute's acceptance of the collection and its prominent display.

I wish to express my appreciation to my publisher, Art Brown of Vandamere Press, and to my editor, Pat Berger. The attractive book design was the work of Larry Converse. The original drawings of the badges were the painstaking work of Holly M. Cooley, and the magnificent photographs of the figures were taken by L.J. Fox. Thanks also to Alice Sufit and Stephanie Brown for their gracious help.

A very special thanks to Mr. James M. Tully, Secretary General of the National Toy Soldier Museum, without whose support this book would not have become a reality.

Finally, I wish to acknowledge my beloved wife Linda for her patience and assistance during the preparation of this book, and to my son Ted for his understanding over the years.

Edward M. Nevins
Strasburg, Virginia
April, 1992

FOREWORD

Over a period of twenty years, Mr. Edward M. Nevins traveled the globe gathering information needed to complete an ambitious project: to create the world's most accurate collection of miniature figures representing the military organization of the British Empire on the eve of World War I in August 1914. Numbering over 400 figures, the collection illustrates the distinctive and colorful full dress uniforms that modern warfare and new technology would soon make obsolete. This book is a guide to the Nevins Collection on display at the Virginia Military Institute in Lexington, Virginia.

Only in the unique Nevins Collection can the student of military history find such a complete survey of uniform details and designs of the British Empire. The 54mm figures are accompanied by complete reference and research materials in addition to brief regimental histories.

Naval forces as well as all of the *regular* regiments and corps of the armies of the British Empire are illustrated on the color plates, with corresponding text showing the badge, dates of formation, description of the uniform, etc. Militia, volunteer, and territorial formations are listed and described, but not illustrated. Researchers seeking unit histories, lineages, etc., should use this book as a first reference and then refer to the bibliography for additional sources. They should also note the various museums and government agencies mentioned on the acknowledgments page.

Most of the figures in the collection were sculpted and cast by Russell Gammage, M.S.I.A., the founder of Rose Miniatures, London, England. Mr. Gammage holds the National Diploma in Design Illustration and the Art Teacher's Diploma from the London University. A member of the Society of Industrial Designers, his figures are considered by many to be among the finest 54mm figures in the field of miniature figures. Mr. Gammage is now retired.

Other models included in the collection were cast by W. Britains, Ltd., Hinchliffe Models, Valient Miniatures, H-R Products, Inc., and Solido.

In 1984, 70 years to the month of the date his collection captures, Mr. Nevins presented his figures to the Virginia Military Institute. As a standard for uniform details of the era, the museum displays the collection and makes it available to students and researchers from around the world. The VMI Museum is pleased to house this outstanding research and reference collection.

Keith E. Gibson
Executive Director
Museum Programs
Virginia Military Institute

CONTENTS

Introduction
13 Introduction by David Chandler

CHAPTER ONE
Naval and Marine Forces of the British Empire, 1914
19 Introduction
20 The Royal Navy
23 The Royal Canadian Navy
23 The Royal Australian Navy
24 The Royal Marine Forces

CHAPTER TWO
Land Forces of Great Britain and Ireland, 1914
27 Introduction
29 Household Cavalry
30 Cavalry of the Line
39 Yeomanry Regiments of the Territorial Force
44 Cavalry Special Reserve
45 Royal Regiment of Artillery
46 Corps of Royal Engineers
47 Foot Guards
49 Infantry of the Line (with affiliated Militia and Territorial Force battalions)
78 Infantry Regiments of the Territorial Force (unaffiliated battalions, cyclist battalions, Inns of Court Officers Training Corps, and the Honourable Artillery Company)
82 Channel Islands Militia
82 Departmental Corps
86 Royal Flying Corps
86 Military Bands

CHAPTER THREE
Land Forces of the Dominion of Canada, 1914
87 Introduction
88 Canadian Permanent Forces
    88 Cavalry
    89 Royal Canadian Artillery
    89 Royal Canadian Engineers
    90 Infantry
    90 Departmental Corps
91 Canadian Militia
    91 Cavalry
    94 Artillery
    95 Engineers
    95 Signal Corps
    95 Corps of Guides
    95 Infantry
    136 Departmental Corps

CHAPTER FOUR
Land Forces of the Commonwealth of Australia, 1914
137 Introduction
139 Australian Permanent Forces
    139 Administrative and Instructional Staff
    139 Royal Australian Artillery
    139 Royal Australian Engineers
    140 Departmental Corps
140 Australian Citizen Military Forces
    140 Light Horse
    142 Artillery
    143 Engineers

143 Intelligence Corps
143 Automobile Corps
143 Infantry
149 Departmental Corps

CHAPTER FIVE
Land Forces of the Dominion of New Zealand, 1914
151 Introduction
152 New Zealand Permanent Forces
    152 New Zealand Staff Corps
    153 New Zealand Permanent Staff
    153 Royal New Zealand Artillery
153 New Zealand Territorial Forces
    153 Mounted Rifles
    154 Artillery
    155 Engineers
    155 Infantry
    157 Departmental Corps

CHAPTER SIX
Land Forces of the Union of South Africa, 1914
159 Introduction
160 South African Permanent Forces
    160 Mounted Riflemen
    193 Artillery Brigade
    193 Medical Section
193 South African Active Citizen Forces
    193 Mounted Rifles
    195 Dismounted Rifles
    196 Artillery
    196 Engineers
    197 Infantry
    198 Departmental Corps

CHAPTER SEVEN
The Army of The Indian Empire, 1914
199 Introduction
201 Bodyguards
202 Corps of Guides
203 Cavalry
215 Artillery
217 Sappers and Miners
218 Infantry
253 Brigade of Gurkhas
256 Departmental Corps
258 Imperial Service Troops
266 Volunteer Forces
    266 Light Horse
    266 Mounted Rifles
    267 Artillery
    267 Engineers
    267 Rifles
270 Frontier Militia
270 Indian State Forces

CHAPTER EIGHT
Land Forces of the Colonies and Protectorates of the British Empire, 1914
273 Permanent Forces
273 Royal Malta Artillery
274 West India Regiment
274 West Africa Regiment
274 West African Frontier Force
275 King's African Rifles
275 Somaliland Camel Corps
275 Northern Rhodesia Police (Military Wing)
275 Malay States Guides
276 Armed Constabulary of North Borneo
276 Sarawak Rangers
276 Johore Military Force
277 Militia and Volunteers of the Colonies and Protectorates
279 Egypt

280 BIBLIOGRAPHY
281 INDEX

INTRODUCTION

by DAVID G. CHANDLER

The year 1914 was a crucial turning point in world, as well as British, history. At the year's start, Great Britain and its Empire, both Dominions and Colonies, held a position of global supremacy. Schoolboys were taught that the Union Jack flew throughout both hemispheres and over large areas of most continents; indeed, so wide were British interests that it was literally possible to say that it was an empire "... upon which the sun never set!" Britons of all classes lustily sang to the rousing music of Elgar's Pomp and Circumstance No. One, the words of *Land of Hope and Glory* with heartfelt conviction:

Land of Hope and Glory, Mother of the Free,
How shall we extol thee, who are born of thee?
Wider still and wider shall thy bounds be set;
God who made thee mighty, make thee mightier yet.

Even in 1914, there were men and women of discernment who realized that there were flaws in the Second British Empire (successor to the First which had foundered in large measure with the loss of the American colonies over a century earlier). Still, some 385 million souls from Canada to Ceylon, from Australasia to the Falklands, from the Isle of Lewis to the huge subcontinent of India, owed allegiance of one sort or another to the King-Emperor, George V, whose unofficial nickname, the Sailor King, highlighted the significance of the powerful Royal Navy, keeper of the *Pax Brittanica* over the oceans and seas of the world. Indeed, as even its critics conceded, the British Empire, although not *good* in every way, was undeniably *great*. How right it must have seemed to be born British! The years 1903 to 1914 were the last flowering of British power.

But all this was to change over the short space of five years. The strains and expense in human and economic terms of the vastest war mankind had ever seen—"the Great War" or "the War to End all Wars" as it came to be called from 1918 to 1939 was to cost Great Britain and the other great nations involved dearly. True, Britain and France, together with their ally (from 1917), the United States, were to emerge the winners in 1918, as evidenced in the terms of the Peace of Versailles concluded the next year. For Great Britain, however, the greatest years were now passed; the costs of the struggle had nigh bankrupted the British nation, and although the main transformation from Empire to independent Commonwealth would come after 1945, the omens were there to be read from 1919.

In early August of 1914, few were likely to guess that this revolution in British imperial fortunes would follow so abruptly.

The two major props of British power in 1914 were its armed forces—the Royal Navy and the Army, and if, in the words of the music hall ditty; "Every nice girl, loves a sailor, Every nice girl, loves a tar ...," the place of the British Army—"We're soldiers of the King, my lads," was also significant even if it was—by continental standards—relatively small. The military power of the British Army was backed by the soldiers of the Empire, who rallied to the aid of the mother-country without question or demur upon the outbreak of war with Germany and Austria. Canadians, Australians and New Zealanders (soon to be dubbed "the ANZACS"), not to forget most South Africans, the peoples of the west, central and east African colonies, and above all the teeming millions of India responded to their mother country's call. Eventually it is estimated that five million Britons and almost four million from overseas served "King and Country" in khaki or navy blue between August 1914 and November 1918. At least 908,000 of them were to pay the supreme sacrifice by the Armistice at the eleventh hour of the eleventh day of the eleventh month, 1918, out of a world total of over 17 million deaths all told (civilians included)—or even 22 million if the victims of the vicious influenza epidemic of 1918-19 are taken into account. By comparison, the share of the United States was four million in uniform and 114,000 casualties; but, the then potentially greatest nation upon earth had only entered the war in mid-1917.

In mid-1914 the British nation and its Empire stood upon the brink of the unknown. The Royal Navy numbered 33 capital ships and 8 more building; the Regular Army (including imperial garrisons) stood at some 250,000 men, of which five divisions (four of infantry and one of cavalry, or some 160,000 soldiers in round numbers) formed the British Expeditionary Force (BEF), ready for a major European war.

That Army was probably the best in terms of quality that Great Britain ever put into the field. By early 1915 it lost almost half its strength, and was replaced successively by, first the Territorial Force, then Kitchener's huge volunteer armies of 1916, and last—for the very first time in British history—by the conscript armies of the last years of the great struggle. The British Regular Army, however, (proudly self-dubbed "the Old Contemptibles" after a derogatory remark of Kaiser Wilhelm II who had spoken of the B.E.F. as forming "a contemptible little army") held the line in France and Flanders alongside our French and Belgian allies during the critical months of late 1914 and early 1915. This was the period that saw on the Western Front, the huge German offensive through Belgium towards Paris—the (modified) Schlieffen Plan—the headlong Allied retreat from Mons, the tough battle of Le Cateau, and the culminating "miracle" of the Marne (which Winston Churchill termed "the greatest battle in the history of the world" in his fine work, *The World Crisis*)—a huge engagement that halted the grey flood of German invaders just a few miles short of their ultimate objective. The BEF (or what was left of it) was reinforced by General Gallieni's garrison of Paris, and sent out to the front in commandeered taxicabs for want of other transport. The German highwater mark was followed by the ebb of the tide, known as "the Race to the Sea", as the Germans retreated to the French and Belgian coast, there to dig in and commence the construction of the notorious trench lines that would soon stretch without a break for 400 miles from the Channel coast to the Swiss frontier. The dying achievement of the "Old Contemptibles" was the First Battle of Ypres.

Already some Canadian troops and a few Indians had reached the front, the precursors of many more. That the BEF had been of sufficient calibre to take the initial strain, thus earning time for new armies to be formed, and the Dominion and Imperial forces been able to send such rapid assistance, was due to important military reforms that had been implemented from 1902 onwards. In the last years of the 19th Century and in the first of the 20th, Great Britain had fought the Great Boer War (1899-1902) in South Africa. To defeat and hold down the two small republics of the Transvaal and Orange Free State (which fielded barely 60,000 men between them) had ultimately required almost half a million British and Dominion soldiers. The Boer field armies, followed by their redoubtable "commandos" who waged a last-stand guerrilla war for 18 months, revealed serious weakness in the late Victorian Army in what was to prove the very nick of time. However suitable for expanding and policing the Empire, the British Army had not faced a European opponent equipped with modern weapons and artillery since the Crimean War in the mid-1850s. Consequently, it had become very out-of-date and needed the hard lessons of the South African War to prick the bubble of Victorian military complacency and create the atmosphere for immediate and drastic reform.

Following the Hartington Commission's work of 1902 and the "Report on the War in South Africa" published in the following year, came the creation of the Imperial General Staff. With it came the reorganization of all forces at home and overseas, including those of the Dominions, on identical establishments, equipment tables and training schedules. Next, from 1904 to 1908, came the reforms associated with the name of Lord Esher—the most significant being the creation of a modern General Staff. Finally came the work of Liberal statesman, Richard Haldane, who between 1906 and 1912, inspired radical changes in equipment and training, set up the Territorial Force as the second-line reserve behind the Regular Army's reservists, and created the British Expeditionary Force. Formal training manuals were written on every aspect of the soldier's trade, including treatises on field fortification. Minimum physical requirements for recruits were raised and all soldiers were required to fire annual musketry classifications to improve their accuracy with, and confidence in, their .303 Lee-Enfield magazine loading rifles. Army exercises were made far more realistic and demanding. All this excellent (and long overdue) work was carried through just in time for the supreme challenge of August 1914.

Some idea of the effectiveness of these timely reforms and the professionalism of the Regular Army they made possible can be illustrated from a German report on the battle of Mons. There the German Imperial Army had for the first time come up against the British Army, positioned amongst the industrial suburbs and behind the canals and waterways of that Belgian city, and encountered its firepower. This was so intense and well directed that German intelligence officers reported that, contrary to their earlier estimates, it was clear that each British infantry battalion was equipped with at least 14 machine guns instead of four as hitherto believed. In fact the British battalions did indeed have only four machine guns apiece. What made the Germans think otherwise was the accuracy and high rate of fire of the ordinary private soldier who, year after year, had been required to fire rifle classifications until by 1914 he was capable of firing what was termed "the mad minute"—18 aimed rounds by bolt action Lee-Enfields in just 60 seconds. This weight of rapid and accurate fire had been mistaken by the German experts as only explainable in terms of machine guns.

By 1914 much of the social stigma that had traditionally been attached to the profession of arms in Great Britain had been replaced with a widespread pride for men in uniform. In the 1870s, the mother of "Wully" Robertson, destined to be the first private soldier to receive the baton of a Field Marshal, had told her son that " . . . I would fain see tha' dead, Wully, than in a red coat." At the end of the century, Rudyard Kipling also pointed out the ambivalence of the popular feeling towards the soldier in several of his famous barrack-room ballads.

> It's "Tommy this" and "Tommy that," and
> "Tommy 'ows yer soul?,"
> but it's "thin red line of 'eroes" when the drums
>   begin to roll,
> It's "Tommy this" and "Tommy that," and "throw
>   'im out the Brute"
> But it's " 'ero of 'is Country," when the guns
>   begin to shoot.

By 1914, however, "Tommy Atkins" had become firmly established in the national consciousness. The millions who rushed forward to enlist as volunteers in response to the appeal of Lord Kitchener, Minister for War, were evidence of this improved reputation of the Army, as well as of the great surge of patriotic feeling unleashed at the time.

This fine new book, therefore, is dedicated to the superb armed forces of Great Britain, its Dominions and Empire on the very eve of Armageddon. The unique collection of military miniatures, reflecting every single regular unit of those British armies in 1914, as well as the Royal Navy, presently housed at the Virginia Military Institute, represents the "labour of love" of Mr. Edward Nevins, over many years of dedicated research, assembling and painting. It encapsulates the British Regular Army in a moment in time—arguably its greatest. To the photographs of each model Mr. Nevins has added a scrupulously researched description of each and every regiment and formation represented, giving the minimum of essential information on the unit concerned from its first raising down to 1914, including the badge it then carried, the Battle Honours it had been awarded (or in the case of the Royal Artillery it's Honour Titles, as *Ubique* ["Everywhere"] is its sole formal Battle Honour as such. As Edward Nevins points out, the Royal Artillery has no Regimental Colours—it's "standard" having been for over three hundred years it's guns. Details of every uniform represented are also to be found.

At a time when the United States is considering ways of adopting some of the best features of the unique British Regimental System, this book may be said to illustrate that same system at its moment of apogee. But I must add one British word of caution; Do not expect to see full results overnight. There is a famous (probably apocryphal) story of a tourist visiting the splendid gardens of St. John's College, Oxford. Seeing an aged gardener leaning on his hoe, he asked him what was the secret of the perfect weed-free lawns of the college. "Nothing much to it, sir," replied the old man, gratefully pocketing the proffered tip. "You see, all you have to do is to mow, water and roll them for two hundred years." Similarly, the British Army of 1914—or of today—only attained its excellence over a long period of evolution and often haphazard development dating back at least to 1660. That year marked the Restoration of King Charles II to the English throne, the traditional starting point for the modern British Army. In other words the British Army, and its famous regimental system, were not the creation of a stroke of a pen. On the other hand, the American Army may be said to have had a "flying start" if it indeed wishes to model its "cohorts" on the British concept. After all, until 1775, all Americans were citizens of the British Crown, and may therefore be said to have inherited the first hundred and fifteen years of British regimental evolution, even if thereafter their ancestors insisted on becoming "departed brethren." It is sometimes overlooked that Colonel George Washington held a commission in the Virginia Militia from King George III.

It was an honour to be asked to contribute this Introduction. I had the privilege to spend the first semester of the academic year 1988-1989 as a visiting professor holding the Mary Moody Northen Chair in the Humanities at the Virginia Military Institute. On my first day there, I was introduced to the Nevins Collection by Keith Gibson, Executive Director of Museum Programs at the Virginia Military Institute. It is therefore doubly an honour to have contributed to this bold publishing project and "labour of love" on the part of Mr. Nevins.

David G. Chandler
Sandhurst and Yateley

18 June 1989
(174th Anniversary of the Battle of Waterloo)

Forces of the British Empire
1914

CHAPTER ONE
Naval Forces of the British Empire, 1914

The foundation of a regular British Navy was laid down in 1546 by King Henry VIII with the establishment of dockyards and a board of commissioners for the management of naval affairs. The prior history of British seamanship dates back to the age of the rowing vessel with bold seamanship learned from the Vikings. From time to time, fleets were raised and then neglected when the need for them passed. The Royal Navy's action against the Spanish Armada (1588) under Henry VIII's daughter Elizabeth I and the exploits of Sir Francis Drake were the first steps leading to British domination of the seas.

The Royal Navy's ability and discipline won the famous battle of Trafalgar (1805) over the combined fleets of France and Spain, thus opening the age of British naval supremacy that was to last into World War II (1939-1945). From 1889, it was British policy that the Royal Navy was more than equal to the combined navies of any other two naval powers. Over the years the oceans of the world became safe and secure because of British sea power. The world's sea-lanes became the "highways" upon which the British Empire was built and maintained.

In 1914, the Royal Navy was at its highest state of strength and efficiency over its long history. When the test of World War I (1914-1918) came, the Royal Navy was in the hands of very capable officers and men. On 18 July 1914, a grand review of the fleet was held off the Hampshire coast at Spithead, probably the largest gathering of naval power in the world to that date. King George V and the First Lord of the Admiralty, Winston Churchill, took the fleet's salute.

Normally after a grand review the fleet would demobilize, generous leave would be given to the regular seamen, and the reservists would be sent home. Churchill, aware of the warlike events taking place in Europe, ordered the fleet not to disperse. On the night of July 28th, orders were given for the fleet to proceed to its war stations. On the next day, the battleships arrived at Scapa Flow in the Orkney Islands north of Scotland and the battle cruisers stood off Rosyth in the Firth of Forth. The Royal Navy was dominant in the North Sea, keeping the German fleet bottled up in its fortified ports.

THE ROYAL NAVY

ORGANIZATION

In 1914, the scope of the Royal Navy spanned the globe. Officers and men numbered over 136,000 with another 58,000 in the reserves. In addition to more than 600 warships and auxiliary ships, there were major naval establishments ashore at Portsmouth, Plymouth, Chatham, Portland, Dover, and Sheerness in England; Rosyth and Scapa Flow in Scotland; Pembroke in Wales; and Haulbowline at Queenstown (Cobh) in Ireland. Overseas bases included Gibraltar, Malta, Sierra Leone and the Gold Coast in West Africa, Simons Bay at the Cape of Good Hope in South Africa, Aden, Colombo, Singapore, Penang Island off the Malay Peninsula, Hong Kong, Wei-Hai-Wei on the north-east coast of China, and Auckland, New Zealand. The government of India maintained dockyards at Bombay and Calcutta. Also, fortified ports on the British colonies, such as Bermuda, Mauritius, Falklands, and St. Helena, provided numerous coaling and wireless stations.

ROYAL NAVAL AIR SERVICE

The Royal Naval Air Service was formed in July 1914 from the Naval Wing of the Royal Flying Corps, with a strength of 830 officers and men, 7 airships, 52 seaplanes, and 39 airplanes. The Naval Flying School was at Eastchurch, England. There were naval air stations at Isle of Grain (near Sheerness), Calshot, Felixstowe, Yarmouth, Farnborough, and Kingsnorth in England, and at Fort George and Dundee in Scotland. The Royal Naval Air Service provided observation and reconnaissance for the Royal Navy; that is, it was the *eyes* of the fleet. In 1914, fighter aircraft and bombers were not yet envisioned.

QUEEN ALEXANDRA'S ROYAL NAVAL NURSING SERVICE

The Naval Nursing Service was founded on 1 April 1885. In 1902, the service was reorganized by Queen Alexandra and renamed Queen Alexandra's Royal Naval Nursing Service. In 1914, this service was the only women's organization in the Royal Navy, with 69 nursing sisters on active duty at naval hospitals in the United Kingdom and overseas.

NAVAL RESERVES AND NAVAL VOLUNTEERS

The Royal Naval Reserve was a force of professional officers and men who attended periods of training in the ships of the Royal Navy and normally served in merchant and fishing ships.

The Royal Fleet Reserve was a force of seamen (no officers) who had enlisted for 12 years of service, including 5 years with the fleet and 7 years in the Royal Fleet Reserve

The Royal Naval Volunteer Reserve consisted of volunteers whose officers were usually yachtsmen. This reserve was formed into companies and divided along territorial lines within the British Isles. An officer of the Royal Navy was assigned to each division as an instructor, together with petty officers to supervise drills and training.

Naval reserves overseas included three companies of the Royal Naval Volunteer Reserve in the Union of South Africa, A and B Companies in the Cape of Good Hope Province, and C Company in Natal Province.

In India, the Calcutta Port Defence Volunteer Corps's Naval Division was raised in 1883. In Newfoundland, the Royal Newfoundland Naval Reserve was raised in 1899.

NAVAL UNIFORMS

The men and junior petty officers of the seaman and stoker branches wore navy blue jumpers with badges of rating on their left sleeves. Skill qualification badges were worn on the right sleeve. The collar was light blue with narrow stripes of white edging. A black silk handkerchief was worn around the neck and tied in front. Other dress included navy blue bell-bottom trousers and navy blue or white round caps with black silk cap ribbons embroidered with the gold letters, H.M.S. (His Majesty's Ship), followed by the name of the ship. A seaman's uniform, outfitted for a landing party is illustrated by figure 1.

Chief petty officers, senior petty officers, and ratings of the artisan, victualling, sick berth, steward and cook branches wore double-breasted navy blue jackets with brass buttons, navy blue trousers, and navy blue or white peaked caps with a distinctive badge.

The naval officer's uniform included a navy blue frock coat or jumper, both with gold rings on the cuffs indicating rank. Colored cloth between the rings indicated certain branches. Executive officers had no colored cloth between the rings; engineers had purple, paymasters had white, doctors had red, and naval instructors had blue. Other dress included navy blue trousers and a navy blue or white peaked cap with a gold badge.

The full dress of a British naval officer included a navy blue swallow-tailed coat with gold buttons, lace, and epaulets. A white gold-edged flap on the sleeve with gold rings indicated rank. Other dress included navy blue trousers with gold stripes, a black silk cocked hat, and a gold embroidered sword belt with sword and scabbard.

Officers and men of the Royal Naval Air Service wore the same uniforms described above. However, an officer's cap badge had a soaring eagle in place of the anchor. A flying officer of the Royal Naval Air Service, together with the Royal Flying Corps, is illustrated by figure 120.

The uniform of Queen Alexandra's Royal Naval Nursing Service included a navy blue ankle-length dress with scarlet cuffs, a navy blue cloak with scarlet lining, and a navy blue straw bonnet with a navy blue velvet bow and ribbons. On the right side of the cloak there was an embroidered badge comprising a red cross on a white background in a gold border. Queen Alexandra's monogram, two red A's, were interlaced with a gold anchor and cable with the imperial crown above. The duty uniform included a white cap and white apron.

Chaplains in the Royal Navy did not wear uniforms or hold rank. On full dress occasions, they wore the clerical garb of their particular denomination.

In warm climates, officers and men wore white uniforms that were very similar in style to the navy blue uniforms described above. Nurses wore white cotton blouses with navy blue ankle-length skirts.

FLAGS OF THE ROYAL NAVY

The distinctive flag of the Royal Navy is the White Ensign, which displays a red St. George's cross on a white field with the Union in the upper-left canton. The White Ensign is flown from the ensign staff at the stern of a warship. The Union flag is flown from the jackstaff at the bow of a warship; this flag is known as a "Jack." The Blue Ensign, a blue flag with the Union in the upper-left canton, is flown from the ensign staff of a merchant ship whose captain and a specified number of the ship's officers and crew belong to the Royal Naval Reserve.

The Union Flag is the British national flag. It combines the crosses of St. George (England), St. Andrew (Scotland), and St. Patrick (Ireland), all on a blue field.

SHIPS OF THE ROYAL NAVY 1914

(Year shown in parenthesis is the year of completion)

DREADNOUGHT BATTLESHIPS

Royal Sovereign (building), *Royal Oak* (building), *Resolution* (building), *Ramillies* (building), *Revenge* (building), *Valient* (building), *Barham* (building), *Malaya* (building), *Queen Elizabeth* (1914), *Warsprite* (1914), *Benbow* (1914), *Emperor of India* (1914), *Iron Duke* (1914), *Marlborough* (1914), *Ajax* (1913), *Audacious* (1913), *King George V* (1913), *Centurion* (1913), *Thunderer* (1912), *Monarch* (1912), *Conqueror* (1912), *Orion* (1912), *Colossus* (1911), *Hercules* (1911), *Neptune* (1911), *Vanguard* (1910), *St. Vincent* (1910), *Collingwood* (1910), *Bellerophon* (1909), *Temeraire* (1909), *Superb* (1909), *Dreadnought* (1906)

H.M.S. *Dreadnought*, combining heavy armor and large caliber guns, made obsolete all previously built battleships in all navies of the world.

BATTLE CRUISERS (DREADNOUGHTS)

Tiger (1914), *Queen Mary* (1913), *Princess Royal* (1912), *Lion* (1912) *New Zealand* (1910), *Indefatigable* (1911), *Invincible* (1908), *Inflexible* (1908), *Indomitable* (1908)

Battle Cruisers (Dreadnoughts) had the firepower of the Dreadnought battleship but sacrificed armor to achieve speed.

BATTLESHIPS (PRE-DREADNOUGHTS)

Lord Nelson (1908), *Agamemnon* (1907), *Hibernia* (1906), *Africa* (1906), *Brittania* (1906), *Zealan-*

dia (1905) *Commonwealth* (1905), *King Edward* (1905), *Dominion* (1905), *Hindustan* (1905), *Swiftsure* (1904), *Triumph* (1904), *Queen* (1904), *Prince of Wales* (1904), *Cornwallis* (1904), *Russell* (1903), *Albemarle* (1903), *Duncan* (1903), *Exmouth* (1903), *London* (1902), *Bulwark* (1902), *Venerable* (1902), *Implacable* (1902), *Albion* (1902), *Irresistible* (1902), *Glory* (1901), *Vengeance* (1901), *Formidable* (1901), *Goliath* (1900), *Ocean* (1900), *Illustrious* (1898), *Mars* (1897), *Caesar* (1897), *Hannibal* (1897), *Victorious* (1897), *Jupiter* (1897), *Prince George* (1896), *Majestic* (1895), *Magnificent* (1895)

CRUISERS

Minotaur (1908), *Defence* (1908), *Shannon* (1908), *Achilles* (1907), *Cochrane* (1907), *Natal* (1907), *Warrior* (1907), *Black Prince* (1906), *Duke of Edinburgh* (1905), *Antrim* (1905), *Argyll* (1905), *Hampshire* (1905), *Roxburgh* (1905), *Devonshire* (1904), *Carnarvon* (1904), *Lancaster* (1904), *Cornwall* (1904), *Cumberland* (1904), *Suffolk* (1904), *Essex* (1903), *Kent* (1903), *Monmouth* (1903), *Berwick* (1903), *Donegal* (1903), *King Alfred* (1903), *Leviathan* (1903), *Euryalus* (1903), *Good Hope* (1902), *Drake* (1902), *Sutlej* (1902), *Aboukir* (1902), *Hogue* (1902), *Bacchante* (1902), *Spartiate* (1902), *Cressy* (1901), *Argonaut* (1901), *Ariadne* (1900), *Amphitrite* (1900), *Diadem* (1899), *Europa* (1899), *Crescent* (1892), *Theseus* (1892), *Grafton* (1892), *Gibraltar* (1892), *Royal Arthur* (1891), *Hawke* (1891), *Endymion* (1891), *Edgar* (1890)

LIGHT CRUISERS

Calliope (building), *Caroline* (building), *Carysfort* (building), *Champion* (building), *Cleopatra* (building), *Comus* (building), *Conquest* (building), *Cordelia* (building), *Arethusa* (1914), *Aurora* (1914), *Galatea* (1914), *Inconstant* (1914), *Royalist* (1914), *Penelope* (1914), *Phaeton* (1914), *Undaunted* (1914), *Nottingham* (1914), *Birmingham* (1914), *Lowestoft* (1914), *Fearless* (1913), *Southampton* (1912), *Dublin* (1912), *Chatham* (1912), *Yarmouth* (1912), *Active* (1912), *Amphion* (1912), *Dartmouth* (1911), *Falmouth* (1911), *Weymouth* (1911), *Bristol* (1911), *Glasgow* (1911), *Gloucester* (1911), *Blonde* (1911), *Liverpool* (1910), *New Castle* (1910), *Blanche* (1910), *Bellona* (1910), *Boadicea* (1909), *Skirmisher* (1905), *Challenger* (1905), *Diamond* (1905), *Sapphire* (1905), *Adventure* (1904), *Attentive* (1904), *Forward* (1904), *Foresight* (1904), *Pathfinder* (1904), *Patrol* (1904), *Sentinel* (1904), *Topaz* (1904), *Amethyst* (1904), *Hyacinth* (1901), *Perseus* (1901), *Hermes* (1900), *Highflyer* (1900), *Pyramus* (1900), *Pioneer* (1900), *Psyche* (1900), *Pegasus* (1899), *Proserpine* (1899), *Pelorus* (1897), *Vindictive* (1897), *Dido* (1896), *Doris* (1896), *Isis* (1896), *Diana* (1895), *Juno* (1895), *Venus* (1895), *Minerva* (1895), *Talbot* (1895), *Eclipse* (1894), *Astraea* (1893), *Charybdis* (1893), *Forte* (1893), *Fox* (1893), *Hermione* (1893), *Sappho* (1891), *Melpomene* (1891), *Sirus* (1890), *Philomel* (1890)

DESTROYERS

Two Special Flotilla Leaders (building)

13 M Class destroyers (building)

20 L Class destroyers, all completed during 1912-1913

20 K Class destroyers, all completed during 1912-1913

23 I Class destroyers, all completed during 1911-1912

20 H Class destroyers, all completed during 1910-1911

16 G Class destroyers, all completed during 1908-1911

12 F Class destroyers, all completed during 1906-1910

One unclassified destroyer, completed in 1907

34 E Class destroyers, all completed during 1902-1906

8 D Class destroyers, all completed during 1900-1904

35 C Class destroyers, all completed during 1897-1900

21 B Class destroyers, all completed during 1895-1901

12 A Class destroyers, all completed during 1893-1895

SUBMARINES

Two ocean going submarines, *Nautilus* and *Swordfish* (building)

Seven of E Class (building)

Four of S Class (building)

Four of V Class (building)

Four of W Class (building)

Eight of F Class, completed during 1913

One of S Class, completed during 1913

11 of E Class, completed during 1912

Seven of D Class, completed during 1911

One of D Class, completed during 1910

Eight of C Class, completed during 1909

12 of C Class, completed during 1908

One of D Class, completed during 1907

Seven of C Class, completed during 1907

Nine of C Class, completed during 1906

Nine of B Class, completed during 1905

Six of A Class, completed during 1904

MISCELLANEOUS WARSHIPS

In 1914, there were 10 sloops (1884-1903); 5 gunboats (1889-1899); 18 torpedo gunboats, most adapted as minesweepers (1889-1894); 7 minesweepers (1911-1912); 7 minelayers (all circa 1891); 97 torpedo boats (1886-1908); 10 river gunboats (1897-1904); and 6 coastguard cruisers (1889-1912). One coastguard cruiser, H.M.S. *Thrush*, had formerly served as a gunboat and was commanded by King George V, the "Sailor King," when he was on active duty in the navy.

FLEET AUXILIARY SHIPS

Auxiliary ships performed supplementary but important services. In some cases, warships of an older class were converted to auxiliary service.

In 1914, there were seven torpedo depot ships (1878-1890); eight submarine depot ships (1885-1911); two fleet repair ships (1905 and 1901); one distillery ship (1902); four petrol or oil ships (all 1903) with two being built; nine miscellaneous special service vessels (1874-1896); eight survey ships (1878-1912); one despatch ship (1885); and one collier (1902).

There was one hospital ship, the *Maine* (1887). It had been outfitted as a hospital ship in service of the United States during the Spanish-American War (1898). It was presented to the British Government in 1901 by the Atlantic Transport Company and renamed in memory of the U.S. battleship, U.S.S. *Maine*, sunk in Havana, Cuba, in 1898. The *Maine* saw service in the South African War (1899-1902). Another hospital ship, *Mediator* was being built in 1914.

There were two royal yachts, the *Victoria and Albert* (1899) and the *Alexandra* (1907). One Admiralty yacht was named the *Enchantress* (1903).

ROYAL INDIAN MARINE

This force was organized in 1892. By 1914, it comprised six armed transport ships (1886-1907) and a survey ship (1907).

THE ROYAL CANADIAN NAVY

The title, Royal Canadian Navy, was granted by royal proclamation on 4 May 1910. In the same year, two men-of-war were purchased and used for training purposes. In 1911, a small naval college opened at Halifax, Nova Scotia, a fortified port and the main base of the Royal Canadian Navy.

UNIFORM

The uniform of the Royal Canadian Navy was identical to that of the Royal Navy, only the silk cap ribbons differed. The ribbons were embroidered with the gold letters, H.M.C.S. (His Majesty's Canadian Ship), followed by the name of the ship.

SHIPS OF THE ROYAL CANADIAN NAVY, 1914
(Year shown in parenthesis is year of completion)

CRUISERS
Niobe (1897), *Rainbow* (1891)

MISCELLANEOUS GUNBOATS AND AUXILIARY SHIPS
Four gunboats (1891-1904), two survey ships (1901 and 1910), one customs cruiser (1914), and five miscellaneous vessels (1880-1904)

THE ROYAL AUSTRALIAN NAVY

The title, Royal Australian Navy, was granted by King George V on 10 July 1911. By 1914, Australia had attained a sizable navy in comparison to its population. The main bases of the Royal Australian Navy were the fortified ports of Sydney, New South Wales, and King George Sound in Western Australia. In the opening months of World War I, the Royal Australian Navy played an important part in the Pacific and Indian Oceans. On the outbreak of war, Australian naval and military forces seized Kaiser Wilhelms Land (northeast New Guinea) and the adjacent islands of the Bismarck Archipelago.

UNIFORM

The uniform of the Royal Australian Navy was basically the same as that of the Royal Navy. However, buttons differed and the silk cap ribbons were embroidered with the gold letters, H.M.A.S. (His Majesty's Australian Ship), followed by the name of the ship. The white naval uniforms were commonly worn in the warmer Pacific and Indian Ocean climates.

SHIPS OF THE ROYAL AUSTRALIAN NAVY, 1914

(Year shown in parenthesis is year of completion)

BATTLE CRUISER (DREADNOUGHT)
Australia (1912)

CRUISERS
Brisbane (building), *Melbourne* (1911), *Sydney* (1911)

LIGHT CRUISER
Encounter (1902)

DESTROYERS
Six, all completed during 1910-1912

SUBMARINES
Two of E Class, both completed in 1912

GUNBOATS
Three, all completed in 1912

ROYAL MARINE FORCES

ROYAL MARINE LIGHT INFANTRY

ROYAL MARINE ARTILLERY

In 1914, there were three divisions of the Royal Marine Light Infantry, headquartered at Gosport, Chatham, and Devonport, totalling 13,425 officers and men. The Royal Marine Artillery was headquartered at Eastney, Southsea near Portsmouth, and totalled 3,393 officers and men. The depot of the Royal Marine Forces was at Walmer. All of these locations are in England. In 1914, King George V was Colonel-in-Chief.

Year	Event
1664	The Lord Admiral's Maritime Regiment raised. Several other maritime regiments were raised and disbanded between 1664 and 1697.
1702	Six maritime regiments were raised and disbanded a few years later. Six infantry regiments became maritime regiments but later reverted to the Army.
1740	Ten marine regiments were raised; all were disbanded by 1748.
1755	50 companies of marines were raised and became a permanent force.
1802	The 50 companies raised in 1755 were designated the Royal Marines.
1804	The Royal Marine Artillery was raised.
1831	The Royal Marine Artillery was abolished, but one company in each division of marines was soon converted to artillery. These companies gradually increased in number.
1855	The Royal Marines became the Royal Marine Light Infantry.
1862	The title Royal Marine Artillery was restored.

THE COLOURS

Each of the three divisions had a King's Colour and a Division Regimental Colour. (See Standards, Guidons, and Colours section of Chapter Two.)

BATTLE HONOURS

The Great Globe was granted to the Royal Marines in 1827 in the belief that the Royal Marines had engaged in too many battles to be included on the colours. However, the battle honour *Gibraltar*, which was on the old colours, remained. The laurel wreath was granted for the capture of Belle Isle in 1761.

ORGANIZATION

Both branches of the Royal Marines provided detachments for service in the ships of the Royal Navy and were administered by the Admiralty. The Royal Marine Light Infantry was an infantry force carried by ship and landed when necessary. They were also used to maintain discipline aboard ship. The Royal Marine Light Infantry and the Royal Marine Artillery served together on board battleships and battle cruisers. Both branches were available for landing parties. At least one of the large caliber gun turrets on battleships and battle cruisers was manned by the Royal Marine Artillery. Cruisers and smaller ships carried only Royal Marine Light Infantry.

When the Royal Marine Forces were ashore and under Army command, they ranked in seniority after the 1st Battalion, Royal Berkshire Regiment, raised in 1744.

UNIFORMS

The uniform of the Royal Marine Light Infantry included a white helmet with a brass ball, a scarlet tunic with blue facings, slashes on the cuffs with three points and three buttons, and blue trousers with red piping. This uniform is illustrated by figure 2.

The uniform of the Royal Marine Artillery included a white helmet with a brass ball, a blue tunic with scarlet facings, and blue trousers with red piping. This uniform is illustrated by figure 3.

The forage caps for both branches were blue Broderick caps with white covers for summer wear.

Each of the three Royal Marine Light Infantry Divisions maintained a military band. The scarlet tunic was worn without a belt and was embroidered with gold lace down the front and across the back seams. The uniform included dark blue trousers with red piping.

The Royal Marine Artillery band wore a blue tunic with scarlet facings, also without a belt, but with gold *frogging* across the front of the tunic similar to that worn by hussars. The uniform included dark blue trousers with red piping.

The Royal Marine Forces assumed responsibility for providing military bands for the Royal Navy in 1903. These bands on board flagships and other large warships wore blue tunics with scarlet facings and dark blue trousers with red piping. All Royal Marine bands wore the white helmet with a brass ball. In 1914, the Royal Marine Band Service at sea and ashore totalled 1,442 officers and men.

CHAPTER TWO
Land Forces of the United Kingdom of Great Britain and Ireland, 1914

The British Army of 1914 was quite small when compared to the conscripted millions of the continental European armies; however, the officers and men of the British Army were keen volunteers, very professional, and well trained. As World War I progressed, Britain was forced to raise a multimillion-man army, but it was the British Expeditionary Force drawn from the Army of 1914 which was lost almost to a man. This Army when added to the gallant French forces completely upset the enemy's plans, saved Paris, and forced the enemy to retreat, dig in, and begin 4 years of trench warfare.

The following sections describe each *regular* regiment and corps of the British Army in 1914. Each regiment or corps is listed in order of seniority. The photographic plates illustrate the appropriate full dress uniform of a private soldier for each regular regiment or corps. The text gives the 1914 station or stations, a brief history, battle honours, and a description of the full dress uniform. The same information is given for the Yeomanry, Militia, and Territorial formations, but these units are not illustrated.

ORGANIZATION

Infantry of the Line regiments with two numbers after the title resulted from the reorganization of 1881. At that time those regiments with only one battalion, that is the 26th to the 109th (with the exception of the 60th and 79th), were linked in pairs. As a result, all Infantry of the Line regiments had at least two regular battalions, one at home and the other abroad. Five Infantry of the Line regiments had four regular battalions. The 79th had only one battalion until 1897, when a second was added. In the Foot Guards, the Grenadier Guards and Coldstream Guards had three battalions each. The Scots Guards had two, and the Irish Guards had one.

The Yeomanry regiments of the Territorial Force and the Cavalry Special Reserve units are listed after the regular cavalry regiments. The Militia (Special Reserve) and Territorial Force infantry battalions are listed on the page of the regular infantry regiments with which they were affiliated. Territorial infantry regiments and battalions not affiliated with regular regiments are listed at the end of the infantry section. Territorial formations of the artillery, engineers, and departmental corps are listed on the page of the regular component of that particular corps. Infantry militia battalions provided drafts to the regular battalions. Yeomanry regiments and Territorial battalions could volunteer to serve as a unit.

It should be noted that unlike cavalry and yeomanry regiments, the infantry regiment has no tactical significance since the number of battalions in the infantry regiment is variable. In fact, during World War I, the British infantry regiments expanded to 1,761 battalions comprising 18 battalions of the Foot Guards regiments, 1,619 battalions of Infantry of the Line regiments, and 124 Territorial infantry battalions.

Militia and Territorial Force formations were part-time organizations. A camp of 14 to 18 days was held once a year, usually during the first part of August. A number of drills were held during the year.

The Territorial Force was created during 1907-08 from existing Yeomanry and Volunteer formations. The Yeomanry regiments dated from the 1790s in most cases, although some were raised as late as 1903. In a Yeomanry regiment, landowners traditionally provided the officers, with tenant farmers providing the other ranks. Each man supplied his own horse. Most infantry Volunteer formations were raised during 1859-60; a few were raised later.

The majority of Yeomanry regiments and Volunteer battalions sent contingents to the South African War (1899-1902), and thus bear the battle honour *South Africa*.

All regular Infantry of the Line regiments had Militia battalions as well as affiliated Territorial battalions, except for the King's Royal Rifle Corps and the Rifle Brigade, which only had Militia (Special Reserve) battalions. Note that use of the words, corps and brigade, mentioned above is a bit misleading. Actually both of these formations were regiments. The Territorial system did not apply to Ireland; thus, all Irish infantry regiments only had Militia (Special Reserve) battalions. The Foot Guards did not have any Militia or Affiliated Territorial battalions.

Cavalry and Yeomanry regiments numbered around 500 men organized into four squadrons. The squadron was divided into four troops. Infantry battalions numbered around 1000 men organized into eight companies. The company was divided into four sections. Horse and Field Artillery were formed into batteries. Garrison Artillery was formed into companies who manned batteries. Engineer and Departmental Corps (Service, Medical, etc.) were formed into companies.

UNIFORMS

The uniforms described and illustrated are those of a private (unless otherwise noted) of the regiment or corps listed, in *full dress*. Regimental accoutrements of *full dress*, the color of the *facings* (collar and cuffs), as well as badges and other distinctions were steeped in tradition and jealously guarded. Forage caps (peaked caps with a visor) and glengarry caps in the case of Scottish regiments are also described together with *full dress* since they would be worn with *walking-out dress* instead of the more elaborate headgear of *full dress*. By 1914, *walking-out dress* had replaced the old undress uniforms of red, blue, etc.

Service dress consisted of a khaki serge uniform. In the British Army, the khaki service dress was an olive-drab color. The jacket was a shooting-coat style with large pockets. Buttons and badges were a dull bronze rather than the bright brass or gilt of most full dress uniforms. A peaked cap and trousers or breeches with puttees were of the same khaki serge material as the jacket. A tan khaki tropical kit was worn in warm climates.

The *full dress* of officers was similar to that of the men but more ornamented. On ceremonial occasions, officers of the Foot Guards wore gold and crimson sashes. Infantry officers of "red-coated" English, Welsh, and Irish regiments wore scarlet tunics and crimson waist sashes.

There were broad edging of gold lace on the officer's uniform collar and cuffs. The lace on the cuffs ended in a small Austrian knot. Officers of rifle regiments wore dark green hussar-type tunics with black embroidery. Officers of Highland and Lowland Scottish regiments had a special sword, the *Claymore*, and a full crimson sash worn over the left shoulder.

The scarlet tunics of other ranks in "red-coated" regiments tended to be redder in color and of a cheaper material. (Scarlet tended to discolor or fade rather quickly.)

Cavalry officers' uniforms were richly decorated with additional lace and sashes over the left shoulder, more elaborate plumes, and other decorative features.

In the 1st and 2nd Life Guards and the Royal Horse Guards, gold *aiguillettes* were worn on the right shoulder indicating that those officers were on the personal staff of the sovereign. Officers' horse furniture was quite elaborate with richly decorated saddlecloths. The 3rd and 7th Hussars had leopard-skin saddlecloths. The 10th and 15th Hussars had leopard-skin saddlecovers.

Mess dress for officers consisted of a jacket with a roll collar, waistcoat, overalls, and Wellington boots. The color of the jacket and facings were the same as *full dress*.

The uniforms of the Yeomanry regiments and Territorial battalions with distinctive uniforms described below are not illustrated.

Yeomanry regiments and the Cavalry Special Reserve had their own full dress uniforms. Militia (Special Reserve) battalions and the majority of affiliated Territorial infantry and cyclist battalions wore the same uniforms as the regiment that they were affiliated with. However, buttons and badges were of a white (silver) metal rather than brass. In the case of rifle battalions, the buttons and badges were bronze instead of black. Officers' lace and non-commissioned officers' chevrons were silver/white rather than gold. In some cases, badges differed considerably from those of the regular battalions. In Territorial battalions, metal titles worn on the shoulder strap were surmounted with the letter T. Forage caps, or glengarry caps in the case of Scottish battalions, were worn in place of the *full dress* head gear of the regular battalions. Battalions in scarlet tunics wore the usual dark blue trousers with red piping. Rifle battalions wore green trousers. As a rule, Territorial units wore brown leather belts rather than the white belts of the regulars.

Some affiliated infantry and cyclist Territorial battalions continued to wear the same old Volunteer uniforms worn before the formation of the Territorial Force. Usually, the differing uniform was strongly identified with that particular battalion. These exceptions are noted on the page describing the regular regiment with which the battalion in question is affiliated. Territorial battalions in grey tunics wore grey trousers. Unaffiliated infantry and cyclist battalions wore distinctive uniforms.

STANDARDS, GUIDONS, COLOURS, AND DRUM BANNERS

Heraldic devices, mottos, and battle honours were embroidered on a regiment's standard, guidon, or colours. Standards were nearly square. They were crimson with a gold fringe and were used by the Household Cavalry and Dragoon Guards. Crimson guidons with a gold fringe (similar to a standard but rounded at the end with a slit in the fly) were used by Dragoons. Hussars and Lancers did not have standards or guidons. In these cases, heraldic devices and battle honours were embroidered on the drum banners of the mounted band's kettledrums. One regiment, the 3rd (King's Own) Hussars, did not have drum banners; the honours and heraldic devices were engraved on the silver kettledrums. Drum banners of cavalry regiments were of the facing colour, except for the 2nd Dragoons (Royal Scots Greys), which were scarlet.

Each battalion of infantry had a *King's Colour* and a *Regimental Colour*, except for rifle battalions who had no colours. The King's Colour was the Union flag. The Regimental Colour was of the facings colour. Regiments with white facings had a white regimental colour with a red St. George's cross as did the one regiment with scarlet facings. In the four regiments of the Foot Guards, the colours were reversed. The King's Colours were crimson and the Regimental Colours were the Union flag. Infantry colours were 3 feet, 9 inches by 3 feet with a gold fringe and crimson and gold tassels.

Many heraldic items embroidered on the banners described above included a red rose, a white rose, or a combination thereof, which represented England. A thistle represented Scotland. The harp and shamrocks represented Ireland. A leek represented Wales.

Units other than cavalry or infantry did not have standards, guidons, or colours. The Mounted Band of the Royal Artillery did have scarlet drum banners.

HOUSEHOLD CAVALRY

1ST LIFE GUARDS

In 1914, this regiment was stationed at Hyde Park, London. King George V was Colonel-in-Chief.

1660 Raised as the 1st or His Majesty's Own Troop of Guards

1685 1st Troop of Life Guards of Horse
1788 1st Life Guards

BATTLE HONOURS: *Dettingen, Peninsula, Waterloo, Tel el Kebir, Egypt 1882, Relief of Kimberley, Paardeberg, South Africa 1899-1900*

The uniform included a white metal (steel) helmet with a white plume. (The mounted band and trumpeters had scarlet plumes.) The scarlet tunic had blue facings. In *review order*, the uniform was a steel cuirass with a crimson flask cord on the pouch belt, white leather breeches, and black jackboots. The saddles were covered with black fur. Farriers wore blue tunics and black helmet plumes. In state dress, the mounted band wore blue jockey caps and long crimson coats laced in gold. The blue forage cap had a scarlet band. There were double 1½ inch scarlet stripes on the blue overalls worn in *walking-out* dress. The *review order* uniform is illustrated by figure 4.

2ND LIFE GUARDS

In 1914, this regiment was stationed at Windsor, England. King George V was Colonel-in-Chief.

1660	Raised as the 3rd or the Duke of Albemarle's Troop of Guards
1670	2nd or the Queen's Troop of Guards
1685	2nd Troop of Life Guards of Horse
1788	2nd Life Guards

BATTLE HONOURS: *Dettingen, Peninsula, Waterloo, Tel el Kebir, Egypt 1882, Relief of Kimberley, Paardeberg, South Africa 1899-1900*

The uniform was the same as the 1st Life Guards, except for a blue flask cord on the pouch belt. Also, the 2nd Life Guards used a white fur saddle cover. The forage cap was also blue with a scarlet band, but the 2nd Life Guards did not wear a badge on the forage cap. State dress for the mounted band was the same as for the 1st Life Guards. The *review order* uniform is illustrated by figure 5.

ROYAL HORSE GUARDS (THE BLUES)

In 1914, this regiment was stationed at Regent's Park, London. King George V was Colonel-in-Chief.

1661	Raised as the Royal Regiment of Horse
1687	Royal Regiment of Horse Guards
1750	Royal Horse Guards Blue
1819	Royal Horse Guards (The Blues)

BATTLE HONOURS: *Dettingen, Warburg, Beaumont, Willems, Peninsula, Waterloo, Tel el Kebir, Egypt 1882, Relief of Kimberley, South Africa 1899-1900*

The uniform included a white (steel) metal helmet with a scarlet plume (including the mounted band, trumpeters, and farriers).

The blue tunic had scarlet facings. In *review order*, the uniform was a steel cuirass with a crimson flask cord on the pouch belt, white leather breeches, and black jackboots. State dress for the mounted band was the same as that described for the 1st Life Guards. The blue forage cap had a scarlet band. There were 2½ inch scarlet stripes on the blue overalls worn in *walking-out dress*. The *review order* uniform is illustrated by figure 6.

Note: All three regiments of the Household Cavalry were mounted exclusively on black horses, except for the trumpeters who were mounted on white horses. The kettle drummers in the mounted bands were mounted on piebalds.

CAVALRY OF THE LINE

1ST (KING'S) DRAGOON GUARDS

In 1914, this regiment was stationed at Lucknow, India. Francis Joseph, Emperor of Austria and King of Hungary, was Colonel-in-Chief. This honorary title was withdrawn at the start of World War I.

1685	Raised as the Queen's or 2nd Regiment of Horse
1714	The King's Own Regiment of Horse
1746	1st (King's) Dragoon Guards

BATTLE HONOURS: *Blenheim, Ramillies, Oudenarde, Malplaquet, Dettingen, Warburg, Beaumont, Waterloo, Sevastopol, Taku Forts, Pekin 1860, South Africa 1879, South Africa 1901-1902*

The uniform included a brass helmet with a scarlet plume. (The mounted band had white plumes.) The scarlet tunic had blue facings, and there were yellow stripes on the blue pantaloons. The blue forage cap had a blue band. This uniform is illustrated by figure 7.

LAND FORCES OF GREAT BRITAIN AND IRELAND 31

2ND DRAGOON GUARDS (QUEEN'S BAYS)

In 1914, this regiment was stationed at Aldershot, England.

1685	Raised as the Earl of Peterborough's Regiment of Horse
1688	3rd Regiment of Horse
1715	Princess of Wales's Own Royal Regiment of Horse
1727	The Queen's Own Royal Regiment of Horse
1746	2nd, or The Queen's, Dragoon Guards
1872	2nd Dragoon Guards (Queen's Bays)

BATTLE HONOURS: *Warburg, Willems, Lucknow, South Africa 1901-02*

The uniform included a brass helmet with a black plume. (The mounted band had white plumes.) The scarlet tunic had buff facings, and there were buff stripes on the blue pantaloons. The blue forage cap had a buff band. Since 1767 this was the only cavalry regiment mounted exclusively on bay horses. This uniform is illustrated by figure 8.

3RD (PRINCE OF WALES'S) DRAGOON GUARDS

In 1914, this regiment was stationed at Cairo, Egypt.

1685	Raised as the Earl of Plymouth's Regiment of Horse
1687	4th Regiment of Horse
1746	3rd Regiment of Dragoon Guards
1765	3rd (Prince of Wales's) Dragoon Guards

BATTLE HONOURS: *Blenheim, Ramillies, Oudenarde, Malplaquet, Warburg, Beaumont, Willems, Talavera, Albuhera, Vittoria, Peninsula, Abyssinia, South Africa 1901-02*

The uniform included a brass helmet with a black and red plume, red underneath. (The mounted band had red and white plumes.) The scarlet tunic had yellow facings, and there were yellow stripes on the blue pantaloons. The blue forage cap had a yellow band. This uniform is illustrated by figure 9.

4TH (ROYAL IRISH) DRAGOON GUARDS

In 1914, this regiment was stationed at Tidworth, England.

1685	Raised as the 6th Horse or the Earl of Arran's Cuirassiers
1690	5th Horse
1746	1st Irish Horse or the Blue Horse
1788	4th (Royal Irish) Dragoon Guards

BATTLE HONOURS: *Peninsula, Balaklava, Sevastopol, Tel el Kebir, Egypt 1882*

The uniform included a brass helmet with a white plume. (The mounted band had black plumes.) The scarlet tunic had blue facings and there were yellow stripes on the blue pantaloons. The blue forage cap had a blue band. This uniform is illustrated by figure 10.

5TH (PRINCESS CHARLOTTE OF WALES'S) DRAGOON GUARDS

In 1914, this regiment was stationed at Aldershot, England.

1685	Raised as the Duke of Shrewsbury's Regiment of Horse
1687	6th Regiment of Horse

1717 2nd Irish Horse
1788 5th Dragoon Guards
1804 5th (Princess Charlotte of Wales's) Dragoon Guards

BATTLE HONOURS: *Blenheim, Ramillies, Oudenarde, Malplaquet, Beaumont, Salamanca, Vittoria, Toulouse, Peninsula, Balaklava, Sevastopol, Defence of Ladysmith, South Africa 1899-1902*

The uniform included a brass helmet with a red and white plume, red underneath. (The mounted band had red plumes.) The scarlet tunic had dark green facings, and there were yellow stripes on the blue pantaloons. The blue forage cap had a dark green band. This uniform is illustrated by figure 11.

6TH DRAGOON GUARDS (CARABINIERS)

In 1914, this regiment was stationed at Canterbury, England.

1685 Raised as the Queen Dowager's Horse
1690 8th Horse
1692 The King's Carabiniers (During the 18th century the term carabinier referred to a type of long horse pistol.)
1745 3rd Irish Horse
1788 6th Dragoon Guards (Carabiniers)

BATTLE HONOURS: *Blenheim, Ramillies, Oudenarde Malplaquet, Warburg, Willems, Sevastopol, Delhi 1857, Afghanistan 1879-80, Relief of Kimberley, Paardeberg, South Africa 1899-1902*

The uniform included a brass helmet with a white plume (The mounted band had red plumes.) The blue tunic had white facings. During the years 1851-1864, this regiment served temporarily as light cavalry wearing the dress of light cavalry, that is, blue; but they continued to wear the helmets of the dragoon guards. The blue tunic is a relic of those days. There were white stripes on the blue pantaloons. The blue forage cap had a white band. This uniform is illustrated by figure 12.

7TH (PRINCESS ROYAL'S) DRAGOON GUARDS

In 1914, this regiment was stationed at Secunderbad, India. Louise, the Princess Royal, was Colonel-in-Chief.

1688 Raised as the Earl of Devonshire's Horse or 10th Horse
1690 Schomberg's Horse
1691 Duke of Leinster's Horse or 8th Horse
1720 Ligonier's Horse, 8th Horse
1749 4th Irish Horse
1788 7th (Princess Royal's) Dragoon Guards

BATTLE HONOURS: *Blenheim, Ramillies, Oudenarde, Malplaquet, Dettingen, Warburg, South Africa 1846-47, Tel el Kebir, Egypt 1882, South Africa 1900-02*

The uniform included a brass helmet with a black and white plume, white underneath. (The mounted band had white plumes.) The scarlet tunic had black facings, and there were yellow stripes on the blue pantaloons. The blue forage cap had a black band. This uniform is illustrated by figure 13.

1ST (ROYAL) DRAGOONS

In 1914, this regiment was stationed at Potchefstroom, Union of South Africa. Wilhelm II, King of Prussia and Emperor of Germany, was Colonel-in-Chief. This honorary title was withdrawn at the start of World War I.

1661 Raised as The Tangiers Horse
1683 The King's Own Royal Regiment of Dragoons
1690 Royal Regiment of Dragoons
1751 1st (Royal) Dragoons

BATTLE HONOURS: *Tangier 1662-80, Dettingen, Warburg, Beaumont, Willems, Fuentes d'Onor, Peninsula, Waterloo, Balaklava, Sevastopol, Relief of Ladysmith, South Africa 1899-1902*

The uniform included a white (steel) metal helmet with a black plume (The mounted band had white plumes.) The scarlet tunic had blue facings, and there were yellow stripes on the blue pantaloons. The blue forage cap had a scarlet band. This uniform is illustrated by figure 14.

2ND DRAGOONS (ROYAL SCOTS GREYS)

In 1914, this regiment was stationed at York, England. Nicholas II, Tsar of Russia, was Colonel-in-Chief.

1681	Raised as the Royal Regiment of Scots Dragoons
1707	Royal North British Dragoons
1751	2nd, or Royal North British Dragoons
1866	2nd Royal North British Dragoons (Scots Greys)
1877	2nd Dragoons (Royal Scots Greys)

BATTLE HONOURS: *Blenheim, Ramillies, Oudenarde, Malplaquet, Dettingen, Warburg, Willems, Waterloo, Balaklava, Sevastopol, Relief of Kimberley, Paardeberg, South Africa 1899-1902*

The uniform included a black bearskin cap with a white plume. There was a brass grenade at the base of the plume. (The kettle-drummer of the mounted band wore a white bearskin cap with a scarlet hackle. The remainder of the mounted band wore scarlet plumes on black bearskin caps.) The scarlet tunic had blue facings, and there were yellow stripes on the blue pantaloons. The blue forage cap had a distinctive white zig-zag on a black band. This uniform is illustrated by figure 15.

Note: This regiment was mounted exclusively on white/grey horses, except for the mounted band's drum horse, which was black. The drum banners were scarlet instead of the usual facing color. This regiment was also permitted to emblazon the Scottish Royal Arms on the trumpet banners.

3RD (KING'S OWN) HUSSARS

In 1914, this regiment was stationed at Shorncliffe, England.

1685	Raised as the Queen Consort's Own Regiment of Dragoons
1692	Queen's Dragoons
1714	King's Own Regiment of Dragoons
1751	3rd (King's Own) Dragoons
1818	3rd (King's Own) Light Dragoons
1861	3rd (King's Own) Hussars

BATTLE HONOURS: *Dettingen, Salamanca, Vittoria, Toulouse, Peninsula, Cabool 1842, Moodkee, Ferozeshah, Sobraon, Chillianwallah, Goojerat, Punjab, South Africa 1902*

The uniform included a black fur hussar busby with a white plume and a garter blue busby-bag. The blue tunic had a scarlet collar and was braided with yellow in front, along the back seams, and on the collar and cuffs. There were double yellow stripes on the blue pantaloons and a red forage cap. This uniform is illustrated by figure 16.

4TH (QUEEN'S OWN) HUSSARS

In 1914, this regiment was stationed at Curragh, Ireland.

1685	Raised as the Princess Anne of Denmark's Dragoons
1751	4th Dragoons
1788	4th or Queen's Own Dragoons
1818	4th or Queen's Own Light Dragoons
1861	4th (Queen's Own) Hussars

BATTLE HONOURS: *Dettingen, Talavera, Albuhera, Salamanca, Vittoria, Toulouse, Peninsula, Ghuznee 1839, Afghanistan 1839, Alma, Balaklava, Inkerman, Sevastopol*

The uniform included a black fur hussar busby with a scarlet plume and a yellow busby-bag. The blue tunic was braided with yellow in front, along the back seams, and on the collar and cuffs. There were double yellow stripes on the blue pantaloons and a red forage cap. This uniform is illustrated by figure 17.

5TH (ROYAL IRISH) LANCERS

In 1914, this regiment was stationed at Dublin, Ireland.

1689	Raised as Wynne's Dragoons
1704	The Royal Dragoons of Ireland
1751	5th Royal Irish Dragoons
1799	Disbanded
1858	Reraised as the 5th Royal Irish Light Dragoons (Lancers)
1861	5th (Royal Irish) Lancers

BATTLE HONOURS: *Blenheim, Ramillies, Oudenarde, Malplaquet, Suakin 1885, Defence of Ladysmith, South Africa 1899-1902.*

The uniform included a black lancer cap (the Polish czapka). The upper part of the cap was scarlet with green plume. The blue tunic had scarlet facings and plastron. There were double yellow stripes on the blue pantaloons. The blue forage cap had a scarlet band. This uniform is illustrated by figure 18.

6TH (INNISKILLING) DRAGOONS

In 1914, this regiment was stationed at Muttra, India. Arthur, Duke of Connaught and Strathearn, was Colonel-in-Chief.

1689	Raised as Cunningham's Dragoons (Albert Cunningham)
1751	6th or Inniskilling Dragoons
1861	6th (Inniskilling) Dragoons

BATTLE HONOURS: *Dettingen, Warburg, Willems, Waterloo, Balaklava, Sevastopol, South Africa 1899-1902*

The uniform included a white (steel) metal helmet with a white plume. (The mounted band had scarlet plumes.) The scarlet tunic had primrose yellow facings. There were yellow stripes on the blue pantaloons. The blue forage cap had a primrose yellow band. This uniform is illustrated by figure 19.

7TH (QUEEN'S OWN) HUSSARS

In 1914, this regiment was stationed at Bangalore, India.

1689	Raised as the Queen's Own Dragoons or Cunningham's Dragoons (Robert Cunningham)
1715	Princess of Wales's Own Royal Dragoons
1727	Queen's Own Dragoons
1751	7th or Queen's Own Dragoons
1784	7th or Queen's Own Light Dragoons
1807	7th or Queen's Own Light Dragoons (Hussars)
1861	7th (Queen's Own) Hussars

BATTLE HONOURS: *Dettingen, Warburg, Beaumont, Willems, Orthes, Peninsula, Waterloo, Lucknow, South Africa 1901-02*

The uniform included a black fur hussar busby with a white plume and a scarlet busby-bag. The blue tunic was braided with yellow in front, along the back seams, and on the collar and cuffs. There were double yellow stripes on the blue pantaloons and a red forage cap. This uniform is illustrated by figure 20.

8TH (KING'S ROYAL IRISH) HUSSARS

In 1914, this regiment was stationed at Amballa, India.

1693	Raised as Cunningham's Dragoons (Henry Cunningham)
1751	8th Dragoons
1775	8th Light Dragoons
1777	8th or the King's Royal Irish Light Dragoons
1822	8th, the King's Royal Irish Light Dragoons (Hussars)
1861	8th (King's Royal Irish) Hussars

BATTLE HONOURS: *Leswarree, Hindustan, Alma, Balaklava, Inkerman, Sevastopol, Central India, Afghanistan 1879-80, South Africa 1900-02*

The uniform included a black fur hussar busby with a white over red plume and a scarlet busby-bag. The blue tunic was braided with yellow in front, along the back seams, and on the collar and cuffs. There were double yellow stripes on the blue pantaloons and a red forage cap. This uniform is illustrated by figure 21.

9TH (QUEEN'S ROYAL) LANCERS

In 1914, this regiment was stationed at Tidworth, England.

1715	Raised as Wynne's Dragoons
1751	9th Dragoons
1783	9th Light Dragoons
1816	9th Light Dragoons (Lancers)
1830	9th Queen's Royal (Light) Dragoons (Lancers)
1861	9th (Queen's Royal) Lancers

BATTLE HONOURS: *Peninsula, Punniar, Sobraon, Chillianwallah, Goojerat, Punjab, Delhi 1857, Lucknow, Charasiah, Kabul 1879, Kandahar 1880, Afghanistan 1878-80, Modder River, Relief of Kimberley, Paardeberg, South Africa 1899-1902*

The uniform included a black lancer cap (the Polish czapka). The upper part of the cap was blue with a black and white plume. The blue tunic had scarlet facings and plastron. There were double yellow stripes on the blue pantaloons. The blue forage cap had a scarlet band. This uniform is illustrated by figure 22.

10TH (PRINCE OF WALES'S OWN ROYAL) HUSSARS

In 1914, this regiment was stationed at Potchefstroon, Union of South Africa. King George V was Colonel-in-Chief.

1715	Raised as Gore's Dragoons
1751	10th Dragoons
1783	10th or Prince of Wales's Own Light Dragoons
1806	10th or Prince of Wales's Own Light Dragoons (Hussars)
1811	10th the Prince of Wales's Own Royal Light Dragoons (Hussars)
1861	10th (Prince of Wales's Own Royal) Hussars

BATTLE HONOURS: *Warburg, Peninsula, Waterloo, Sevastopol, Ali Masjid, Afghanistan 1878-79, Egypt 1884, Relief of Kimberley, Paardeberg, South Africa 1899-1902*

The uniform included a black fur busby with a white over black plume and a scarlet busby-bag. The blue tunic was braided with yellow in front, along the back seams, and on the collar and cuffs. There were double yellow stripes on the blue pantaloons and a red forage cap. This uniform is illustrated by figure 23.

11TH (PRINCE ALBERT'S OWN) HUSSARS

In 1914, this regiment was stationed at Aldershot, England. The Crown Prince of the German Empire was Colonel-in-Chief. This honorary title was withdrawn at the start of World War I.

1715   Raised as Honeywood's Dragoons
1751   11th Dragoons
1783   11th Light Dragoons
1840   11th (Prince Albert's Own) Hussars

BATTLE HONOURS: *Egypt (with the Sphinx), Warburg, Beaumont, Willems, Salamanca, Peninsula, Waterloo, Bhurtpore, Alma, Balaklava, Inkerman, Sevastopol*

The uniform included a black fur busby with a white over crimson plume and a crimson busby-bag. (The mounted band wore busbies of grey fur rather than the usual black.) The blue tunic was braided with yellow in front, along the back seams, and on the collar and cuffs. There were double yellow stripes on the crimson pantaloons and a crimson forage cap. The *full dress* crimson pantaloons and the overalls for *walking-out* dress were unique in the British Army. This uniform is illustrated by figure 24.

12TH (PRINCE OF WALES'S ROYAL) LANCERS

In 1914, this regiment was stationed at Norwich, England.

1715   Raised as Bowles' Dragoons
1751   12th Dragoons
1768   12th or Prince of Wales's Light Dragoons
1816   12th or the Prince of Wales's Light Dragoons (Lancers)
1817   12th (Prince of Wales's Royal) Lancers

BATTLE HONOURS: *Egypt (with the Sphinx), Peninsula, Waterloo, South Africa 1851-52-53, Sevastopol, Central India, Relief of Kimberley, South Africa 1899-1902*

The uniform included a black lancer cap (the Polish czapka) The upper part of the cap was scarlet with a scarlet plume. The blue tunic had scarlet facings and plastron. There were double yellow stripes on the blue pantaloons. The scarlet forage cap had a scarlet band. This uniform is illustrated by figure 25.

13TH HUSSARS

In 1914, this regiment was stationed at Meerut, India.

1715   Raised as Munden's Dragoons
1751   13th Dragoons
1783   13th Light Dragoons
1861   13th Hussars

BATTLE HONOURS: *Albuhera, Vittoria, Orthes, Toulouse, Peninsula, Waterloo, Alma, Balaklava, Inkerman, Sevastopol, Relief of Ladysmith, South Africa 1900-02*

The uniform included a black fur hussar busby with a white plume and a buff busby-bag. The blue hussar tunic had a buff collar and was braided with yellow in front, along the back seams, and on the collar and cuffs. There were double buff stripes on the blue pantaloons. The forage cap was white with a blue band. The color buff, in this case, was almost white. This uniform is illustrated by figure 26.

14TH (KING'S) HUSSARS

In 1914, this regiment was stationed at Mhow, India.

1715   Raised as Dormer's Dragoons

1720 14th Dragoons
1776 14th Light Dragoons
1798 14th or Duchess of York's Own Light Dragoons
1830 14th King's Light Dragoons
1861 14th (King's) Hussars

BATTLE HONOURS: *Douro, Talavera, Fuentes d'Onor, Salamanca, Vittoria, Pyrenees, Orthes, Peninsula, Chillianwallah, Goojerat, Punjaub, Persia, Central India, Relief of Ladysmith, South Africa 1900-02*

The uniform included a black fur hussar busby with a white plume and a yellow busby-bag. The blue tunic was braided with yellow in front, along the back seams, and on the collar and cuffs. There were double yellow stripes on the blue pantaloons and a red forage cap. This uniform is illustrated by figure 27.

15TH (THE KING'S) HUSSARS

In 1914, this regiment was stationed at Longmoor Camp, England.

1759 Raised as the 15th Light Dragoons or Elliott's Light Horse
1766 1st or the King's Royal Light Dragoons
1769 15th or the King's Royal Light Dragoons
1806 15th the King's Light Dragoons (Hussars)
1861 15th (The King's) Hussars

BATTLE HONOURS: *Emsdorf, Villarers-en-Cauchies, Willems, Egmont-op-Zee, Sahagun, Vittoria, Peninsula, Waterloo, Afghanistan 1878-80*

The uniform included a black fur hussar busby with a scarlet plume and a scarlet busby-bag. The blue tunic was braided with yellow in front, along the back seams, and on the collar and cuffs. There were double yellow stripes on the blue pantaloons and a scarlet forage cap. This uniform is illustrated by figure 28.

16TH (THE QUEEN'S) LANCERS

In 1914, this regiment was stationed at Curragh, Ireland. Alfonso XIII, King of Spain, was Colonel-in-Chief.

1759 Raised as The 16th Light Dragoons or Burgoyne's Light Horse
1766 2nd or Queen's Light Dragoons
1769 16th or Queen's Light Dragoons
1816 16th, Queens Light Dragoons (Lancers)
1861 16th (The Queen's) Lancers

BATTLE HONOURS: *Beaumont, Willems, Talavera, Fuentes d'Onor, Salamanca, Vittoria, Nive, Peninsula, Waterloo, Bhurtpore, Ghuznee 1839, Afghanistan 1839, Maharajpore, Aliwal, Sobraon, Relief of Kimberley, Paardeberg, South Africa 1900-02*

The uniform included a black lancer cap (the Polish czapka). The upper part of the cap was blue with a black plume. The scarlet tunic had blue facings and plastron. There were double yellow stripes on the blue pantaloons. The scarlet forage cap had a blue band. This uniform is illustrated by figure 29.

17TH (DUKE OF CAMBRIDGE'S OWN) LANCERS

In 1914, this regiment was stationed at Sialkot, India.

1759 Raised as the 18th Light Dragoons
1763 17th Light Dragoons
1766 3rd Light Dragoons
1769 17th Light Dragoons
1822 17th Light Dragoons (Lancers)
1876 17th (Duke of Cambridge's Own) Lancers

BATTLE HONOURS: *Alma, Balaklava, Inkerman, Sevastopol, Central India, South Africa 1879, South Africa 1899-1902*

The uniform included a black lancer cap (the Polish czapka). The upper part of the cap was white with a white plume. The blue tunic had white facings and plastron. There were double white stripes on the blue pantaloons. The blue forage cap had a white band. This uniform is illustrated by figure 30.

18TH (QUEEN MARY'S OWN) HUSSARS

In 1914, this regiment was stationed at Tidworth, England. Queen Mary was Colonel-in-Chief.

1759	Raised as the 19th Light Dragoons
1763	18th Light Dragoons
1807	18th King's Irish Hussars
1821	Disbanded
1858	Reraised as the 18th Light Dragoons (Hussars)
1910	18th (Queen Mary's Own) Hussars

BATTLE HONOURS: *Peninsula, Waterloo, Defence of Ladysmith, South Africa 1899-1902*

The uniform included a black fur hussar busby with a white over scarlet plume and a blue busby-bag. The blue tunic was braided with yellow in front, along the back seams, and on the collar and cuffs. There were double yellow stripes on the blue pantaloons and a red forage cap. This uniform is illustrated by figure 31.

19TH (QUEEN ALEXANDRA'S OWN ROYAL) HUSSARS

In 1914, this regiment was stationed at Hounslow, England. Queen Alexandra was Colonel-in-Chief.

1781	Raised as the 23rd Light Dragoons
1786	19th Light Dragoons
1817	19th Lancers
1821	Disbanded
1858	Reraised as the Honorable East India Company's 1st Bengal European Cavalry
1860	Returned to the British Army as the 19th Light Dragoons (Title was changed to "hussars" in the same year.)
1885	19th (Princess of Wales's Own) Hussars
1902	19th, Alexandra (Princess of Wales's Own) Hussars
1908	19th (Queen Alexandra's Own Royal) Hussars

BATTLE HONOURS: *Assaye (with the elephant), Mysore, Seringapatam, Niagara, Tel el Kebir, Egypt 1882-84, Abu Klea, Nile 1884-85, Defence of Ladysmith, South Africa 1899-1902*

The uniform included a black fur hussar busby with a white plume and a white busby bag. The blue tunic was braided with yellow in front, along the back seams, and on the collar and cuffs. There were double yellow stripes on the blue pantaloons and a red forage cap. This uniform is illustrated by figure 32.

20TH HUSSARS

In 1914, this regiment was stationed at Colchester, England.

1759	Raised as the 20th Inniskilling Light Dragoons (disbanded in the same year)
1779	Reraised as the 20th Light Dragoons (disbanded again in the same year)
1791	Reraised as the 20th Jamaica Light Dragoons
1802	20th Light Dragoons
1819	Disbanded
1858	Reraised as the Honorable East India Company's 2nd Bengal European Light Cavalry
1860	Returned to the British Army as the 20th Light Dragoons (Title changed to the 20th Hussars in the same year)

BATTLE HONOURS: *Vimiera, Peninsula, Suakin 1885, South Africa 1901-02*

The uniform included a black fur busby with a yellow plume and a crimson busby-bag. The blue tunic was braided with yellow in front, along the back seams, and on the collar and cuffs. There were double yellow stripes on the blue pantaloons and a red forage cap. This uniform is illustrated by figure 33.

21ST (EMPRESS OF INDIA'S) LANCERS

In 1914, this regiment was stationed at Rawalpindi, India.

1759	Raised as the 21st Light Dragoons or the Royal Windsor Foresters
1763	Disbanded
1779	Reraised as the 21st Light Dragoons
1783	Disbanded
1794	Reraised again as the 21st Light Dragoons
1819	Disbanded
1858	Reraised as the Honorable East India Company's 3rd Bengal European Light Cavalry
1860	Returned to the British Army as the 21st Light Dragoons (Title changed to the 21st Hussars in the same year.)
1897	21st Lancers
1898	21st (Empress of India's) Lancers

BATTLE HONOUR: *Khartoum*

The uniform included a black lancer cap (the Polish czapka). The upper part of the cap was French-grey with a white plume. The blue tunic had French-grey facings and plastron. There were double yellow stripes on the blue pantaloons. The blue forage cap had a French-grey band. This uniform is illustrated by figure 34.

YEOMANRY REGIMENTS OF THE TERRITORIAL FORCE

THE ROYAL WILTSHIRE YEOMANRY (PRINCE OF WALES'S OWN ROYAL REGIMENT) (HUSSARS)

The regiment was raised in 1794 and headquartered at Chippenham. The uniform included a brown fur hussar busby with a scarlet plume and busby-bag. The blue tunic had scarlet facings and white braid. There were double white stripes on the blue pantaloons.

BATTLE HONOUR: *South Africa 1900-01*

THE WARWICKSHIRE YEOMANRY (HUSSARS)

This regiment was raised in 1794 and headquartered at St. John's, Warwick. The uniform included a brown fur hussar busby with a white plume and busby-bag. The blue tunic had white facings and white braid. There were double white stripes on the blue pantaloons.

BATTLE HONOUR: *South Africa 1900-01*

THE YORKSHIRE HUSSARS (ALEXANDRA PRINCESS OF WALES'S OWN)

This regiment was raised in 1794 and headquartered at York. The uniform included a brown fur hussar busby with a black over scarlet plume and a scarlet busby-bag. The blue tunic had white braid, and there were double white stripes on the blue pantaloons.

BATTLE HONOUR: *South Africa 1900-02*

THE NOTTINGHAMSHIRE (SHERWOOD RANGERS) YEOMANRY (HUSSARS)

This regiment was raised in 1794 and headquartered at Retford. The uniform included a brown fur hussar busby with a green plume and a scarlet busby-bag. The green tunic had white braid, and there were double white stripes on the green pantaloons.

BATTLE HONOUR: *South Africa 1900-01*

THE STAFFORDSHIRE YEOMANRY (QUEEN'S OWN ROYAL REGIMENT) (HUSSARS)

This regiment was raised in 1794 and headquartered at Stafford. The uniform included a brown fur hussar busby with a white plume and a scarlet busby-bag. The blue tunic had scarlet facings and white braid. There were double white stripes on the blue pantaloons.

BATTLE HONOUR: *South Africa 1900-01*

THE SHROPSHIRE YEOMANRY (DRAGOONS)

This regiment was raised in 1795 and headquartered at Shrewsbury. The uniform included a white (steel) metal helmet with a white over red plume. The blue tunic had scarlet facings, and there were scarlet stripes on the blue pantaloons.

BATTLE HONOUR: *South Africa 1900-02*

THE AYRSHIRE (EARL OF CARRICK'S OWN) YEOMANRY (HUSSARS)

This regiment was raised in 1803 and headquartered at Ayr. The uniform included a brown fur hussar busby with a white over scarlet plume and a scarlet busby-bag. The blue tunic had scarlet facings and white braid. There were double white stripes on the blue pantaloons.

BATTLE HONOUR: *South Africa 1900-02*

THE CHESHIRE (THE EARL OF CHESTER'S) YEOMANRY (HUSSARS)

This regiment was raised in 1797 and headquartered at Chester. The uniform included a brown fur hussar busby with white over scarlet plume and a white busby-bag. The blue tunic had scarlet facings and white braid. There were double white stripes on the blue pantaloons.

BATTLE HONOUR: *South Africa 1900-01*

THE QUEEN'S OWN YORKSHIRE DRAGOONS

This regiment was raised in 1794 and headquartered at Doncaster. The uniform included a white (steel) metal helmet with a white plume. The blue tunic had white facings, and there were white stripes on the blue pantaloons.

BATTLE HONOUR: *South Africa 1900-02*

THE LEICESTERSHIRE YEOMANRY (PRINCE ALBERT'S OWN) (HUSSARS)

This regiment was raised in 1794, disbanded in 1802, and reraised in 1803. The headquarters were in Leicester. The uniform included a brown fur hussar busby with a white plume and a red busby-bag. The blue tunic had scarlet facings and white braid. There were double white stripes on the blue pantaloons.

BATTLE HONOUR: *South Africa 1900-02*

THE NORTH SOMERSET YEOMANRY (DRAGOONS)

This regiment was raised in 1798 and headquartered at Bath. The uniform included a white (steel) metal helmet with a white plume. The blue tunic had white facings, and there were white stripes on the blue pantaloons.

BATTLE HONOUR: *South Africa 1900-01*

THE DUKE OF LANCASTER'S OWN YEOMANRY (DRAGOONS)

This regiment was raised in 1819 and headquartered at Manchester. King George V was Colonel-in-Chief. The uniform included a white (steel) metal helmet with a white plume. The scarlet tunic had blue facings, and there were scarlet stripes on the blue pantaloons.

BATTLE HONOUR: *South Africa 1900-02*

THE LANARKSHIRE YEOMANRY (LANCERS)

This regiment was raised in 1819 and headquartered at Lanark. The uniform included a black lancer cap (the Polish *czapka*); the upper part of the cap was also black with a black plume. The blue tunic had scarlet facings and plastron. There were double white stripes on the blue pantaloons.

BATTLE HONOUR: *South Africa 1900-02*

THE NORTHUMBERLAND HUSSARS

This regiment was raised in 1797 and headquartered at Newcastle-on-Tyne. The uniform included a brown fur hussar busby with a white over red plume and a scarlet busby-bag. The blue tunic had white braid, and there were double white stripes on the blue pantaloons.

BATTLE HONOURS: *Imperial Service, South Africa 1900-02*

THE SOUTH NOTTINGHAMSHIRE HUSSARS

This regiment was raised in 1795 and headquartered at Nottingham. The uniform included a brown fur hussar busby with a white over red plume and a scarlet busby-bag. The blue tunic had white braid, and there were double white stripes the on blue pantaloons.

BATTLE HONOUR: *South Africa 1900-02*

THE DENBIGHSHIRE YEOMANRY (HUSSARS)

This regiment was raised in 1795 and headquartered at Wrexham. The uniform included a brown fur hussar busby with a white plume and a scarlet busby-bag. The blue tunic had scarlet facings and white braid. There were double white stripes on the blue pantaloons.

BATTLE HONOUR: *South Africa 1900-01*

THE WESTMORLAND AND CUMBERLAND YEOMANRY (HUSSARS)

This regiment was raised in 1819 and headquartered at Penrith. The uniform included a brown fur hussar busby with a white over red plume and a scarlet busby-bag. The scarlet tunic had white facings and white braid. There were double white stripes on the blue pantaloons.

BATTLE HONOUR: *South Africa 1900-01*

THE PEMBROKE YEOMANRY (HUSSARS)

This regiment was raised in 1797 and headquartered at Tenby. The uniform included a brown fur hussar busby with a white plume and busby-bag. The blue tunic had white facings and white braid. There were double white stripes on the blue pantaloons.

BATTLE HONOURS: *Fishguard, South Africa 1901*

THE ROYAL EAST KENT YEOMANRY (THE DUKE OF CONNAUGHT'S OWN) (MOUNTED RIFLES)

This regiment was raised in 1830 and was headquartered at Canterbury. The uniform included a brown fur hussar busby with a green over red plume. The green tunic had scarlet facings and white braid. There were double white stripes on the green pantaloons.

BATTLE HONOUR: *South Africa 1900-01*

THE HAMPSHIRE CARABINIERS YEOMANRY

This regiment was raised in 1830 and headquartered at Winchester. The uniform included a white (steel) metal helmet with a white plume. The blue tunic had white facings, and there were white stripes on the blue pantaloons.

BATTLE HONOUR: *South Africa 1900-01*

THE BUCKINGHAMSHIRE YEOMANRY (ROYAL BUCKS HUSSARS)

This regiment was raised in 1794 and headquartered at Buckingham. The uniform included a brown fur hussar busby with a white plume and a scarlet busby-bag. The green tunic had scarlet facings and white braid. There were double white stripes on the green pantaloons.

BATTLE HONOUR: *South Africa 1900-01*

THE DERBYSHIRE YEOMANRY (DRAGOONS)

This regiment was raised in 1794 and headquartered at Derby. The uniform included a white (steel) metal helmet with a white over red plume. The blue tunic had scarlet facings, and there were scarlet stripes on the blue pantaloons.

BATTLE HONOUR: *South Africa 1900-01*

THE QUEEN'S OWN DORSET YEOMANRY (HUSSARS)

This regiment was raised in 1830 and headquartered at Sherborne. The uniform included a brown fur hussar busby with a white plume and a scarlet busby-bag. The blue tunic had scarlet facings and white braid. There were double white stripes on the blue pantaloons.

BATTLE HONOUR: *South Africa 1900-01*

THE ROYAL GLOUCESTERSHIRE HUSSARS

This regiment was raised in 1830 and headquartered at Gloucester. The uniform included a brown fur hussar busby with a white over scarlet plume and a scarlet busby-bag. The blue tunic had white braid, and there were double white stripes on the blue pantaloons.

BATTLE HONOUR: *South Africa 1900-01*

THE HERTFORDSHIRE YEOMANRY (DRAGOONS)

This regiment was raised in 1830 and headquartered at Hertford. The uniform included a white (steel) metal helmet with a black plume. The scarlet tunic had white facings, and there were scarlet stripes on the blue pantaloons.

BATTLE HONOUR: *South Africa 1900-01*

THE BERKSHIRE YEOMANRY (DRAGOONS)

This regiment was raised in 1831 and headquartered at Reading. The uniform included a white (steel) metal helmet with a white plume. The blue tunic had scarlet facings, and there were scarlet stripes on the blue pantaloons.

BATTLE HONOUR: *South Africa 1900-01*

1ST COUNTY OF LONDON (MIDDLESEX, DUKE OF CAMBRIDGE'S HUSSARS)

This regiment was raised in 1797 and headquartered at Chelsea, London. The uniform included a brown fur hussar busby with a green over scarlet plume and a scarlet busby-bag. The green tunic had black facings and white braid. There were double white stripes on the green pantaloons.

BATTLE HONOUR: *South Africa 1900-01*

THE ROYAL 1ST DEVONSHIRE YEOMANRY (HUSSARS)

This regiment was raised in 1793 and headquartered at Exeter. The uniform included a brown fur hussar busby with a white over scarlet plume and a scarlet busby-bag. The scarlet tunic had blue facings and white braid. There were double white stripes on the blue pantaloons.

BATTLE HONOUR: *South Africa 1900-01*

THE DUKE OF YORK'S OWN LOYAL SUFFOLK HUSSARS

This regiment was raised in 1793 and headquartered at Bury St. Edmunds. King George V was Colonel-in-Chief. The uniform included a brown fur hussar busby with a white plume and a scarlet busby-bag. The green tunic had scarlet facings and white braid. There were double white stripes on the green pantaloons.

BATTLE HONOUR: *South Africa 1900-01*

THE ROYAL NORTH DEVON YEOMANRY (HUSSARS)

This regiment was raised in 1798 and headquartered at Barnstaple. The uniform included a brown fur hussar busby with a white over scarlet plume and a scarlet busby-bag. The blue tunic had scarlet facings and white braid. There were double white stripes on the blue pantaloons.

BATTLE HONOUR: *South Africa 1900-01*

THE QUEEN'S OWN WORCESTERSHIRE HUSSARS

This regiment was raised in 1831 and headquartered at Worcester. The uniform included a brown fur hussar busby with a scarlet plume and busby-bag. The blue tunic had scarlet facings and white braid. There were double white stripes on the blue pantaloons.

BATTLE HONOUR: *South Africa 1900-02*

THE QUEEN'S OWN WEST KENT YEOMANRY (HUSSARS)

This regiment was raised in 1831 and headquartered at Maidstone. The uniform included a brown fur hussar busby with a white over red plume and a scarlet busby-bag. The blue tunic had scarlet facings and white braid. There were double white stripes on the blue pantaloons.

BATTLE HONOUR: *South Africa 1900-01*

THE WEST SOMERSET YEOMANRY (HUSSARS)

This regiment was raised in 1798 and headquartered at Taunton. The uniform included a brown fur hussar busby with a white plume and a red busby-bag. The blue tunic had scarlet facings and white braid. There were double white stripes on the blue pantaloons.

BATTLE HONOUR: *South Africa 1900-01*

THE QUEEN'S OWN OXFORDSHIRE HUSSARS

This regiment was raised in 1798 and headquartered at Oxford. The uniform included a brown fur hussar busby with a white over purple plume and a purple busby-bag. The blue tunic had purple facings and white braid. There were double white stripes on the blue pantaloons.

BATTLE HONOUR: *South Africa 1900-01*

THE MONTGOMERYSHIRE YEOMANRY (DRAGOONS)

This regiment was raised in 1803, disbanded in 1828, and reraised in 1831. The headquarters were in Welshpool. The uniform included white (steel) metal helmet with a yellow plume. The blue tunic had yellow facings, and there were yellow stripes on the blue pantaloons.

BATTLE HONOUR: *South Africa 1901*

THE LOTHIANS AND BORDER HORSE YEOMANRY (DRAGOONS)

This regiment was raised in 1797 and headquartered at Edinburgh. The uniform included a white (steel) metal helmet with a white plume. The scarlet tunic had blue facings, and there were scarlet stripes on the blue pantaloons.

BATTLE HONOUR: *South Africa 1900-01*

THE QUEEN'S OWN ROYAL GLASGOW AND LOWER WARD OF LANARKSHIRE YEOMANRY (DRAGOONS)

This regiment was raised in 1848 and headquartered at Glasgow. The uniform included a white (steel) metal helmet with a black plume. The blue tunic had scarlet facings, and there were scarlet stripes on the blue pantaloons.

BATTLE HONOUR: *South Africa 1900-01*

THE LANCASHIRE HUSSARS YEOMANRY

This regiment was raised in 1798 and headquartered at Liverpool. The uniform included a brown fur hussar busby with a white over crimson plume and a crimson busby-bag. The blue tunic with white braid, and there were double white stripes on the blue pantaloons.

BATTLE HONOUR: *South Africa 1900-02*

THE SURREY YEOMANRY (QUEEN MARY'S REGIMENT) (LANCERS)

This regiment was raised in 1794, disbanded in 1848, and reraised in 1901. The headquarters were in Clapham Park. The unique uniform included a blue forage cap with a red band. The blue-wrap around tunic was fastened on the right with five rows of black braid. The pantaloons were blue.

THE FIFE AND FORFAR YEOMANRY (DRAGOONS)

This regiment was raised in 1797. It was twice disbanded, reraised, and reraised again in 1900. The headquarters were in Kirkcaldy. The uniform included a white (steel) metal helmet with a white plume. The scarlet tunic had blue facings, and there were scarlet stripes on the blue pantaloons.

BATTLE HONOUR: *South Africa 1900-01*

THE NORFOLK YEOMANRY (THE KING'S OWN ROYAL REGIMENT) DRAGOONS

This regiment was raised in 1901 and headquartered at Norwich. The uniform included a white (steel) helmet with a yellow plume. The blue tunic had yellow facings, and there were yellow stripes on the blue pantaloons.

THE SUSSEX YEOMANRY (DRAGOONS)

This regiment was raised in 1901 and headquartered at Brighton. The uniform included a blue forage cap. The blue tunic had yellow facings, and there were yellow stripes on the blue pantaloons.

THE GLAMORGAN YEOMANRY (DRAGOONS)

This regiment was raised in 1902 and headquartered at Bridgend. The uniform included a white (steel) metal helmet with a white plume. The blue tunic had white facings, and there were white stripes on the blue pantaloons.

THE LINCOLNSHIRE YEOMANRY (LANCERS)

This regiment was raised in 1902 and headquartered at Lincoln. The uniform included a black lancer cap (the Polish czapka); the upper part of the cap and plume were green. The green tunic had white facings and plastron. There were double white stripes on the green pantaloons.

THE CITY OF LONDON YEOMANRY (ROUGH RIDERS) (LANCERS)

This regiment was raised in 1900 and headquartered at Finsbury, London. The uniform included a black lancer cap (the Polish czapka); the upper part of the cap was purple with a light blue plume. The blue-grey tunic had purple facings and plastron. There were double purple stripes on the blue pantaloons.

BATTLE HONOUR: *South Africa 1900-02*

2ND COUNTY OF LONDON YEOMANRY (WESTMINSTER DRAGOONS)

This regiment was raised in 1901 and headquartered at Westminster, London. The uniform included a white (steel) metal helmet with a white plume. The scarlet tunic had purple facings, and there were purple stripes on the blue pantaloons.

BATTLE HONOUR: *South Africa 1902*

3RD COUNTY OF LONDON YEOMANRY (SHARPSHOOTERS) (HUSSARS)

This regiment was raised in 1900 and headquartered at St. John's Wood, London. The uniform included a brown fur hussar busby with a white plume and green busby-bag. The green tunic had white braid, and there were double white stripes on the green pantaloons.

BATTLE HONOUR: *South Africa 1900-02*

THE BEDFORDSHIRE YEOMANRY (LANCERS)

This regiment was raised in 1902 and headquartered at Bedford. The uniform included a black lancer cap (the Polish czapka); the upper part of the cap was white with a black and white plume. The blue tunic had white facings and plastron. There were double white stripes on the blue pantaloons.

THE ESSEX YEOMANRY (DRAGOONS)

This regiment was raised in 1902 and headquartered at Colchester. The uniform included a white (steel) metal helmet with a scarlet plume. The green tunic had scarlet facings, and there were scarlet stripes on the green pantaloons.

THE NORTHAMPTONSHIRE YEOMANRY (DRAGOONS)

This regiment was raised in 1902 and headquartered at Northampton. The uniform included a white (steel) metal helmet with a light blue and white plume. The blue tunic had light blue facings, and there were light blue stripes on the blue pantaloons.

THE EAST RIDING OF YORKSHIRE YEOMANRY (LANCERS)

This regiment was raised in 1903 and headquartered at Beverly. The uniform included a black lancer cap (the Polish czapka); the upper part of the cap was light blue with a light blue and white plume. The maroon tunic had light blue facings and plastron. There were double light blue stripes on the blue pantaloons.

1ST LOVAT'S SCOUTS YEOMANRY
2ND LOVAT'S SCOUTS YEOMANRY

Lovat's Scouts were raised in 1900, by the 16th Baron Lovat. The unit was a corps of Scottish deerstalkers and gamekeepers raised for the South African War (1899-1902) as reconnaissance and intelligence specialists as well as mounted infantry. In 1903, Lovat's Scouts were formed into two Yeomanry regiments. The headquarters for both regiments were at Beauly. The uniform for both regiments included a blue Balmoral bonnet with a blue-and-white diced border. The khaki tunic had three button slash cuffs, and there were blue stripes on the khaki breeches.

BATTLE HONOUR: *South Africa 1900-02* for both regiments

1ST SCOTTISH HORSE
2ND SCOTTISH HORSE

The Scottish Horse was raised in 1900 in South Africa by the Marquis of Tullibardine. It was disbanded in 1902 at the end of the South African War. In 1903, the unit was reraised as two Yeomanry regiments. The headquarters for the 1st Scottish Horse were in Dunkeld. Headquarters for the 2nd Scottish Horse were in Aberdeen. The uniform for both regiments included a grey slouch hat with a plume of blackcock's feathers. The grey tunic had yellow facings, and the breeches were grey.

BATTLE HONOUR: *South Africa 1900-02* for both regiments

CAVALRY SPECIAL RESERVE

KING EDWARD'S HORSE (THE KING'S OVERSEAS DOMINIONS REGIMENT)

This regiment was raised in 1901 as the 4th County of London (The King's Colonials) Yeomanry. This regiment consisted of Canadians, Australians, New Zealanders, South Africans, and Anglo-Indians resident in Great Britain, mainly in the London area. The headquarters were in London. The uniform included a khaki forage cap with a scarlet band. The khaki tunic had scarlet piping, and there were scarlet stripes on the khaki breeches.

THE NORTH IRISH HORSE (HUSSARS)

This regiment was raised in 1902 and headquartered at Belfast. The uniform included a brown fur hussar busby with a green plume and busby-bag. A black slouch hat with a green puggaree and a green plume was also worn. The green hussar tunic had white facings, and there were double white stripes on the green pantaloons.

THE SOUTH IRISH HORSE (DRAGOONS)

This regiment was raised in 1902 and headquartered at Dublin. The uniform included a white (steel) metal helmet with a green plume. A green slouch hat was also worn. The green tunic had red facings, and there were red stripes on the green pantaloons.

ARTILLERY

ROYAL REGIMENT OF ARTILLERY

In 1914, the Royal Regiment of Artillery was headquartered at Woolwich, London. King George V was Colonel-in-Chief, and Field Marshal Lord Roberts was Master Gunner.

1716   Raised as the Royal Regiment of Artillery. Prior to 1716 artillery was raised when needed and then disbanded.

1793   The Royal Horse Artillery raised, adding considerable mobility to light artillery.

1899   The Royal Regiment of Artillery, excluding the Royal Horse Artillery, was divided into two distinct branches: (1) the Royal Field Artillery consisting of field batteries and (2) the Royal Garrison Artillery, consisting of companies, heavy batteries, and mountain batteries.

BATTLE HONOUR: *Ubique* (Artillery had participated in almost every battle or campaign for which a battle honour was granted). As a result, King William IV bestowed the honour *Ubique* (Everywhere) upon the Royal Artillery.

Many batteries and companies of the Royal Artillery have Honour Titles. These titles were bestowed upon them to mark some aspect of their history. For example, Q Battery, (*Sanna's Post*) Royal Horse Artillery, marked a particular battle. The 56th (*Olphert's Battery*), Royal Field Artillery, recalled the name of a famous commander. Honour titles could also have historical or special significance, such as O Battery (*The Rocket Troop*), Royal Horse Artillery, and A Battery (*The Chestnut Troop*), Royal Horse Artillery. A Battery was the senior battery of the Royal Horse Artillery. The title, *The Chestnut Troop*, was granted by King Edward VII in 1902. It should be noted that horse artillery batteries were lettered. Field batteries and garrison artillery companies were numbered.

UNIFORMS OF THE ROYAL REGIMENT OF ARTILLERY

The uniform of the Royal Horse Artillery included a black fur horse artillery busby (similar to a hussar busby) with a white plume and a scarlet busby-bag. The blue shell jacket had a scarlet collar and 18 rows of yellow braid on the front of the jacket and yellow braid on the cuffs. There were wide scarlet stripes on the blue pantaloons. The forage cap was blue with a scarlet band. This uniform, together with a 13-pounder gun and limber, is illustrated by figure 35.

The uniform of the Royal Field Artillery included a blue helmet with a brass ball. The blue tunic had a scarlet collar and piping down the front of the tunic. There were yellow shoulder cords and yellow piping around the collar and on the cuffs. A red girdle with a yellow center edged blue was also worn. There were wide scarlet stripes on the blue pantaloons. The forage cap was blue with a scarlet band. This uniform, together with an 18-pounder gun and limber, is illustrated by figure 36.

The uniform of the Royal Garrison Artillery was the same as for the Royal Field Artillery, except for white infantry-style waist belts and trousers instead of breeches. The usual wide scarlet stripes were worn on the trousers. The forage cap was blue with a scarlet band. The uniforms of a sergeant and privates, together with a 6-inch gun, are illustrated by figure 37.

The same uniform, together with an 8-inch Mark VI howitzer being towed by a 45-horsepower Thornycroft Military Oil Tractor (driven by an Army Service Corps driver), is illustrated by figure 38.

Bandsmen of the Royal Artillery Mounted Band wore the horse artillery busby with a scarlet busby-bag and a scarlet, rather than a white, plume. The dark blue tunic had scarlet facings and yellow piping similar to as for the field and garrison artillery. A white waist belt was worn as well as a white pouch belt worn over the left shoulder. The dark blue breeches had wide scarlet stripes. In 1914, the mounted band was stationed at Aldershot.

Dismounted bandsmen of the Royal Artillery Band wore the horse artillery busby with a scarlet busby-bag and plume. The dark blue tunic had scarlet facings and yellow piping. No waist belt was worn. Five yellow brandenburgs, ornamental loops, were worn on the front of the tunic in the place of buttons. The dark blue trousers had wide scarlet stripes. In 1914, the Royal Artillery Band was stationed at headquarters, Woolwich, London.

The Royal Garrison Artillery maintained *outstation* bands at Gibraltar, Dover, Plymouth and Portsmouth. These bands were uniformed the same as the Royal Artillery Band.

GUNS AND ORGANIZATION

The Royal Horse Artillery was armed with 13-pounder, breech-loading, quick-firing guns. These guns could move at a gallop and keep up with cavalry. There were six guns and limbers with 12 ammunition and supply wagons in a battery of horse artillery. The men were all mounted. There were three drivers for each gun as well as five gunners and the sergeant in charge of the gun. The rank and file of a horse artillery battery was somewhat larger than a field battery as horse holders had to be provided for the mounted gunners. In 1914, there were 28 batteries of the Royal Horse Artillery; 12 were stationed in India along with nine ammunition columns. In the Territorial Force, there were 14 batteries, including two batteries in the Honourable Artillery Company. (See Honourable Artillery Company.)

The Royal Field Artillery was armed with 18-pounder, breech-loading, quick-firing guns and 4.7-inch howitzers. These guns could move at a trot. A battery of field artillery consisted of six guns and limbers with 12 ammunition and supply wagons. There were three drivers for each gun and five gunners. The gunners rode on the limbers and ammunition wagons. The sergeant in charge of the gun was mounted. Three batteries formed a brigade (18 guns). In 1914, there were 147 batteries of the Royal Field Artillery, including 32 howitzer batteries. Forty-five batteries were stationed in India along with 12 ammunition columns, and there were three batteries stationed in South Africa. In the Territorial Force, there were 55 brigades, 14 of which were howitzer brigades.

The Royal Garrison Artillery dealt with a variety of heavy guns: 6-, 8-, and 9.4-inch howitzers; 4.7-, 6-, and 9.2-inch guns and the 60-pounder gun. These guns were mobile but needed many teams of horses to move them. By 1914, however, the Army Service Corps was providing mechanical transport and drivers to the Royal Garrison Artillery. (See Army Service Corps.) A variety of experimental tractors was used as the prime mover. (A 45-horsepower Thornycroft Military Oil Tractor is illustrated in figure 38.) Many of these heavy guns were in garrison mountings in the fortresses of defended ports. The Royal Garrison Artillery also maintained nine mountain batteries. These batteries were armed with the light 10-pounder breech-loading, quick-firing guns that could be broken down and carried on the backs of mules.

The organization of the Royal Garrison Artillery differed from that of horse or field artillery. In 1914, the personnel of the Royal Garrison Artillery were organized into 87 companies and 12 heavy batteries. Eighteen companies and five heavy batteries were stationed in India. There were eight companies stationed at Malta, seven at Gibraltar, three at Aden, three at Hong Kong, two at Bermuda, two at Singapore, and two in South Africa. There was one company each stationed at Sierra Leone, Mauritius, Jamaica, and Ceylon. Mountain artillery was formed into batteries rather than companies. There were nine batteries of mountain artillery; eight were stationed in India and one at Cairo, Egypt. In the Territorial Force, there were 14 heavy batteries, three mountain batteries, and 82 companies assigned to coast defence.

In addition to the above, the Royal Garrison Artillery also maintained the Hong Kong-Singapore Battalion, headquartered in Hong Kong with three companies, a fourth company in Singapore, and a fifth company in Mauritius. The Royal Garrison Artillery provided the officers. The other ranks were Sikhs and Muslims recruited in India. There was also a local company of the Royal Garrison Artillery in Sierra Leone, West Africa. The other ranks were Africans recruited locally. These troops wore the uniform of the Royal Garrison Artillery. The Indians wore turbans.

It should be noted that the Royal Horse Artillery, the Royal Field Artillery, and the Royal Garrison Artillery made up the Royal Regiment of Artillery. The word regiment had no tactical significance. The Royal Regiment of Artillery was an entire branch of the army.

ENGINEERS

CORPS OF ROYAL ENGINEERS

In 1914, the Corps of Royal Engineers was headquartered at Chatham, England. King George V was Colonel-in-Chief.

1716	The Officer Corps of Engineers raised from the ancient Board of Ordnance (originally formed circa 1414 to include the king's military engineers)
1772	The Soldier Artificer Company (other ranks) raised
1787	The Officer Corps of Engineers given the title *Royal Corps* of Engineers (The Corps of Royal Military Artificers (other ranks) is raised and absorbs the Soldier Artificer Company.)
1812	The Corps of Royal Military Artificers given the title the Corps of Royal Sappers and Miners
1856	The Corps of Royal Engineers (officers) and the Corps of Royal Sappers and Miners (other ranks) merged as the Corps of Royal Engineers.

BATTLE HONOURS: *Ubique* (Like the Royal Regiment of Artillery, the Corps of Royal Engineers has served in almost every battle and campaign for which a battle honour has been granted. *Ubique* (Everywhere) includes them all.)

The uniform of the Corps of Royal Engineers included a blue helmet with a brass spike. The scarlet tunic had blue facings and piping down the front of the tunic. There was yellow braid on the shoulders, around the collar, and on the cuffs. White infantry-style waist belts were worn. There were wide scarlet stripes on the blue trousers or pantaloons in the case of mounted formations. The blue forage cap had a scarlet band. This uniform of an officer (with blueprint) and two privates is illustrated by figure 39.

Bandsmen of the Corps of Royal Engineers wore a bearskin cap similar to that of the Foot Guards. There was no plume. The scarlet tunic had blue facings and yellow piping. No waist belt was worn. Five yellow brandenbergs were on the front of the tunic with no visible buttons. The dark blue trousers had wide scarlet stripes. In 1914, there were two bands: one at Chatham, England, the Corps headquarters, and another at Aldershot, England.

ORGANIZATION

In 1914, the Corp of Royal Engineers consisted of 15 field companies, 28 fortress companies (including works and electric light sections), two bridging trains, three survey companies, two railway companies, a railway depot, one works (line of communication) company, one printing company, a field squadron (mounted), and a field troop (mounted). There were eight signal companies, one wireless signal company, a signal squadron (mounted), and four signal troops (mounted). There were nine depot companies at Corps headquarters and one depot company at Army Headquarters in India. The Indian Army maintained a separate engineering establishment consisting of three corps of Sappers and Miners with officers assigned from the Corps of Royal Engineers.

Of the companies mentioned above, the following were overseas: four fortress companies at Gibraltar, two at Malta, two at Hong Kong, and one fortress company each stationed at Bermuda, Ceylon, Sierra Leone, Singapore, Mauritius, Jamaica, and Simonstown, Union of South Africa. There was one field company at Cairo, Egypt, and one at Pretoria, Union of South Africa. There was one signal company in the Union of South Africa and a survey section at Penang, Malay States. The Corps of Royal Engineers also maintained the School of Military Engineering at Chatham, the School of Signalling at Aldershot, and the Schools of Electric Lighting at Plymouth and Portsmouth. In the Territorial Force, there were 43 fortress companies (24 designated works companies and 19 designated electric light companies). There were also 28 field companies, 29 signal companies, 10 electrical engineer companies, and an Engineer and Railway Staff Corps.

It should be noted that since 1878, the Corps of Royal Engineers had been involved with balloons and later with airplanes. Balloon detachments went on active service in Bechuanaland in 1884 and in the Sudan in 1885. During the South African War (1899-1902), four balloon sections were in operation. In 1907, the first British Army airship, a dirigible, was in service. In 1911, the Air Battalion of the Corps of Royal Engineers was formed. In 1912, however, the Royal Flying Corps was raised and absorbed the Air Battalion. (See Royal Flying Corps.)

FOOT GUARDS

GRENADIER GUARDS

In 1914, the 1st Battalion was stationed at Warley, England, the 2nd Battalion at Chelsea Barracks, London, and the 3rd Battalion at Wellington Barracks, London. King George V was Colonel-in-Chief.

1656   Raised as the Royal Regiment of Guards by King Charles II at Bruges, Flanders (now Belgium). On his return to England. Charles II raised another regiment: the King's Royal Regiment of Foot Guards.
1665   The two regiments raised by Charles II amalgamated into the Royal Regiment of Foot Guards
1685   The First Regiment of Foot Guards
1815   1st or Grenadier Guards

BATTLE HONOURS: *Tangier 1680, Namur 1695, Gibraltar 1704-05, Blenheim, Ramillies, Oudenarde, Malplaquet, Dettingen, Lincelles, Egmont-op-Zee, Corunna, Barrosa, Nive, Peninsula, Waterloo, Alma, Inkerman, Sevastopol, Tel el Kebir, Egypt 1882, Suakin 1885, Khartoum, Modder River, South Africa 1899-1902*

The uniform included a black bearskin cap with a white plume on the left. The scarlet tunic had blue facings, and there were slashes on the cuffs with three points and three buttons. Buttons on the front of the tunic were evenly spaced. The blue trousers had red piping, and the blue forage cap a scarlet band. This uniform is illustrated by figure 40.

COLDSTREAM GUARDS

In 1914, the 1st Battalion was stationed at Aldershot, England, the 2nd Battalion at Windsor, England, and the 3rd Battalion at Chelsea Barracks, London. King George V was Colonel-in-Chief.

- 1650 Raised as Colonel Monck's Regiment of Foot in the service of Parliament
- 1661 Disbanded and immediately reraised as the Lord General's Regiment of Foot Guards in the service of the Crown
- 1670 Coldstream Regiment of Foot Guards
- 1817 Coldstream Guards

BATTLE HONOURS: *Egypt (with the Sphinx), Tangier 1680, Namur 1695, Gibraltar 1704-05, Oudenarde, Malplaquet, Dettingen, Lincelles, Talavaera, Barrosa, Fuentes d'Onor, Nive, Peninsula, Waterloo, Alma, Inkerman, Sevastopol, Tel el Kebir, Egypt 1882 Suakin 1885, Modder River, South Africa 1899-1902*

The uniform included a black bearskin cap with a red plume on the right side. The scarlet tunic had blue facings, and there were slashes on the cuffs with three points and three buttons. The buttons on the front of the tunic were in sets of two. The blue trousers had red piping, and the blue forage cap had a white band. This uniform is illustrated by figure 41.

SCOTS GUARDS

In 1914, the 1st Battalion was stationed at Aldershot, England, and the 2nd Battalion at the Tower of London. King George V was Colonel-in-Chief.

- 1660 Raised as the Scots Regiment of Guards
- 1712 The 3rd Foot Guards
- 1831 The Scots Fusilier Guards
- 1877 Scots Guards

BATTLE HONOURS: *Egypt (with the Sphinx), Namur 1695, Dettingen, Lincelles, Talavera, Barrosa, Fuentes d'Onor, Nive, Peninsula, Waterloo, Alma, Inkerman, Sevastopol, Tel el Kebir, Egypt 1882, Suakin 1885, Modder River, South Africa 1899-1902.*

The uniform included a black bearskin cap without a plume. The scarlet tunic had blue facings, and there were slashes on the cuffs with three points and three buttons. The buttons on the front of the tunic were in sets of three. The blue trousers had red piping, and the blue forage cap had a red-and-white diced band. This uniform is illustrated by figure 42.

The pipers wore black feather bonnets with red over blue plumes. The doublets were blue with kilts of Royal Stuart tartan. The hose was scarlet and green.

IRISH GUARDS

In 1914, the one battalion of the Irish Guards was stationed at Wellington Barracks, London. King George V was Colonel-in-Chief.

- 1900 Raised in April 1900 by order of Queen Victoria to commemorate the devotion and bravery shown by the Irish regiments serving in the South African War

The uniform included a black bearskin cap with a blue plume on the right. The scarlet tunic had blue facings, and there were slashes on the cuffs with three points and three buttons. The buttons on the front of the tunic were in sets of four. The blue trousers had red piping, and the blue forage cap had a green band. This uniform is illustrated by figure 43.

Note: Although beyond the scope of this book, it should be mentioned that a fifth regiment of Foot Guards, the Welsh Guards was raised in 1915, by order of King George V. Thus, every nationality within the British Isles was represented. The full dress uniform of the Welsh Guards was the same as the other regiments of Foot Guards. The regimental distinctions were a white-green-white plume on the left of the bearskin cap and buttons in sets of five on the front of the tunic.

INFANTRY OF THE LINE

THE ROYAL SCOTS (LOTHIAN REGIMENT) (1ST FOOT)

In 1914, the 1st Battalion was stationed at Allahbad, India, and the 2nd Battalion at Plymouth, England. The 3rd Battalion, the Edinburgh Light Infantry Militia, was headquartered at Edinburgh. The Territorial Force comprised the 4th Battalion (Queen's Edinburgh Rifles), the 5th Battalion (Queen's Edinburgh Rifles), and the 6th Battalion, headquartered at Edinburgh. The 7th Battalion, was headquartered at Leith, the 8th Battalion at Haddington, the 9th (Highlanders) Battalion at Edinburgh, and the 10th (Cyclist) Battalion at Linlithgow.

1633	Raised in Scotland for the service of France, and known as *Le Regiment d'Hebron*
1637	*Le Regiment d'Douglas* in French service
1669	Taken into *English* service
1678	The Earl of Dumbarton's Regiment of Foot
1684	The Royal Regiment of Foot
1751	1st or Royal Regiment of Foot
1812	1st or Royal Scots
1821	1st or Royal Regiment
1871	1st or Royal Scots Regiment
1881	Lothian Regiment (Royal Scots)
1882	Royal Scots (Lothian Regiment)

BATTLE HONOURS: *Egypt (with the Sphinx), Tangier 1680, Namur 1695, Blenheim, Ramillies, Oudenarde, Malplaquet, Louisburg, Havannah, Egmont-op-Zee, St. Lucia 1803, Corunna, Busaco, Salamanca, Vittoria, St. Sebastian, Nive, Peninsula, Niagara, Waterloo, Nagpore, Maheidpore, Ava, Alma, Inkerman, Sevastopol, Taku Forts, Pekin 1860, South Africa, 1899-1902*

4th, 5th, and 7th Battalions *South Africa 1900-02* 6th, 9th, and 10th Battalions *South Africa 1901-02* 8th Battalion *South Africa 1901*

The uniform included a blue Kilmarnock bonnet with a red-white-blue diced border, a red pom-pom, and blackcock's feathers. The scarlet doublet had blue facings, and the trews were of Hunting Stuart tartan. This uniform is illustrated by figure 44.

The pipers wore a glengarry cap with a red-white-blue diced border and blackcock's feathers. A blue doublet was worn with kilts of Hunting Stuart tartan.

The 4th and 5th Battalions (Queen's Edinburgh Rifles) wore a blue glengarry cap. The dark grey tunic had black facings, and the trousers were dark grey.

The 9th Battalion (Highlanders) were uniformed the same as the other territorial battalions but wore kilts of Hunting Stuart Tartan rather than trews.

THE QUEEN'S (ROYAL WEST SURREY REGIMENT) (2ND FOOT)

In 1914, the 1st Battalion was stationed at Bordon Camp, England, and the 2nd Battalion at Robert's Heights, Transvaal, Union of South Africa. The 3rd Battalion, the 2nd Royal Surrey Militia, was headquartered at Guildford. The Territorial Force comprised the 4th Battalion, headquartered at Croydon, and the 5th Battalion, at Guildford.

1661	Raised as the Tangier Regiment of Foot
1684	Queen's Regiment
1715	Princess of Wales's Own Regiment of Foot
1727	Queen's Own Royal Regiment of Foot
1751	2nd or Queen's Royal Regiment of Foot
1881	Queen's (Royal West Surrey Regiment)

BATTLE HONOURS: *1st of June 1794 (with a Naval Crown), Egypt (with the Sphinx), Tangier 1662-80, Namur 1695, Vimiera, Corunna, Salamanca, Vittoria, Pyrenees, Nivelle, Toulouse, Peninsula, Ghuznee 1839, Khelat, Afghanistan 1839, South Africa 1851-2-3, Taku Forts, Pekin 1860, Burma 1885-87, Tirah, Relief of Ladysmith, South Africa 1900-02* (Note: The battle honour *1st June 1794 (with a Naval Crown)*, denotes service as marines.)

4th and 5th Battalions *South Africa 1900-02*

The uniform included a blue helmet with a brass spike. The scarlet tunic had blue facings. The blue trousers had red piping and the blue forage cap had a scarlet band. This uniform is illustrated by figure 45.

The 5th Battalion wore a rifle green tunic with scarlet facings, rifle green trousers and forage cap.

THE BUFFS (EAST KENT REGIMENT) (3RD FOOT)

In 1914, the 1st Battalion was stationed at Fermoy, Ireland, and the 2nd Battalion at Madras, India. The 3rd Battalion (East Kent Militia) was headquartered at Canterbury. The Territorial Force comprised the 4th Battalion, headquartered at Canterbury, and the 5th (Weald of Kent) Battalion at Ashford. King Christian X of Denmark was Colonel-in-Chief.

1572	Raised as the Holland Regiment in the service of Holland
1665	The Holland Regiment in the service of King Charles II
1689	Prince George of Denmark's Regiment
1708	First known as the *Buffs*
1751	3rd or the Buffs Regiment of Foot
1772	3rd (East Kent-The Buffs) Regiment of Foot
1881	The Buffs (East Kent Regiment)

BATTLE HONOURS: *Blenheim, Ramillies, Oudenarde, Malplaquet, Dettingen, Guadaloupe 1759, Douro, Talavera, Albuhera, Vittoria, Pyrenees, Nivelle, Nive, Orthes, Toulouse, Peninsula, Punniar, Sevastopol, Taku Forts, South Africa 1879, Chitral, Relief of Kimberley, Paardeberg, South Africa 1900-02*

4th and 5th Battalions *South Africa 1900-02*

The uniform included a blue helmet with brass spike. The scarlet tunic had buff facings. The blue trousers had red piping, and there was a blue forage cap. This uniform is illustrated by figure 46.

THE KING'S OWN (ROYAL LANCASTER REGIMENT) (4TH FOOT)

In 1914, the 1st Battalion was stationed at Dover, England, and the 2nd Battalion at Lebong Island, Malay Peninsula. The 3rd Battalion, 1st Royal Lancashire Militia, was headquartered at Lancaster. The Territorial Force comprised the 4th Battalion, headquartered at Ulverston, and the 5th Battalion at Lancaster. King George V was Colonel-in-Chief.

1680	Raised as the 2nd Tangier Regiment
1684	Duchess of York and Albany's Regiment
1685	Queen's Regiment
1702	Queen's Marine Regiment
1715	King's Own Regiment
1751	4th or King's Own Regiment
1867	4th (The King's Own Royal) Regiment
1881	King's Own (Royal Lancaster Regiment)

BATTLE HONOURS: *Namur 1695, Gibraltar 1704-05, Guadaloupe 1759, St. Lucia 1778, Corunna, Badajoz, Salamanca, Vittoria, St. Sebastian, Nive, Peninsula, Bladensburg, Waterloo, Alma, Inkerman, Sevastopol, Abyssinia, South Africa 1879, Relief of Ladysmith, South Africa 1899-1902*

4th and 5th Battalions *South Africa 1900-02*

The uniform included a blue helmet with a brass spike. The scarlet tunic had blue facings. The blue trousers had red piping, and the blue forage cap had a scarlet band. This uniform is illustrated by figure 47.

THE NORTHUMBERLAND FUSILIERS (5TH FOOT)

In 1914, the 1st Battalion was stationed at Portsmouth, England, and the 2nd Battalion at Sabathu, India. The 3rd Battalion, Northumberland Militia, was headquartered at Newcastle-on-Tyne. The Territorial Force comprised the 4th Battalion, headquartered at Hexham, the 5th and 6th Battalions at Newcastle-on-Tyne, and the 7th Battalion at Alnwick.

1674	Raised as the Irish Regiment in the service of the Prince of Orange
1685	Taken into *English* service
1751	5th Foot
1782	5th or Northumberland Regiment of Foot
1836	5th or Northumberland Fusiliers
1881	Northumberland Fusiliers

BATTLE HONOURS: *Wilhelmstahl, St. Lucia 1778, Rolica, Vimiera, Corunna, Busaco, Ciudad Rodrigo, Badajoz, Salamanca, Vittoria, Nivelle, Orthes, Toulouse, Peninsula, Lucknow, Afghanistan 1879-80, Khartoum, Modder River, South Africa 1899-1902*

4th, 5th, and 6th Battalions *South Africa 1900-02*

The uniform included a raccoon skin fusilier cap with a scarlet over white plume on the left. The scarlet tunic had gosling green facings. The blue trousers had red piping, and the forage cap was blue. This uniform is illustrated by figure 48.

THE ROYAL WARWICKSHIRE REGIMENT (6TH FOOT)

In 1914, the 1st Battalion was stationed at Shorncliffe, England, and the 2nd Battalion at Malta. The 3rd Battalion, 1st Warwickshire Militia, and the 4th Battalion, 2nd Warwickshire Militia, were headquartered at Warwick. The Territorial Force comprised the 5th and 6th Battalions, headquartered at Birmingham, the 7th Battalion at Coventry, and the 8th Battalion at Birmingham.

1673	Raised as Vane's Regiment in the service of Holland
1685	Taken into *English* service
1751	6th Foot
1782	6th (1st Warwickshire) Regiment
1832	6th (Royal 1st Warwickshire) Regiment
1881	Royal Warwickshire Regiment

BATTLE HONOURS: *Namur 1695, Martinique 1794, Rolica, Vimiera, Corunna, Vittoria, Pyrenees, Nivelle, Orthes, Peninsula, Niagara, South Africa 1846-47, 1851-2-3, Atbara, Khartoum, South Africa 1899-1902*

5th, 6th, and 7th Battalions *South Africa 1900-02*

The uniform included a blue helmet with a brass spike. The scarlet tunic had blue facings. The blue trousers had red piping, and the blue forage cap had a scarlet band. This uniform is illustrated by figure 49.

THE ROYAL FUSILIERS (CITY OF LONDON REGIMENT) (7TH FOOT)

In 1914, the 1st Battalion was stationed at Kinsale, Ireland, the 2nd Battalion at Calcutta, India, the 3rd Battalion at Lucknow, India, and the 4th Battalion on the Isle of Wight, England. The 5th Battalion, Royal Westminster Militia, and the 6th Battalion, Royal South Middlesex Militia, were headquartered at Hounslow. The 7th Battalion, Royal London Militia, was headquartered at Finsbury, London. The Territorial Force comprised the 1st, 2nd, 3rd, and 4th (City of London) Battalions, the London Regiment (Royal Fusiliers). (See the *London Regiment*.) King George V was Colonel-in-Chief.

1685	Raised as the Royal Regiment of Fusiliers or the Ordnance Regiment
1751	7th Foot (Royal Fusiliers)
1881	Royal Fusiliers (City of London Regiment)

BATTLE HONOURS: *Namur 1695, Martinique 1809, Talavera, Busaco, Albuhera, Badajos, Salamanca, Vittoria, Pyrenees, Orthes, Toulouse, Peninsula, Alma, Inkerman, Sevastopol, Kandahar 1880, Afghanistan 1879-80, Relief of Ladysmith, South Africa 1899-1902*

See the *London Regiment* for battle honours of the four affiliated Territorial Force battalions.

The uniform included a raccoon skin fusilier cap (officers had bearskin caps) with a white plume on the right. The scarlet tunic had blue facings. The blue trousers had red piping, and the blue forage cap had a scarlet band. This uniform is illustrated by figure 50.

THE KING'S (LIVERPOOL REGIMENT) (8TH FOOT)

In 1914, the 1st Battalion was stationed at Aldershot, England, and the 2nd Battalion at Peshawar, India. The 3rd and 4th Battalions, 2nd Royal Lancashire Militia, were headquartered at Seaforth. The Territorial Force comprised the 5th and 6th (Rifles) Battalions, headquartered at Liverpool, the 7th Battalion at Bootle and the 8th (Irish) Battalion, 9th Battalion, and 10th (Scottish) Battalions all headquartered at Liverpool. In addition, there was a *Volunteer* battalion on the Isle of Man.

1685	Raised as Princess Anne of Denmark's Regiment
1702	Queen's Regiment
1716	King's Regiment
1751	8th (The King's) Regiment
1881	King's (Liverpool Regiment)

BATTLE HONOURS: *Egypt (with the Sphinx), Blenheim, Ramillies, Oudenarde, Malplaquet, Dettingen, Martinique 1809, Niagara, Delhi 1857, Lucknow, Peiwar Kotal, Afghanistan 1878-80, Burma 1885-87, Defence of Ladysmith, South Africa 1899-1902*

5th, 7th, and 8th Battalions *South Africa 1900-02* 6th and 9th Battalions *South Africa 1900-01* 10th Battalion *South Africa 1902*

The uniform included a blue helmet with a brass spike. The scarlet tunic had blue facings. The blue trousers had red piping, and the blue forage cap had a scarlet band. This uniform is illustrated by figure 51.

The 5th Battalion wore a rifle green tunic with black facings, rifle green trousers, and forage cap.

The 6th (Rifles) Battalion wore a rifle green tunic with scarlet facings, rifle green trousers, and forage cap.

The 8th (Irish) Battalion wore a rifle green tunic with black facings, rifle green trousers, and forage cap.

The 10th (Scottish) Battalion wore a blue glengarry cap, a khaki doublet with scarlet facings, a kilt of Forbes tartan, and a grey sporran with two black tails.

THE NORFOLK REGIMENT (9TH FOOT)

In 1914, the 1st Battalion was stationed at Holywood, Ireland, and the 2nd Battalion at Belgaum, India. The 3rd Battalion, Norfolk Militia, was headquartered at Norwich. The Territorial Force comprised the 4th Battalion, headquartered at Norwich, the 5th Battalion at East Dereham, and the 6th (Cyclist) Battalion at Norwich. King George V was Colonel-in-Chief.

1685	Raised as Cornwell's Regiment
1751	9th Foot
1782	9th (East Norfolk) Regiment of Foot
1881	Norfolk Regiment

BATTLE HONOURS: *Havannah, Martinique 1794, Rolica, Vimiera, Corunna, Busaco, Salamanca, Vittoria, St. Sebastian, Nive, Peninsula, Cabool 1842, Moodkee, Ferozeshah, Sobraon, Sevastopol, Kabul 1879, Afghanistan 1879-80, Paardeberg, South Africa 1900-02*

4th and 5th Battalions *South Africa 1900-02*

The uniform included a blue helmet with a brass spike. The scarlet tunic had yellow facings, and the blue trousers had red piping. The forage cap was blue. This uniform is illustrated by figure 52.

THE LINCOLNSHIRE REGIMENT (10TH FOOT)

In 1914, the 1st Battalion was stationed at Portsmouth, England, and the 2nd Battalion at Bermuda. The 3rd Battalion, Royal North Lincolnshire Militia, was headquartered at Lincoln. The Territorial Force comprised the 4th Battalion, headquartered at Grimsby, and the 5th Battalion at Lincoln.

1685	Raised as Greville's Regiment
1751	10th Foot
1782	10th or North Lincolnshire Regiment
1881	Lincolnshire Regiment

BATTLE HONOURS: *Egypt (with the Sphinx), Blenheim, Ramillies, Oudenarde, Malplaquet, Peninsula, Sobraon, Mooltan, Goojerat, Punjaub, Lucknow, Atbara, Khartoum, Paardeberg, South Africa 1900-02.*

4th and 5th Battalions *South Africa 1900-02.*

The uniform included a blue helmet with a brass spike. The scarlet tunic had white facings, and the blue trousers had red piping. The forage cap was blue. This uniform is illustrated by figure 53.

THE DEVONSHIRE REGIMENT (11TH FOOT)

In 1914, the 1st Battalion was stationed on the Island of Jersey, and the 2nd Battalion at Cairo, Egypt. The 3rd Battalion, Devon Militia, was headquartered at Exeter. The Territorial Force comprised the 4th Battalion, headquartered at Exeter, the 5th (Prince of Wales's) Battalion at Plymouth, the 6th Battalion at Barnstaple, and the 7th (Cyclist) Battalion at Exeter.

1685 Raised as the Duke of Beaufort's Regiment
1751 11th Foot
1782 11th or North Devonshire Regiment
1881 Devonshire Regiment

BATTLE HONOURS: *Dettingen, Salamanca, Pyrenees, Nivelle, Nive, Orthes, Toulouse, Peninsula, Afghanistan 1879-80, Tirah, Defence of Ladysmith, Relief of Ladysmith, South Africa 1899-1902*

4th, 5th, and 6th Battalions *South Africa 1900-01*

The uniform included a blue helmet with a brass spike. The scarlet tunic had Lincoln green facings, and the blue trousers had red piping. The forage cap was blue. This uniform is illustrated by figure 54.

The 4th Battalion wore a rifle green tunic with black facings, rifle green trousers, and forage cap.

THE SUFFOLK REGIMENT (12TH FOOT)

In 1914, the 1st Battalion was stationed at Khartoum, Anglo-Egyptian Sudan, and the 2nd Battalion at Curragh, Ireland. The 3rd Battalion, West Suffolk Militia, was headquartered at Bury St. Edmunds. The Territorial Force comprised the 4th Battalion headquartered at Ipswich, the 5th Battalion at Bury St. Edmunds, and the 6th (Cyclist) Battalion at Ipswich.

1685 Raised as the Duke of Norfolk's Regiment
1751 12th Foot
1782 12th or East Suffolk Regiment
1881 Suffolk Regiment

BATTLE HONOURS: *Gibraltar 1779-83 (with the Castle and Key), Dettingen, Minden, Seringapatam, India, South Africa 1851-2-3, New Zealand, Afghanistan 1878-80, South Africa 1899-1902*

4th and 5th Battalions *South Africa 1900-02*

The uniform included a blue helmet with a brass spike. The scarlet tunic had yellow facings, and the blue trousers had red piping. The forage cap was blue. This uniform is illustrated by figure 55.

PRINCE ALBERT'S (SOMERSET LIGHT INFANTRY) (13TH FOOT)

In 1914, the 1st Battalion was stationed at Colchester, England, and the 2nd Battalion at Quetta, India. The 3rd Battalion, Somerset Militia, was headquartered at Taunton. The Territorial Force comprised the 4th Battalion, headquartered at Bath, and the 5th Battalion at Taunton.

1685 Raised as the Earl of Huntingdon's Regiment
1751 13th Foot
1782 13th or First Somersetshire Regiment
1822 13th or First Somersetshire Regiment, Light Infantry
1842 13th or 1st Somersetshire, Prince Albert's Light Infantry
1881 Prince Albert's (Somerset Light Infantry)

BATTLE HONOURS: *Egypt (with the Sphinx), Jellalabad (with a Mural Crown), Gibraltar 1704-05, Dettingen, Martinique 1809, Ava, Ghuznee 1839, Afghanistan 1839, Cabool 1842, Sevastopol, South Africa 1878-79, Burma 1885-87, Relief of Ladysmith, South Africa 1899-1902*

4th and 5th Battalions *South Africa 1900-01*

The uniform included a green helmet with a brass spike. The scarlet tunic had blue facings, and the blue trousers had red piping. The forage cap was green. This uniform is illustrated by figure 56.

THE PRINCE OF WALES'S OWN (WEST YORKSHIRE REGIMENT) (14TH FOOT)

In 1914, the 1st Battalion was stationed at Lichfield, England, and the 2nd Battalion at Malta. The 3rd Battalion, 2nd West York Militia, and the 4th Battalion, 4th West York Militia, were headquartered at York. The Territorial Force comprised the 5th Battalion, headquartered at York, the 6th Battalion at

Bradford, and the 7th (Leeds Rifles) and 8th (Leeds Rifles) Battalions at Leeds.

1685	Raised as Hales's Regiment
1751	14th Foot
1782	14th or Bedfordshire Regiment
1809	14th or Buckinghamshire Regiment
1876	14th (Buckinghamshire, The Prince of Wales's Own) Regiment
1881	Prince of Wales's Own (West Yorkshire Regiment)

BATTLE HONOURS: *India (with the Royal Tiger), Namur 1695, Tournay, Corunna, Java, Waterloo, Bhurtpore, Sevastopol, New Zealand, Afghanistan 1879-80, Relief of Ladysmith, South Africa 1899-1902*

5th, 6th, 7th (Leeds Rifles) and 8th (Leeds Rifles) Battalions *South Africa 1900-02*

The uniform included a blue helmet with a brass spike. The scarlet tunic had buff facings, and the blue trousers had red piping. The forage cap was blue. This uniform is illustrated by figure 57.

The 7th (Leeds Rifles) Battalion and the 8th (Leeds Rifles) Battalion wore a rifle green tunic with black facings, rifle green trousers, and forage cap.

THE EAST YORKSHIRE REGIMENT (15TH FOOT)

In 1914, the 1st Battalion was stationed at York, England, and the 2nd Battalion at Kamptee, India. The 3rd Battalion, East York Militia, was headquartered at Beverly. The Territorial Force comprised the 4th and the 5th (Cyclist) Battalions, headquartered at Hull.

1685	Raised as Clifton's Regiment
1751	15th Foot
1782	15th or York, East Riding, Regiment
1881	East Yorkshire Regiment

BATTLE HONOURS: *Blenheim, Ramillies, Oudenarde, Malplaquet, Louisburg, Quebec 1759, Martinique 1762, Havannah, St. Lucia 1778, Martinique 1794, 1809, Guadaloupe 1810, Afghanistan 1879-80, South Africa 1900-02*

4th Battalion *South Africa 1900-01*

The uniform included a blue helmet with a brass spike. The scarlet tunic had white facings, and the blue trousers had red piping. The forage cap was blue. This uniform is illustrated by figure 58.

The 5th (Cyclist) Battalion wore a rifle green tunic with scarlet facings, rifle green trousers, and forage cap.

THE BEDFORDSHIRE REGIMENT (16TH FOOT)

In 1914, the 1st Battalion was stationed at Mullingar, Ireland, and the 2nd Battalion at Robert's Heights, Transvaal, Union of South Africa. The 3rd Battalion, the Bedfordshire Militia, was headquartered at Bedford. The 4th Battalion, the Hertfordshire Militia, was headquartered at Hertford. The Territorial Force comprised the 5th Battalion headquartered at Bedford.

1688	Raised as Douglass's Regiment
1751	16th Foot
1782	16th or Buckinghamshire Regiment
1809	16th or Bedfordshire Regiment
1881	Bedfordshire Regiment

BATTLE HONOURS: *Namur 1695, Blenheim, Ramillies, Oudenarde, Malplaquet, Surinam, Chitral, South Africa 1900-02*

5th Battalion *South Africa 1900-02*

The uniform included a blue helmet with a brass spike. The scarlet tunic had white facings, and the blue trousers had red piping. The forage cap was blue. This uniform is illustrated by figure 59.

THE LEICESTERSHIRE REGIMENT (17TH FOOT)

In 1914, the 1st Battalion was stationed at Fermoy, Ireland, and the 2nd Battalion at Raniket, India. The 3rd Battalion, the Leicestershire Militia, was headquartered at Leicester. The Territorial Force comprised the 4th Battalion, headquartered at Leicester, and the 5th Battalion at Loughborough.

1688 Raised as Richards's Regiment
1751 17th Foot
1782 17th or Leicestershire Regiment
1881 Leicestershire Regiment

BATTLE HONOURS: *Hindoostan (with the Royal Tiger), Namur 1695, Louisburg, Martinique 1762, Havannah, Ghuznee 1839, Khelat, Afghanistan 1839, Sevastopol, Ali Masjid, Afghanistan 1878-79, Defence of Ladysmith, South Africa 1899-1902*

4th and 5th Battalions *South Africa 1900-02*

The uniform included a blue helmet with a brass spike. The scarlet tunic had white facings, and the blue trousers had red piping. The forage cap was blue. This uniform is illustrated by figure 60.

THE ROYAL IRISH REGIMENT (18TH FOOT)

In 1914, the 1st Battalion was stationed at Nasirabad, India, and the 2nd Battalion at Devonport, England. The 3rd Battalion, the North Tipperary Militia, was headquartered at Clonmel, and the 4th Battalion, the Kilkenny Militia, at Kilkenny. Field Marshal, Sir John French, was Colonel-in-Chief.

1684 Raised as the Earl of Granard's Regiment
1695 The Royal Regiment of Ireland
1751 18th or Royal Irish Regiment
1881 Royal Irish Regiment

BATTLE HONOURS: *Egypt (with the Sphinx), China (with the Dragon), Namur 1695, Blenheim, Ramillies, Oudenarde, Malplaquet, Pegu, Sevastopol, New Zealand, Afghanistan 1879-80, Tel el Kebir, Egypt 1882, Nile 1884-85, South Africa 1900-02*

The uniform included a blue helmet with a brass spike. The scarlet tunic had blue facings. The blue trousers had red piping, and the blue forage cap had a scarlet band. This uniform is illustrated by figure 61.

ALEXANDRA, PRINCESS OF WALES'S OWN (YORKSHIRE REGIMENT) (19TH FOOT)

In 1914, the 1st Battalion was stationed at Barian, India, and the 2nd Battalion on the Island of Guernsey. The 3rd Battalion, the 5th West York Militia, was headquartered at Richmond. The Territorial Force comprised the 4th Battalion, headquartered at Northallerton, and the 5th Battalion at Scarborough. Queen Alexandra was Colonel-in-Chief.

1688 Raised as Luttrell's Regiment
1751 19th Foot
1782 19th or 1st Yorkshire, North Riding, Regiment
1875 19th (1st Yorkshire North Riding, Princess of Wales's Own) Regiment
1881 The Princess of Wales's Own (Yorkshire Regiment)
1902 Alexandra, Princess of Wales's Own (Yorkshire Regiment)

BATTLE HONOURS: *Malplaquet, Alma, Inkerman, Sevastopol, Tirah, Relief of Kimberley, Paardeberg, South Africa 1899-1902*

4th and 5th Battalions *South Africa 1900-02*

The uniform included a blue helmet with a brass spike. The scarlet tunic had grass green facings, and the blue trousers had red piping. The forage cap was blue. This uniform is illustrated by figure 62.

THE LANCASHIRE FUSILIERS (20TH FOOT)

In 1914, the 1st Battalion was stationed at Karachi, India, and the 2nd Battalion at Dover, England. The 3rd and 4th Battalions, 7th Royal Lancashire Militia, was headquartered at Bury. The Territorial Force comprised the 5th Battalion, headquartered at Bury, the 6th Battalion, at Rochdale, and the 7th and 8th Battalions at Salford.

1688	Raised as Peyton's Regiment
1751	20th Foot
1782	20th or East Devonshire Regiment
1881	Lancashire Fusiliers

BATTLE HONOURS: *Egypt (with the Sphinx), Dettingen, Minden, Egmont op Zee, Maida, Vimiera, Corunna, Vittoria, Pyrenees, Orthes, Toulouse, Peninsula, Alma, Inkerman, Sevastopol, Lucknow, Khartoum, Relief of Ladysmith, South Africa 1899-1902*

5th, 6th, 7th, and 8th Battalions *South Africa 1900-02*

The uniform included a raccoon skin fusilier cap with a primrose-yellow plume on the left side. The scarlet tunic had white facings, and the blue trousers had red piping. The forage cap was blue. This uniform is illustrated by figure 63.

THE ROYAL SCOTS FUSILIERS (21ST FOOT)

In 1914, the 1st Battalion was stationed at Gosport, England, and the 2nd Battalion at Gibraltar. The 3rd Battalion, Royal Ayr and Wigtown Militia, was headquartered at Ayr. The Territorial Force comprised the 4th Battalion, headquartered at Kilmarnock, the 5th Battalion, at Ayr, and the Ardeer Company (attached to the 4th Battalion) at Ardeer.

1678	Raised as the Earl of Mar's Regiment or the Scots Fusiliers in the service of Holland
1688	Taken into *English* service
1707	North British Fusiliers
1712	21st or Royal North British Fusiliers
1877	21st Foot (Royal Scots Fusiliers)
1881	Royal Scots Fusiliers

BATTLE HONOURS: *Blenheim, Ramillies, Oudenarde, Malplaquet, Dettingen, Martinique 1794, Bladensburg, Alma, Inkerman, Sevastopol, South Africa 1879, Burma 1885-87, Tirah, Relief of Ladysmith, South Africa 1899-1902*

4th Battalion *South Africa 1900-02* 5th Battalion *South Africa 1900-01*

The uniform included a seal skin fusilier cap with a white plume on the right. The scarlet doublet had blue facings, and the trews were of Sutherland tartan. The blue glengarry cap had a scarlet-green-white diced border. This uniform is illustrated by figure 64.

The pipers wore a blue glengarry cap with a scarlet-greenwhite diced border and feathers and a blue doublet with kilts of Sutherland tartan.

THE CHESHIRE REGIMENT (22ND FOOT)

In 1914, the 1st Battalion was stationed at Londonderry, Ireland, and the 2nd Battalion at Jubbulpore, India. The 3rd Battalion, Royal Cheshire Militia, was headquartered at Chester. The Territorial Force comprised the 4th Battalion, headquartered at Birkenhead, the 5th (Earl of Chester's) Battalion at Chester, the 6th Battalion at Stockport, and the 7th Battalion at Macclesfield.

1689	Raised as the Duke of Norfolk's Regiment
1751	22nd Foot
1782	22nd or The Cheshire Regiment
1881	Cheshire Regiment

BATTLE HONOURS: *Louisburg, Martinique 1762, Havannah, Meeanee, Hyderabad, Scinde, South Africa 1900-02*

4th Battalion *South Africa 1901-02*

5th and 6th Battalions *South Africa 1900-02*

The uniform included a blue helmet with a brass spike. The scarlet tunic had buff facings, and the blue trousers had red piping. The forage cap was blue. This uniform is illustrated by figure 65.

The 4th Battalion wore a grey tunic with scarlet facings. The grey trousers had red piping, and the grey forage cap had a scarlet band.

THE ROYAL WELSH FUSILIERS (23RD FOOT)

In 1914, the 1st Battalion was stationed on Malta, and the 2nd Battalion at Portland, England. The 3rd Battalion, Royal Denbigh and Flint Militia, was headquartered at Wrexham. The Territorial Force comprised the 4th (Denbighshire) Battalion, headquartered at Wrexham, the 5th (Flintshire) Battalion at Flint, the 6th (Carnarvonshire and Anglesey) Battalion at Carnarvon, and the 7th (Merioneth and Montgomery) Battalion, at Newtown, Montgomery. King George V was Colonel-in-Chief.

1689	Raised as Lord Herbert's Regiment
1714	Prince of Wales's Own Royal Welsh Fusiliers
1727	The Royal Welsh Fusiliers
1751	23rd or Royal Welsh Fusiliers
1881	Royal Welsh Fusiliers

BATTLE HONOURS: *Egypt (with the Sphinx), Namur 1695, Blenheim, Ramillies, Oudenarde, Malplaquet, Dettingen, Minden, Corunna, Martinique 1809, Albuhera, Badajos, Salamanca, Vittoria, Pyrenees, Nivelle, Orthes, Toulouse, Peninsula, Waterloo, Alma, Inkerman, Sevastopol, Lucknow, Ashantee 1873-4, Burma 1885-87, Relief of Ladysmith, South Africa 1899-1902, Pekin 1900*

4th, 5th and 6th Battalions *South Africa 1900-02*

7th Battalion *South Africa 1900-01*

The uniform included a raccoon skin fusilier cap with a white plume on the right. The scarlet tunic had blue facings. The *flash* on the back of the collar was a bunch of black ribbons formerly worn to tie the queue. The blue trousers had red piping, and the blue forage cap had a scarlet band. This uniform is illustrated by figures 66 and 66A.

THE SOUTH WALES BORDERERS (24TH FOOT)

In 1914, the 1st Battalion was stationed at Bordon, England, and the 2nd Battalion at Tientsin, China. The 3rd Battalion, the Royal South Wales Borderers Militia, was headquartered at Wrexham. The Territorial Force comprised the Brecknockshire Battalion headquartered at Brecon.

1689	Raised as Dering's Regiment
1751	24th Foot
1881	South Wales Borderers

BATTLE HONOURS: *Egypt (with the Sphinx). Blenheim, Ramillies, Oudenarde, Malplaquet, Cape of Good Hope 1806, Talavera, Busaco, Fuentes d'Onor, Salamanca, Vittoria, Pyrenees, Nivelle, Orthes, Peninsula, Chillianwallah, Goojerat, Punjaub, South Africa 1877-8-9, Burma 1885-87, South Africa 1900-02*

The Brecknockshire Battalion *South Africa 1900-01*

The uniform included a blue helmet with a brass spike. The scarlet tunic had grass green facings, and the blue trousers had red piping. The forage cap was blue. This uniform is illustrated by figure 67.

THE KING'S OWN SCOTTISH BORDERERS (25TH FOOT)

In 1914, the 1st Battalion was stationed at Lucknow, India, and the 2nd Battalion at Dublin, Ireland. The 3rd Battalion, the Scottish Borderers Militia, was headquartered at Dumfries. The Territorial Force comprised the 4th (Border) Battalion, headquartered at Galashiels, and the 5th (Dumfries and Galloway) Battalion at Dumfries.

1689	Raised as the Earl of Levan's Regiment
1751	25th or the Edinburgh Regiment
1805	25th or the King's Own Borderers Regiment
1887	King's Own Scottish Borderers

BATTLE HONOURS: *Egypt (with the Sphinx), Namur 1695, Minden, Egmont op Zee, Martinique 1809, Afghanistan 1878-80, Chitral, Tirah, Paardeberg, South Africa 1900-02*

4th and 5th Battalions *South Africa 1900-02*

The uniform included a blue Kilmarnock bonnet with a red-white-blue diced border, a red pom-pom, and a plume of blackcock's feathers. The scarlet doublet had blue facings, and the trews were of Leslie tartan. This uniform is illustrated by figure 68.

The pipers wore a blue glengarry cap with a red-white-blue diced border and a blue doublet with kilts of Royal Stuart tartan.

THE CAMERONIANS (SCOTTISH RIFLES) (26TH AND 90TH FOOT)

In 1914, the 1st Battalion was stationed at Glasgow, Scotland, and the 2nd Battalion on Malta. The 3rd and 4th Battalions, the 2nd Royal Lanark Militia, were headquartered at Hamilton. The Territorial Force comprised the 5th Battalion, headquartered at Glasgow, the 6th Battalion at Hamilton, and the 7th and 8th Battalions at Glasgow.

26TH FOOT

1689	Raised as the Earl of Angus's Regiment, The Cameronians
1751	26th Foot
1786	26th or The Cameronians
1881	1st Battalion, Cameronians (Scottish Rifles)

90TH FOOT

1794	Raised as the 90th or Perthshire Volunteers
1815	*Light Infantry* added to the title
1881	2nd Battalion, Cameronians (Scottish Rifles)

BATTLE HONOURS: *Egypt (with the Sphinx), China (with the dragon), Blenheim, Ramillies, Oudenarde, Malplaquet, Mandora, Corunna, Martinique 1809, Guadaloupe 1810, South Africa 1846-7, Sevastopol, Lucknow, Abyssinia, South Africa 1877-8-9, Relief of Ladysmith, South Africa 1899-1902*

5th, 6th, 7th, and 8th Battalions *South Africa 1900-02*

The uniform included a green shako with a green plume. The rifle green doublet had black piping and black buttons. The trews were of Douglas tartan and the glengarry cap was green. This uniform is illustrated by figure 69.

The pipers wore a green glengarry cap, a green doublet, and kilts of Douglas tartan. Like other rifle regiments, the Cameronians (Scottish Rifles) band did not have drums (see *Military Bands* for explanation). However, because it was a Scottish regiment with bagpipes, there were drums in the pipe band.

The 5th Battalion wore a grey tunic with blue facings. The grey trousers had blue piping, and the glengarry cap was blue.

THE ROYAL INNISKILLING FUSILIERS (27TH AND 108TH FOOT)

In 1914, the 1st Battalion was stationed at Trimulgherry, India, and the 2nd Battalion at Dover, England. The 3rd Battalion, Royal Tyrone Militia, was headquartered at Omagh, and the 4th Battalion, Fermanagh Militia at Enniskillen.

27TH FOOT

1690	Raised as Tiffin's Regiment
1751	27th or Enniskillen (spelling changed in 1840) Regiment
1881	1st Battalion, Royal Inniskilling Fusiliers

108TH FOOT

1854	Raised as the 3rd Madras European Infantry of the Honorable East India Company
1861	Taken into the British Army as the 3rd (Madras) Regiment Designation changed to 108th (Madras Infantry) Regiment
1881	2nd Battalion, Royal Inniskilling Fusiliers

BATTLE HONOURS: *Egypt (with the Sphinx), Martinique 1762, Havannah, St. Lucia 1778, 1796, Maida, Badajos, Salamanca, Vittoria, Pyrenees, Nivelle, Orthes, Toulouse, Peninsula, Waterloo, South Africa 1835, 1846-47, Central India, Relief of Ladysmith, South Africa 1899-1902*

The uniform included a raccoon skin fusilier cap with a grey plume on the left. The scarlet tunic had blue facings. The blue trousers scarlet piping, and the blue forage cap had a scarlet band. This uniform is illustrated by figure 70.

THE GLOUCESTERSHIRE REGIMENT
(28TH and 61ST FOOT)

In 1914, the 1st Battalion was stationed at Bordon Camp, England, and the 2nd Battalion at Tientsin, China. The 3rd Battalion, Royal South Gloucester Militia, was headquartered at Bristol. The Territorial Force comprised the 4th (City of Bristol) Battalion, headquartered at Bristol, the 5th Battalion, at Gloucester, and the 6th Battalion, at Bristol.

28TH FOOT

1694	Raised as Gibson's Regiment
1751	28th Foot
1782	28th or North Gloucestershire Regiment
1881	1st Battalion, Gloucestershire Regiment

61ST FOOT

1756	Raised as the 2nd Battalion of the 3rd Foot
1758	61st Foot
1782	61st or South Gloucestershire Regiment
1881	2nd Battalion, Gloucestershire Regiment

BATTLE HONOURS: *Egypt (with the Sphinx), Ramillies, Louisburg, Guadaloupe 1759, Quebec 1759, Martinique 1762, Havannah, St. Lucia 1778, Maida, Corunna, Talavera, Busaco, Barrosa, Albuhera, Salamanca, Vittoria, Pyrenees, Nivelle, Nive, Orthes, "Toulouse", Peninsula, Waterloo, Chillianwallah, Goojerat, Punjaub, Alma, Inkerman, Sevastopol, Delhi 1857, Defence of Ladysmith, Relief of Kimberley, Paardeberg, South Africa 1899-1902*

4th and 5th Battalions *South Africa 1900-02*

The uniform included a blue helmet with a brass spike. The scarlet tunic had white facings, and the blue trousers had red piping. The forage cap was blue. A small Sphinx badge was worn on the back of the headdress, an honour granted for distinguished conduct at Alexandria, Egypt, in 1801 when attacked by the enemy in the front and rear simultaneously. This uniform is illustrated by figure 71.

The 5th Battalion wore a rifle green tunic with scarlet facings, rifle green trousers, and forage cap.

THE WORCESTERSHIRE REGIMENT
(29TH AND 36TH FOOT)

In 1914, the 1st Battalion was stationed at Cairo, Egypt. The 2nd Battalion was stationed at Aldershot, England, the 3rd Battalion at Tidworth, England, and the 4th Battalion at Meiktila, Burma. The 5th and 6th Battalions, Worcester Militia, were headquartered at Worcester. The Territorial Force comprised the 6th Battalion, headquartered at Kidderminster, and the 8th Battalion at Worcester.

29TH FOOT

1694	Raised as Farrington's Regiment
1751	29th Foot
1782	29th or Worcestershire Regiment
1881	1st Battalion, Worcestershire Regiment

36TH FOOT

1701	Raised as Charlemont's Regiment
1751	36th Foot
1782	36th or Herefordshire Regiment
1881	2nd Battalion, Worcestershire Regiment

The 3rd and 4th Battalions were added after 1881.

BATTLE HONOURS: *1st June 1794 (with a Naval Crown), Ramillies, Mysore, Hindoostan, Rolica, Vimiera, Corunna, Talavera, Albuhera, Salamanca, Pyrenees, Nivelle, Nive, Orthes, Toulouse, Peninsula, Ferozeshah, Sobraon, Chillianwallah, Goojerat, Punjaub", South Africa 1900-02* (Note: The battle honour *1st June 1794* (with a Naval Crown) denotes service as marines.)

7th Battalion *South Africa 1900-01* 8th Battalion *South Africa 1900-02*

The uniform included a blue helmet with a brass spike. The scarlet tunic had white facings, and the blue trousers had red piping. The forage cap was blue. This uniform is illustrated by figure 72.

THE EAST LANCASHIRE REGIMENT (30TH AND 59TH FOOT)

In 1914, the 1st Battalion was stationed at Colchester, England, and the 2nd Battalion at Wynberg, Cape Province, Union of South Africa. The 3rd Battalion, the 5th Royal Lancashire Militia, was headquartered at Preston. The Territorial Force comprised the 4th Battalion, headquartered at Blackburn, and the 5th Battalion at Burnley.

30TH FOOT
1694	Raised and known by the Colonel's name
1751	30th Foot
1782	30th or Cambridgeshire Regiment
1881	1st Battalion, Lancashire Regiment

59TH FOOT
1741	Raised as the 59th Foot
1782	59th or 2nd Nottinghamshire Regiment
1881	2nd Battalion, Lancashire Regiment

BATTLE HONOURS: *Egypt (with the Sphinx). Gibraltar 1704-5, Cape of Good Hope 1806, Corunna, Java, Badajos, Salamanca, Vittoria, St. Sebastian, Nive, Peninsula, Waterloo, Bhurtpore, Alma, Inkerman, Sevastopol, Canton, Ahmed Khel, Afghanistan 1878-80, Chitral, South Africa, 1900-02*

4th and 5th Battalions *South Africa 1900-02*

The uniform included a blue helmet with brass spike. The scarlet tunic had white facings, and the blue trousers had red piping. The forage cap was blue. This uniform is illustrated by figure 73.

The facings of the 5th Battalion were black rather than white.

THE EAST SURREY REGIMENT (31ST AND 70TH FOOT)

In 1914, the 1st Battalion was stationed at Dublin, Ireland, and the 2nd Battalion at Chaubattia, India. The 3rd Battalion, 1st Royal Surrey Militia, and the 4th Battalion, 3rd Royal Surrey Militia, were headquartered at Kingston-on-Thames. The Territorial Force comprised the 5th Battalion, headquartered at Wimbledon, and the 6th Battalion at Kingston-on-Thames.

31ST FOOT
1702	Raised as Villier's Regiment of Marines
1714	Goring's Regiment of Foot
1751	31st Foot
1782	31st or Huntingdonshire Regiment
1881	1st Battalion, East Surrey Regiment

70TH FOOT
1756	Raised as the 2nd Battalion, 31st Foot
1758	70th Foot
1782	70th or Surrey Regiment
1813	70th or Glasgow Lowland Regiment
1825	70th or Surrey Regiment
1881	2nd Battalion, East Surrey Regiment

BATTLE HONOURS: *Gibraltar 1704-5, Dettingen, Martinique 1794, Talavera, Guadaloupe 1810, Albuhera, Vittoria, Pyrenees, Nivelle, Nive, Orthes, Peninsula, Cabool 1842, Moodkee, Ferozeshah, Aliwal, Sobraon, Sevastopol, Taku Forts, New Zealand, Afghanistan 1878-79, Suakin 1885, Relief of Ladysmith, South Africa 1899-1902*

5th Battalion *South Africa 1900-02* 6th Battalion *Imperial Service, South Africa 1900-02*

The uniform included a blue helmet with a brass spike. The scarlet tunic had white facings, and the blue trousers had red piping. The forage cap was blue. This uniform is illustrated by figure 74.

The 6th Battalion wore a rifle green tunic with scarlet facings, rifle green trousers, and forage cap.

THE DUKE OF CORNWALL'S LIGHT INFANTRY (32ND and 46TH FOOT)

In 1914, the 1st Battalion was stationed at Curragh, Ireland, and the 2nd Battalion at Hong Kong. The 3rd Battalion, the Royal Cornwall Rangers Militia, was headquartered at Bodmin. The Territorial Force comprised the 4th Battalion, headquartered at Truro, and the 5th Battalion at Bodmin.

32ND FOOT

1702	Raised as Fox's Regiment of Marines
1751	32nd Foot
1782	32nd or Cornwall Regiment
1858	32nd or Cornwall Regiment, Light Infantry
1881	1st Battalion, Duke of Cornwall's Light Infantry

46TH FOOT

1741	Raised as Price's Regiment
1751	46th Foot
1782	46th or South Devonshire Regiment
1881	2nd Battalion, Duke of Cornwall's Light Infantry

BATTLE HONOURS: *Gibraltar 1704-05, Dettingen, St. Lucia 1778, Dominica, Rolica, Vimiera, Corunna, Salamanca, Pyrenees, Nivelle, Nive, Orthes, Peninsula, Waterloo, Mooltan, Goojerat, Punjaub, Sevastopol, Lucknow, Tel el Kebir, Egypt 1882, Nile 1884-85, Paardeberg, South Africa 1899-1902*

4th and 5th Battalions *South Africa 1900-01*

The uniform included a green helmet with a brass spike. The scarlet tunic had white facings, and the blue trousers had red piping. The forage cap was green. This uniform is illustrated by figure 75.

THE DUKE OF WELLINGTON'S (WEST RIDING REGIMENT) (33RD AND 76TH FOOT)

In 1914, the 1st Battalion was stationed at Lahore, India, and the 2nd Battalion at Dublin, Ireland. The 3rd Battalion, the 6th West York Militia, was headquartered at Halifax. The Territorial Force comprised the 4th Battalion, headquartered at Halifax, the 5th Battalion at Huddersfield, the 6th Battalion at Skipton-in-Craven, and the 7th Battalion at Milnsbridge.

33RD FOOT

1702	Raised as Huntingdon's Regiment
1751	33rd Foot
1782	33rd or 1st York, West Riding Regiment (Arthur Wellesley, 1st Duke of Wellington (1769-1852) was made colonel of the 33rd Foot in 1796 after serving as a major and lieutenant colonel in the regiment.)
1853	33rd (Duke of Wellington's Regiment)
1881	1st Battalion, Duke of Wellington's (West Riding Regiment)

76TH FOOT

1787	Raised as the 76th Foot
1807	76th or Hindoostan Regiment
1812	76th Foot
1881	2nd Battalion, Duke of Wellington's (West Riding Regiment)

BATTLE HONOURS: *Hindoostan (with the Elephant), Dettingen, Mysore, Seringapatam, Ally Ghur, Delhi 1803, Leswarree, Deig, Corunna, Nive, Peninsula, Waterloo, Alma, Inkerman, Sevastopol, Abyssinia, Relief of Kimberley, Paardeberg, South Africa 1900-02*

4th, 5th, 6th and 7th Battalions *South Africa 1900-02*

The uniform included a blue helmet with a brass spike. The scarlet tunic had scarlet facings (the only scarlet-coated regiment with scarlet facings), blue trousers with red piping, and a blue forage cap. This uniform is illustrated by figure 76.

THE BORDER REGIMENT
(34TH AND 55TH FOOT)

In 1914, the 1st Battalion was stationed at Maymyo, Burma, and the 2nd Battalion at Pembroke Dock, Wales. The 3rd Battalion, Royal Cumberland Militia, was headquartered at Carlisle. The Territorial Force comprised the 4th (Cumberland and Westmorland) Battalion, headquartered at Carlisle, and the 5th (Cumberland) Battalion at Workington.

34TH FOOT
1702   Raised as Lord Lucas's Regiment
1751   34th Foot
1782   34th or Cumberland Regiment
1881   1st Battalion, The Border Regiment

55TH FOOT
1742   Raised as the 55th Foot
1782   55th or Westmorland Regiment
1881   2nd Battalion, The Border Regiment

BATTLE HONOURS: *China (with the Dragon). Havannah, St. Lucia 1778, Albuhera, Arroyo dos Molinos, Vittoria, Pyrenees, Nivelle, Nive, Orthes, Peninsula, Alma, Inkerman, Sevastopol, Lucknow, Relief of Ladysmith, South Africa 1899-1902*

4th Battalion *South Africa 1900-02* 5th Battalion *South Africa 1901-02*

The uniform included a blue helmet with a brass spike. The scarlet tunic had yellow facings, and the blue trousers had red piping. The forage cap was blue. This uniform is illustrated by figure 77.

THE ROYAL SUSSEX REGIMENT
(35TH AND 107TH FOOT)

In 1914, the 1st Battalion was stationed at Peshawur, India, and the 2nd Battalion at Woking, England. The 3rd Battalion, Royal Sussex Militia, was headquartered at Chichester. The Territorial Force comprised the 4th Battalion, headquartered at Horsham, the 5th (Cinque Ports) Battalion at Hastings, and the 6th (Cyclist) Battalion at Brighton.

35TH FOOT
1701   Raised as the Earl of Donegal's Regiment
1751   35th Foot
1782   35th or Dorsetshire Regiment
1805   35th or Sussex Regiment
1832   35th (Royal Sussex) Regiment
1881   1st Battalion, Royal Sussex Regiment

107TH FOOT
1854   Raised as the 3rd Bengal European Light Infantry of the Honorable East India Company
1858   3rd Bengal Light Infantry
1862   Taken into the British Army as the 107th Bengal Infantry
1881   2nd Battalion, Royal Sussex Regiment

BATTLE HONOURS: *Gibraltar 1704-05, Louisburg, Quebec 1759, Martinique 1762, Havannah, St. Lucia 1778, Maida, Egypt 1882, Abu Klea, Nile 1884-85, South Africa 1900-02*

4th and 5th Battalions *South Africa 1900-02*

The uniform included a blue helmet with a brass spike. The scarlet tunic had blue facings. The blue trousers had red piping, and the blue forage cap had scarlet band. This uniform is illustrated by figure 78.

THE HAMPSHIRE REGIMENT
(37TH AND 67TH FOOT)

In 1914, the 1st Battalion was stationed at Colchester, England, and the 2nd Battalion at Mhow, India. The 3rd Battalion, Hampshire Militia, was headquartered at Winchester. The Territorial Force comprised the 4th Battalion, headquartered at Winchester, the 5th Battalion at Southampton, the 6th (Duke of Connaught's Own) Battalion at Portsmouth, the 7th Battalion at Bournemouth, the 8th (Isle of Wight Rifles, Princess Beatrice's) Battalion at Newport, and the 9th (Cyclist) Battalion at Southampton.

37TH FOOT

1702	Raised as Meredith's Regiment
1751	37th Foot
1782	37th or North Hampshire Regiment
1881	1st Battalion, Hampshire Regiment

67TH FOOT

1758	Raised as the 67th Foot
1782	67th or South Hampshire Regiment
1881	2nd Battalion, Hampshire Regiment

BATTLE HONOURS: *India (with the Royal Tiger), Blenheim, Ramillies, Oudenarde, Malplaquet, Dettingen, Minden, Tournay, Barrosa, Peninsula, Taku Forts, Pekin 1860, Charasia, Kabul 1879, Afghanistan 1878-80, Burma 1885-87, Paardeberg, South Africa 1900-02*

4th, 5th, and 6th Battalions *South Africa 1900-02*

8th Battalion *South Africa 1900-01*

The uniform included a blue helmet with a brass spike. The scarlet tunic had yellow facings, and the blue trousers had red piping. The forage cap was blue. This uniform is illustrated by figure 79.

The 8th (Isle of Wight Rifles, Princess Beatrice's) Battalion wore a rifle green tunic with black facings, rifle green trousers and forage cap. King George V was Colonel-in-Chief of the 8th Battalion.

THE SOUTH STAFFORDSHIRE REGIMENT (38TH AND 80TH FOOT)

In 1914, the 1st Battalion was stationed at Pietermaritzburg, Natal, Union of South Africa, and the 2nd Battalion at Aldershot, England. The 3rd and 4th Battalions, the 1st King's Own Stafford Militia, were headquartered at Lichfield. The Territorial Force comprised the 5th Battalion, headquartered at Walsall, and the 6th Battalion at Wolverhampton.

38TH FOOT

1702	Raised as Lillingstone's Regiment
1751	38th Foot
1782	38th or 1st Staffordshire Regiment
1881	1st Battalion, South Staffordshire Regiment

80TH FOOT

| 1793 | Raised as the 80th or Staffordshire Volunteers Regiment |
| 1881 | 2nd Battalion, South Staffordshire Regiment |

BATTLE HONOURS: *Egypt (with the Sphinx), Guadaloupe 1759, Martinique 1762, Monte Video, Rolica, Vimiera, Corunna, Busaco, Badajos, Salamanca, Vittoria, St. Sebastian, Nive, Peninsula, Ava, Inkerman, Sevastopol, Lucknow, Central India, South Africa 1878-79, Egypt 1882, Kirbekan, Nile 1884-85, South Africa 1900-02*

5th and 6th Battalions *South Africa 1900-02*

The uniform included a blue helmet with a brass spike. The scarlet tunic had white facings, and the blue trousers had red piping. The forage cap was blue. This uniform is illustrated by figure 80.

THE DORSETSHIRE REGIMENT (39TH AND 54TH FOOT)

In 1914, the 1st Battalion was stationed at Belfast, Ireland, and the 2nd Battalion at Poona, India. The 3rd Battalion, Dorset Militia, was headquartered at Dorchester. The Territorial Force comprised the 4th Battalion, also headquartered at Dorchester.

39TH FOOT

1702	Raised as Coote's Regiment
1751	39th Foot
1782	39th or East Middlesex Regiment
1807	39th or Dorsetshire Regiment
1881	1st Battalion, Dorsetshire Regiment

54TH FOOT

1755	Raised as the 56th Foot
1757	Renumbered 54th
1782	54th or West Norfolk Regiment
1881	2nd Battalion, Dorsetshire Regiment

BATTLE HONOURS: *Gibraltar 1779-83, (with the Castle and Key), Egypt (with the Sphinx), Plassey, Martinique 1794, Marabout, Albuhera, Vittoria, Pyrenees, Nivelle, Nive, Orthes, Peninsula, Ava, Maharajpore, Sevastopol, Tirah, Relief of Ladysmith, South Africa 1899-1902*

4th Battalion *South Africa 1900-01*

The uniform included a blue helmet with a brass spike. The scarlet tunic had grass green facings, and the blue trousers had red piping. The forage cap was blue. This uniform is illustrated by figure 81.

THE PRINCE OF WALES'S VOLUNTEERS (SOUTH LANCASHIRE REGIMENT) (40TH AND 82ND FOOT)

In 1914, the 1st Battalion was stationed at Quetta, India, and the 2nd Battalion at Tidworth, England. The 3rd Battalion, the 4th Royal Lancashire Militia, was headquartered at Warrington. The Territorial Force comprised the 4th Battalion, headquartered at Warrington, and the 5th Battalion at St. Helens.

40TH FOOT

1717	Raised as Phillip's Regiment
1751	40th Foot
1782	40th or 2nd Somersetshire Regiment
1881	1st Battalion, Prince of Wales's Volunteers (South Lancashire Regiment)

82ND FOOT

1793	Raised as the 82nd or Prince of Wales's Volunteer Regiment
1881	2nd Battalion, Prince of Wales's Volunteers (South Lancashire Regiment

BATTLE HONOURS: *Egypt (with the Sphinx), Louisburg, Martinique 1762, Havannah, St. Lucia 1778, Monte Video, Rolica, Vimiera, Corunna, Talavera, Badajos, Salamanca, Vittoria, Pyrenees, Nivelle, Orthes, Toulouse, Peninsula, Niagara, Waterloo, Candahar 1842, Ghuznee 1842, Cabool 1842, Maharajpore, Sevastopol, Lucknow, New Zealand, Relief of Ladysmith, South Africa 1899-1902*

4th Battalion *South Africa 1900-02*

5th Battalion *South Africa 1900-01*

The uniform included a blue helmet with a brass spike. The scarlet tunic had white facings, and the blue trousers had red piping. The forage cap was blue. This uniform is illustrated by figure 82.

The 5th Battalion wore a rifle green tunic with scarlet facings, rifle green trousers, and forage cap.

THE WELSH REGIMENT (41ST AND 69TH FOOT)

In 1914, the 1st Battalion was stationed at Chakrata, India, and the 2nd Battalion at Bordon Camp, England. The 3rd Battalion, Royal Glamorgan Militia, was headquartered at Cardiff. The Territorial Force comprised the 4th Battalion, headquartered at Carmarthen, the 5th Battalion at Pontypridd, the 6th (Glamorgan) Battalion at Swansea, and the 7th (Cyclist) Battalion at Cardiff.

41ST FOOT

1719	Raised as the 41st Royal Invalids
1787	41st Foot
1822	41st or Welsh Regiment
1881	1st Battalion, Welsh Regiment

69TH FOOT

1756	Raised as the 2nd Battalion 24th Foot
1758	69th Foot
1782	69th or South Lincolnshire Regiment
1881	2nd Battalion, Welsh Regiment

BATTLE HONOURS: *12th April 1782 (with a Naval Crown), Martinique 1762, St. Vincent, India, Bourbon, Java, Detroit, Queenstown, Miami, Niagara, Waterloo, Ava, Candahar 1842, Ghuznee 1842, Cabool 1842, Alma, Inkerman, Sevastopol, Relief of Kimberley, Paardeberg, South Africa 1899-1902.* Note: The battle honour *12th April 1782 (with a Naval Crown)*, denotes service as marines.

4th, 5th, and 6th Battalions *South Africa 1900-02*

The uniform included a blue helmet with a brass spike. The scarlet tunic had white facings, and the blue trousers had red piping. The forage cap was blue. This uniform is illustrated by figure 83.

The 7th (Cyclist) Battalion wore a rifle green tunic with scarlet facings, rifle green trousers, and forage cap.

THE BLACK WATCH (ROYAL HIGHLAND REGIMENT) (42ND AND 73RD FOOT)

In 1914, the 1st Battalion was stationed at Aldershot, England, and the 2nd Battalion at Bareilly India. The 3rd Battalion, Royal Perth Militia, was headquartered at Perth. The Territorial Force comprised the 4th (City of Dundee) Battalion, headquartered at Dundee, the 5th (Angus and Dundee) Battalion at Arbroath, the 6th (Perthshire) Battalion at Perth, and the 7th (Fife) Battalion at St. Andrews. King George V was Colonel-in-Chief.

42ND FOOT

1725	Independent companies of Highlanders raised in Scotland
1739	The Highland Regiment of Foot
1751	42nd or Highland Regiment
1758	42nd or Royal Highland Regiment
1861	42nd or Royal Highland Regiment (Black Watch)
1881	1st Battalion, Black Watch (Royal Highlanders)

73RD FOOT

1758	Raised as the 2nd Battalion 42nd or Royal Highland Regiment
1780	73rd Highland Regiment
1809	73rd Foot
1881	2nd Battalion, Black Watch (Royal Highlanders)

BATTLE HONOURS: *Egypt (with the Sphinx). Guadaloupe 1759, Martinique 1762, Havannah, North America 1763-64, Mangalore, Mysore, Seringapatam, Corunna, Busaco, Fuentes d'Onor, Pyrenees, Nivelle, Nive, Orthes, Toulouse, Peninsula, Waterloo, South Africa 1846-7, 1851-2-3, Alma, Sevastopol, Lucknow, Ashantee 1873-4, Tel el Kebir, Egypt 1882, 1884, Kirbekan, Nile 1884-85, Paardeberg, South Africa 1899-1902*

4th, 5th, and 6th Battalions *South Africa 1900-02*

The uniform included a black feather bonnet with a scarlet hackle and a red and white diced border. The scarlet doublet had blue facings, and the kilt was of Black Watch or *Government* tartan. The white sporran had five black tassels, and the hose was red and black. The glengarry cap was blue. This uniform is illustrated by figure 84.

The pipers wore a black feather bonnet with a scarlet hackle and a red and white diced border (the only Scottish regiment whose pipers wore the feather bonnet, other than pipers of the Scots Guards). The doublet was blue with a kilt of Royal Stuart tartan. The hose was red and black.

THE OXFORDSHIRE AND BUCKINGHAMSHIRE LIGHT INFANTRY (43RD AND 52ND FOOT)

In 1914, the 1st Battalion was stationed at Ahmednagar, India, and the 2nd Battalion at Aldershot, England. The 3rd Battalion, Oxford Militia, was headquartered at Oxford. The Territorial Force comprised the 4th Battalion, headquartered at Oxford, and the Buckinghamshire Battalion at Aylesbury.

43RD FOOT

1741	Raised as Fowke's Regiment
1751	43rd Foot
1782	43rd or Monmouthshire Regiment
1803	43rd or Monmouthshire Light Infantry
1881	1st Battalion, Oxfordshire Light Infantry
1908	1st Battalion, Oxfordshire and Buckinghamshire Light Infantry

52ND FOOT

1755	Raised as the 54th Foot
1757	Renumbered 52nd Foot
1782	52nd or Oxfordshire Regiment
1803	52nd or Oxfordshire Light Infantry
1881	2nd Battalion, Oxfordshire Light Infantry
1908	2nd Battalion, Oxfordshire and Buckinghamshire Light Infantry

BATTLE HONOURS: *Quebec 1759, Martinique 1762, Havannah, Mysore, Hindoostan, Martinique 1794, Vimiera, Corunna, Busaco, Fuentes d'Onor, Ciudad Rodrigo, Badajos, Salamanca, Vittoria, Pyrenees, Nivelle, Nive, Orthes, Toulouse, Peninsula, Waterloo, South Africa 1851-2-3, Delhi 1857, New Zealand, Relief of Kimberley, Paardeberg, South Africa 1900-02*

4th Battalion *South Africa 1900-01*

Buckinghamshire Battalion *South Africa 1900-02*

The uniform included a green helmet with a brass spike. The scarlet tunic had white facings, and the blue trousers had red piping. The forage cap was green. This uniform is illustrated by figure 85.

The Buckinghamshire Battalion wore a dark grey tunic with scarlet facings and dark grey trousers with red piping. The dark grey forage cap had a scarlet band.

THE ESSEX REGIMENT (44TH AND 56TH FOOT)

In 1914, the 1st Battalion was stationed on Mauritius, and the 2nd Battalion at Chatham, England. The 3rd Battalion Essex (Rifles) Militia, was headquartered at Warley. The Territorial Force comprised the 4th Battalion, headquartered at Brentwood, the 5th Battalion at Chelmsford, the 6th Battalion at West Ham, the 7th Battalion at Walthamstow, and the 8th (Cyclist) Battalion at Colchester.

44TH FOOT

1741	Raised as Long's Regiment
1751	44th Foot
1782	44th or East Essex Regiment
1881	1st Battalion, Essex Regiment

56TH FOOT

1755	Raised as the 58th Foot
1757	Renumbered 56th Foot
1782	56th or West Essex Regiment
1881	2nd Battalion, Essex Regiment

BATTLE HONOURS: *Gibraltar 1779-83 (with the Castle and Key), Egypt (with the Sphinx), Moro, Havannah, Badajos, Salamanca, Peninsula, Bladensburg, Waterloo, Ava, Alma, Inkerman, Sevastopol, Taku Forts, Nile 1884-85, Relief of Kimberley, Paardeberg, South Africa 1899-1902*

4th, 5th, 6th, and 7th Battalions *South Africa 1900-02*

The uniform included a blue helmet with a brass spike. The scarlet tunic had white facings, and the blue trousers had red piping. The forage cap was blue. This uniform is illustrated by figure 86.

Note: Although rifles appears in the title of the 3rd Essex (Rifles) Militia Battalion, this battalion was uniformed in scarlet tunics and white facings as were the other battalions.

THE SHERWOOD FORESTERS (NOTTINGHAMSHIRE AND DERBYSHIRE REGIMENT) (45TH AND 95TH FOOT)

In 1914, the 1st Battalion was stationed at Bombay, India, and the 2nd Battalion at Sheffield, England. The 3rd Battalion, the 1st and 2nd Derby Militia, and the 4th Battalion, Royal Sherwood Foresters Militia, were headquartered at Derby. The Territorial Force comprised the 5th Battalion, headquartered at Derby, the 6th Battalion at Chesterfield, the 7th (Robin Hood) Battalion at Nottingham, and the 8th Battalion at Newark.

45TH FOOT

1741	Raised as Houghton's Regiment
1782	45th or Nottinghamshire Regiment
1866	45th or Nottinghamshire-Sherwood Foresters Regiment
1881	1st Battalion, Sherwood Foresters (Derbyshire Regiment)
1902	1st Battalion, Sherwood Foresters (Nottinghamshire and Derbyshire Regiment)

95TH FOOT

1823	Raised as the 95th Foot
1825	95th or Derbyshire Regiment
1881	2nd Battalion, Sherwood Foresters (Derbyshire Regiment)
1902	2nd Battalion, Sherwood Foresters (Nottinghamshire and Derbyshire Regiment)

BATTLE HONOURS: *Louisburg, Rolica, Vimera, Talavera, Busaco, Fuentes d'Onor, Ciudad Rodrigo, Badajos, Salamanca, Vittoria, Pyrenees, Nivelle, Orthes, Toulouse, Peninsula, Ava, South Africa 1846-47, Alma, Inkerman, Sevastopol, Central India, Abyssinia, Egypt 1882, Tirah, South Africa 1899-1902*

5th, 6th, 7th, and 8th Battalions *South Africa 1900-02*

The uniform included a blue helmet with a brass spike. The scarlet tunic had Lincoln green facings, and the blue trousers had red piping. The forage cap was blue. This uniform is illustrated by figure 87.

The 5th Battalion had white facings rather than Lincoln green.

The 7th (Robin Hood) Battalion wore a Lincoln green tunic with black facings, green trousers, and forage cap.

THE LOYAL NORTH LANCASHIRE REGIMENT (47TH AND 81ST FOOT)

In 1914, the 1st Battalion was stationed at Aldershot, England, and the 2nd Battalion at Bangalore, India. The 3rd Battalion, the 3rd Royal Lancashire Militia, was headquartered at Preston. The Territorial Force comprised the 4th Battalion, headquartered at Preston, and the 5th Battalion at Bolton.

47TH FOOT

1740	Raised as Mordaunt's Regiment
1751	47th Foot
1782	47th or Lancashire Regiment
1881	1st Battalion, Loyal North Lancashire Regiment

81ST FOOT

1793	Raised as the 81st or Loyal Lincoln Volunteers Regiment
1794	81st Foot
1832	81st or Loyal Lincoln Volunteers Regiment
1881	2nd Battalion, Loyal North Lancashire Regiment

BATTLE HONOURS: *Louisburg, Quebec 1759, Maida, Corunna, Tarifa, Vittoria, St. Sebastian, Nive, Peninsula, Ava, Alma, Inkerman, Sevastopol, Ali Masjid, Afghanistan 1878-79, Defence of Kimberley, South Africa 1899-1902*

4th and 5th Battalions *South Africa 1900-02*

The uniform included a blue helmet with a brass spike. The scarlet tunic had white facings, and the blue trousers had red piping. The forage cap was blue. This uniform is illustrated by figure 88.

THE NORTHAMPTONSHIRE REGIMENT (48TH AND 58TH FOOT)

In 1914, the 1st Battalion was stationed at Blackdown Camp, England, and the 2nd Battalion at Alexandria, Egypt. The 3rd Battalion, Northampton and Rutland Militia, was headquartered at Northampton. The Territorial Force comprised the 4th Battalion, headquartered at Northampton.

48TH FOOT

1741	Raised as Cholmondeley's Regiment
1751	48th Foot
1782	48th or Northamptonshire Regiment
1881	1st Battalion, Northamptonshire Regiment

58TH FOOT

1740	Raised as the 58th Regiment of Foot
1755	Renumbered 56th, then 60th Foot
1755	Reverted to the 58th Foot
1782	58th or Rutlandshire Regiment
1881	2nd Battalion, Northamptonshire Regiment

BATTLE HONOURS: *Gibraltar 1779-83 (with the Castle and Key), Egypt (with the Sphinx), Louisburg, Quebec 1759, Martinique 1762, Havannah, Martinique 1794, Maida, Douro, Talavera, Albuhera, Badajos, Salamanca, Vittoria, Pyrenees, Nivelle, Orthes, Toulouse, Peninsula, New Zealand, Sevastopol, South Africa 1879, Tirah, Modder River, South Africa 1899-1902*

4th Battalion *South Africa 1899-1902*

The uniform included a blue helmet with a brass spike. The scarlet tunic had white facings, and the blue trousers had red piping. The forage cap was blue. This uniform is illustrated by figure 89.

PRINCESS CHARLOTTE OF WALES'S (ROYAL BERKSHIRE REGIMENT) (49TH AND 66TH FOOT)

In 1914, the 1st Battalion was stationed at Aldershot, England, and the 2nd Battalion at Jhansi, India. The 3rd Battalion, Royal Berkshire Militia, was headquartered at Reading. The Territorial Force comprised the 4th Battalion, headquartered at Reading.

49TH FOOT

1744	Raised as Trelawney's Regiment
1751	49th Foot
1782	49th or Hertfordshire Regiment

1816	49th or Hertfordshire-Princess Charlotte of Wales's Regiment
1881	1st Battalion, Princess Charlotte of Wales's (Berkshire Regiment)
1885	1st Battalion, Princess Charlotte of Wales's (Royal Berkshire Regiment)

66TH FOOT

1755	Raised as the 2nd Battalion of the 19th Foot
1758	66th Foot
1782	66th or Berkshire Regiment
1881	2nd Battalion, Princess Charlotte of Wales's (Berkshire Regiment)
1885	2nd Battalion, Princess Charlotte of Wales's (Royal Berkshire Regiment)

BATTLE HONOURS: *China (with the Dragon), St. Lucia 1778, Egmont op Zee, Copenhagen, Douro, Talavera, Albuhera, Queenstown, Vittoria, Pyrenees, Nivelle, Nive, Orthes, Peninsula, Alma, Inkerman, Sevastopol, Kandahar 1880, Afghanistan 1879-82, Egypt 1882, Tofrek, Suakin 1885, South Africa 1899-1902*

4th Battalion *South Africa 1900-02*

The uniform included a blue helmet with a brass spike. The scarlet tunic had blue facings. The blue trousers had red piping, and the blue forage cap had a scarlet band. This uniform is illustrated by figure 90.

THE QUEEN'S OWN (ROYAL WEST KENT REGIMENT) (50TH AND 97TH FOOT)

In 1914, the 1st Battalion was stationed at Dublin, Ireland, and the 2nd Battalion at Multan, India. The 3rd Battalion, West Kent Militia, was headquartered at Maidstone. The Territorial Force comprised the 4th Battalion, headquartered at Maidstone, and the 5th Battalion at Bromley.

50TH FOOT

1755	Raised as the 52nd Foot
1757	Renumbered 50th Foot
1782	50th or West Kent Regiment
1827	50th or Duke of Clarence's Regiment
1831	50th or Queen's Own Regiment
1881	1st Battalion, Queen's Own (Royal West Kent Regiment)

97TH FOOT

1824	Raised as the 97th Foot
1826	97th or Earl of Ulster's Regiment
1881	2nd Battalion, Queen's Own (Royal West Kent Regiment)

BATTLE HONOURS: *Egypt (with the Sphinx), Vimiera, Corunna, Almaraz, Vittoria, Pyrenees, Nive, Orthes, Peninsula, Punniar, Moodkee, Ferozeshah, Aliwal, Sobraon, Alma, Inkerman, Sevastopol, Lucknow, New Zealand, Egypt 1882, Nile 1884-85, South Africa 1900-02*

4th and 5th Battalions *South Africa 1900-02*

The uniform included a blue helmet with a brass spike. The scarlet tunic had blue facings. The blue trousers had red piping, and the blue forage cap had a scarlet band. This uniform is illustrated by figure 91.

THE KING'S OWN (YORKSHIRE LIGHT INFANTRY) (51ST AND 105TH FOOT)

In 1914, the 1st Battalion was stationed at Singapore, and the 2nd Battalion at Dublin, Ireland. The 3rd Battalion, the 1st York Militia, was headquartered at Pontefract. The Territorial Force comprised the 4th Battalion, headquartered at Wakefield, and the 5th Battalion at Doncaster.

51ST FOOT

1755	Raised as the 53rd Foot
1757	Renumbered 51st Foot
1782	51st or 2nd Yorkshire, West Riding Regiment
1809	51st or 2nd Yorkshire, West Riding, Light Infantry
1821	51st or 2nd Yorkshire, West Riding, King's Own Light Infantry
1881	1st Battalion, King's Own (Yorkshire Light Infantry)

105TH FOOT

1839	Raised as the 2nd Madras (European Light Infantry) Regiment of the Honorable East India Company
1858	2nd Madras (Light Infantry)
1861	Taken into the British Army as the 105th (Madras Light Infantry) Regiment
1881	2nd Battalion, King's Own (Yorkshire Light Infantry)

BATTLE HONOURS: *Minden, Corunna, Fuentes d'Onor, Salamanca, Vittoria, Pyrenees, Nivelle, Orthes, Peninsula, Waterloo, Pegu, Ali Masjid, Afghanistan 1878-80, Burma 1885-87, Modder River, South Africa 1899-1902*

4th and 5th Battalions *South Africa 1899-1902*

The uniform included a green helmet with a brass spike. The scarlet tunic had blue facings. The blue trousers had red piping, and the forage cap was green. This uniform is illustrated by figure 92.

THE KING'S (SHROPSHIRE LIGHT INFANTRY) (53RD AND 85TH FOOT)

In 1914, the 1st Battalion was stationed at Tipperary, Ireland, and the 2nd Battalion at Trimulgherry, India. The 3rd Battalion, Shropshire Militia, was headquartered at Shrewsbury. The Territorial Force comprised the 4th Battalion, headquartered at Shrewsbury.

53RD FOOT

1755 Raised as the 55th Foot
1757 Renumbered the 53rd Foot
1782 53rd or Shropshire Regiment
1881 1st Battalion, King's (Shropshire Light Infantry)

85TH FOOT

1794 Raised as the 85th or Buckinghamshire Volunteers Regiment
1808 85th or Buckinghamshire Volunteers Light Infantry
1815 85th or Buckinghamshire Volunteers, Duke of York's Own Light Infantry
1821 85th or Buckinghamshire Volunteers, The King's Light Infantry
1881 2nd Battalion, King's (Shropshire Light Infantry)

BATTLE HONOURS: *Nieuport, Tournay, St. Lucia 1796, Talavera, Fuentes d'Onor, Salamanca, Vittoria, Pyrenees, Nivelle, Nive, Toulouse, Peninsula, Bladensburg, Aliwal, Sobraon, Goojerat, Punjaub, Lucknow, Afghanistan 1879-80, Egypt 1882, Suakin 1885, Paardeberg, South Africa 1899-1902*

4th Battalion *South Africa 1900-02*

The uniform included a green helmet with a brass spike. The scarlet tunic had blue facings, and the blue trousers had red piping. The forage cap was green. This uniform is illustrated by figure 93.

THE DUKE OF CAMBRIDGE'S OWN (MIDDLESEX REGIMENT) (57TH AND 77TH FOOT)

In 1914, the 1st Battalion was stationed at Woolwich, England, and the 2nd Battalion on Malta, the 3rd Battalion at Cawnpore, India, and the 4th Battalion at Devonport, England. The 5th Battalion, Royal Elthorne Militia, and the 6th Battalion, Royal East Middlesex Militia, were headquartered at Mill Hill. The Territorial Force comprised the 7th Battalion, headquartered at Hornsey, the 8th Battalion at Hounslow, the 9th Battalion at Willesden Green, and the 10th Battalion at Hammersmith.

57TH FOOT

1741 Raised as the 57th Foot
1782 57th or West Middlesex Regiment
1881 1st Battalion, Duke of Cambridge's Own Middlesex Regiment)

77TH FOOT

1787 Raised as the 77th Foot
1807 77th or East Middlesex Regiment
1876 77th or East Middlesex, Duke of Cambridge's Own Regiment
1881 2nd Battalion, Duke of Cambridge's Own (Middlesex Regiment)

The 3rd and 4th Battalions were raised after 1881.

BATTLE HONOURS: *Mysore, Seringapatam, Albuhera, Ciudad Rodrigo, Badajos, Vittoria, Pyrenees, Nivelle, Nive, Peninsula, Alma, Inkerman, Sevastopol, New Zealand, South Africa 1879, Relief of Ladysmith, South Africa 1900-02*

7th and 8th Battalions *Imperial Service, South Africa 1900-02*

9th Battalion *South Africa 1900-02*

The uniform included a blue helmet with a brass spike. The scarlet tunic had lemon-yellow facings, and the blue trousers had red piping. The forage cap was blue. This uniform is illustrated by figure 94.

THE KING'S ROYAL RIFLE CORPS (60TH FOOT)

In 1914, the 1st Battalion was stationed at Aldershot, England, the 2nd Battalion at Blackdown, England, the 3rd Battalion at Meerut, India, and the 4th Battalion at Gharial, India. The 5th Battalion, Huntingdon Militia, and the 6th Battalion Royal Middlesex Militia, were headquartered at Winchester. King George V was Colonel-in-Chief.

1755	Raised in Virgina, Maryland and Pennsylvania as the 62nd or Royal American Regiment
1757	Renumbered 60th or Royal American Regiment
1824	60th or the Duke of York's Rifle Corps
1830	60th King's Royal Rifle Corps
1881	King's Royal Rifle Corps

BATTLE HONOURS: *Louisburg, Quebec 1759, Martinique 1762, Havannah, North America 1763-64, Rolica, Vimiera, Martinique 1809, Talavera, Busaco, Fuentes d'Onor, Albuhera, Ciudad Rodrigo, Badajos, Salamanca, Vittoria, Pyrenees, Nivelle, Nive, Orthes, Toulouse, Peninsula, Mooltan, Goojerat, Punjaub, South Africa 1851-2-3, Delhi 1857, Taku Forts, Pekin 1860, South Africa 1879, Ahmad Khel, Kandahar 1880, Afghanistan 1878-80, Tel el Kebir, Egypt 1882, 1884, Chitral, Defence of Ladysmith, Relief of Ladysmith, South Africa 1899-1902*

The uniform included a black rifle busby with scarlet piping. An officer's plume was scarlet on a black base; other ranks displayed black on a scarlet base. The rifle green tunic had scarlet facings and piping. (Officers had scarlet cuffs; other ranks had green cuffs with scarlet piping.) Buttons were black. The trousers and forage cap were rifle green. This uniform is illustrated by figure 95.

Note: The word corps in the title is misleading. The King's Royal Rifle Corps was a regiment.

THE DUKE OF EDINBURGH'S (WILTSHIRE REGIMENT) (62ND AND 99TH FOOT)

In 1914, the 1st Battalion was stationed at Tidworth, England, and the 2nd Battalion at Gibraltar. The 3rd Battalion, Royal Wiltshire Militia, was headquartered at Devizes. The Territorial Force comprised the 4th Battalion, headquartered at Trowbridge.

62ND FOOT

1756	Raised as the 2nd Battalion of the 4th Foot
1758	Became the 62nd Foot
1782	62nd or Wiltshire Regiment
1881	1st Battalion, Duke of Edinburgh's (Wiltshire Regiment)

99TH FOOT

1824	Raised as the 99th or Lanarkshire Regiment
1874	99th (Duke of Edinburgh's Regiment)
1881	2nd Battalion, Duke of Edinburgh's (Wiltshire Regiment)

BATTLE HONOURS: *Louisburg, Nive, Peninsula, New Zealand, Ferozeshah, Sobraon, Sevastopol, Pekin 1860, South Africa, 1879, South Africa 1900-02*

4th Battalion *South Africa 1900-02*

The uniform included a blue helmet with a brass spike. The scarlet tunic had buff facings, and the blue trousers had red piping. The forage cap was blue. This uniform is illustrated by figure 96.

The 4th Battalion wore a rifle green tunic with black facings, rifle green trousers, and forage cap. The Duke of Somerset was Honorary Colonel of the 4th Battalion

THE MANCHESTER REGIMENT (63RD AND 96TH FOOT)

In 1914, the 1st Battalion was stationed at Jullundur, India, and the 2nd Battalion at Curragh, Ireland. The 3rd and 4th Battalions, the 6th Royal Lancashire Militia, were headquartered at Ashton. The Territorial Force comprised the 5th Battalion, headquartered at Wigan, the 6th and 7th Battalions, both at Manchester, the 8th (Ardwick) Battalion at Ardwick, the 9th Battalion at Ashton-under-Lyne, and the 10th Battalion at Oldham.

63RD FOOT

1757	Raised as the 2nd Battalion of the 8th Foot
1758	Became the 63rd Foot
1782	63rd or West Suffolk Regiment
1881	1st Battalion, Manchester Regiment

96TH FOOT

1824	Raised as the 96th Foot
1881	2nd Battalion, Manchester Regiment

BATTLE HONOURS: *Egypt (with the Sphinx), Guadaloupe 1759, Egmont op Zee, Peninsula, Martinique 1809, Guadaloupe 1810, New Zealand, Alma, Inkerman, Sevastopol, Afghanistan 1879-80, Egypt 1882, Defence of Ladysmith, South Africa 1899-1902*

5th, 6th, 7th, 8th, and 9th Battalions *South Africa 1900-02*

10th Battalion *South Africa 1901-02*

The uniform included a blue helmet with a brass spike. The scarlet tunic had white facings, and the blue trousers had red piping. The forage cap was blue. This uniform is illustrated by figure 97.

The 6th Battalion had yellow facings rather than white.

THE PRINCE OF WALES'S (NORTH STAFFORDSHIRE REGIMENT) (64TH AND 98TH FOOT)

In 1914, the 1st Battalion was stationed at Buttevant, Ireland, and the 2nd Battalion at Rawalpindi, India. The 3rd Battalion, the 2nd King's Own Stafford Militia, and the 4th Battalion, the 3rd King's Own Stafford Militia, were headquartered at Lichfield. The Territorial Force comprised the 5th Battalion, headquartered at Hanley, and the 6th Battalion at Burton-on-Trent.

64TH FOOT

1756	Raised as the 2nd Battalion of the 11th Foot
1758	Became the 64th Foot
1782	64th or 2nd Staffordshire Regiment
1881	1st Battalion, Prince of Wales's (North Staffordshire Regiment)

98TH FOOT

1824	Raised as the 98th Foot
1876	98th (The Prince of Wales's) Regiment
1881	2nd Battalion, Prince of Wales's (North Staffordshire Regiment)

BATTLE HONOURS: *China (with the Dragon), Guadaloupe 1759, Martinique 1794, St. Lucia 1803, Surinam, Punjaub, Reshire, Bushire, Koosh-ab, Persia, Lucknow, Hafir, South Africa 1900-02*

5th and 6th Battalions *South Africa 1900-02*

The uniform included a blue helmet with a brass spike. The scarlet tunic white facings, and the blue trousers had red piping. The forage cap was blue. This uniform is illustrated by figure 98.

The 6th Battalion had blue facings rather than white.

THE YORK AND LANCASTER REGIMENT (65TH AND 84TH FOOT)

In 1914, the 1st Battalion was stationed at Jubbulpore, India, and the 2nd Battalion at Limerick, Ireland. The 3rd Battalion, the 3rd West York Militia, was headquartered at Pontefract. The Territorial Force comprised the 4th (Hallamshire) Battalion, headquartered at Sheffield, and the 5th Battalion at Rotherham.

65TH FOOT

1756	Raised as the 2nd Battalion of the 12th Foot
1758	Became the 65th Foot
1782	65th or 2nd Yorkshire North Riding Regiment
1881	1st Battalion, York and Lancaster Regiment

84TH FOOT

1793	Raised as the 84th Foot
1809	84th or York and Lancaster Regiment
1881	2nd Battalion, York and Lancaster Regiment

BATTLE HONOURS: *India (with the Royal Tiger). Guadaloupe 1759, Martinique 1794, India 1796-1819, Nive, Peninsula, Arabia, New Zealand, Lucknow, Tel el Kebir, Egypt 1882, 1884, Relief of Ladysmith, South Africa 1899-1902*

4th and 5th Battalions *South Africa 1900-02*

THE DURHAM LIGHT INFANTRY (68TH AND 106TH FOOT)

In 1914, the 1st Battalion was stationed at Nowshera, India, and the 2nd Battalion at Lichfield, England. The 3rd Battalion, the 2nd Durham Militia, was headquartered at Newcastle-on-Tyne and the 4th Battalion, the 1st Durham Militia was headquartered at Barnard Castle. The Territorial Force comprised the 5th Battalion, headquartered at Stockton-on-Tees, the 6th Battalion at Bishop Auckland, the 7th Battalion at Sunderland, the 8th Battalion at Durham, and the 9th Battalion at Gateshead.

68TH FOOT

- 1756 Raised as the 2nd Battalion of the 23rd Foot
- 1758 Became the 68th Foot
- 1782 68th or Durham Regiment
- 1808 68th or Durham Regiment, Light Infantry
- 1881 1st Battalion, Durham Light Infantry

106TH FOOT

- 1826 Raised as the 2nd Bombay European Light Infantry of the Honorable East India Company
- 1858 2nd Bombay Light Infantry
- 1861 Taken into the British Army as the 106th Bombay Light Infantry
- 1881 2nd Battalion, Durham Light Infantry

BATTLE HONOURS: *Salamanca, Vittoria, Pyrenees, Nivelle, Orthes, Peninsula, Alma, Inkerman, Sevastopol, Reshire, Bushire, Koosh-ab, Persia, New Zealand, Relief of Ladysmith, South Africa 1899-1902*

5th, 6th, 7th, 8th, and 9th Battalions *South Africa 1900-02*

The uniform included a green helmet with a brass spike. The scarlet tunic had dark green facings, and the blue trousers had red piping. The forage cap was green. This uniform is illustrated by figure 100.

THE HIGHLAND LIGHT INFANTRY (71ST AND 74TH FOOT)

In 1914, the 1st Battalion was stationed at Ambala, India, and the 2nd Battalion at Aldershot, England. The 3rd and 4th Battalions, the 1st Royal Lanark Militia, were headquartered at Hamilton. The Territorial Force comprised the 5th (City of Glasgow) Battalion, the 6th (City of Glasgow) Battalion, and the 7th (Blythswood) Battalion, all headquartered at Glasgow. The 8th (Lanark) Battalion was headquartered at Lanark, and the 9th (Glasgow Highlanders) Battalion was headquartered at Glasgow. Field Marshal Arthur, Duke of Connaught and Strathern, was Colonel-in-Chief.

71ST FOOT

- 1777 Raised as the 73rd Foot (McLeod's Highlanders)
- 1786 Renumbered the 71st Highland Regiment
- 1808 71st or Glasgow Highland Regiment
- 1809 71st or Glasgow Highland Light Infantry
- 1810 71st Highland Regiment, Light Infantry
- 1881 1st Battalion, Highland Light Infantry

74TH FOOT

- 1787 Raised as the 74th Highland Regiment
- 1803 Also known as the Assaye Regiment
- 1816 74th Foot
- 1845 74th Highlanders
- 1881 2nd Battalion, Highland Light Infantry

BATTLE HONOURS: *Gibraltar 1780-83 (with the Castle and Key), Assaye (with the Elephant), Carnatic, Hindoostan, Sholingur, Mysore, Seringapatam, Cape of Good Hope 1806, Rolica, Vimiera, Corunna, Busaco, Fuentes d'Onor, Ciudad Rodrigo, Badajos, Almaraz, Salamanca, Vittoria, Pyrenees, Nivelle, Nive, Orthes, Toulouse, Peninsula, Waterloo, South Africa 1851-2-3, Sevastopol, Central India, Tel el Kebir, Egypt 1882, Modder River, South Africa 1899-1902*

5th, 6th, 7th, 8th, and 9th Battalions *South Africa 1900-02*

The uniform included a blue shako with a red-white-green diced border, a green ball, and black cords. The scarlet doublet had buff facings. The trews were of Mackenzie tartan, and the glengarry cap was green. This uniform is illustrated by figure 101.

The bandsmen wore feather bonnets with scarlet hackles.

The pipers wore a green glengarry cap with black-tipped feathers. The doublet was green. The kilt and hose tops were of Mackenzie tartan.

The 9th (Glasgow Highlanders) Battalion wore kilts of Black Watch or *Government* tartan, and the facings were blue rather than buff. The glengarry cap was blue.

SEAFORTH HIGHLANDERS (ROSS-SHIRE BUFFS, THE DUKE OF ALBANY'S) (72ND AND 78TH FOOT)

In 1914, the 1st Battalion was stationed at Agra, India, and the 2nd Battalion at Shorncliffe, England. The 3rd Battalion, the Highland (Rifle) Militia, was headquartered at Fort George. The Territorial Force comprised the 4th (Ross Highland) Battalion, headquartered at Dingwall, the 5th (Sutherland and Caithness) Battalion at Golspie, and the 6th (Morayshire) Battalion at Elgin. The Duke of Albany was Colonel-in-Chief.

72ND FOOT

- 1778 Raised as the 2nd Battalion of the 78th Highland Regiment (Seaforth's Highlanders)
- 1786 Became the 72nd Highland Regiment
- 1823 72nd or Duke of Albany's Own Highlanders
- 1881 1st Battalion, Seaforth Highlanders (Ross-shire Buffs, The Duke of Albany's)

78TH FOOT

- 1778 Raised as the 1st Battalion of the 78th Highland Regiment
- 1793 78th Highland Regiment or the Ross-shire Buffs
- 1881 2nd Battalion, Seaforth Highlanders (Ross-shire Buffs, The Duke of Albany's)

BATTLE HONOURS: *Assaye (with the Elephant), Carnatic, Hindoostan, Mysore, Cape of Good Hope 1806, Maida, Java, South Africa 1835, Sevastopol, Koosh-ab, Persia, Lucknow, Central India, Peiwar Kotal, Charasiah, Kabul 1879, Kandahar 1880, Afghanistan 1878-80, Tel el Kebir, Egypt 1882, Chitral, Atbara, Khartoum, Paardeberg, South Africa 1899-1902*

4th, 5th, and 6th Battalions *South Africa 1900-02*

The uniform included a black feather bonnet with a red and white diced border and a white hackle. The scarlet doublet had buff facings, and the kilt was of Mackenzie tartan. The sporran was white with two black tassels. The hose was scarlet and white, and the blue glengarry cap had a red-white-blue diced border. This uniform is illustrated by figure 102.

The bandsmen wore scarlet hackles on the feather bonnet rather than white.

The pipers wore a blue glengarry cap with a red-white-blue diced border and feathers, a blue doublet, and a kilt of Mackenzie tartan.

The 5th (Sutherland and Caithness Highland) Battalion had yellow facings rather than buff.

THE GORDON HIGHLANDERS (75TH AND 92ND FOOT)

In 1914, the 1st Battalion was stationed at Plymouth, England, and the 2nd Battalion at Cairo, Egypt. The 3rd Battalion, Royal Aberdeenshire Militia, was headquartered at Aberdeen. The Territorial Force comprised the 4th Battalion, headquartered at Aberdeen, the 5th (Buchan and Formartin) Battalion at Peterhead, the 6th (Banff and Donside) Battalion at Keith, the 7th (Deeside Highland) Battalion at Banchory, and the Shetland Islands Companies at Lerwick.

75TH FOOT

- 1787 Raised as the 75th Highland Regiment, Abercrombie's Highlanders
- 1809 75th Foot
- 1862 75th Stirlingshire Regiment
- 1881 1st Battalion, Gordon Highlanders

92ND FOOT

- 1794 Raised as the 100th (Gordon Highlanders) Regiment of Foot
- 1798 Renumbered 92nd
- 1861 92nd Foot, Gordon Highlanders
- 1881 2nd Battalion, Gordon Highlanders

BATTLE HONOURS: *India (with the Royal Tiger), Egypt (with the Sphinx), Mysore, Seringapatam, Egmont op Zee, Mandora, Corunna, Fuentes d'Onor, Almaraz, Vittoria, Pyrenees, Nive, Orthes, Peninsula, Waterloo, South Africa 1835, Delhi 1857, Lucknow, Charasiah, Kabul 1879, Kandahar 1880, Afghanistan 1878-80, Tel el Kebir, Egypt 1882, 1884, Nile 1884-85, Chitral, Tirah, Defence of Ladysmith, Paardeberg, South Africa 1899-1902*

4th, 6th, and 7th Battalions *South Africa 1900-02*

5th Battalion *South Africa 1900-01*

The uniform included a black feather bonnet with a red and white diced border and a white hackle. The scarlet doublet had yellow facings, and the kilt was of Gordon tartan. The sporran was white with two black tassels. The hose was scarlet and black, and the blue glengarry cap had a red-white-blue diced border. This uniform is illustrated by figure 103.

The bandsmen wore scarlet over white hackles on the feather bonnet.

The pipers wore a blue glengarry cap with a red-white-blue diced border and a blue doublet with a kilt of Gordon tartan.

THE QUEEN'S OWN CAMERON HIGHLANDERS (79TH FOOT)

In 1914, the 1st Battalion was stationed at Edinburgh, Scotland, and the 2nd Battalion at Poona, India. The 3rd Battalion, Highland (Light Infantry) Militia, was headquartered at Inverness. The Territorial Force comprised the 4th Battalion, headquartered at Aberdeen. King George V was Colonel-in-Chief.

1793	Raised as the 79th Regiment of Foot (The Cameronian Volunteers)
1807	79th Foot or Cameron Highlanders
1873	79th Foot, Queen's Own Cameron Highlanders
1881	Queen's Own Cameron Highlanders
1897	2nd Battalion raised

BATTLE HONOURS: *Egypt (with the Sphinx), Egmont op Zee, Corunna, Busaco, Fuentes d'Onor, Salamanca, Pyrenees, Nivelle, Nive, Toulouse, Peninsula, Waterloo, Alma, Sevastopol, Lucknow, Tel el Kebir, Egypt 1882, Nile 1884-85, Atbara, Khartoum, South Africa 1900-02*

4th Battalion *South Africa 1900-02*

The uniform included a black feather bonnet with a red and white diced border and a white hackle. The scarlet doublet had blue facings, and the kilt was of Cameron of Erracht tartan. The sporran was black with two white tails. The hose was scarlet and green, and the blue glengarry cap was plain without a diced border.

This uniform is illustrated by figure 104.

The pipers wore a plain blue glengarry cap with feathers and a blue doublet with a kilt of Cameron of Erracht tartan.

THE ROYAL IRISH RIFLES (83RD AND 86TH FOOT)

In 1914, the 1st Battalion was stationed at Aden, and the 2nd Battalion at Tidworth, England. The 3rd Battalion, Royal Antrim Militia was headquartered at Belfast, the 4th Battalion Royal North Down Militia at Newtown, and the 5th Battalion, Royal South Down Militia at Downpatrick.

83RD FOOT

1793	Raised as Fitch's Corps
1794	83rd Foot
1859	83rd (County of Dublin) Regiment
1881	1st Battalion, Royal Irish Rifles

86TH FOOT

1793	Raised as Cuyler's Shropshire Volunteers
1794	86th or Shropshire Volunteers
1806	86th or (Leinster) Regiment of Foot
1812	86th or Royal County Down Regiment
1881	2nd Battalion, Royal Irish Rifles

BATTLE HONOURS: *Egypt (with the Sphinx), India, Cape of Good Hope 1806, Talavera, Bourbon, Busaco, Fuentes d'Onor, Ciudad Rodrigo, Badajos, Salamanca, Vittoria, Nivelle, Orthes, Toulouse, Peninsula, Central India, South Africa 1899-1902*

The uniform included a black rifle busby with a black plume on a green base. The rifle green tunic had green facings and the buttons were black. The trousers and forage cap were rifle green. This uniform is illustrated by figure 105.

PRINCESS VICTORIA'S (ROYAL IRISH FUSILIERS) (87TH AND 89TH FOOT)

In 1914, the 1st Battalion was stationed at Shorncliffe, England and the 2nd Battalion at Quetta, India. The 3rd Battalion, Armagh Militia, was headquartered at Armagh, and the 4th Battalion, Cavan Militia, at Cavan. King George V was Colonel-in-Chief.

87TH FOOT

1793	Raised as the 87th or The Prince of Wales's Irish Regiment
1811	87th or Prince of Wales's Own
1827	87th or Royal Irish Fusiliers
1881	1st Battalion, Princess Victoria's (Royal Irish Fusiliers)

89TH FOOT

1794	Raised as the 89th Foot
1866	89th (Princess Victoria's) Regiment
1881	2nd Battalion, Princess Victoria's (Royal Irish Fusiliers)

BATTLE HONOURS: *Egypt (with the Sphinx), Montevideo, Talavera, Barrosa, Java, Tarifa, Vittoria, Nivelle, Niagara, Orthes, Toulouse, Peninsula, Ava, Sevastopol, Tel el Kebir, Egypt 1882-1884, Relief of Ladysmith, South Africa 1899-1902*

The uniform included a raccoon skin fusilier cap with a green plume on the left side. The scarlet tunic had blue facings. The blue trousers had red piping, and the blue forage cap had a scarlet band. This uniform is illustrated by figure 106.

THE CONNAUGHT RANGERS (88TH AND 94TH FOOT)

In 1914, the 1st Battalion was stationed at Ferozepore, India, and the 2nd Battalion at Aldershot, England. The 3rd Battalion, Galway Militia, was headquartered at Galway, and the 4th Battalion, Roscommon Militia, at Boyle.

88TH FOOT

1793	Raised as the 88th Foot or The Connaught Rangers
1881	1st Battalion, Connaught Rangers

94TH FOOT

1823	Raised as the 94th Foot
1881	2nd Battalion, Connaught Rangers

BATTLE HONOURS: *Egypt (with the Sphinx), Seringapatam, Talavera, Busaco, Fuentes d'Onor, Ciudad Rodrigo, Badajos, Salamanca, Vittoria, Pyrenees, Nivelle, Orthes, Toulouse, Peninsula, Alma, Inkerman, Sevastopol, Central India, South Africa 1877-8-9, Relief of Ladysmith, South Africa 1899-1902*

The uniform included a blue helmet with a brass spike. The scarlet tunic had green facings. The blue trousers had red piping, and the blue forage cap had a green band. This uniform is illustrated by figure 107.

PRINCESS LOUISE'S (ARGYLL AND SUTHERLAND HIGHLANDERS) (91ST AND 93RD FOOT)

In 1914, the 1st Battalion was stationed at Dinapore, India, and the 2nd Battalion at Fort George, Scotland. The 3rd Battalion, Highland Borderers Militia, was headquartered at Stirling, and the 4th Battalion, Royal Renfrew Militia, at Paisley. The Territorial Force comprised the 5th (Renfrewshire) Battalion, headquartered at Greenock, the 6th (Renfrewshire) Battalion at Paisley, the 7th Battalion at Stirling, the 8th (Argyllshire) Battalion at Dunoon, and the 9th (Dumbartonshire) Battalion at Dumbarton. Princess Louise, Duchess of Argyll was Colonel-in-Chief, and the Duke of Argyll was the Honorary Colonel of the 8th (Argyllshire) Battalion.

91ST FOOT

1794	Raised as the 98th Argyllshire Highlanders
1798	Renumbered 91st Argyllshire Highlanders
1809	91st Foot
1821	91st Argyllshire Regiment
1864	91st Argyllshire Highlanders
1872	91st (Princess Louise's Argyllshire Highlanders)
1881	1st Battalion, Princess Louise's (Argyll and Sutherland Highlanders)

93RD FOOT

1799	Raised as the 93rd Highlanders
1861	93rd (Sutherland Highlanders)
1881	2nd Battalion, Princess Louise's (Argyll and Sutherland Highlanders)

BATTLE HONOURS: *Cape of Good Hope 1806, Rolica, Vimiera, Corunna, Pyrenees, Nivelle, Nive, Orthes, Toulouse, Peninsula, South Africa 1846-47, 1851-2-3, Alma, Balak-*

Iava, Sevastopol, Lucknow, South Africa 1879, Modder River, Paardeberg, South Africa 1899-1902

5th, 6th, 7th, 8th, and 9th Battalions *South Africa 1900-02*

The uniform included a black feather bonnet with a red and white diced border and a white hackle. The scarlet doublet had yellow facings and the kilt was of Sutherland tartan. The sporran was black with six white tassels. (Officers and sergeants wore a badger's head sporran.) The hose was scarlet and white, and the glengarry cap was blue with a red and white diced border. This uniform is illustrated by figure 108.

The bandsmen wore a scarlet hackle in the feather bonnet rather than a white one.

The pipers wore a blue glengarry cap with a red and white diced border and feathers and a blue doublet with kilts of Sutherland tartan.

THE PRINCE OF WALES'S LEINSTER REGIMENT (ROYAL CANADIANS) (100TH AND 109TH FOOT)

In 1914, the 1st Battalion was stationed at Fyzabad, India, and the 2nd Battalion at Cork, Ireland. The 3rd Battalion, King's County Militia, was headquartered at Birr, the 4th Battalion, Queen's County Militia, at Maryborough, and the 5th Battalion, Royal Meath Militia, at Drogheda.

100TH FOOT

- 1858 Raised in Canada as the 100th Prince of Wales's Royal Canadian Regiment from Canadian volunteers for service in India but on the British Army establishment
- 1881 1st Battalion, Prince of Wales's Leinster Regiment (Royal Canadians)

109TH FOOT

- 1854 Raised as the 3rd Bombay European Regiment of the Honorable East India Company
- 1858 3rd (Bombay) Regiment
- 1861 Taken into the British Army as the 109th (Bombay Infantry)
- 1881 2nd Battalion, Prince of Wales's Leinster Regiment (Royal Canadians)

BATTLE HONOURS: *Niagara* (inherited from the 100th Prince of Wales's Tipperary Regiment of Foot which this regiment perpetuated). *Central India, South Africa 1900-02*

The uniform included a blue helmet with a brass spike. The scarlet tunic had blue facings. The blue trousers had red piping, and the blue forage cap had a scarlet band. This uniform is illustrated by figure 109.

THE ROYAL MUNSTER FUSILIERS (101ST AND 104TH FOOT)

In 1914, the 1st Battalion was stationed at Rangoon, Burma, and the 2nd Battalion at Aldershot, England. The 3rd Battalion, Kerry Militia, was headquartered at Tralee, the 4th Battalion, South Cork Militia, at Kinsale, and the 5th Battalion, Royal Limerick Militia, at Limerick.

101ST FOOT

- 1759 Raised as the Bengal European Regiment of the Honorable East India Company
- 1840 1st Bengal (European) Regiment
- 1841 1st (Bengal European) Light Infantry
- 1846 1st (Bengal European) Fusiliers
- 1861 Taken into the British Army as the 101st Royal Bengal Fusiliers
- 1881 1st Battalion, Royal Munster Fusiliers

104TH FOOT

- 1839 Raised as the 2nd Bengal (European) Regiment of the Honorable East India Company
- 1850 2nd Bengal (European) Fusiliers
- 1858 2nd Bengal Fusiliers
- 1861 Taken into the British Army as the 104th Bengal Fusiliers
- 1881 2nd Battalion, Royal Munster Fusiliers

BATTLE HONOURS: *Plassey, Condore, Masulipatam, Badara, Buxar, Rohilcund 1774, Sholinghur, Carnatic, Rohilcund 1794, Guzerat, Deig, Bhurtpore, Ghuznee, Afghanistan 1839, Ferozeshah, Sobraon, Chillianwallah, Goojerat, Punjaub, Pegu, Delhi 1857, Lucknow, Burma 1885-87, South Africa 1899-1902*

The uniform included a raccoon skin fusilier cap with a white over green plume on the left side. The scarlet tunic had blue facings. The blue trousers had red piping, and the blue forage cap had a scarlet band. This uniform is illustrated by figure 110.

THE ROYAL DUBLIN FUSILIERS
(102ND AND 103RD FOOT)

In 1914, the 1st Battalion was stationed at Madras, India, and the 2nd Battalion at Gravesend, England. The 3rd Battalion, Kildare Militia, was headquartered at Naas, the 4th Battalion, Royal Dublin City Militia, at Dublin, and the 5th Battalion, Dublin County Militia, also at Dublin. Field Marshal Arthur, Duke of Connaught and Strathearn, was Colonel-in-Chief.

102ND FOOT

1746	Raised as the Honorable East India Company's European Regiment
1830	Madras (European) Regiment
1839	1st Madras (European) Regiment
1843	1st Madras (European) Fusiliers
1858	1st Madras Fusiliers
1861	Taken into the British Army as the 102nd (Royal Madras) Fusiliers
1881	1st Battalion, Royal Dublin Fusiliers

103RD FOOT

1661	Raised as The Bombay Regiment
1668	The Bombay (European) Regiment of the Honorable East India Company
1839	1st Bombay (European) Regiment
1843	1st Bombay (European) Fusiliers
1858	1st Bombay Fusiliers
1861	Taken into the British Army as the 103rd (Royal Bombay) Fusiliers
1881	2nd Battalion, Royal Dublin Fusiliers

BATTLE HONOURS: *Plassey and Buxar (with the Royal Tiger), Carnatic and Mysore (with the Elephant), Arcot, Condore, Wandiwash, Pondicherry, Guzerat, Sholinghur, Nundy Droog, Amboyna, Ternate, Banda, Seringapatam, Kirkee, Maheidpore, Beni Boo Ali, Ava, Aden, Mooltan, Goojerat, Punjaub, Pegu, Lucknow, Relief of Ladysmith, South Africa 1899-1902*

The uniform included a raccoon skin fusilier cap with a bright blue plume on the left side. The scarlet tunic had blue facings. The blue trousers had red piping, and the forage cap was of a distinct bright blue with a scarlet band. This uniform is illustrated by figure 111.

THE RIFLE BRIGADE
(THE PRINCE CONSORT'S OWN)

In 1914, the 1st Battalion was stationed at Colchester, England, the 2nd Battalion was stationed at Kuldana, India; the 3rd Battalion at Cork, Ireland, and the 4th Battalion at Dagshai, India. The 5th Battalion, Queen's Own Royal Tower Hamlets Militia, and the 6th Battalion, King's Own Tower Hamlets Militia, were headquartered at Winchester. Field Marshal Arthur, Duke of Connaught and Strathearn, was Colonel-in-Chief.

1800	Raised as the Rifle Corps or Manninham's Sharpshooters
1802	95th Foot, the Rifle Corps
1816	Rifle Brigade, an unnumbered regiment (The 95th was reraised in 1823 but not as part of the Rifle Brigade.)
1862	Prince Consort's Own, The Rifle Brigade
1881	The Rifle Brigade (The Prince Consort's Own)

BATTLE HONOURS: *Copenhagen, Montevideo, Rolica, Vimiera, Corunna, Busaco, Barrosa, Fuentes d'Onor, Ciudad Rodrigo, Badajos, Salamanca, Vittoria, Pyrenees, Nivelle, Nive, Orthes, Toulouse, Peninsula, Waterloo, South Africa 1847-48, 1851-2-3, Alma, Inkerman, Sevastopol, Lucknow, Ashantee 1873-74, Ali Masjid, Afghanistan 1878-79, Burma 1885-87, Khartoum, Defence of Ladysmith, Relief of Ladysmith, South Africa 1899-1902*

The uniform included a black rifle busby with a black plume. The rifle green tunic had black facings, and the buttons were black. The trousers and forage cap were rifle green This uniform is illustrated by figure 112.

Note: The word brigade in the title is misleading. The Rifle Brigade was a regiment. The Rifle Brigade considered itself unique because it had no regimental number and was last in the order of precedence among the infantry regiments.

INFANTRY REGIMENTS OF THE TERRITORIAL FORCE

THE LONDON REGIMENT, TERRITORIAL FORCE

The first four battalions of the London Regiment, Territorial Force, were affiliated with The Royal Fusiliers (City of London Regiment) and were uniformed as the Royal Fusiliers with Territorial accoutrements.

1ST (CITY OF LONDON) BATTALION (ROYAL FUSILIERS)

This battalion was headquartered at Bloomsbury, London.
BATTLE HONOUR: *South Africa 1900-02.*

2ND (CITY OF LONDON) BATTALION (ROYAL FUSILIERS)

This battalion was headquartered at Westminster, London.
BATTLE HONOUR: *South Africa 1900-02.*

3RD (CITY OF LONDON) BATTALION (ROYAL FUSILIERS)

This battalion was headquartered at St. Pancras, London.
BATTLE HONOUR: *South Africa 1900-02.*

4TH (CITY OF LONDON) BATTALION (ROYAL FUSILIERS)

This battalion was headquartered at Shoreditch, London.
BATTLE HONOUR: *South Africa 1900.*

Note: The following infantry and cyclists formations of the Territorial Force were not affiliated with regular Infantry of the Line regiments.

5TH (CITY OF LONDON) BATTALION (LONDON RIFLE BRIGADE)

This battalion was raised in 1859 and headquartered at Finsbury, London. The uniform included a rifle green tunic with black facings. The trousers and forage cap were also rifle green.
BATTLE HONOUR: *South Africa 1900-02*

6TH (CITY OF LONDON) BATTALION (RIFLES)

This battalion was raised in 1860 and headquartered at Finsbury, London. Field Marshal Earl Roberts of Kandahar, Pretoria, and Waterford was the Honorary Colonel. The uniform included a rifle green tunic with scarlet facings. The trousers and forage cap were also rifle green.
BATTLE HONOUR: *South Africa 1900-02*

7TH (CITY OF LONDON) BATTALION

This battalion was raised in 1861 and headquartered at Shoreditch, London. The uniform included a scarlet tunic with buff facings, blue trousers with red piping, and a blue forage cap.
BATTLE HONOUR: *South Africa 1900-02*

8TH (CITY OF LONDON) BATTALION (POST OFFICE RIFLES)

This battalion was raised in 1868 and headquartered at Finsbury, London. Most of the personnel were Post Office employees. The uniform included a rifle green tunic with black facings. The trousers and forage cap were also rifle green.
BATTLE HONOURS: *Egypt 1882, South Africa 1899-1902*

9TH (COUNTY OF LONDON) BATTALION (QUEEN VICTORIA'S RIFLES)

This battalion was raised in 1853 and headquartered at Westminster, London. The uniform included a rifle green tunic with scarlet facings. The trousers and forage cap were also rifle green.
BATTLE HONOUR: *South Africa 1900-02*

10TH (COUNTY OF LONDON) BATTALION (HACKNEY)

This battalion was raised in 1912 and headquartered at Hackney, London. The uniform included a scarlet tunic with white facings. The blue trousers had red piping, and the forage cap was blue.

11TH (COUNTY OF LONDON) BATTALION (FINSBURY RIFLES)

This battalion was raised in 1860 and headquartered at Finsbury, London. The uniform included a rifle green tunic with scarlet facings. The trousers and forage cap were also rifle green.

BATTLE HONOUR: *South Africa 1900-02*

12TH (COUNTY OF LONDON) BATTALION (THE RANGERS)

This battalion was raised in 1860 and headquartered at Holborn, London. The uniform included a rifle green tunic with scarlet facings. The trousers and forage cap were also rifle green.

BATTLE HONOUR: *South Africa 1900-02*

13TH (COUNTY OF LONDON) BATTALION (KENSINGTON)

This battalion was raised in 1859 and headquartered at Kensington, London. The uniform included a grey tunic with scarlet facings. The trousers were grey with red piping, and the forage cap was grey with a scarlet band.

BATTLE HONOUR: *South Africa 1900-02*

14TH (COUNTY OF LONDON) BATTALION (LONDON SCOTTISH)

This battalion was raised in 1859 and headquartered at Westminster, London. The uniform included an Elcho grey doublet with blue facings and an Elcho grey kilt. The hose was also Elcho grey with a grey sporran with two black tails and a blue glengarry cap with blackcock's feathers. This uniform was unique in the British Army.

BATTLE HONOUR: *South Africa 1900-02*

15TH (COUNTY OF LONDON) BATTALION (PRINCE OF WALES'S OWN, CIVIL SERVICE RIFLES)

This battalion was raised in 1860 and headquartered at Westminster, London. Most of the personnel were government civil service employees. The uniform included a grey tunic with blue facings. The grey trousers had blue piping, and the grey forage cap had a blue band.

BATTLE HONOUR: *South Africa 1900-02*

16TH (COUNTY OF LONDON) BATTALION (QUEEN'S WESTMINSTER RIFLES)

This battalion was raised in 1860 and headquartered at Westminster, London. The uniform included a grey tunic with scarlet facings. The grey trousers had red piping, and the grey forage cap had a scarlet band.

BATTLE HONOUR: *South Africa 1900-02*

17TH (COUNTY OF LONDON) BATTALION (POPLAR AND STEPNEY RIFLES)

This battalion was raised in 1860 and headquartered at Poplar, London. The uniform included a rifle green tunic with black facings. The trousers and forage cap were also rifle green.

BATTLE HONOUR: *South Africa 1900-02*

18TH (COUNTY OF LONDON) BATTALION (LONDON IRISH RIFLES)

This battalion was raised in 1860 and headquartered at Chelsea, London. The uniform included a rifle green tunic with light green facings. The trousers and forage cap were also rifle green.

BATTLE HONOUR: *South Africa 1900-02*

19TH (COUNTY OF LONDON) BATTALION (ST. PANCRAS)

This battalion was raised in 1860 and headquartered at Camden Town, St. Pancras, London. The uniform included a scarlet tunic with green facings. The blue trousers had red piping, and the forage cap was blue.

BATTLE HONOUR: *South Africa 1900-02*

20TH (COUNTY OF LONDON) BATTALION (BLACKHEATH AND WOOLWICH)

This battalion was raised in 1859 and headquartered at Blackheath, London. The uniform included a scarlet tunic with black facings. The blue trousers had red piping, and the forage cap was blue.

BATTLE HONOUR: *South Africa 1900-02*

21ST (COUNTY OF LONDON) BATTALION (FIRST SURREY RIFLES)

This battalion was raised in 1859 and headquartered at Camberwell, London. The uniform included a rifle green tunic with scarlet facings. The trousers and forage cap were also rifle green.

BATTLE HONOUR: *South Africa 1900-02*

22ND (COUNTY OF LONDON) BATTALION (THE QUEEN'S)

This battalion was raised in 1860 and headquartered at Bermondsey, London. The uniform included a scarlet tunic with blue facings. The blue trousers had red piping, and the blue forage cap had a scarlet band.

BATTLE HONOUR: *South Africa 1900-02*

23RD (COUNTY OF LONDON) BATTALION

This battalion was raised in 1859 and headquartered at Battersea, London. The uniform included a scarlet tunic with white facings. The blue trousers had red piping, and the forage cap was blue.

BATTLE HONOUR: *South Africa 1900-02*

24TH (COUNTY OF LONDON) BATTALION (THE QUEEN'S)

This battalion was raised in 1860 and headquartered at Southwark, London. The uniform included a scarlet tunic with blue facings. The blue trousers had red piping, and the blue forage cap had a scarlet band.

BATTLE HONOUR: *South Africa 1900-02*

25TH (COUNTY OF LONDON) CYCLIST BATTALION

This battalion was raised in 1888 and headquartered at Fulham, London. The uniform included a grey tunic with scarlet facings. The grey trousers had red piping, and the grey forage cap had a scarlet band.

26TH—See the Inns of Court Officer's Training Corps.

27TH—See the Honourable Artillery Company.

28TH (COUNTY OF LONDON) BATTALION (ARTISTS RIFLES)

This battalion was raised in 1860 and headquartered at St. Pancras, London. Most of the personnel were in the arts, including painters, sculptors, writers, actors, etc. The uniform included a grey tunic with white facings. The grey trousers white piping, and the grey forage cap had a white band.

BATTLE HONOUR: *South Africa 1900-01*

INNS OF COURT OFFICERS TRAINING CORPS, TERRITORIAL FORCE

This corps was raised in 1859 as a rifle corps of volunteers, but the corps traces its lineage back to 1660. In 1908, it became the 26th (County of London) Battalion (Inns of Court) headquartered at Lincoln's Inn, London. Most of the personnel were in the legal profession. In 1909, the battalion was converted to an officer's training corps with one cavalry squadron and three infantry companies. The uniforms included a blue tunic with green facings, blue pantaloons, and a blue forage cap for the cavalry squadron. The infantry companies were uniformed in a grey tunic with scarlet facings. The grey trousers had red piping, and the grey forage cap had a scarlet band.

BATTLE HONOUR: *South Africa 1900-01*

THE HONOURABLE ARTILLERY COMPANY, TERRITORIAL FORCE

The Honourable Artillery Company is probably the oldest military unit in the world with a continuous existence. It was granted a charter in 1537 by King Henry VIII, although the unit dated prior to that year. Part of the charter reads: "To the ... Fraternity or Guylde of Saint George: Maisters and Rulars of the science of Artillary as aforesaid rehearsed for Longbows, Cros-bows and Hand-gonnes." It should be noted that "artillary" (artillery) in those days referred to any instrument that shot a projectile. The title company refers to a body of men rather than a tactical formation.

In 1914, the Company was headquartered at Finsbury, London, and consisted of two batteries of horse artillery, each with an ammunition column and an infantry battalion of four companies. King George V was the Captain-General and Colonel.

The artillery uniform was the same as the Royal Horse Artillery, except for the white over red plumes, buttons, and badges. The infantry uniform was the same as the Grenadier Guards but with white metal buttons and badges, rather than brass, and silver lace, rather than gold, for the officers. The red band of the blue forage cap also differed in having a narrow blue band superimposed in the center.

BATTLE HONOUR: *South Africa 1900-02*

Note: The battalion number 27 of the London Regiment was reserved for the Honourable Artillery Company, but it was never used.

THE MONMOUTHSHIRE REGIMENT, TERRITORIAL FORCE

This regiment was raised in 1860. The 1st Battalion was headquartered at Newport. The uniform included a rifle green tunic with black facings. The trousers and forage cap were also rifle green.

The 2nd Battalion was headquartered at Pontypool. The uniform included a scarlet tunic with green facings, and the blue trousers had red piping. The forage cap was blue.

The 3rd Battalion was headquartered at Abergavenny. The uniform was the same as for the 2nd Battalion.

BATTLE HONOUR: *South Africa 1900-02* (for all three battalions.)

THE CAMBRIDGESHIRE REGIMENT, TERRITORIAL FORCE

This regiment was raised in 1861 and consisted of only one battalion headquartered at Cambridge. The uniform included a scarlet tunic with blue facings. The blue trousers had red piping, and the blue forage cap had a scarlet band.

BATTLE HONOUR: *South Africa 1900-01*

THE HERTFORDSHIRE REGIMENT, TERRITORIAL FORCE

This regiment was raised in 1859 and consisted of only one battalion headquartered at Hertford. The uniform included a scarlet tunic with white facings. The blue trousers had red piping, and the forage cap was blue.

BATTLE HONOUR: *South Africa 1900-02*

THE HEREFORDSHIRE REGIMENT, TERRITORIAL FORCE

This regiment was raised in 1860 and consisted of only one battalion headquartered at Hereford. The uniform included a scarlet tunic with grass green facings. The blue trousers had red piping, and the forage cap was blue.

BATTLE HONOUR: *South Africa 1900-02*

THE NORTHERN CYCLIST BATTALION, TERRITORIAL FORCE

This battalion was raised in 1908 and headquartered at Newcastle-on-Tyne. The uniform included a scarlet tunic with green facings. The blue trousers had red piping, and the forage cap was blue.

THE HIGHLAND CYCLIST BATTALION, TERRITORIAL FORCE

This battalion was raised in 1908 and was headquartered at Kirkcaldy. The uniform included a grey tunic with scarlet facings. The grey trousers had red piping, and the glengarry cap was blue.

BATTLE HONOUR: *South Africa 1900-02* (inherited from an earlier volunteer unit perpetuated by this battalion.)

THE KENT CYCLIST BATTALION, TERRITORIAL FORCE

This battalion was raised in 1908 and was headquartered at Tonbridge. The uniform included a scarlet tunic with black facings. The blue trousers had red piping, and the forage cap was blue.

THE HUNTINGDONSHIRE CYCLIST BATTALION, TERRITORIAL FORCE

This battalion was raised in 1914 and was headquartered at Huntingdon. The uniform included a scarlet tunic with white facings. The blue trousers had red piping, and the forage cap was blue.

CHANNEL ISLANDS MILITIA

THE ROYAL MILITIA OF THE ISLAND OF JERSEY

This regiment was raised in 1860 and consisted of three battalions: the 1st or West Battalion (Light Infantry), the 2nd or East Battalion (Light Infantry), and the 3rd or South Battalion (Light Infantry). The uniform for all three battalions included a scarlet tunic with blue facings. The blue trousers had red piping and the forage cap was green.

BATTLE HONOUR: *Jersey 1781* (inherited from an earlier volunteer unit.)

THE ROYAL GUERNSEY MILITIA

This regiment was raised in 1860 and consisted of two battalions: the 1st Battalion (Light Infantry) and the 2nd Battalion (Light Infantry). The uniform for both battalions included a scarlet tunic with blue facings. The blue trousers had red piping, and the forage cap was green.

Note: The Channel Islands Militia also maintained small formations of artillery, engineers, and medical personnel on Jersey. The uniforms were the same as their regular *counterparts but with white metal accoutrements, white lace for officers, etc. These units included the Jersey Artillery, Medical Corps (Jersey), the Guernsey Artillery, the Guernsey Engineers, and the Alderney Artillery.*

DEPARTMENTAL CORPS

CORPS OF MILITARY POLICE

In 1914, The Corps of Military Police was headquartered at Aldershot, England.

1855	Military Mounted Police raised
1885	Military Foot Police raised
1901	Military Provost Staff Corps raised

The uniform included a blue helmet with a brass spike. The blue tunic had scarlet facings with scarlet piping on the front edge of the tunic. There were yellow shoulder cords and yellow piping on the cuffs. The belts were brown leather. There were scarlet stripes on the blue trousers or pantaloons, if worn by the mounted police. White gauntlets were worn by the mounted police, and white gloves were worn by the foot police. The forage cap was red with a blue band. This uniform is illustrated by figure 113.

ORGANIZATION

In order to join the Corps of Military Police, a man had to have an excellent character, proper recommendations, and 4 years of service in some branch of the army. (For the mounted police, service had to be in the cavalry). Other ranks in the military police were all noncommissioned officers. If a private were accepted, he would be given one stripe. The Military Provost Staff Corps was responsible for military prisons. All members of this corps held the rank of sergeant or higher. In 1914, detachments of this Corps were stationed at most military establishments in the United Kingdom. Overseas, there was one detachment in Egypt.

ARMY PAY CORPS AND DEPARTMENT

1878	Army Pay Department raised (officers)
1899	Army Pay Corps raised (other ranks)

The uniform included a blue helmet with a brass spike. The blue tunic had yellow facings and piping. There were double yellow stripes on the blue trousers. The blue forage cap had a blue band piped in yellow on the top and bottom. This uniform is illustrated by figure 114.

ORGANIZATION

The Army Pay Corps consisted of other ranks directed by the officers of the Army Pay Department. The officers and other ranks were volunteers selected from other branches of the army. They transferred into the department or corps and were not directly enlisted. In 1914, detachments of this Corps and Department were assigned to all army commands.

ARMY ORDNANCE DEPARTMENT AND ARMY ORDNANCE CORPS

In 1914, the Army Ordnance Department and Corps were headquartered at Aldershot, England.

1875	Army Ordnance Department raised (officers)
1881	Army Ordnance Corps raised (other ranks)

The uniform included a blue helmet with a brass spike. The blue tunic had scarlet facings and piping. There were double scarlet stripes on the blue trousers. The blue forage cap had a blue band piped in scarlet on the top and bottom. This uniform is illustrated by figure 115.

ORGANIZATION

The men of the Army Ordnance Corps, directed by the officers of the Army Ordnance Department, supplied and maintained all armaments from heavy artillery to bayonets, as well as all types of horse-drawn and motor vehicles, including harnesses and spare parts. Ordnance was also responsible for all kinds of clothing and equipment. In 1914, eight companies were stationed in the United Kingdom. One was stationed overseas with detachments at Gibraltar, Malta, Cairo, and at Pretoria and Capetown in the Union of South Africa. There were independent detachments at Hong Kong, Tientsin, Singapore, Ceylon, Sierra Leone, Mauritius, Jamaica, and Bermuda. The Indian Army maintained a separate ordnance establishment.

ARMY VETERINARY CORPS

In 1914, the Army Veterinary Corps was headquartered at Aldershot, England.

1881	Army Veterinary Department raised (officers)
1903	Army Veterinary Corps raised (other ranks)
1906	The Department and Corps amalgamated into the Army Veterinary Corps

The uniform included a blue helmet with a silver ball on brass fittings. The blue tunic had maroon facings and piping. There was yellow piping on the cuffs double maroon stripes on the blue trousers or pantaloons. The forage cap was blue with a maroon band. This uniform is illustrated by figure 116.

ORGANIZATION

The Army Veterinary Corps was responsible for the medical care and treatment of all animals, mainly horses and mules in army service. The corps also supervised the remount companies of the Army Service Corps. Detachments of the Army Veterinary Corps were stationed wherever there were concentrations of troops, especially cavalry, horse and field artillery, and various transport formations, all of which used large numbers of horses. In addition to the regular Army Veterinary Corps, there were also Territorial Force personnel. The Army Veterinary School was at Aldershot.

ARMY SERVICE CORPS

In 1914, the Army Service Corps was headquartered at Aldershot, England. Field Marshal Arthur, Duke of Connaught and Strathearn, was Colonel-in-Chief.

1794-1795	Royal Waggoners
1799-1833	Royal Waggon Corps and Train

84   FORCES OF THE BRITISH EMPIRE—1914

1855 Land Transport Corps
1857 Military Train, and Commissariat Staff Corps
1869 Army Service Corps under the Control Department and the Commissariat and Transport Department
1881 Commissariat and Transport Staff and the Commissariat and Transport Corps
1888 Army Service Corps

Note: Gaps in the dates above indicate periods when there was no supply or transport service

The uniform included a blue helmet with a brass ball. The blue tunic had white facings and piping. A blue girdle was worn with two white stripes in the center and two yellow outer stripes. There were double white stripes on the trousers or pantaloons. The blue forage cap had a blue band edged in white on the top and bottom. This uniform of a sergeant and drivers, together with a General Service Waggon and a Wolseley 3 Ton Lorry, is illustrated by figure 117. (See also figures 118 and 38.)

ORGANIZATION

In 1914, the Army Service Corps included 43 horse transport companies, 21 motor transport companies, five supply companies, and four remount companies. (The first motor transport company of the Army Service Corps was formed in 1903.) (The remount companies were under the supervision of the Army Veterinary Corps.) The Army Service Corps Training Establishment was at Aldershot. Thirty-eight horse transport companies were in the United Kingdom, one company was at Gibraltar, one was on the island of Malta, one was at Cairo, Egypt, and two were in the Union of South Africa. The Indian Army maintained a separate supply and transport service as well as a separate remount service.

The Territorial Force included 70 companies of the Army Service Corps organized into 14 mounted brigade transport and supply columns and 14 divisional transport and supply columns.

The Army Service Corps had extensive experience with all types of transport: animals, including horses, mules, camels, oxen, etc., used as pack and draft transport, as well as canal boats, steam engines, and internal-combustion motor vehicles. The Army Service Corps also provided drivers for the horse-drawn and motor ambulances of the Royal Army Medical Corps and tractor drivers for various types of tractors used to pull the heavy guns of the Royal Artillery.

Transport in the field was divided into first-line and second-line. The first-line accompanied the fighting troops and consisted of ammunition, engineer, and medical vehicles. The second-line followed at a distance and consisted of baggage and supply vehicles as well as additional ammunition, engineer, and medical vehicles. In 1914, mechanical transport was used to a considerable extent in the second-line.

In addition to transport duties, the Army Service Corps provided rations to the army, maintaining and operating bakeries and butcheries. The corps also provided grain and forage to the great numbers of horses then in service.

ROYAL ARMY MEDICAL CORPS

In 1914, the Royal Army Medical Corps was headquartered at Aldershot, England.

1660 Regimental *surgeons* permanently appointed under an Inspector-General of Hospitals. (Although this statement seems impressive, it should be remembered that until the beginning of the 20th century, medical care of the sick and wounded was most rudimentary.)
1854 Hospital Conveyance Corps raised (stretcher-bearers and orderlies)
1855 Medical Staff Corps raised
1857 Army Hospital Corps raised
1873 Medical Department (Regimental medical officers came under the direction of this department; regimental hospitals and personnel were also taken over by this department.)
1898 Medical Department (medical officers) and the Army Hospital Corps (other ranks) amalgamated to form the Royal Army Medical Corps

The uniform included a blue helmet with a brass ball. The blue tunic had dull cherry-red facings and piping. There were triple dull cherry-red stripes on the blue trousers, and the blue forage cap had a dull cherry-red band. This uniform of a sergeant and orderlies, together with an ambulance driven by an Army Service Corps driver, is illustrated by figure 118.

ORGANIZATION

In 1914, there were 38 *regular* companies of the Royal Army Medical Corps including 3 depot companies at Aldershot. These companies were designated *field ambulance, hospital,* or *sanitary* companies. Twenty-three companies were in the United Kingdom. Eleven companies were stationed overseas at Wynberg and Pretoria in the Union of South Africa and in Bermuda, Ceylon, Hong Kong, Gibraltar, Jamaica, Malta, Mauritius, Singapore, and Cairo, Egypt. The Indian Army maintained a separate medical establishment. The Royal Army Medical Corps also maintained the Royal Army Medical College.

In the Territorial Force, there were 14 mounted brigade field ambulance companies, 42 divisional field ambulance companies, 37 hospital companies, and 2 sanitary companies.

Sick or wounded men were first attended by the battalion medical officer and carried, if necessary, by the battalion stretcher-bearers. (Bandsmen were trained in first aid and doubled as stretcher-bearers.) Once the patient was off the immediate battlefield, stretcher-bearers of the Royal Army Medical Corps removed the patient to a field dressing station operated by a field ambulance company at the first line of assistance. Any emergency operations were performed at this point. The patient was then transported by ambulance to a field hospital at the second line of assistance. From there, the patient was transferred by a hospital train (if available) or by ambulance to the general hospital at the advance base of operations. The patient would then be transported to the hospital at the base of operations, usually on the coast. At base hospitals, nursing sisters were usually available to assist the medical personnel. (See Queen Alexandra's Imperial Military Nursing Service.) Invalids were sent home by hospital ship.

Note: Ambulance drivers were provided by the Army Service Corps. Locomotive crews manning hospital trains were provided by the Corps of Royal Engineers. Hospital ships were manned by the Royal Navy.

QUEEN ALEXANDRA'S IMPERIAL MILITARY NURSING SERVICE

In 1914, Queen Alexandra was President of the military nursing service.

1881   The Army Nursing Service raised
1902   Queen Alexandra's Imperial Military Nursing Service
1907   Territorial Force Nursing Service formed

The uniform included a white raised cap and veil. The grey ankle length dress had a white collar and cuffs. A starched white apron with a bib front and crossover straps at the back was worn over the dress. The cape was scarlet. Nurses of the Territorial Force were similarly uniformed, except that the cape was grey with a red border. This uniform is illustrated by figure 119.

ORGANIZATION

In 1914, Queen Alexandra's Imperial Military Nursing Service was the only woman's service in the army. The ranks were matron, sister, and staff nurse. A candidate for the nursing service had to be between 25 and 35 years of age, unmarried or a widow of good social status, and have at least 3 years of training in a general hospital. There was a general list of nurses who were posted to hospitals in the United Kingdom and overseas along with companies of the Royal Army Medical Corps.

Note: A volunteer unit known as the First Aid Nursing Yeomanry was raised in 1907. Members were upper-class women who were mounted. It was intended that they would ride onto the battlefield and aid the wounded. The War Office refused to recognize this unit and it was not part of the Territorial Force in 1914. When World War I began, the First Aid Nursing Yeomanry offered its services but was rejected. Many of the women went to France on their own and drove motor ambulances for the French and Belgians, and eventually for the British. This women's service was finally accepted by the Army Council in 1927! Their full dress uniform in 1914 consisted of a dark blue forage cap, scarlet tunic, dark blue ankle-length skirt, and riding boots. When mounted, the women rode sidesaddle. This unit is not illustrated.

CHAPLAINS' DEPARTMENT

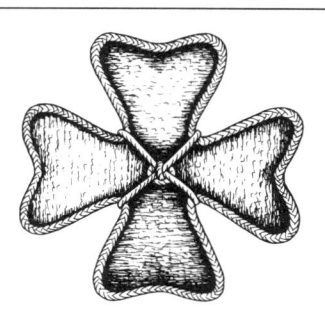

The Chaplains' Department was instituted in 1796. There was no *full dress* for chaplains; civilian clerical dress was worn on *full dress* occasions. On active service, chaplains wore the ordinary *service dress* of officers with plain black buttons, white dog collar, a black scarf, and black badges of rank.

ORGANIZATION

The Chaplain General ranked as a major-general. First class chaplains ranked as colonels, second class as lieutenant colonels, third class as majors, and fourth class as captains. Denominations mentioned in the Army List of August 1914 were Church of England, Roman Catholic, and Presbyterian.

FLYING CORPS

ROYAL FLYING CORPS

In 1914, The headquarters of the Royal Flying Corps was at South Farnborough, England.

- 1883   A balloon factory and school of instruction set up and operated by the Corps of Royal Engineers
- 1890   Balloon Section, Corps of Royal Engineers
- 1911   Air Battalion, Corps of Royal Engineers
- 1912   Royal Flying Corps formed as a separate branch, including a Military Wing and a Naval Wing
- 1914   In July 1914, the Naval Wing became the Royal Naval Air Service. (See Royal Naval Air Service.) The Military Wing of the Royal Flying Corps remained as part of the Army.

Flying officers of the Royal Flying Corps were seconded from the regiments and corps of the army and wore the uniforms of their regiments or corps. However, *full dress* regulations for officers and other ranks of the Royal Flying Corps were published in November 1913. This *full dress* was hardly authorized when World War I began and *service dress* was the order of the day. The 1913, *full dress* uniform included a blue forage cap with a scarlet band. The blue tunic had scarlet facings and piping on the front edge of the tunic. A dark blue girdle was worn as a belt with three gilded wire toggles as fasteners; there were scarlet stripes on the blue trousers. The khaki serge *service dress* jacket differed from that worn by other branches of the army. It was a double-breasted jacket with a turnover collar and no visible buttons. On 1 April 1918, the Royal Flying Corps became the Royal Air Force, an independent service with a new *full dress* uniform. The 1913, *full dress* uniforms of an officer and a private, together with a flying officer of the Royal Naval Air Service and a Sopwith-Tabloid airplane, are illustrated by figure 120.

ORGANIZATION

On 1 August 1914, the Royal Flying Corps consisted of 105 officers and 755 other ranks. There were 63 airplanes and an airship (dirigible) detachment. The Royal Flying Corps maintained the Central Flying School at Upavon, Salisbury Plain, England. The Airship Detachment, the 1st, 5th, 6th, and 7th Squadrons and the Aircraft Park were at South Farnborough; the 3rd, and 4th Squadrons were at Upavon, Salisbury Plain; and the 2nd Squadron at Montrose, Scotland. The mission of the Royal Flying Corps was to provide observation and reconnaissance, that is, to be the *eyes* of the army. In 1914, fighter aircraft and bombers were not yet envisioned.

MILITARY BANDS

Infantry battalions maintained a military band and a corps of drums (fifes and drums) or, in the case of Scottish battalions, pipes and drums. Rifle and Light Infantry battalions did not have fifes and drums; they maintained bugle bands without drums. However, Light Infantry battalions had drums in their military bands. The Highland Light Infantry had pipes and drums in addition to their military and bugle bands. Rifle battalions had no drums at all, except for the Cameronians (Scottish Rifles), who had pipes and drums.

Infantry bandsmen wore distinctive *wings* on the shoulders of the tunic. Drummers wore additional lace on the sleeves. Foot Guard drummers wore bands of white lace on the fronts of the tunics. Scottish pipers, drummers, and bandsmen had various regimental distinctions that are noted on the appropriate pages of this book.

By 1914, some Irish battalions had revived the Irish bagpipe. Irish pipers existed in the following battalions in place of fifers: 2nd and 4th Battalions, the Royal Inniskilling Fusiliers; 2nd and 4th Battalions, the Royal Irish Fusiliers; 3rd Battalion, the Royal Irish Regiment; 1st, 2nd, and 4th Battalions, the Prince of Wales's Own Leinster Regiment (Royal Canadians); 2nd Battalion, the Royal Dublin Fusiliers; and the 18th (County of London) Battalion (London Irish Rifles), the London Regiment, Territorial Force. Irish pipers wore the normal *full dress* of their particular regiments. However, in 1913, pipers of the 4th Battalion, Royal Irish Fusiliers, appeared in Irish *caubeens* (bonnets) and saffron (brownish-yellow) kilts. By the 1920s, all Irish pipers had adopted saffron kilts, caubeens, and cutaway jackets of green or blue, depending on the regiment, with green or blue hose. Irish pipers did not wear sporrans or spats.

Cavalry regiments and the Royal Regiment of Artillery maintained mounted bands. These bands were smaller than infantry bands. The centerpiece of the mounted band was the drum horse with two kettle drums, one on either side of the saddle. The drum horse was usually a distinctive color. For example, the 2nd Dragoons (Royal Scots Greys) were all mounted on greys except for the drum horse, which was black. Drum horses in other regiments tended to be greys or piebalds (spotted horses of various colors.) Mounted bandsmen wore yellow aiguillettes on the left shoulder in addition to white pouch belts.

Military bands of the dominions and colonies followed the British example. Scottish regiments of the dominions, needless to say, maintained pipe bands. It is interesting to note that the bagpipe was taken up with enthusiasm by a number of Indian regiments as well as by the Gurkhas. The 17th Cavalry of the Indian Army even had a mounted pipe band.

CHAPTER THREE
Land Forces of the Dominion of Canada, 1914

In 1914, the permanent army of the Dominion of Canada consisted of only a few squadrons of cavalry, an infantry battalion, a few batteries of artillery, and the permanent departmental corps for a total of about 3,000 men.

The bulk of Canada's land forces was in a part-time militia. The origins of the militia dated back to French colonial times. Officers holding French commissions were allowed to continue serving, even after the British conquest of Canada, providing they accepted a British commission. The Canadian Militia served well during the War of 1812 (1812-14) but deteriorated later to an almost nonexistent state. Officers were commissioned but rarely held drills, and military equipment was stored away. The defence of Canada rested with British troops that garrisoned the country.

In 1854, the Crimean War drew off a great number of the British troops stationed in Canada. As a result, the Canadian government passed the Militia Act of 1855. The militia was now to be properly trained and equipped to take on the major share of the defence of Canada. It should be noted that to this day the Canadian government will not officially recognize any militia unit other than those created after the Militia Act of 1855, even though the forerunners of many units dated back to colonial times.

The Dominion of Canada came into being 1 July 1867 with the union of Ontario, Quebec, Nova Scotia, and New Brunswick. Between 1867 and 1905, other provinces joined until the Dominion of Canada spanned North America from the Atlantic to the Pacific Oceans. Newfoundland remained a British colony until it finally joined Canada in 1949.

The last British troops, mostly garrison artillery formations at defended ports, were withdrawn from Canada in 1906.

Certain regiments of the militia saw active service during the Fenian raids of 1866 and 1870 as well as the Red River rebellion in 1870. In 1885, the militia also dealt with Louis Riel's rebellion in northwest Canada. Cavalry and infantry of the small permanent force as well as contingents of volunteers from the militia served again with distinction in the South African War (1899-1902). The Canadians at their request made the final attack at Paardeberg.

At the outbreak of World War I in August 1914, the militia units, although well-organized, were mostly under strength. It was therefore decided to enroll volunteers in new, full-strength battalions consisting of 1,000 men each. These battalions were numbered and known as the Canadian Expeditionary Force. For the most part, these battalions were raised by the Militia units. For example, the 15th, 92nd, and 134th Highland Battalions were in essence the 2nd, 3rd, and 4th Battalions of the 48th Highlanders that raised them. The 1st Battalion, or the regiment, remained at home and theoretically served as a depot. The cavalry regiments of the militia raised mounted rifle formations as well as infantry battalions. The artillery, engineers, and departmental corps of both the permanent force and the militia were expanded many times over. The two permanent force cavalry regiments, one militia cavalry regiment, and the permanent force infantry regiment served as units.

The senior Dominion of the British Empire sent nearly 620,000 volunteers to World War I. In October

1914, the first contingent of 33,000 Canadians arrived in England to complete their training. By the end of the war, Canada counted more than 200,000 dead and wounded. In 1918, Canadian troops were the first to break Germany's famed Hindenburg Line.

It should be mentioned that before the United States entered World War I in 1917, many Americans crossed the border and joined the Canadian Expeditionary Force and, in some cases, even formed their own battalions.

UNIFORMS

The permanent force formations of each branch of the Canadian Army are listed and illustrated, followed by a list of militia formations.

The uniforms described are that of a private of the regiment or corps listed in *full dress*. Regiments and corps of the permanent force had both *full dress* and *service dress* issued. Militia formations had only an allowance for *service dress*. *Full dress*, even if authorized, was at the unit's expense. As a result, many units, other than senior officers, did not possess *full dress*. Most urban units had at least some men, bands, colour parties, etc., in *full dress* for parades and ceremonial occasions. Rural units usually only had *service dress*. Infantry regiments, other than Scottish or rifles, were authorized a white helmet in *full dress*; however, some regiments dispensed with *full dress* head-gear, wearing only the forage cap for economy. Many rifle regiments wore a *wedge* cap rather than the *rifle busby*. The *wedge* cap was similar in appearance to an overseas or garrison cap. This book will describe the authorized full dress, whether the unit wore it or not.

Full dress of Canadian formations followed the British Army very closely. In the Canadian Militia, *hussars*, with one exception, copied the dress of the 13th Hussars; *rifle* regiments copied the King's Royal Rifle Corps (60th Foot). Most militia infantry regiments had blue facings. In the British Army, blue facings indicated a *royal* regiment. Queen Victoria had referred to the Canadian Militia as her "... trusted *royal* Canadian Militia," resulting in the blue facings

STANDARDS, GUIDONS, AND COLOURS

Permanent Force: The Royal Canadian Dragoons carried the usual crimson guidon. Each squadron of Lord Strathcona's Horse (Royal Canadians) carried a red-white-red triangular pennon presented to the regiment upon its formation. Lord Strathcona's coat of arms and motto were in the upper right corner. The phrase, Strathcona's Horse, was on the middle white strip in red letters. The squadron letter was in the lower right corner. A proper guidon was not presented until 1932. The Royal Canadian Regiment carried a King's and Regimental Colour.

Militia: The Governor General's Horse Guards and Princess Louise's Dragoon Guards carried standards. All other militia cavalry carried guidons, except for hussars who had none. Infantry battalions carried the King's and Regimental Colours, except for *rifles* who did not have colours. The Regimental Colour was of the *facings colour*.

Regimental heraldic devices and battle honours were embroidered in gold on the Regimental Colour within a wreath of maple leaves. (The Maple leaf is the symbol of Canada.)

After the South African War (1899-1902), the King's Banner, which was a Union flag with a gold fringe, was presented to those Canadian regiments that had served in South Africa. These flags were considered honorary banners for services rendered to the Empire.

CANADIAN PERMANENT FORCES

THE ROYAL CANADIAN DRAGOONS

In 1914, Headquarters was at Toronto, Ontario. A Squadron was stationed at St. Jean, Quebec, and B Squadron at Toronto, Ontario. King George V was the Honorary Colonel.

1883	Raised as the Cavalry School Corps
1887	Royal School of Cavalry
1892	Canadian Dragoons
1893	Royal Canadian Dragoons

BATTLE HONOURS: *Northwest Canada 1885, South Africa 1900*

The uniform included a white (steel) metal helmet with a black plume. The scarlet tunic had blue facings, and there were yellow stripes on the blue pantaloons. The blue forage cap had a scarlet band. This uniform is illustrated by figure 121.

LORD STRATHCONA'S HORSE (ROYAL CANADIANS)

In 1914, Headquarters and A and B Squadrons were all at Winnipeg, Manitoba.

1900   Privately raised in January 1900 by Sir Donald Alexander Smith, Lord Strathcona and Baron Mount Royal (1820-1914). (The regiment was irregular cavalry, 600 strong, and fully equipped. The regiment was presented to the British government for service in South Africa as mounted rifles.)
1901   Placed on the Canadian Army list as a permanent regiment known as the Canadian Mounted Rifles
1903   Royal Canadian Mounted Rifles
1909   Strathcona's Horse (Royal Canadians)
1911   Lord Strathcona's Horse (Royal Canadians)

BATTLE HONOUR: *South Africa 1900-01*

The uniform included a white (steel) metal helmet with a red and white plume with red underneath. The scarlet tunic had myrtle green facings, and there were yellow stripes on the blue pantaloons. The blue forage cap had a myrtle green band. This uniform is illustrated by figure 122.

ROYAL CANADIAN ARTILLERY

In 1914, Headquarters and A and B Batteries of the Royal Canadian Horse Artillery were at Kingston, Ontario. Headquarters, No. 1 Company (Coast Defence), and No. 2 Company (Coast Defence) of the Royal Canadian Garrison Artillery were at Halifax, Nova Scotia; No. 3 Company (Heavy Company) and No. 4 Company (Coast Defence) were at Quebec City, Quebec; and No. 5 Company (Coast Defence) was at Esquimalt, British Columbia. Field Marshal Earl Roberts of Kandahar, Pretoria, and Waterford was the Honorary Colonel.

1871   Raised with two batteries of garrison artillery (A Battery at Kingston, Ontario, and B Battery at Quebec City, Quebec)
1880   The Royal Schools of Gunnery formed around A and B Batteries at Kingston and Quebec City
1883   Now known as the Royal Schools of Artillery (Also, C Battery raised at Victoria, British Columbia)
1898   The three existing *regular* batteries now known as the Regiment of Canadian Artillery
1905   The Royal Canadian Horse Artillery was raised. Garrison Artillery formations (now numbered companies instead of batteries) known as the Royal Canadian Garrison Artillery)

Note: All Canadian field artillery was in the Militia.

The uniform of the Royal Canadian Horse Artillery was the same as the British Royal Horse Artillery, except for badges and buttons. This uniform is illustrated by figure 123.

The uniform of the Royal Canadian Garrison Artillery included a *full dress* white helmet with a brass ball. Other than the white helmet, badges, and buttons, the uniform was the same as the British Royal Garrison Artillery. This uniform is illustrated by figure 124.

ROYAL CANADIAN ENGINEERS

In 1914, Corps Headquarters was at Ottawa, Ontario. Personnel were stationed at various posts across Canada. Field Marshal Kitchener of Khartoum was the Honorary Colonel.

1903   Raised as the Canadian Engineer Corps
1904   Royal Canadian Engineers

The uniform included a *full dress* white helmet with a brass spike. Other than the white helmet, buttons, and badges, the uniform was the same as the British Corps of Royal Engineers. This uniform is illustrated by figure 125.

THE ROYAL CANADIAN REGIMENT

In 1914, Regimental Headquarters was at Halifax, Nova Scotia; Companies A, B, C, D, E, and F were also at Halifax; G Company was at Quebec City, Quebec; H Company was at Fredericton, New Brunswick; I Company was at Toronto, Ontario; and K Company was at London, Ontario.

1883 Raised as the Infantry School Corps
1892 Canadian Regiment of Infantry
1893 Royal Regiment of Canadian Infantry
1899 Royal Canadian Regiment of Infantry
1901 Royal Canadian Regiment

BATTLE HONOURS: *Saskatchewan, North West Canada, 1885, Paardeberg, South Africa 1899-1900*

The uniform included a white Wolseley helmet with a brass spike and a scarlet puggaree. (The regiment also wore the regular white helmet with a brass spike.) The scarlet tunic had blue facings. The blue trousers had red piping, and the blue forage cap had a scarlet band. This uniform is illustrated by figure 126.

CANADIAN ORDNANCE CORPS

In 1914, Corps Headquarters was at Ottawa, Ontario. The personnel were stationed at posts across Canada.

1903 Raised as the Ordnance Store Corps
1907 Canadian Ordnance Corps

The uniform included a *full dress* white helmet with a brass spike. Other than the white helmet, buttons, and badges, the uniform was essentially the same as the British Army Ordnance Department and Corps. This uniform is illustrated by figure 127.

CANADIAN PERMANENT ARMY SERVICE CORPS

In 1914, Corps Headquarters was at Ottawa, Ontario. There were detachments stationed at posts across Canada.

1903 Raised as the Canadian Army Service Corps
1906 The Canadian Permanent Army Service Corps

The uniform included a *full dress* white helmet with a brass ball. Other than the white helmet, buttons, and badges, the uniform was essentially the same as the British Army Service Corps. This uniform is illustrated by figure 128.

CANADIAN ARMY MEDICAL CORPS

In 1914, Corps Headquarters was at Ottawa, Ontario. There were detachments stationed at posts across Canada.

1904 Raised as the Permanent Active Militia Army Medical Corps
1909 Canadian Army Medical Corps

The uniform included a *full dress* white helmet with a brass ball. Other than the white helmet, buttons, and badges, the uniform was essentially the same as the British Royal Army Medical Corps. This uniform is illustrated by figure 129.

CANADIAN ARMY PAY CORPS

In 1914, Corps Headquarters was at Ottawa, Ontario. The personnel were stationed at various posts across Canada.

1907   Raised as the Canadian Army Pay Corps

The uniform included a *full dress* white helmet with a brass spike. Other than the white helmet, buttons, and badges, the uniform was essentially the same as the British Army Pay Corps and Department. This uniform is illustrated by figure 130.

CANADIAN PERMANENT ARMY VETERINARY CORPS

In 1914, Corps Headquarters was at Ottawa, Ontario. There were personnel stationed at various posts across Canada.

1910   Raised as the Canadian Permanent Army Veterinary Corps

The uniform included a *full dress* white helmet with a ball. Other than the white helmet, buttons and badges, the uniform was essentially the same as the British Army Veterinary Corps. This uniform is illustrated by figure 131.

CORPS OF MILITARY STAFF CLERKS

This corps was raised April 1st 1912, at Militia Headquarters, Ottawa, Ontario. On April 15th of the same year the Corps organized into two sections. Section A comprised officers and noncommissioned officers on administrative and clerical duties. The uniform included a blue tunic with white facings, blue trousers, and a blue forage cap. Section B comprised noncommissioned officers and men stationed at Militia Headquarters who performed orderly and clerical duties for the General Staff. The uniform included a blue tunic without any facings, blue trousers, and a blue forage cap. The uniform of Section B is illustrated by figure 132.

CANADIAN MILITIA

CAVALRY REGIMENTS OF THE CANADIAN MILITIA

THE GOVERNOR GENERAL'S BODYGUARD

This regiment was raised in 1855 and headquartered at Toronto, Ontario. The uniform included a white (steel) metal helmet with a white plume. The blue tunic had white facings, and there were white stripes on the blue pantaloons.

BATTLE HONOURS: *North West Canada 1885, South Africa 1900*

1ST HUSSARS

This regiment was raised in 1872 and headquartered at London, Ontario. The uniform included a hussar busby with a white plume and a buff busby-bag. The blue hussar tunic had buff facing, a buff collar, and yellow braid. There were double buff stripes on blue pantaloons.

BATTLE HONOUR: *South Africa 1900*

2ND DRAGOONS

This regiment was raised in 1872 and headquartered at St. Catherines, Ontario. The uniform included a white (steel) metal helmet with a white plume. The blue tunic had white facings, and there were white stripes on the blue pantaloons.

3RD (THE PRINCE OF WALES'S) CANADIAN DRAGOONS

This regiment was raised in 1875 and headquartered at Peterborough, Ontario. The uniform included a white (steel) metal helmet with a red and black plume. The scarlet tunic had yellow facings, and there were yellow stripes on the blue pantaloons.

4TH HUSSARS

This regiment was raised in 1875 and headquartered at Prescott, Ontario. The uniform included a hussar busby with a white plume and a buff busby-bag. The blue tunic had buff facings, a buff collar, and yellow braid. There were double buff stripes on the blue pantaloons.

5TH PRINCESS LOUISE'S DRAGOON GUARDS

This regiment was raised in 1872 and headquartered at Ottawa, Ontario. Princess Louise, Duchess of Argyll, was the Honorary Colonel. The uniform included a white (steel) metal helmet with a white plume. The blue tunic had white facings, and there were white stripes on the blue pantaloons.
BATTLE HONOUR: *South Africa 1900*

6TH DUKE OF CONNAUGHT'S ROYAL CANADIAN HUSSARS

This regiment was raised in 1885 and headquartered at Montreal, Quebec. The uniform included a hussar busby with red over white plume and a scarlet busby-bag. The blue tunic had buff facings, a buff collar, and yellow braid. There were double buff stripes on the blue pantaloons.

7TH HUSSARS

This regiment was raised in 1867 as infantry, converted to cavalry in 1903, and headquartered at Bury, Quebec. The uniform included a blue forage cap with a buff band. The blue tunic had buff facings, a buff collar, and yellow braid. There were double buff stripes on the blue pantaloons.

8TH PRINCESS LOUISE'S NEW BRUNSWICK HUSSARS

This regiment was raised in 1866 and headquartered at Sussex, New Brunswick. The uniform included a blue forage cap with a buff band. The blue tunic had buff facings, a buff collar, and yellow braid. There were double buff stripes on the blue pantaloons.

9TH MISSISSAUGA HORSE

This regiment was raised in 1901 and headquartered at Toronto, Ontario. The uniform included a khaki slouch hat with a myrtle green puggaree. The scarlet tunic had myrtle green facings, and there were yellow stripes on the blue pantaloons.

10TH—Vacant in 1914

11TH HUSSARS

This regiment was raised in 1867 as infantry. It was converted to cavalry in 1903 and headquartered at Richmond, Quebec. The uniform included a blue forage cap with a buff band. The blue tunic had buff facings, a buff collar, and yellow braid. There were double buff stripes on the blue pantaloons.

12TH MANITOBA DRAGOONS

This regiment was raised in 1903 and perpetuated a squadron in the Canadian Mounted Rifles, originally a company in the Winnipeg Battalion of Infantry raised in 1885. The regiment was headquartered at Brandon, Manitoba. The uniform included a white (steel) metal helmet with a white plume. The scarlet tunic had white facings. There were yellow stripes on the blue pantaloons.
BATTLE HONOURS: *North West Canada 1885, South Africa 1900* (inherited from the earlier formations)

13TH SCOTTISH LIGHT DRAGOONS

This regiment was raised in 1904 from two infantry regiments: the 52nd raised in 1866 and the 79th raised in 1872. They were amalgamated in 1903. The regiment was converted to cavalry in 1904 and headquartered at Waterloo, Ontario. The uniform included a white topi helmet in mounted review order. The blue forage cap had a red and white diced band. The scarlet tunic had yellow facings, and there were yellow stripes on the blue pantaloons.

14TH KING'S CANADIAN HUSSARS

This regiment was raised in 1874 and headquartered in Middleton, Nova Scotia. The uniform included a blue forage cap with a buff band. The blue tunic had buff facings, a buff collar, and yellow braid. There were double buff stripes on the blue pantaloons.

15TH LIGHT HORSE

This regiment was raised in 1905 and perpetuated an earlier formation raised in 1885. The regiment was headquartered at Calgary, Alberta. The uniform included a blue forage cap with a yellow band. The scarlet tunic had yellow facings, and there were yellow stripes on the blue pantaloons.

BATTLE HONOUR: *North West Canada 1885* (inherited from the earlier unit.)

16TH LIGHT HORSE

This regiment was raised in 1905 and perpetuated an earlier formation raised in 1885. The regiment was headquartered at Regina, Saskatchewan. The uniform included a blue forage cap with a yellow band. The scarlet tunic had yellow facings, and there were yellow stripes on blue pantaloons.

BATTLE HONOUR: *North West Canada* (inherited from the earlier unit)

17TH DUKE OF YORK'S ROYAL CANADIAN HUSSARS (ARGENTEUIL RANGERS)

This regiment was raised in 1897 and headquartered at Montreal, Quebec. The uniform included a hussar busby with a white plume and a buff busby-bag. The blue tunic had buff facings, a buff collar, and yellow braid. There were double buff stripes on the blue pantaloons.

BATTLE HONOUR: *South Africa 1900*

18TH MOUNTED RIFLES

This regiment was raised in 1907 and headquartered at Portage la Prairie, Manitoba. The uniform included a blue forage cap with a yellow band. The scarlet tunic had yellow facings, and there were yellow stripes on the blue pantaloons.

19TH ALBERTA DRAGOONS

This regiment was raised in 1908 and headquartered at Edmonton, Alberta. The uniform included a blue forage cap with a yellow band. The scarlet tunic had yellow facings, and there were yellow stripes on the blue pantaloons.

20TH BORDER HORSE

This regiment was raised in 1908 and headquartered at Pipestone, Manitoba. The uniform included a blue forage cap with a yellow band. The scarlet tunic had yellow facings, and there were yellow stripes on the blue pantaloons.

21ST ALBERTA HUSSARS

This regiment was raised in 1908 perpetuating an earlier formation raised in 1885. The regiment was headquartered at Medicine Hat, Alberta. The uniform included a blue forage cap with a white band. The scarlet tunic had white facings and braid, and there double white stripes on the blue pantaloons.

BATTLE HONOUR: *North West Canada 1885* (inherited from the earlier unit)

22ND SASKATCHEWAN LIGHT HORSE

This regiment was raised in 1908 and headquartered at Lloydminster, Saskatchewan. The uniform included a blue forage cap with a white band. The scarlet tunic had white facings, and there were yellow stripes on the blue pantaloons.

23RD ALBERTA RANGERS

This regiment was raised in 1908 and headquartered at Pincher Creek, Alberta. The uniform included a blue forage cap with a white band. The scarlet tunic had white facings, and there were yellow stripes on the blue pantaloons.

24TH REGIMENT (GREY'S HORSE)

This regiment was raised in 1908 and headquartered at Ingersoll, Ontario. The uniform included a khaki slouch hat with a tan puggaree with blue and yellow folds. Blackcock's feathers were worn in the hat band. The scarlet tunic had yellow facings, and there were yellow stripes on the blue pantaloons.

25TH BRANT DRAGOONS

This regiment was raised in 1910 and headquartered at Brantford, Ontario. The uniform included a brass helmet with a red plume. The scarlet tunic had yellow facings, and there were yellow stripes on the blue breeches.

26TH STANSTEAD DRAGOONS

This regiment was raised in 1910 and headquartered at Coaticook, Quebec. The uniform included a blue forage cap with a black band. The scarlet tunic had black facings, and there were yellow stripes on the blue pantaloons.

27TH LIGHT HORSE

This regiment was raised in 1910 and headquartered at Moosejaw, Saskatchewan. The uniform included a blue forage cap with a white band. The scarlet tunic had white facings, and there were white stripes on the blue pantaloons.

28TH NEW BRUNSWICK DRAGOONS

This regiment was raised in 1911 and headquartered at St. John, New Brunswick. The uniform included a blue forage cap with a yellow band. The scarlet tunic had yellow facings, and there were yellow stripes on the blue pantaloons.

29TH LIGHT HORSE

This regiment was raised in 1911 and headquartered at Saskatoon, Saskatchewan. The uniform included a blue forage cap with a yellow band. The scarlet tunic had yellow facings, and there were yellow stripes on the blue pantaloons.

30TH REGIMENT (BRITISH COLUMBIA HORSE)

This regiment was raised in 1911 and headquartered at Vernon, British Columbia. The uniform included a blue forage cap with a yellow band. The scarlet tunic had yellow facings, and there were yellow stripes on the blue pantaloons.

31ST REGIMENT (BRITISH COLUMBIA HORSE)

This regiment was raised in 1911 and headquartered at Merrit, British Columbia. The uniform included a blue forage cap with a yellow band. The scarlet tunic had yellow facings, and there were yellow stripes on the blue pantaloons.

32ND MANITOBA HORSE

This regiment was raised in 1912 perpetuating an earlier formation raised in 1885. The regiment was headquartered at Roblin, Manitoba. The uniform included a blue forage cap with a yellow band. The scarlet tunic had yellow facings, and there were yellow stripes on the blue pantaloons.

BATTLE HONOURS: *Fish Creek, Batoche, North West Canada 1885* (inherited from the earlier unit)

33RD VAUDREVIL AND SOULANGES HUSSARS

This regiment was raised in 1912 and headquartered at Rigaud, Quebec. The uniform included a blue forage cap with a buff band. The blue tunic had buff facings, a buff collar, and yellow braid. There were double buff stripes on the blue pantaloons.

34TH FORT GARRY HORSE

This regiment was raised in 1912 and headquartered at Winnipeg, Manitoba. The uniform included a blue forage cap with a yellow band. The scarlet tunic had yellow facings, and there were yellow stripes on the blue pantaloons. (Note: This regiment, like the two cavalry and one infantry regiments of the permanent force, served as a unit in the Canadian Expeditionary Force.)

35TH CENTRAL ALBERTA HORSE

This regiment was raised in 1913 and headquartered at Red Deer, Alberta. The uniform included a blue forage cap with a white band. The scarlet tunic had white facings, and there were yellow stripes on the blue pantaloons.

36TH PRINCE EDWARD ISLAND LIGHT HORSE

This regiment was raised in 1901 and headquartered at Charlottetown, Prince Edward Island. The uniform included a white (steel) metal helmet with a red and white plume. The scarlet tunic had yellow facings, and there were yellow stripes on the blue pantaloons.

CANADIAN ARTILLERY (MILITIA)

FIELD ARTILLERY

1855   The militia component of the Canadian Artillery raised with the formation of the Volunteer Militia Battery of Quebec

In 1914, there were 39 batteries of field artillery divided into brigades and independent batteries, and there were 12 ammunition columns attached to the brigades. The uniform included a *full dress* white helmet with a brass ball. The blue tunic had red facings, and there were wide red stripes on the blue pantaloons. The forage cap was blue with a red band.

GARRISON ARTILLERY

In 1914, there were four regiments and two companies of garrison artillery. The 1st (Halifax) Regiment consisted of four companies, the 3rd (New Brunswick) Regiment consisted of three companies, the 5th (British Columbia) Regiment consisted of three companies; and the 6th (Quebec and Levis) Regiment consisted of three companies. The No. 1 Siege Company was at Halifax, Nova Scotia, and the Montreal Siege Company was at Montreal, Quebec. The uniform included a *full dress* white helmet with a brass ball. The blue tunic had red facings, and there were wide red stripes on the blue trousers. The forage cap was blue with a red band.

CANADIAN ENGINEERS (MILITIA)

1861 The militia component of the Canadian Engineers was originally raised with the formation of the Volunteer Militia Engineer Company of Quebec

In 1914, there were four field troops (mounted) and nine field companies with headquarters at Ottawa, Ontario. The uniform included a *full dress* white helmet with a brass spike. The scarlet tunic had blue facings. The blue trousers, or pantaloons for mounted personnel, had wide scarlet stripes. The forage cap was blue.

CANADIAN SIGNAL CORPS (MILITIA)

This corps was raised in 1903 and headquartered at Ottawa, Ontario. In 1914, there were seven signal sections in the militia. It should be noted that in 1914, Canada was the only part of the British Empire military forces that maintained a signal corps separate from the engineers.

The uniform included a *full dress* white helmet with a brass spike. The blue tunic had French grey facings. The blue trousers, or pantaloons for mounted personnel, had double French grey stripes. The blue forage cap had a French grey band.

CANADIAN CORPS OF GUIDES (MILITIA)

This corps was raised in 1903 and headquartered at Ottawa, Ontario. The corps was administered by the General Staff at Military Headquarters, Ottawa. In 1914, there were nine detachments. The Guides were responsible for field security and some aspects of military intelligence.

The uniform included a *full dress* white helmet with a brass spike and a puggaree of six folds; the two center folds were scarlet, and the two top and bottom folds were khaki. The khaki tunic had a scarlet collar and cuffs and a *lancer* plastron. The khaki pantaloons (the Corps was mounted) had scarlet stripes, and the forage cap was khaki.

INFANTRY REGIMENTS OF THE CANADIAN MILITIA

In 1914, infantry regiments of the Canadian Militia had only one battalion, except for the 2nd Regiment (Queen's Own Rifles of Canada) and the 5th Regiment (Royal Highlanders of Canada), which had two battalions. Most battalions consisted of eight companies, although there were some with six and a few with only four.

THE GOVERNOR GENERAL'S FOOT GUARDS

This regiment was raised in 1872 and headquartered at Ottawa, Ontario. The Governor General of Canada was the Honorary Colonel. The uniform included a black bearskin cap with a red plume on the right side. The scarlet tunic had blue facings. The blue trousers had red piping, and the blue forage cap had a white band.

BATTLE HONOURS: *North West Canada 1885, South Africa 1899-1900*

1ST REGIMENT (THE GRENADIER GUARDS OF CANADA)

This regiment was raised in 1859 and headquartered at Montreal, Quebec. The uniform included a black bearskin cap with a white plume, tipped red on the left side. The scarlet tunic had blue facings. The blue trousers had red piping, and the forage cap was blue.

BATTLE HONOUR: *South Africa 1899-1900*

2ND REGIMENT (QUEEN'S OWN RIFLES OF CANADA)

This regiment was raised in 1860 and headquartered at Toronto, Ontario. Field Marshal Earl Roberts of Kandahar, Pretoria, and Waterford was the Honorary Colonel. The uniform included a black rifle busby with scarlet piping and a scarlet and black plume, a rifle green tunic with scarlet facings and piping, and rifle green trousers.

BATTLE HONOURS: *North West Canada 1885, South Africa 1899-1900*

3RD REGIMENT (VICTORIA RIFLES OF CANADA)

This regiment was raised in 1862 and headquartered at Montreal, Quebec. The uniform included a black rifle busby with scarlet piping and a scarlet and black plume, a rifle green tunic with scarlet facings and piping, and rifle green trousers.

BATTLE HONOURS: *Eccles Hill, South Africa 1899-1900*

4TH REGIMENT (CHASSEURS CANADIENS)

This regiment was raised in 1901 and headquartered at Ste. Ann de la Perade, Quebec. The uniform included a blue forage cap, scarlet tunic with blue facings, and blue trousers with red piping.

5TH REGIMENT (ROYAL HIGHLANDERS OF CANADA)

This regiment was raised in 1862 and headquartered at Montreal, Quebec. Except for badges and buttons, the uniform was essentially the same as the Black Watch (Royal Highlanders) of the British Army, including a black feather bonnet with a red and white diced border and a scarlet hackle. The scarlet doublet had blue facings, and the kilt was of Black Watch or *Government* tartan. The hose was red and black. Pipers had the same uniform, including a blue doublet with a kilt of Royal Stuart tartan. Instead of the feather bonnet, the pipers wore a black glengarry cap with a blackcock's feather.

BATTLE HONOUR: *South Africa 1899-1900*

6TH REGIMENT (THE DUKE OF CONNAUGHT'S OWN RIFLES)

This regiment was raised in 1899 and headquartered at Vancouver, British Columbia. Field Marshal Arthur Duke of Connaught and Strathearn, was the Honorary Colonel. The uniform included a black rifle busby with scarlet piping and a scarlet and black plume, a rifle green tunic with scarlet facings and piping, and rifle green trousers.

BATTLE HONOUR: *South Africa 1899-1900*

7TH REGIMENT (FUSILIERS)

This regiment was raised in 1866 and headquartered at London, Ontario. The uniform included a sealskin fusilier cap with a red over white plume. The scarlet tunic had blue facings, and the blue trousers had red piping. The forage cap was blue.

BATTLE HONOURS: *North West Canada 1885, South Africa 1899-1900*

8TH REGIMENT (ROYAL RIFLES)

This regiment was raised in 1862 and headquartered at Quebec City, Quebec. The uniform included a black rifle busby with scarlet piping and a scarlet and black plume, a rifle green tunic with scarlet facings and piping, and rifle green trousers.

BATTLE HONOUR: *South Africa 1899-1900*

9TH REGIMENT (VOLTIGEURS DE QUEBEC)

This regiment was raised in 1862 and headquartered at Quebec City, Quebec. The uniform included a blue forage cap, a scarlet tunic with blue facings, and blue trousers with red piping.

BATTLE HONOUR: *North West Canada 1885*

10TH REGIMENT (ROYAL GRENADIERS)

This regiment was raised in 1862 and headquartered at Toronto, Ontario. The Earl of Aberdeen was the Honorary Colonel. The uniform included a black bearskin cap with a red over white plume. The scarlet tunic had blue facings, and the blue trousers had red piping. The forage cap was blue with a scarlet band.

BATTLE HONOURS: *Fish Creek, Batoche, North West Canada 1885, South Africa 1899-1900*

11TH REGIMENT (IRISH FUSILIERS OF CANADA)

This regiment was raised in 1913 and headquartered at Vancouver, British Columbia. The uniform included a blue forage cap, a scarlet tunic with blue facings, and blue trousers with red piping.

12TH REGIMENT (YORK RANGERS)

This regiment was raised in 1866 and headquartered at Aurora, Ontario. The uniform included a blue forage cap with a green band, a scarlet tunic with green facings, and blue trousers with red piping.

BATTLE HONOUR: *North West Canada 1885*

13TH ROYAL REGIMENT

This regiment was raised in 1862 and headquartered at Hamilton, Ontario. The uniform included a blue forage cap with a scarlet band, a scarlet tunic with blue facings, and blue trousers with red piping.

BATTLE HONOUR: *South Africa 1900*

14TH REGIMENT (THE PRINCESS OF WALES'S OWN RIFLES)

This regiment was raised in 1863 and headquartered at Kingston, Ontario. The uniform included a black rifle busby with scarlet piping and a scarlet and black plume, a rifle green tunic with scarlet facings and piping, and rifle green trousers.

BATTLE HONOUR: *South Africa 1900*

HIS MAJESTY GEORGE THE FIFTH
1865–1936
**KING OF GREAT BRITAIN AND IRELAND
AND OF THE BRITISH DOMINIONS BEYOND THE SEAS
EMPEROR OF INDIA**

The "Sailor King" in the uniform of an admiral of the Royal Navy.

George V was born in London on June 3, 1865, the second son of the Prince of Wales, later King Edward VII. In 1877, George, together with his older brother Albert Victor became naval cadets. In 1879, they made a voyage to the West Indies during which they were rated midshipmen. In 1880, both brothers made a prolonged cruise visiting South America, South Africa, Australia, Fiji, Japan, Ceylon, Egypt, Palestine, and Greece. At the close of this cruise the brothers separated. George remained in the navy serving on H.M.S. *Canada* on the North American and West Indian station where he was promoted sub-lieutenant. Upon his return home he passed through the Royal Naval College at Greenwich, and the gunnery and torpedo schools. In 1886 the was assigned to the Mediterranean station serving on three ships. In 1889 he joined the flagship of the Channel Squadron, H.M.S. *Northumberland* and in that year was in command of torpedo boat No. 79. In 1890 he was put in command of the gunboat, H.M.S. *Thrush* on the North American and West Indian station. He was promoted commander in 1891 and commissioned H.M.S. *Melampus*. In 1892, upon the death of his brother he relinquished his command. As heir to the throne, his new duties prevented him from devoting himself exclusively to the navy. He remained a navy man, promoted to captain in 1893, rear-admiral in 1901, and vice-admiral in 1903. The habits and outlooks he formed in the Royal Navy regulated the daily routine of the "Sailor King."

In 1892, he was created Duke of York, Earl of Inverness and Baron Killarney. In 1893, he married Princess Victoria Mary of Teck. In 1899, the duke and duchess visited Ireland. In 1901, they traveled to Australia and New Zealand returning home by way of South Africa and Canada. In November 1901, the duke was created Prince of Wales

Upon the death of his father, Edward VII in 1910 he succeeded to the throne as George V, his consort becoming Queen Mary. The coronation was held on June 22, 1911 followed by visits to Ireland, Wales, and Scotland. In December 1911, the King and Queen visited Delhi where a coronation *durbar* was held.

During World War I frequent Royal visits were made to the French and Belgian fronts, as well as visits to the fleet, shipyards, factories, hospitals, and other facilities engaged in the war effort. George's second son, later King George VI (1895-1952) followed in his father's footsteps, serving in the Royal Navy, and was present as a sub-lieutenant at the Battle of Jutland.

George V remained a popular and well loved monarch to the end of his reign. In 1935, his Silver Jubilee was marked by expressions of enthusiasm and loyalty from his subjects throughout the Empire. He died on 20 January 1936 and was buried in St. George's Chapel, Windsor.

FORCES OF THE BRITISH EMPIRE—1914   99

ROYAL NAVY & ROYAL MARINE FORCES

Fig. 1. Royal Navy

Fig. 2. Royal Marine Light Infantry

Fig. 3. Royal Marine Artillery

Photo: Imperial War Museum, London   Q21184

H.M.S Dreadnought, under way leaving Portsmouth harbour.

GREAT BRITAIN AND IRELAND
HOUSEHOLD CAVALRY

Fig. 4. 1st Life Guards

Fig. 5. 2nd Life Guards

Fig. 6. Royal Horse Guards (The Blues)

CAVALRY OF THE LINE

Fig. 7. 1st (King's) Dragoon Guards

Fig. 8. 2nd Dragoon Guards (Queen's Bays)

Fig. 9. 3rd (Prince of Wales's) Dragoon Guards

FORCES OF THE BRITISH EMPIRE—1914   101

GREAT BRITAIN AND IRELAND

Fig. 10. 4th (Royal Irish) Dragoon Guards

Fig. 11. 5th (Princess Charlotte of Wales's) Dragoon Guards

Fig. 12. 6th Dragoon Guards (Carabiniers)

Fig. 13. 7th (Princess Royal's) Dragoon Guards

Fig. 14. 1st (Royal) Dragoons

Fig. 15. 2nd Dragoons (Royal Scots Greys)

102 FORCES OF THE BRITISH EMPIRE—1914

GREAT BRITAIN AND IRELAND

Fig. 16. 3rd (King's Own) Hussars

Fig. 17. 4th (Queen's Own) Hussars

Fig. 18. 5th (Royal Irish) Lancers

Fig. 19. 6th (Inniskilling) Dragoons

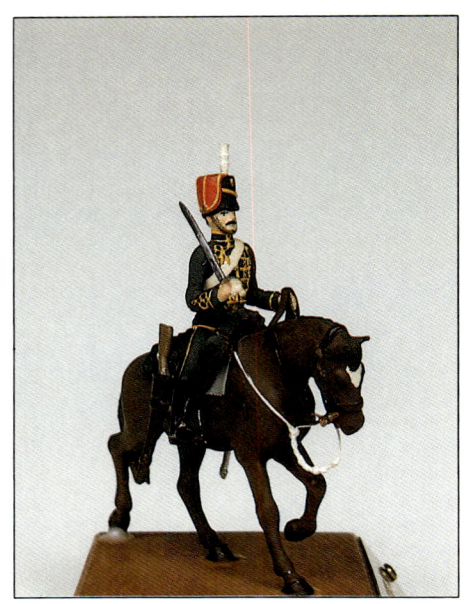

Fig. 20. 7th (Queen's Own) Hussars

Fig. 21. 8th (King's Royal Irish) Hussars

GREAT BRITAIN AND IRELAND

Fig. 22. 9th (Queen's Royal) Lancers

Fig. 23. 10th (Prince of Wales's Own Royal) Hussars

Fig. 24. 11th (Prince Albert's Own) Hussars

Fig. 25. 12th (Prince of Wales's Royal) Lancers

Fig. 26. 13th Hussars

Fig. 27. 14th (King's) Hussars

GREAT BRITAIN AND IRELAND

Fig. 28. 15th (The King's) Hussars

Fig. 29. 16th (The Queen's) Lancers

Fig. 30. 17th (Duke of Cambridge's Own) Lancers

Fig. 31. 18th (Queen Mary's Own) Hussars

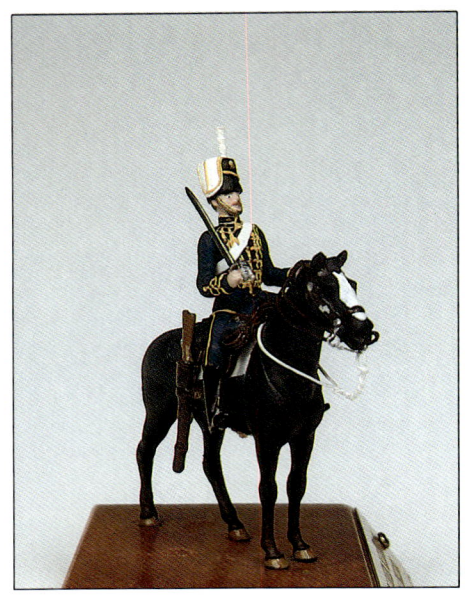

Fig. 32. 19th (Queen Alexandra's Own Royal) Hussars

Fig. 33. 20th Hussars

FORCES OF THE BRITISH EMPIRE—1914   105

GREAT BRITAIN AND IRELAND

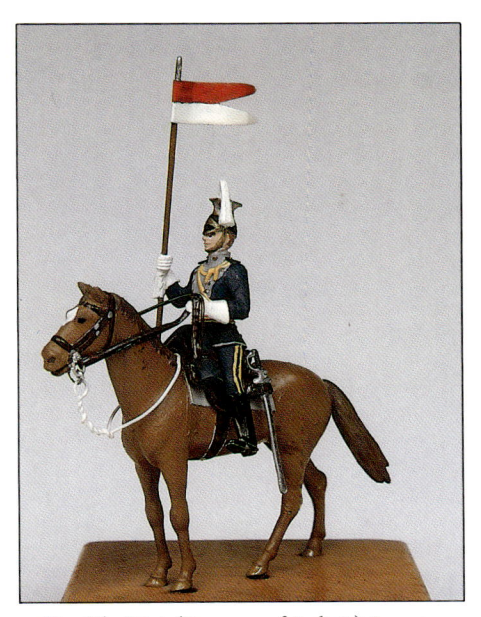

Fig. 34. 21st (Empress of India's) Lancers

ARTILLERY

Fig. 35. Royal Horse Artillery

106 FORCES OF THE BRITISH EMPIRE—1914

GREAT BRITAIN AND IRELAND

Fig. 36. Royal Field Artillery

Fig. 37. Royal Garrison Artillery

FORCES OF THE BRITISH EMPIRE—1914

GREAT BRITAIN AND IRELAND

Fig. 38. Royal Garrison Artillery

ENGINEERS

Fig. 39. Corps of Royal Engineers

108 FORCES OF THE BRITISH EMPIRE—1914

GREAT BRITAIN AND IRELAND
FOOT GUARDS

Fig. 40. Grenadier Guards

Fig. 41. Coldstream Guards

Fig. 42. Scots Guards

Fig. 43. Irish Guards

INFANTRY OF THE LINE

Fig. 44. The Royal Scots (Lothian Regiment)

Fig. 45. The Queen's (Royal West Surrey) Regiment

Fig. 46. The Buffs (East Kent Regiment)

Fig. 47. The King's Own (Royal Lancaster Regiment)

FORCES OF THE BRITISH EMPIRE—1914   109

GREAT BRITAIN AND IRELAND

Fig. 48. The Northumberland Fusiliers

Fig. 49. The Royal Warwickshire Regiment

Fig. 50. The Royal Fusiliers (City of London Regiment)

Fig. 51. The King's (Liverpool Regiment)

Fig. 52. The Norfolk Regiment

Fig. 53. The Lincolnshire Regiment

Fig. 54. The Devonshire Regiment

Fig. 55. The Suffolk Regiment

110 FORCES OF THE BRITISH EMPIRE—1914

GREAT BRITAIN AND IRELAND

Fig. 56. Prince Albert's (Somerset Light Infantry)

Fig. 57. The Prince of Wales's Own (West Yorkshire Regiment)

Fig. 58. The East Yorkshire Regiment

Fig. 59. The Bedfordshire Regiment

Fig. 60. The Leicestershire Regiment

Fig. 61. The Royal Irish Regiment

Fig. 62. Alexandra, Princess of Wales's Own (Yorkshire Regiment)

Fig. 63. The Lancashire Fusiliers

FORCES OF THE BRITISH EMPIRE—1914 111

GREAT BRITAIN AND IRELAND

Fig. 64. The Royal Scots Fusiliers

Fig. 65. The Cheshire Regiment

Fig. 66. The Royal Welsh Fusiliers

Fig. 66A. The Royal Welsh Fusiliers (back view)

Fig. 67. The South Wales Borderers

Fig. 68. The King's Own Scottish Borderers

Fig. 69. The Cameronians (Scottish Rifles)

Fig. 70. The Royal Inniskilling Fusiliers

112   FORCES OF THE BRITISH EMPIRE—1914

GREAT BRITAIN AND IRELAND

Fig. 71. The Gloucestershire Regiment

Fig. 72. The Worcestershire Regiment

Fig. 73. The East Lancashire Regiment

Fig. 74. The East Surrey Regiment

Fig. 75. The Duke of Cornwall's Light Infantry

Fig. 76. The Duke of Wellington's (West Riding Regiment)

Fig. 77. The Border Regiment

Fig. 78. The Royal Sussex Regiment

FORCES OF THE BRITISH EMPIRE—1914   113

GREAT BRITAIN AND IRELAND

Fig. 79. The Hampshire Regiment

Fig. 80. The South Staffordshire Regiment

Fig. 81. The Dorsetshire Regiment

Fig. 82. The Prince of Wale's Volunteers (South Lancashire Regiment)

Fig. 83. The Welsh Regiment

Fig. 84. The Black Watch (Royal Highland Regiment)

Fig. 85. The Oxfordshire and Buckinghamshire Light Infantry

Fig. 86. The Essex Regiment

114   FORCES OF THE BRITISH EMPIRE—1914

GREAT BRITAIN AND IRELAND

Fig. 87. The Sherwood Foresters (Nottinghamshire and Derbyshire Regiment)

Fig. 88. The Loyal North Lancashire Regiment

Fig. 89. The Northamptonshire Regiment

Fig. 90. Princess Charlotte of Wales's (Royal Berkshire Regiment)

Fig. 91. The Queen's Own (Royal West Kent Regiment)

Fig. 92. The King's Own (Yorkshire Light Infantry)

Fig. 93. The King's (Shropshire Light Infantry)

Fig. 94. The Duke of Cambridge's Own (Middlesex Regiment)

FORCES OF THE BRITISH EMPIRE—1914 115

GREAT BRITAIN AND IRELAND

Fig. 95. The King's Royal Rifle Corps

Fig. 96. The Duke of Edinburgh's (Wiltshire Regiment)

Fig. 97. The Manchester Regiment

Fig. 98. The Prince of Wales's (North Staffordshire Regiment)

Fig. 99. The York and Lancaster Regiment

Fig. 100. The Durham Light Infantry

Fig. 101. The Highland Light Infantry

Fig. 102. Seaforth Highlanders (Ross-shire Buffs, The Duke of Albany's)

GREAT BRITAIN AND IRELAND

Fig. 103. The Gordon Highlanders

Fig. 104. The Queen's Own Cameron Highlanders

Fig. 105. The Royal Irish Rifles

Fig. 106. Princess Victoria's (Royal Irish Fusiliers)

Fig. 107. The Connaught Rangers

Fig. 108. Princess Louise's (Argyll and Sutherland Highlanders)

Fig. 109. The Prince of Wales Leinster Regiment (Royal Canadians)

Fig. 110. The Royal Munster Fusiliers

FORCES OF THE BRITISH EMPIRE—1914 117

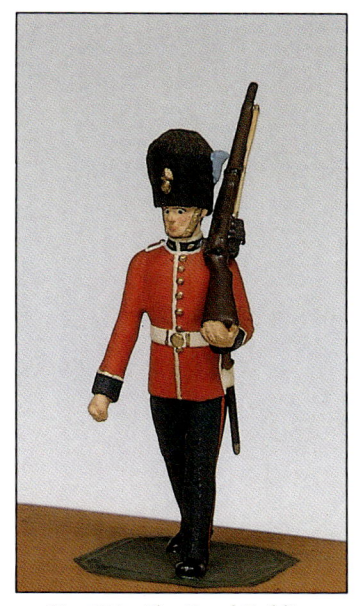

GREAT BRITAIN AND IRELAND

Fig. 111. The Royal Dublin
Fusiliers

Fig. 112. The Rifle Brigade
(The Prince Consort's Own)

DEPARTMENTAL CORPS

Fig. 113. Corps of Military Police
(Mounted & Foot)

Fig. 114. Army Pay Corps

GREAT BRITAIN AND IRELAND

Fig. 115. Army Ordnance Corps

Fig. 116. Army Veterinary Corps

Fig. 117. Army Service Corps

GREAT BRITAIN AND IRELAND

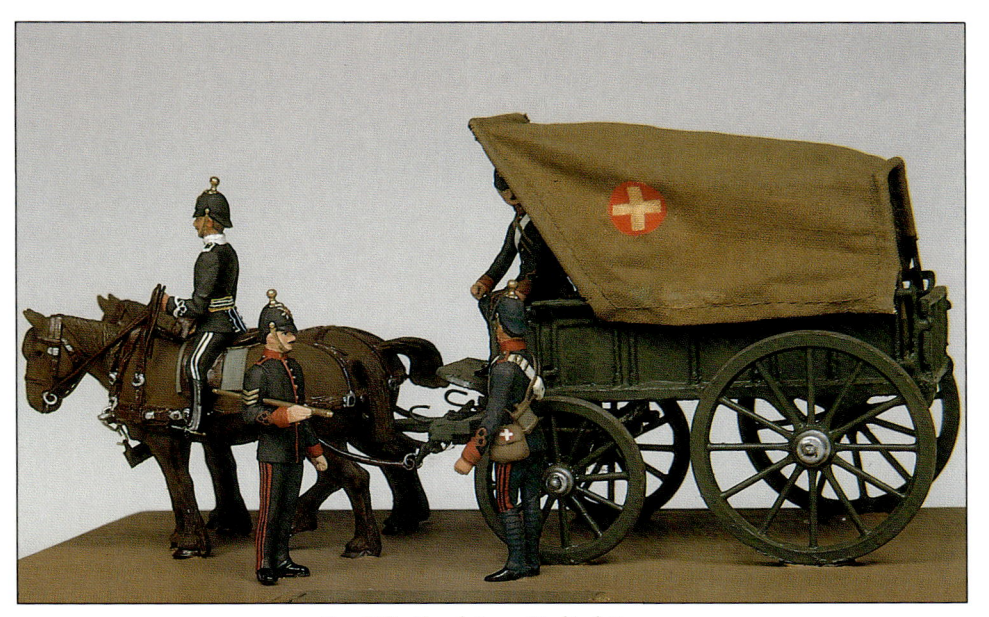

Fig. 118. Royal Army Medical Corps

Fig. 119. Queen Alexandra's Imperial Military Nursing Service

Fig. 120. Royal Flying Corps and Royal Naval Air Service

120 FORCES OF THE BRITISH EMPIRE—1914

CANADA

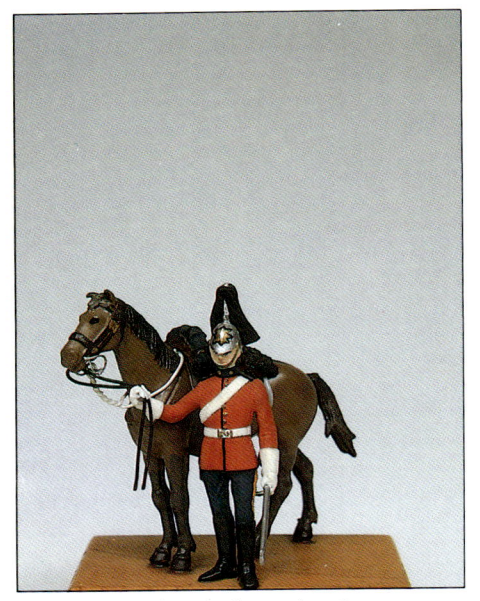

Fig. 121. The Royal Canadian Dragoons

Fig. 122. Lord Strathcona's Horse (Royal Canadians)

Fig. 123. Royal Canadian Horse Artillery

Fig. 124. Royal Canadian Garrison Artillery

Fig. 125. Royal Canadian Engineers

Fig. 126. The Royal Canadian Regiment

CANADA

Fig. 127. Canadian Ordnance Corps

Fig. 128. Canadian Army Service Corps

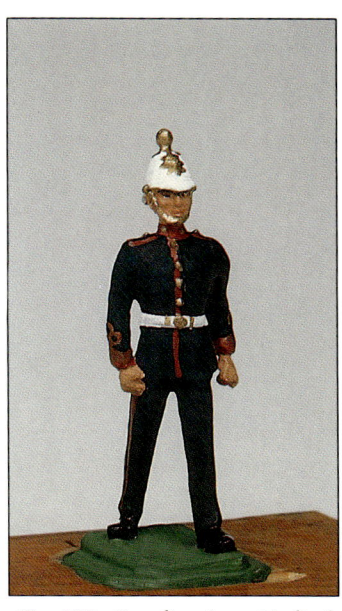

Fig. 129. Canadian Army Medical Corps

Fig. 130. Canadian Army Pay Corps

Fig. 131. Canadian Army Veterinary Corps

Fig. 132. Corps of Military Staff Clerks, Section *B*

AUSTRALIA & NEW ZEALAND

Fig. 133. Administrative and Instructional Staff (Australia)

Fig. 134. Royal Australian Field Artillery

Fig. 135. Royal Australian Garrison Artillery

Fig. 136. Royal Australian Engineers

Fig. 137. Australian Army Medical Corps (Permanent Section)

Fig. 138. Australian Army Service Corps (Permanent Section)

AUSTRALIA & NEW ZEALAND

Fig. 139. Australian Army Veterinary Corps (Permanent Section)

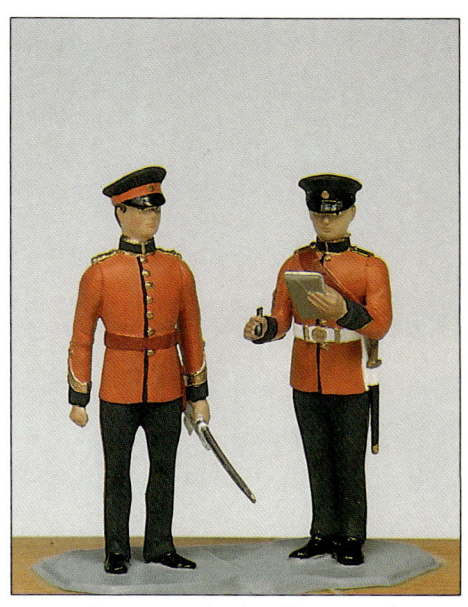

Fig. 140. New Zealand Staff Corps and New Zealand Permanent Staff

SOUTH AFRICA

Fig. 141. Royal New Zealand Artillery

Fig. 142. South African Mounted Riflemen

INDIA
BODYGUARDS AND GUIDES

Fig. 143. The Governor General's Bodyguard (India)

Fig. 144. The Governor's Bodyguard, Madras

Fig. 145. The Governor's Bodyguard, Bombay

Fig. 146. The Governor's Bodyguard, Bengal

Fig. 147. Escort to the British Resident, Nepal Cavalry & Infantry

Fig. 148. Queen Victoria's Own Corps of Guides (Frontier Force) (Lumsden's) Cavalry & Infantry

FORCES OF THE BRITISH EMPIRE—1914 125

INDIA
CAVALRY

Fig. 149. 1st Duke of York's Own Lancers (Skinner's Horse)

Fig. 150. 2nd Lancers (Gardner's Horse)

Fig. 151. 3rd Skinner's Horse

Fig. 152. 4th Cavalry

Fig. 153. 5th Cavalry

Fig. 154. 6th King Edward's Own Cavalry

INDIA

Fig. 155. 7th Hariana Lancers

Fig. 156. 8th Cavalry

Fig. 157. 9th Hodson's Horse

Fig. 158. 10th Duke of Cambridge's Own Lancers (Hodson's Horse)

Fig. 159. 11th King Edward's Own Lancers (Probyn's Horse)

Fig. 160. 12th Cavalry

FORCES OF THE BRITISH EMPIRE—1914 127

INDIA

Fig. 161. 13th Duke of Connaught's Lancers (Watson's Horse)

Fig. 162. 14th Murray's Jat Lancers

Fig. 163. 15th Lancers (Cureton's Multanis)

Fig. 164. 16th Cavalry

Fig. 165. 17th Cavalry

Fig. 166. 18th King George's Own Lancers

INDIA

Fig. 167. 19th Lancers (Fane's Horse)

Fig. 168. 20th Deccan Horse

Fig. 169. 21st Prince Albert Victor's Own Cavalry (Frontier Force) (Daly's Horse)

Fig. 170. 22nd Sam Browne's Cavalry (Frontier Force)

Fig. 171. 23rd Cavalry (Frontier Force)

Fig. 172. 25th Cavalry (Frontier Force)

15TH REGIMENT (ARGYLL LIGHT INFANTRY)

This regiment was raised in 1863 and headquartered at Belleview, Ontario. The uniform included a blue forage cap, a scarlet tunic with blue facings, and blue trousers with red piping. Although the regiment was very Scottish-oriented, it never wore Scottish dress. It did maintain a pipe band. The pipers wore kilts of Erskine tartan and blue glengarry caps. The regiment finally adopted a red and white diced hat band in 1923.

16TH PRINCE EDWARD REGIMENT

This regiment was raised in 1863 and headquartered at Picton, Ontario. The uniform included a blue forage cap, a scarlet tunic with blue facings, and blue trousers with red piping.

17TH REGIMENT

This regiment was raised in 1863, disbanded in 1900, and reraised in 1902 with headquarters at Levis, Quebec. The uniform included a blue forage cap, a scarlet tunic with blue facings, and blue trousers with red piping.

18TH SAGUENAY REGIMENT

This regiment was raised in 1900 and headquartered at Chicoutimi, Quebec. The uniform included a blue forage cap, a scarlet tunic with blue facings, and blue trousers with red piping.

19TH LINCOLN REGIMENT

This regiment was raised in 1863 and headquartered at St. Catherines, Ontario. The uniform included a blue forage cap, a scarlet tunic with blue facings, and blue trousers with red piping.

20TH REGIMENT (HALTON RIFLES)

This regiment was raised in 1866 and headquartered at Milton, Ontario. The uniform included a black rifle busby with scarlet piping and a scarlet and black plume, a rifle green tunic with scarlet facings and piping, and rifle green trousers.

21ST REGIMENT (ESSEX FUSILIERS)

This regiment was raised in 1855 and headquartered at Windsor, Ontario. The uniform included a blue forage cap, a scarlet tunic with blue facings, and blue trousers with red piping.

22ND REGIMENT (THE OXFORD RIFLES)

This regiment was raised in 1863 and headquartered at Woodstock, Ontario. The uniform included a black rifle busby with scarlet piping and a scarlet and black plume, a rifle green tunic with scarlet facings and piping, and rifle green trousers.

23RD REGIMENT (THE NORTHERN PIONEERS)

This regiment was raised in 1903 and headquartered at Parry Sound, Ontario. The uniform included a blue forage cap, a scarlet tunic with blue facings, and blue trousers with red piping.

24TH KENT REGIMENT

This regiment was raised in 1866, disbanded in 1892, reraised in 1901, and headquartered at Chatham, Ontario. The uniform included a blue forage cap, a scarlet tunic with blue facings, and blue trousers with red piping.

25TH REGIMENT

This regiment was raised in 1866 and headquartered at St. Thomas, Ontario. The uniform included a blue forage cap, a scarlet tunic with blue facings, and blue trousers with red piping.

26TH REGIMENT (MIDDLESEX LIGHT INFANTRY)

This regiment was raised in 1866 and headquartered at Strathroy, Ontario. The uniform included a blue forage cap, a scarlet tunic with blue facings, and blue trousers with red piping.
BATTLE HONOUR: *South Africa 1899-1900*

27TH LAMBTON REGIMENT (ST. CLAIR BORDERERS)

This regiment was raised in 1866 and headquartered at Sarnia, Ontario. The uniform included a blue forage cap, scarlet tunic with blue facings, and blue trousers with red piping.

28TH PERTH REGIMENT

This regiment was raised in 1866 and headquartered at Stratford, Ontario. The uniform included a blue forage cap, a scarlet tunic with blue facings, and blue trousers with red piping.

29TH WATERLOO REGIMENT

This regiment was raised in 1866 and headquartered at Galt, Ontario. The uniform included a blue forage cap, scarlet tunic with blue facings, and blue trousers with red piping.

30TH REGIMENT (WELLINGTON RIFLES)

This regiment was raised in 1866 and headquartered at Guelph, Ontario. The uniform included a black rifle busby with scarlet piping and a scarlet and black plume, a rifle green tunic with scarlet facings and piping, and rifle green trousers.

31ST GREY REGIMENT

This regiment was raised in 1866 and headquartered at Owen Sound, Ontario. The uniform included a blue forage cap, a scarlet tunic with blue facings, and blue trousers with red piping.

32ND BRUCE REGIMENT

This regiment was raised in 1866 and headquartered at Walkerton, Ontario. The uniform included a blue forage cap, a scarlet tunic with blue facings, and blue trousers with red piping.

33RD HURON REGIMENT

This regiment was raised in 1866 and headquartered at Goderich, Ontario. The uniform included a blue forage cap, a scarlet tunic with blue facings, and blue trousers with red piping.

34TH ONTARIO REGIMENT

This regiment was raised in 1866 and headquartered at Whitby, Ontario. The uniform included a blue forage cap, a scarlet tunic with blue facings, and blue trousers with red piping.

35TH REGIMENT (SIMCOE FORESTERS)

This regiment was raised in 1866 and headquartered at Barrie, Ontario. The uniform included a blue forage cap, a scarlet tunic with blue facings, and blue trousers with red piping.
BATTLE HONOUR: *North West Canada 1885*

36TH PEEL REGIMENT

This regiment was raised in 1866 and headquartered at Brampton, Ontario. The uniform included a blue forage cap with a white band, a scarlet tunic with white facings, and blue trousers with red piping.

37TH REGIMENT (HALDIMAND RIFLES)

This regiment was raised in 1866 and headquartered at York, Ontario. The uniform included a black rifle busby with scarlet piping and a scarlet and black plume, a rifle green tunic with scarlet facings and piping, and rifle green trousers.

38TH REGIMENT (DUFFERIN RIFLES OF CANADA)

This regiment was raised in 1866 and headquartered at Brantford, Ontario. The Marquess of Dufferin and Ava was the Honorary Colonel. The uniform included a black rifle busby with scarlet piping and a scarlet and black plume, a rifle green tunic with scarlet facings and piping, and rifle green trousers.

39TH REGIMENT (NORFOLK RIFLES)

This regiment was raised in 1866 and headquartered at Simcoe, Ontario. The uniform included a black rifle busby with scarlet piping and a black and scarlet plume, a rifle green tunic with scarlet facings and piping, and rifle green trousers.

40TH NORTHUMBERLAND REGIMENT

This regiment was raised in 1866 and headquartered at Coburg, Ontario. The uniform included a blue forage cap, a scarlet tunic with blue facings, and blue trousers with red piping. There was another *Northumberland* regiment, the 73rd in New Brunswick.

41ST REGIMENT (BROCKVILLE RIFLES)

This regiment was raised in 1866 and headquarterd at Brockville, Ontario. The uniform included a black rifle busby with scarlet piping and a black and scarlet plume, a rifle green tunic with scarlet facings and piping, and rifle green trousers.

42ND LANARK AND RENFREW REGIMENT

This regiment was raised in 1866 and headquartered at Perth, Ontario. The uniform included a blue forage cap, a scarlet tunic with blue facings, and blue trousers with red piping.

43RD REGIMENT
(THE DUKE OF CORNWALL'S OWN RIFLES)

This regiment was raised in 1881 and headquartered at Ottawa, Ontario. King George V was the Honorary Colonel. The uniform included a black rifle busby with scarlet piping and a scarlet and black plume, a rifle green tunic with scarlet facings and piping, and rifle green trousers.

BATTLE HONOUR: *South Africa 1899-1900*

44TH LINCOLN AND WELLAND REGIMENT

This regiment was raised in 1866 and headquartered at Niagara Falls, Ontario. The uniform included a blue forage cap, a scarlet tunic with blue facings, and blue trousers with red piping.

45TH VICTORIA REGIMENT

This regiment was raised in 1866 and headquartered at Lindsay, Ontario. The uniform included a blue forage cap, a scarlet tunic with blue facings, blue trousers with red piping.

46TH DURHAM REGIMENT

This regiment was raised in 1866 and headquartered at Port Hope, Ontario. The uniform included a blue forage cap, a scarlet tunic with blue facings, and blue trousers with red piping.

BATTLE HONOUR: *North West Canada 1885*

47TH FRONTENAC REGIMENT

This regiment was raised in 1866 and headquartered at Kingston, Ontario. The uniform included a blue forage cap, a scarlet tunic with blue facings, and blue trousers with red piping.

48TH REGIMENT (HIGHLANDERS)

This regiment was raised in 1891 and headquartered at Toronto, Ontario. The uniform included a black feather bonnet with a red and white diced border and a white hackle. The scarlet doublet had blue facings, and the kilt was of Davidson tartan. The sporran was black with two white tails, and the hose was red and black hose. The pipers wore blue glengarry caps with blackcocks feathers, blue doublets, and kilts of Fingask tartan.

BATTLE HONOUR: *South Africa 1899-1900*

49TH REGIMENT (HASTINGS RIFLES)

This regiment was raised in 1866 and headquartered at Belleville, Ontario. The uniform included a black rifle busby with scarlet piping and a scarlet and black plume, a rifle green tunic with scarlet facings and piping, and rifle green trousers.

50TH REGIMENT (GORDON HIGHLANDERS)

This regiment was raised in 1913 and headquartered at Victoria, British Columbia. Except for badges and buttons, the uniform was essentially the same as the Gordon Highlanders of the British Army. The pipers wore blue glengarry caps with red-white-blue diced borders, blue doublets, and kilts of Lennox tartan.

51ST REGIMENT (THE SOO RIFLES)

This regiment was raised in 1913 and headquartered at Sault Ste. Marie, Ontario. The uniform included a black rifle busby with scarlet piping and a scarlet and black plume, a rifle green tunic with scarlet facings and piping, and rifle green trousers.

52ND REGIMENT (PRINCE ALBERT VOLUNTEERS)

This regiment was raised in 1913 and headquarterd at Prince Albert, Saskatchewan. This regiment perpetuated an earlier unit, *the Prince Albert Volunteers* of 1885. The battle honour is inherited. The uniform included a blue forage cap, a scarlet tunic with blue facings, and blue trousers with red piping.

BATTLE HONOUR: *North West Canada 1885*

53RD SHERBROOKE REGIMENT

This regiment was raised in 1867 and headquartered at Sherbrooke, Quebec. The uniform included a blue forage cap, a scarlet tunic with blue facings, and blue trousers with red piping.

54TH REGIMENT (CARABINIERS DE SHERBROOKE)

This regiment was raised in 1910 and headquartered at Sherbrooke, Quebec. The uniform included a blue forage cap, a scarlet tunic with blue facings, and blue trousers with red piping.

55TH Regiment—Vacant in 1914

56TH GRENVILLE REGIMENT (LISGAR RIFLES)

This regiment was raised in 1867 and headquartered at Prescott, Ontario. The uniform included a black rifle busby with scarlet piping and a scarlet and black plume, a rifle green tunic with scarlet facings and piping, and the trousers were rifle green.

57TH REGIMENT (PETERBOROUGH RANGERS)

This regiment was raised in 1867 and headquartered at Peterborough, Ontario. The uniform included a blue forage cap, a scarlet tunic with blue facings, and blue trousers with red piping.

58TH Regiment—Vacant in 1914

59TH STORMONT AND GLENGARRY REGIMENT

This regiment was raised in 1868 and headquartered at Alexandria, Ontario. The uniform included a blue glengarry cap with a red and white diced border, a scarlet doublet with blue facings, and trews of Sutherland tartan. The pipers wore blue glengarry caps with red and white diced borders, blue doublets, and kilts of MacDonald tartan.

60TH RIFLES OF CANADA

This regiment was raised in 1913 and headquartered at Moosejaw, Saskatchewan. The uniform included a black rifle busby with scarlet piping and a scarlet and black plume, a rifle green tunic with scarlet facings and piping, and rifle green trousers.

61ST MONTMAGNY AND L'ISLET REGIMENT

This regiment was raised in 1869 and headquartered at Montmagny, Quebec. The uniform included a blue forage cap, a scarlet tunic with blue facings, and blue trousers with red piping.

62ND REGIMENT (ST. JOHN FUSILIERS)

This regiment was raised in 1872 and headquartered at St. John, New Brunswick. The uniform included a sealskin fusilier cap without a plume, a scarlet tunic with blue facings, and blue trousers with red piping. The forage cap was blue.
BATTLE HONOUR: *South Africa 1899-1900, 1902*

63RD REGIMENT (HALIFAX RIFLES)

This regiment was raised in 1860 and headquartered at Halifax, Nova Scotia. The uniform included a black rifle busby with scarlet piping and a scarlet and black plume, a rifle green tunic with scarlet facings and piping, and rifle green trousers.
BATTLE HONOURS: *North West Canada 1885, South Africa 1899-1900*

64TH CHATEAUGUAY AND BEAUHARNOIS REGIMENT

This regiment was raised in 1869 and headquartered at Beauharnois, Quebec. The uniform included a blue forage cap, a scarlet tunic with blue facings, and blue trousers with red piping.

65TH REGIMENT (MOUNT ROYAL RIFLES)

This regiment was raised in 1869 and headquartered at Montreal, Quebec. The uniform included a black rifle busby with scarlet piping and a scarlet and black plume, a rifle green tunic with scarlet facings and piping, and rifle green trousers.
BATTLE HONOUR: *North West Canada 1885*

66TH REGIMENT (PRINCESS LOUISE'S FUSILIERS)

This regiment was raised in 1869 and headquartered at Halifax, Nova Scotia. The uniform included a sealskin fusilier cap with a red over white plume, a scarlet tunic with blue facings, and blue trousers with red piping. The forage cap was blue.

67TH REGIMENT (CARLETON LIGHT INFANTRY)

This regiment was raised in 1869 and headquartered at Woodstock, New Brunswick. The uniform included a blue forage cap, a scarlet tunic with blue facings, and blue trousers with red piping.

68TH Regiment—Vacant in 1914. See Earl Grey's Own Rifles at the end of the Canadian infantry list.

69TH ANNAPOLIS REGIMENT

This regiment was raised in 1869 and headquartered at Middleton, Nova Scotia. The uniform included a blue forage cap, a scarlet tunic with blue facings, and blue trousers with red piping.

70TH Regiment—Vacant in 1914

71ST YORK REGIMENT

This regiment was raised in 1869 and headquartered at Fredericton, New Brunswick. The uniform included a blue forage cap, a scarlet tunic with blue facings, and blue trousers with red piping.

BATTLE HONOUR: *South Africa 1900*

72ND (SEAFORTH HIGHLANDERS OF CANADA)

This regiment was raised in 1910 and headquartered at Vancouver, British Columbia. Except for badges and buttons, the uniform was essentially the same as the Seaforth Highlanders of the British Army: a black feather bonnet with a red and white diced border and a white hackle. The scarlet tunic had buff facings, and the kilt was of Mackenzie tartan. The pipers wore blue glengarry caps with a red-white-blue diced border and blue doublets.

73RD NORTHUMBERLAND REGIMENT

This regiment was raised in 1870 and headquartered at Chatham, New Brunswick. The uniform included a blue forage cap, a scarlet tunic with blue facings, and blue trousers with red piping. There was another *Northumberland* regiment, the 40th in Ontario.

74TH REGIMENT (NEW BRUNSWICK RANGERS)

This regiment was raised in 1870 and headquartered at Sussex, New Brunswick. The uniform included a blue forage cap, a scarlet tunic with blue facings, and blue trousers with red piping.

75TH LUNENBURG REGIMENT

This regiment was raised in 1870 and headquartered at Lunenburg, Nova Scotia. The uniform included a blue forage cap, a scarlet tunic with blue facings, and blue trousers with red piping.

76TH COLCHESTER AND HANTS RIFLES

This regiment was raised in 1910 and headquartered at Truro, Nova Scotia. The uniform included a black rifle busby with scarlet piping and a scarlet and black plume, a rifle green tunic with scarlet facings and piping, and rifle green trousers.

77TH WENTWORTH REGIMENT

This regiment was raised in 1872 and headquartered at Dundas, Ontario. The uniform included a blue forage cap, a scarlet tunic with blue facings, and blue trousers with red piping.

78TH PICTOU REGIMENT (HIGHLANDERS)

This regiment was raised in 1871 and headquartered at Pictou, Nova Scotia. The uniform included a blue Kilmarnock bonnet with a red-white-blue diced border. The scarlet doublet had buff facings, and the kilt was of Mackenzie tartan. The pipers wore blue glengarry caps with a red-white-blue diced border, and blue doublets.

79TH (CAMERON HIGHLANDERS OF CANADA)

This regiment was raised in 1910 and headquartered at Winnipeg, Manitoba. Except for badges and buttons, the uniform was essentially the same as the Queen's Own Cameron Highlanders of the British Army: a black feather bonnet with a red and white diced border and a white hackle. The scarlet doublet had blue facings and the kilt was of Cameron of Erracht tartan. The pipers wore plain blue glengarry caps without a diced border and blue doublets.

80TH NICOLET REGIMENT

This regiment was raised in 1875 and headquartered at Nicolet, Quebec. The uniform included a blue forage cap, a scarlet tunic with blue facings, and blue trousers with red piping.

81ST HANTS REGIMENT

This regiment was raised in 1869, disbanded in 1912, reraised in 1914, and headquartered at Windsor, Nova Scotia. The uniform included a blue forage cap, a scarlet tunic with blue facings, and blue trousers with red piping.

82ND (ABEGWEIT LIGHT INFANTRY) REGIMENT

This regiment was raised in 1875 and headquartered at Charlottetown, Prince Edward Island. The uniform included a blue forage cap, a scarlet tunic with blue facings, and blue trousers with red piping.

BATTLE HONOUR: *South Africa 1900*

83RD JOLIETTE REGIMENT

This regiment was raised in 1871 and headquartered at Joliette, Quebec. The uniform included a blue forage cap, a scarlet tunic with blue facings, and blue trousers with red piping.

84TH ST.HYACINTHE REGIMENT

This regiment was raised in 1871 and headquartered at St. Hyacinthe, Quebec. The uniform included a blue forage cap, a scarlet tunic with blue facings, and blue trousers with red piping.

85TH REGIMENT

This regiment was raised in 1880 and headquartered at Montreal, Quebec. The uniform included a blue forage cap, a scarlet tunic with blue facings, and blue trousers with red piping.

86TH Regiment—Vacant in 1914

87TH QUEBEC REGIMENT

This regiment was raised in 1869 and headquartered at Ancienne Lorette, Quebec. The uniform included a blue forage cap, a scarlet tunic with blue facings, and blue trousers with red piping.

88TH REGIMENT (VICTORIA FUSILIERS)

This regiment was raised in 1912 and headquartered at Victoria, British Columbia. The uniform included a blue forage cap, a scarlet tunic with blue facings, and blue trousers with red piping.

89TH TEMISCOUATA AND RIMOUSKI REGIMENT

This regiment was raised in 1883 and headquartered at Ste. Germain de Rimouski, Quebec. The uniform included a blue forage cap, a scarlet tunic with blue facings, and blue trousers with red piping.

90TH REGIMENT (WINNIPEG RIFLES)

This regiment was raised in 1883 and headquartered at Winnipeg, Manitoba. The Earl of Minto was the Honorary Colonel. The uniform included a black rifle busby with scarlet piping and a scarlet and black plume, a rifle green tunic with scarlet facings and piping, and rifle green trousers.

BATTLE HONOURS: *Fish Creek, Batoche, North West Canada 1885, South Africa 1899-1900*

91ST REGIMENT (CANADIAN HIGHLANDERS)

This regiment was raised in 1903 and headquartered at Hamilton, Ontario. Except for badges and buttons, the uniform was essentially the same as for Princess Louise's (Argyll and Sutherland Highlanders) of the British Army: a black feather bonnet with a red and white diced border and a white hackle. The scarlet doublet had yellow facings and the kilt was of Sutherland tartan. The pipers wore blue glengarry caps with a red and white diced border and blue doublets.

92ND DORCHESTER REGIMENT

This regiment was raised in 1869 and headquartered at St. Isidore, Quebec. The uniform included a blue forage cap, a scarlet tunic with blue facings, and blue trousers with red piping.

93RD CUMBERLAND REGIMENT

This regiment was raised in 1871 and headquartered at Spring Hill, Nova Scotia. It was a Scottish regiment without a Scottish title. The word *Highlanders* was added to the title in 1917. The uniform included a blue glengarry cap with a red and white diced border. The scarlet doublet had blue facings, and the kilt was of Murray of Atholl tartan. The pipers wore blue doublets.

94TH VICTORIA REGIMENT (ARGYLL HIGHLANDERS)

This regiment was raised in 1871 and headquartered at Baddeck, Nova Scotia. Except for badges and buttons, the uniform was essentially the same as for Princess Louise's (Argyll and Sutherland Highlanders) of the British Army: a black feather bonnet with a red and white diced border and a white hackle. The scarlet doublet had yellow facings and the kilt was of Sutherland tartan. The pipers wore blue glengarry caps with a red and white diced border and blue doublets.

95TH SASKATCHEWAN RIFLES

This regiment was raised in 1905 and headquartered at Regina, Saskatchewan. The uniform included a black rifle busby with scarlet piping and a scarlet and black plume, a rifle green tunic with scarlet facings and piping, and rifle green trousers.

96TH LAKE SUPERIOR REGIMENT

This regiment was raised in 1905 and headquartered at Port Arthur, Ontario. The uniform included a blue forage cap, a scarlet tunic with blue facings, and blue trousers with red piping.

97TH REGIMENT (ALGONQUIN RIFLES)

This regiment was raised in 1900 and headquartered at Sudbury, Ontario. The uniform included a black rifle busby with scarlet piping and a scarlet and black plume, a rifle green tunic with scarlet facings and piping, and rifle green trousers.

98TH REGIMENT

This regiment was raised in 1908 and headquartered at Kenora, Ontario. The uniform included a blue forage cap, a scarlet tunic with blue facings, and blue trousers with red piping.

99TH MANITOBA RANGERS

This regiment was raised in 1908 and headquartered at Brandon, Manitoba. The uniform included a blue forage cap with a Lincoln green band, a scarlet tunic with Lincoln green facings, and blue trousers with red piping.

100TH WINNIPEG GRENADIERS

This regiment was raised in 1908 and headquartered at Winnipeg, Manitoba. The uniform included a black bearskin cap with a white plume on the left side, a scarlet tunic with blue facings, and blue trousers with red piping.

101ST REGIMENT (EDMONTON FUSILIERS)

This regiment was raised in 1908 and headquartered at Edmonton, Alberta. The uniform included a blue forage cap, a scarlet tunic with blue facings, and blue trousers with red piping.

102ND REGIMENT (ROCKY MOUNTAIN RANGERS)

This regiment was raised in 1908 and headquartered at Nelson, British Columbia. The uniform included a blue forage cap, a scarlet tunic with blue facings, and blue trousers with red piping.

103RD REGIMENT (CALGARY RIFLES)

This regiment was raised in 1910 and headquartered at Calgary, Alberta. The uniform included a black rifle busby with scarlet piping and a scarlet and black plume, a rifle green tunic with scarlet facings and piping, and rifle green trousers.

104TH REGIMENT (WESTMINSTER FUSILIERS OF CANADA)

This regiment was raised in 1910 and headquartered at New Westminster, British Columbia. The uniform included a blue forage cap, a scarlet tunic with blue facings, and blue trousers with red piping.

105TH REGIMENT (SASKATOON FUSILIERS)

This regiment was raised in 1912 and headquartered at Saskatoon, Saskatchewan. The uniform included a blue forage cap, a scarlet tunic with blue facings, and blue trousers with red piping.

106TH REGIMENT (WINNIPEG LIGHT INFANTRY)

This regiment was raised in 1912 and headquartered at Winnipeg, Manitoba. The uniform included a blue forage cap, a scarlet tunic with blue facings, and blue trousers with red piping.

107TH EAST KOOTENAY REGIMENT

This regiment was raised in 1914 and headquartered at Cranbrook, British Columbia. The uniform included a blue forage cap, a scarlet tunic with blue facings, and blue trousers with red piping.

EARL GREY'S OWN RIFLES

This regiment was raised in 1910 and headquartered at Prince Rupert, British Columbia. The uniform included a blue forage cap, a scarlet tunic with blue facings, and blue trousers with red piping. Evidently, this unit did not wear the traditional *rifle* uniform. This regiment of only four companies was without a number until November 1914, when it took the vacant number 68.

CANADIAN DEPARTMENTAL CORPS (MILITIA)

CANADIAN ARMY SERVICE CORPS (MILITIA)

This corps was raised in 1903 and headquartered at Ottawa, Ontario. In 1914, there were 19 companies. The uniform was essentially the same as the Canadian Permanent Army Service Corps.

CANADIAN ARMY MEDICAL CORPS (MILITIA)

This corps was raised in 1904 and headquartered at Ottawa, Ontario. In 1914, there were 21 field ambulance companies and two hospital companies. The uniform was essentially the same as the Canadian Army Medical Corps of the permanent force. Nurses wore a white cap and veil, an ankle-length dark blue dress with a white collar and cuffs, and an elbow-length scarlet cape.

CANADIAN ARMY VETERINARY CORPS (MILITIA)

This corps was raised in 1910 and headquartered at Ottawa, Ontario. The uniform was essentially the same as the Canadian Permanent Army Veterinary Corps.

CANADIAN POSTAL CORPS (MILITIA)

This corps was raised in 1911. The Director of Supplies and Transport at Militia Headquarters, Ottawa, was also the director of the military postal services. The uniform was the same as the Canadian Army Service Corps; however, the badge differed.

CANADIAN ORDNANCE CORPS (MILITIA)

This corps was raised in 1912 and headquartered at Ottawa, Ontario. In 1914, there were three ordnance detachments. The uniform was essentially the same as Canadian Army Ordnance Corps of the permanent force.

CHAPTER FOUR

Land Forces of the Commonwealth of Australia, 1914

In 1914, the Permanent Force of the Commonwealth of Australia consisted of about 2,600 men in small formations of artillery and engineers, a departmental corps, and an administrative and instructional staff.

The majority of Australia's land forces was in a part-time force known as the Citizen Military Forces. All cavalry (known as light horse), all infantry, and the greater part of artillery, engineer, and departmental corps formations were in these forces.

For many years after the establishment of colonies in Australia, there was no military establishment other than a few volunteer units. Military formations up to the year 1870 consisted of British garrisons in the major cities. The military history differs from that of Canada or South Africa in that Australia was able to develop in peaceful isolation from 1788 until the rise of Japan in the 20th century.

When British troops were withdrawn from Australia in 1870, the need arose for a local defence force. The colonies of New South Wales, Queensland, Victoria, Tasmania, South Australia, and Western Australia each raised a force of volunteers or militia. The only permanent forces were primarily garrison artillery formations at defended ports.

An imperial act, dated 9 July 1900, federated the Australian colonies into the Commonwealth of Australia. The need for a national defence was taken under consideration. In 1903, regiments of light horse, battalions of infantry, and units of the other arms and departments were formed from the existing militia and volunteers of the former Australian colonies, now called states.

Troops from New South Wales had served with British forces in the Sudan as early as 1885. Units descended from these early formations carry the battle honour, *Suakin 1885*. Later, volunteers from many Australian militia units, together with civilian volunteers, formed contingents for service in the South African War (1899-1902). Formations descended from these contingents carry the battle honour, *South Africa*.

In 1912, there was a reorganization of the Citizen Military Forces in Australia following the introduction of compulsory service. New formations were raised or existing units split to form new ones. This was an ongoing process with new units being formed in 1913 and 1914. There were to be 29 light horse regiments and 93 battalions of infantry. Not all of these units had been formed by 1914, and many regimental numbers were vacant.

For administrative purposes, Australia was divided into six military districts corresponding roughly to the boundaries of the states. The 1st Military District (Queensland) was headquartered at Brisbane, the 2nd Military District (New South Wales) was headquartered at Sydney, the 3rd Military District (Victoria) was headquartered at Melbourne, the 4th Military District (South Australia) was headquartered at Adelaide, and the 5th Military District (Tasmania) was headquartered at Hobart. The central administration was at Melbourne, the temporary administrative capital of Australia in 1914.

The Australian Commonwealth Defence Act of 1909 imposed military training on every male citizen between the ages of 12 and 26 years; however, the Citizen Military Forces created by the Defence Act of 1909 could not serve outside Australia. At the outbreak of World War I in August 1914, the Australian government raised a new volunteer army for overseas service. This force, known as the Australian Imperial Force, eventually mobilized more than 330,000 volunteers in five divisions of consecutively numbered light horse regiments (1-15), infantry battalions (1-70), pioneer battalions (1-5), and machine gun battalions (1-5). The artillery, the engineers, and the departmental corps elements of both the Permanent Force and the Citizen Military Forces were expanded many times over. Initially, the majority of officers for the Australian Imperial Force came from the Permanent Force and the Citizen Military Forces.

Because they were able fighters the Australians were involved in some of the most bitter fighting of World War I. As a result, the Australians suffered the highest percentage of casualties in comparison to their population of all the British Empire forces involved in the war.

The Citizen Military Forces listed in this book are those of 1914. In 1918, the designations were altered to conform to the numbers borne by the Australian Imperial Forces to maintain the traditions and perpetuate the records of those units in World War I.

UNIFORMS

The Permanent Force formations of each branch of the Australian Army are listed and illustrated, followed by a list of the Citizen Military Forces units. The uniforms described and illustrated are those of a private (unless otherwise stated).

Before 1906, some earlier formations had worn a full dress uniform similar to British units. Orders for dress and clothing appeared in 1906. The Royal Australian Artillery, Royal Australian Engineers, and the Australian Army Service Corps retained a *full dress* based on their British counterparts. A new khaki uniform was ordered for all Citizen Military Forces. In 1912, new orders issued for the Citizen Military Forces greatly simplified the khaki uniform. A khaki slouch hat, looped up on the left side, was worn with a colored hatband to denote the arm of service. A khaki tunic or woolen shirt was worn with khaki trousers and puttees; mounted personnel wore breeches with leather leggings. Regimental numerals or badges were worn on the front of the slouch hat. Officers were issued forage caps with the colored hatband. Officers wore leather leggings when on duty; at other times, they wore boots, together with swords, sword belts, and slings. In 1913, officers obtained approval to wear open-necked khaki jackets with shirts and ties.

BANNERS AND COLOURS

Between 1903 and 1909, the King's Banner, a Union flag with a gold fringe, was presented to those units descended from the Australian contingents that had served in the South African War (1899-1902), including the Royal Australian Artillery and the Australian Army Medical Corps. These flags were considered honorary banners for service in South Africa.

Orders issued in 1913 and amended in 1914 authorized King's and Regimental Colours for the Australian infantry regiments. The King's Colour was the Union flag. Regimental colours for all infantry regiments (including those with *rifle* in the title) were dark green with the regimental number embroidered in gold in the upper left corner nearest the staff. Regimental heraldic devices and battle honours were embroidered in gold on the colour, all within a wreath of wattle leaves embroidered in light green. The wattle shrub was unique to Australia. Records indicate that only some infantry regiments had been presented with colours by 1914. Light horse regiments were entitled to carry guidons but none were presented until 1927.

AUSTRALIAN PERMANENT FORCES

THE ADMINISTRATIVE AND INSTRUCTIONAL STAFF

In 1903, a permanent staff was raised from officers, warrant officers, and noncommissioned officers of the Permanent Instruction and Headquarters Staff. In 1914, personnel of the Administrative and Instructional Staff were assigned to each of the six military districts and were responsible for administration and instruction of the formations of the Citizen Military Forces. Headquarters for this staff was at Melbourne.

The uniform included a khaki forage cap with a scarlet band. The khaki tunic had scarlet gorget patches on the collar, scarlet piping on the cuffs, and double scarlet stripes on the shoulder straps. Personnel wore khaki breeches with khaki puttees or leather leggings when mounted. The Administrative and Instructional Staff wore the *rising sun* badge (see badge), which was originally adopted in 1904. A sergeant major's uniform is illustrated by figure 133.

ROYAL AUSTRALIAN FIELD ARTILLERY AND ROYAL AUSTRALIAN GARRISON ARTILLERY

In 1914, there were three batteries of the Royal Australian Field Artillery that served as a nucleus for the field artillery formations of the Citizen Military Forces. These three batteries were stationed at Brisbane, Sydney, and Melbourne, respectively. Field artillery headquarters was at Melbourne.

The Royal Australian Garrison Artillery comprised 21 companies stationed at defended ports in each of the six military districts. Eight companies were stationed in the Sydney area protecting the approaches to Port Jackson, the main naval anchorage of Australia. Five companies were stationed in the Melbourne area protecting the approaches to Port Phillip. The remaining companies were stationed at defended ports in Queensland, Western Australia, and Tasmania. Garrison artillery headquarters was at Melbourne.

1871	The first permanent batteries of artillery were raised after the departure of British forces in 1870
1899	The permanent batteries of New South Wales, Victoria, and Queensland amalgamated and known as the Royal Australian Artillery
1911	The Royal Australian Artillery redesignated the Royal Australian Garrison Artillery and the Royal Australian Field Artillery

The uniform included a *full dress* white helmet with a brass ball. Other than the white helmet, buttons, and badges, the uniform was essentially the same as the Royal Field Artillery and Royal Garrison Artillery of the British Army.

The Royal Australian Field Artillery uniform is illustrated by figure 134. The Royal Australian Garrison Artillery uniform is illustrated by figure 135.

ROYAL AUSTRALIAN ENGINEERS

The Royal Australian Engineers were raised in 1907 as a permanent force. In 1914, the Royal Australian Engineers were headquartered at Melbourne and were concerned mainly with electric lights and telephones and with maintaining the facilities related to defended ports. The Royal Australian Engineers also maintained a survey section. The uniform included a *full dress* white helmet with a brass spike. Other than the white helmet, buttons, and badges, the uniform was essentially the same as the Corps of Royal Engineers of the British Army. This uniform is illustrated by figure 136.

AUSTRALIAN ARMY MEDICAL CORPS, PERMANENT SECTION

This corps was raised in 1902 as the Permanent Section of the Australian Army Medical Corps. In 1914, personnel of this corps were stationed in each of the six military districts with headquarters at Melbourne. The Permanent Section was uniformed the same as medical units in the Citizen Force. The uniform included a khaki slouch hat with a chocolate-brown band, a khaki tunic or woolen shirt, and khaki breeches and puttees. This uniform is illustrated by figure 137.

AUSTRALIAN ARMY SERVICE CORPS, PERMANENT SECTION

This corps was raised in 1903 as the Permanent Section of the Australian Army Service Corps. In 1914, personnel of this corps were stationed in each of the six military districts with headquarters at Melbourne. The uniform included a *full dress* white helmet with a brass ball. Officers wore blue tunics with white facings (collar and cuffs) edged with gold lace. Other ranks wore a blue tunic with white piping around the collar, down the front of the tunic, and on the cuffs. The white shoulder straps had blue center stripes, and there were double white stripes on dark blue trousers for both officers and other ranks. This uniform is illustrated by figure 138.

AUSTRALIAN ARMY VETERINARY CORPS, PERMANENT SECTION

This corps was raised in 1909 as the Permanent Section of The Australian Army Veterinary Corps. In 1914, personnel of this corps were stationed in each of the six military districts with headquarters at Melbourne. The Permanent Section was uniformed the same as veterinary officers of the Citizen Force. The uniform included a khaki slouch hat with a maroon band, a khaki tunic or woolen shirt, and khaki breeches with leather leggings. It appears that there was no badge in 1914. This uniform is illustrated by figure 139.

AUSTRALIAN CITIZEN MILITARY FORCES

LIGHT HORSE REGIMENTS OF THE AUSTRALIAN CITIZEN MILITARY FORCE

In 1914, the uniform for all light horse regiments included a khaki slouch hat with a white band, a khaki tunic or woolen shirt, khaki breeches, and leather leggings. Badges or numerals worn on the front of the slouch hat identified the regiment. Light horse regiments from New South Wales wore a black cock's plume in the hat band; Victoria regiments wore a single eagle's feather. The Western Australia regiment wore a black swan's feather; regiments from Queensland, South Australia, and Tasmania wore emu feathers. Regiments with lancer in the title carried lances with a red and white pennon for ceremonial purposes.

1ST (CENTRAL QUEENSLAND) LIGHT HORSE

This regiment descended from part of the Queensland Mounted Infantry, which was consolidated as a regiment from existing militia units in 1900. This regiment was headquartered at Gympie, Queensland.

BATTLE HONOUR: *South Africa 1899-1902*

2ND LIGHT HORSE (QUEENSLAND MOUNTED INFANTRY)

This regiment descended from part of the Queensland Mounted Infantry, which was consolidated as a regiment from existing militia units in 1900. This regiment was headquartered at Brisbane, Queensland.

BATTLE HONOUR: *South Africa 1899-1902*

3RD (DARLING DOWNS) LIGHT HORSE

This regiment descended from part of the Queensland Mounted Infantry, which was consolidated as a regiment from existing militia units in 1900. This regiment was headquartered at Toowoomba, Queensland.

BATTLE HONOUR: *South Africa 1899-1902*

4TH LIGHT HORSE (NORTHERN RIVER LANCERS)

This regiment descended from part of the New South Wales Lancers, which was raised in 1885 from part of the New South Wales Mounted Rifles raised in 1893. This regiment was headquartered at Lismore, New South Wales.

BATTLE HONOUR: *South Africa 1899-1902*

5TH LIGHT HORSE (NEW ENGLAND LIGHT HORSE)

This regiment was descended from part of the Australian Horse, which was raised in 1897. This regiment was headquartered at Armidale, New South Wales.

BATTLE HONOUR: *South Africa 1899-1900*

6TH LIGHT HORSE (HUNTER RIVER LANCERS)

This regiment descended from part of the New South Wales Lancers, which was raised in 1885 and originally known as the Sydney Light Horse. This regiment was headquartered at West Maitland, New South Wales.

BATTLE HONOUR: *South Africa 1899-1902*

7TH LIGHT HORSE (NEW SOUTH WALES LANCERS)

This regiment descended from part of the New South Wales Lancers, which was raised in 1885 and originally known as the Sydney Light Horse. This regiment was headquartered at Parramatta, New South Wales.

BATTLE HONOUR: *South Africa 1899-1902*

8TH Light Horse—Vacant in 1914.

9TH LIGHT HORSE (NEW SOUTH WALES MOUNTED RIFLES)

This regiment descended from part of the New South Wales Mounted Rifles, which was raised in 1893. This regiment was headquartered at Sydney, New South Wales.

BATTLE HONOUR: *South Africa 1899-1902*

10TH Light Horse—Vacant in 1914.

11TH LIGHT HORSE (AUSTRALIAN HORSE)

This regiment descended from part of the Australian Horse, which was raised in 1897. This regiment was headquartered at Goulbum, New South Wales.

BATTLE HONOUR: *South Africa 1899-1900*

12TH Light Horse—Vacant in 1914.

13TH (GIPPSLAND) LIGHT HORSE

This regiment descended from part of the Victorian Mounted Rifles, which was raised in 1885. This regiment was headquartered at Wanagul, Victoria.

BATTLE HONOUR: *South Africa 1899-1902*

14TH Light Horse—Vacant in 1914.

15TH LIGHT HORSE (VICTORIAN MOUNTED RIFLES)

This regiment descended from part of the Victorian Mounted Rifles, which was raised in 1885. This regiment was headquartered at Seymour, Victoria.

BATTLE HONOUR: *South Africa 1899-1902*

16TH LIGHT HORSE (INDI LIGHT HORSE)

This regiment descended from part of the Victorian Mounted Rifles, which was raised in 1885. This regiment was headquartered at Benalla, Victoria.

BATTLE HONOUR: *South Africa 1899-1902*

17TH LIGHT HORSE (CAMPASPE VALLEY LIGHT HORSE)

This regiment descended from part of the Victorian Mounted Rifles, which was raised in 1885. This regiment was headquartered at Bendigo, Victoria.

BATTLE HONOUR: *South Africa 1899-1902*

18TH Light Horse—Vacant in 1914.

19TH (YARROWEE) LIGHT HORSE

This regiment descended from part of the Victorian Mounted Rifles, which was raised in 1885. This regiment was headquartered at Ballarat, Victoria.

BATTLE HONOUR: *South Africa 1899-1902*

20TH LIGHT HORSE (CORANGAMITE LIGHT HORSE)

This regiment descended from part of the Victorian Mounted Rifles, which was raised in 1885. This regiment was headquartered at Colac, Victoria.

BATTLE HONOUR: *South Africa 1899-1902*

21ST Light Horse—Vacant in 1914.

22ND LIGHT HORSE (SOUTH AUSTRALIAN MOUNTED RIFLES)

This regiment descended from part of the South Australian Mounted Rifles, which was raised around 1886-87. This regiment was headquartered at Adelaide, South Australia.

BATTLE HONOUR: *South Africa 1899-1902*

23RD (BAROSSA) LIGHT HORSE

This regiment was raised in 1912 and headquartered at Adelaide, South Australia.

24TH LIGHT HORSE (FLINDERS LIGHT HORSE)

This regiment descended from part of the South Australian Mounted Rifles, which was raised around 1886-87. This regiment was headquartered at Port Pirie, South Australia.

BATTLE HONOUR: *South Africa 1899-1902*

25TH LIGHT HORSE (WESTERN AUSTRALIAN MOUNTED INFANTRY)

This regiment descended from the Western Australian Mounted Infantry, which was consolidated as a regiment from existing volunteer units in 1900. This regiment was headquartered at Perth, Western Australia.

26TH LIGHT HORSE (TASMANIAN MOUNTED INFANTRY)

This regiment descended from the Tasmanian Mounted Infantry, which was raised around 1898. This regiment was headquartered at Launceston, Tasmania.

27TH (NORTH QUEENSLAND) LIGHT HORSE

This regiment descended from part of the Queensland Mounted Infantry, which was consolidated as a regiment from existing militia units in 1900. This regiment was headquartered at Ayr, Queensland.

BATTLE HONOUR: *South Africa 1899-1902.*

28TH (ILLAWARRA) LIGHT HORSE

This regiment descended from part of the New South Wales Lancers raised in 1885. This regiment was headquartered at Albion Park, New South Wales.

BATTLE HONOUR: *South Africa 1899-1902.*

29TH LIGHT HORSE (PORT PHILLIP HORSE)

This regiment descended from part of the Victorian Mounted Rifles raised in 1885. This regiment was headquartered at South Melbourne, Victoria.

BATTLE HONOUR: South Africa 1899-1902.

ARTILLERY OF THE AUSTRALIAN CITIZEN MILITARY FORCES

Volunteer artillery batteries were formed in New South Wales as early as the 1850s. In 1914, headquarters was at Melbourne. The Australian Field Artillery was formed into brigades of three batteries each. There was one brigade in Queensland, three brigades in New South Wales, two brigades in Victoria, one brigade in South Australia, one brigade in Western Australia, and one brigade in Tasmania. The Australian Garrison Artillery was formed into companies with two companies in Queensland, four companies in New South

Wales, three companies in Victoria, one company in South Australia, two companies in Western Australian, and one company in Tasmania.

The uniform included a khaki slouch hat with a scarlet band, a khaki tunic or woolen shirt, with khaki trousers and puttees, or khaki breeches and leather leggings, if personnel were mounted.

ENGINEERS OF THE AUSTRALIAN CITIZEN MILITARY FORCES

The first company of engineers was raised in New South Wales in 1867. In 1877, torpedo and signal detachments were added, and in 1890 a second company was raised. In 1914, there were engineer and signal companies in all six military districts and an Engineer and Railway Staff Corps. Headquarters was at Melbourne. The uniform included a khaki slouch hat with a blue band (signal companies wore purple hat bands), a khaki tunic or woolen shirt, with khaki trousers and puttees, or khaki breeches and leather leggings, if personnel were mounted.

INTELLIGENCE CORPS OF THE AUSTRALIAN CITIZEN MILITARY FORCES

This small corps was raised in 1907. In 1914, there were detachments of this corps in all six military districts. The uniform included a khaki slouch hat with a light blue band, a khaki tunic or woolen shirt, with khaki trousers and puttees, or khaki breeches with leather leggings, if personnel were mounted.

VOLUNTEER AUTOMOBILE CORPS OF THE AUSTRALIAN CITIZEN MILITARY FORCES

This very small formation was raised in 1913 and consisted of only 29 officers and other ranks, mostly owners of motorcars and mechanics. The uniform included a khaki slouch hat with a brown leather hat band, a khaki tunic or woolen shirt, and khaki breeches with leather leggings.

INFANTRY REGIMENTS OF THE AUSTRALIAN CITIZEN MILITARY FORCES

In 1914, the uniform for all infantry regiments included a khaki slouch hat with a green band, a khaki tunic or woolen shirt, khaki trousers, and puttees. Badges or numerals worn on the front of the slouch hat identified the regiment. Infantry regiments of the Australian Citizen Military Forces comprised only one battalion.

1ST Regiment—Vacant in 1914, allotted to Queensland

2ND INFANTRY (KENNEDY REGIMENT)

This regiment descended from the 3rd Queensland (Kennedy) Regiment, which was consolidated as a regiment from existing Queensland militia units in 1893. This regiment was headquartered at Charters Towers, Queensland.

BATTLE HONOUR: *South Africa 1901*

3RD (PORT CURTIS) INFANTRY

This regiment descended from the 5th Queensland (Port Curtis) Regiment, which was consolidated as a regiment from existing Queensland militia units in 1900. This regiment was headquartered at Rockhampton, Queensland.

4TH (WIDE BAY) INFANTRY

This regiment descended from the 2nd Queensland (Wide Bay and Burnett) Regiment, which was consolidated as a regiment from existing Queensland militia units in 1893. This regiment was headquartered at Maryborough, Queensland.

5TH Infantry—Vacant in 1914, allotted to Queensland

6TH Infantry—Vacant in 1914, allotted to Queensland

7TH INFANTRY (MORETON REGIMENT)

This regiment descended from part of the 1st Queensland (Moreton) Regiment, which was consolidated as a regiment from existing Queensland militia units in 1893. This regiment was headquartered at Brisbane, Queensland.

BATTLE HONOUR: *South Africa 1899-1902*

8TH INFANTRY (OXLEY BATTALION)

This regiment descended from part of the 1st Queensland (Moreton) Regiment, which was consolidated as a regiment from existing Queensland militia units in 1893. This regiment was headquartered at South Brisbane, Queensland.

BATTLE HONOUR: *South Africa 1900-02*

9TH (LOGAN AND ALBERT) INFANTRY

This regiment was raised in 1912 and headquartered at Annerley, Queensland.

10TH Infantry—Vacant in 1914, allotted to Queensland

11TH INFANTRY (DARLING DOWNS REGIMENT)

This regiment descended from the 4th Queensland (Darling Downs) Regiment which was consolidated as a regiment from existing Queensland militia units in 1900. This regiment was headquartered at Toowoomba, Queensland.

BATTLE HONOUR: *South Africa 1899-1902*

12TH INFANTRY

This regiment was raised in 1914 and headquartered at Lismore, Queensland.

13TH INFANTRY

This regiment was raised in 1914 and headquartered at Armidale, New South Wales.

14TH (HUNTER RIVER) INFANTRY

This regiment descended from the part of the 4th Regiment, New South Wales Infantry raised in 1884. This regiment was headquartered at Armidale, New South Wales.

BATTLE HONOUR: *South Africa 1899-1902.*

15TH Infantry—Vacant in 1914, allotted to New South Wales

16TH INFANTRY (NEWCASTLE REGIMENT)

This regiment descended from parts of the 4th Regiment, New South Wales Infantry, raised in 1884, the 5th Regiment, New South Wales Infantry, raised in 1885, and the 6th Regiment, New South Wales Infantry, raised in 1896. This regiment was headquartered at Newcastle, New South Wales.

17TH INFANTRY

This regiment was raised in 1914 and headquartered at Mosman, New South Wales.

18TH (NORTH SYDNEY) INFANTRY

This regiment descended from parts of the 1st Regiment, New South Wales Infantry, raised in 1878, the 3rd Regiment, New South Wales Infantry, a consolidation of western New South Wales militia companies around 1880, and the 7th Regiment, New South Wales Infantry, raised in 1896. This regiment was headquartered at North Sydney, New South Wales.

BATTLE HONOURS: *Suakin 1885, South Africa 1899-1902*

19TH (KURING-GAI) INFANTRY

This regiment was formed in 1913 from part of the 18th (North Sydney) Infantry. This regiment was headquartered at Gladesville, New South Wales.

20TH (PARRAMATTA) INFANTRY

This regiment was raised in 1914 and headquartered at Parramatta, New South Wales.

21ST (WOOLLAHRA) INFANTRY

This regiment descended from part of the 1st Regiment, New South Wales Infantry, raised in 1878. From 1912 to 1913, this regiment was known as the Sydney Battalion. This regiment was headquartered at Paddington, New South Wales.

BATTLE HONOURS: *Suakin 1885, South Africa 1899-1902*

22ND Infantry—Vacant in 1914, allotted to New South Wales

23RD Infantry—Vacant in 1914, allotted to New South Wales

24TH INFANTRY (EAST SYDNEY REGIMENT)

This regiment descended from part of the 2nd Regiment, New South Wales Infantry, raised in 1878. This regiment was headquartered at Paddington, New South Wales.

BATTLE HONOURS: *Suakin 1885, South Africa 1899-1902*

25TH INFANTRY (CITY OF SYDNEY)

This regiment descended from part of the 5th Regiment, New South Wales Infantry, raised in 1885. From 1903 to 1912, this regiment was known as the New South Wales Scottish Rifles. This regiment was headquartered at Sydney, New South Wales.

BATTLE HONOUR: *South Africa 1899-1902.*

26TH INFANTRY

This regiment was formed in 1913 from four companies of the 25th Infantry (City of Sydney). This regiment was headquartered at Sydney, New South Wales.

27TH Infantry—Vacant in 1914, allotted to New South Wales

28TH Infantry—Vacant in 1914, allotted to New South Wales

29TH INFANTRY (AUSTRALIAN RIFLES)

This regiment descended from part of the 6th Regiment, New South Wales Infantry, raised in 1896. This regiment was headquartered at Sydney, New South Wales.

BATTLE HONOUR: *South Africa 1899-1902*

30TH Infantry—Vacant in 1914, allotted to New South Wales

31ST (LEICHARDT) INFANTRY

This regiment descended from part of the 7th Regiment, New South Wales Infantry, raised in 1896. From 1903 to 1912, this regiment was known as St. George's English Rifle Regiment. This regiment was headquartered at Sydney, New South Wales.

BATTLE HONOUR: *South Africa 1901-02.*

32ND Infantry—Vacant in 1914, allotted to New South Wales

33RD INFANTRY

This regiment descended from the 8th Regiment, New South Wales Infantry, raised in 1896. From 1903 to 1912 this regiment was known as the New South Wales Irish Rifle Regiment. This regiment was headquartered at Camperdown, New South Wales.

BATTLE HONOUR: *South Africa 1901.*

34TH INFANTRY

This regiment was raised in 1913 and headquartered at Sydney, New South Wales.

35TH Infantry—Vacant in 1914, allotted to New South Wales

36TH Infantry—Vacant in 1914, allotted to New South Wales

37TH (ILLAWARRA) INFANTRY

This regiment was formed in 1913 from part of the 39th Infantry and headquartered at Kiama, New South Wales.

38TH INFANTRY

This regiment was raised in 1913 and headquartered at Kogarah, New South Wales.

39TH INFANTRY

This regiment descended from parts of the 1st Regiment, New South Wales Infantry, raised in 1878, and the 7th Regiment, New South Wales Infantry, raised in 1896. This regiment was headquartered at Burwood, New South Wales.

BATTLE HONOUR: *South Africa 1901-02.*

40TH Infantry—Vacant in 1914, allotted to New South Wales

41ST (BLUE MOUNTAINS) INFANTRY

This regiment descended from part of the 3rd Regiment, New South Wales Infantry, a consolidation of western New South Wales militia companies around 1880. This regiment was headquartered at Richmond, New South Wales.

BATTLE HONOURS: *Suakin 1885, South Africa 1899-1902.*

42ND (LACHLAN MACQUARIE) INFANTRY

This regiment was raised in 1914 and headquartered at Orange, New South Wales.

43RD (WERRIWA) INFANTRY

This regiment descended from part of the 2nd Regiment, New South Wales Infantry, raised in 1878, and headquartered at Goulbum, New South Wales.
BATTLE HONOURS: *Suakin 1885, South Africa 1899-1902.*

44TH (RIVERINA) INFANTRY

This regiment was raised in 1914 and headquartered at Albury, New South Wales.

SYDNEY UNIVERSITY SCOUTS

This unnumbered regiment was raised in 1900 as the University Volunteer Rifle Corps. The name became Sydney University Scouts in 1903. This regiment was headquartered at Sydney University, Sydney, New South Wales.

45TH Infantry—Vacant in 1914, allotted to Victoria

46TH INFANTRY (BRIGHTON RIFLES)

This regiment descended from part of the Victorian Rangers, raised in 1889 and headquartered at Elsternwick, Victoria.

47TH Infantry—Vacant in 1914, allotted to Victoria

48TH (KOOYONG) INFANTRY

This regiment was formed in 1913 from part of the 46th Infantry (Brighton Rifles) and headquartered at Surrey Hills, Victoria.

49TH (PRAHAN) INFANTRY

This regiment descended from part of the 2nd Battalion, Victorian Militia Infantry Brigade, raised in 1884, and headquartered at Prahan, Victoria.
BATTLE HONOUR: *South Africa 1899-1902*

50TH Infantry—Vacant in 1914, allotted to Victoria

51ST (ALBERT PARK) INFANTRY

This regiment descended from part of the Victorian Militia Infantry Brigade, raised in 1884, and headquartered at Albert Park, Victoria.
BATTLE HONOUR: *South Africa 1899-1902*

52ND (HOBSON'S BAY) INFANTRY

This regiment descended from the Victorian Scottish Regiment, raised in 1898, and headquartered at South Melbourne, Victoria.

53RD Infantry—Vacant in 1914, allotted to Victoria

54TH Infantry—Vacant in 1914, allotted to Victoria

55TH (COLLINGWOOD) INFANTRY

This regiment was formed in 1913 from part of the 56th Infantry (Yarra Borderers) and headquartered at Collingwood, Victoria.

56TH (YARRA BORDERERS)

This regiment descended from part of the 2nd Battalion, Victorian Militia Infantry Brigade, raised in 1884, and headquartered at Richmond, Victoria.
BATTLE HONOUR: *South Africa 1899-1902*

57TH Infantry—Vacant in 1914, allotted to Victoria

58TH INFANTRY (ESSENDON RIFLES)

This regiment descended from part of the 1st Battalion, Victorian Militia Infantry Brigade, raised in 1884, and headquartered at Essendon, Victoria.

59TH Infantry—Vacant in 1914, allotted to Victoria

60TH (PRINCES HILL) INFANTRY

This regiment descended from part of the 1st Battalion, Victorian Militia Infantry Brigade, raised in 1884, and headquartered at North Carlton, Victoria.
BATTLE HONOUR: *South Africa 1899-1902*

61ST Infantry—Vacant in 1914, allotted to Victoria

62ND Infantry—Vacant in 1914, allotted to Victoria

63RD INFANTRY
(THE EAST MELBOURNE REGIMENT)

This regiment descended from part of the 2nd Battalion, Victorian Militia Infantry Brigade, raised in 1884, and headquartered at East Melbourne, Victoria.

BATTLE HONOUR: *South Africa 1899-1902*

64TH INFANTRY
(CITY OF MELBOURNE REGIMENT)

This regiment descended from part of the 1st Battalion, Victorian Militia Infantry Brigade, raised in 1884, and headquartered at Melbourne, Victoria.

BATTLE HONOUR: *South Africa 1899-1902*

65TH Infantry—Vacant in 1914, allotted to Victoria

66TH (MOUNT ALEXANDER) INFANTRY

This regiment descended from the 4th Battalion, Victorian Militia Infantry Brigade, raised in 1884, and headquartered at Castlemaine, Victoria.

BATTLE HONOUR: *South Africa 1899-1902*

67TH (BENDIGO) INFANTRY

This regiment descended from the 5th Battalion, Victorian Militia Infantry Brigade, raised in 1884, and headquartered at Bendigo, Victoria.

BATTLE HONOUR: *South Africa 1899-1902*

68TH Infantry—Vacant in 1914, allotted to Victoria

69TH Infantry—Vacant in 1914, allotted to Victoria

70TH INFANTRY (BALLARAT REGIMENT)

This regiment descended from part of the 3rd Battalion, Victorian Militia Infantry Brigade, raised in 1884, and headquartered at Ballarat, Victoria.

BATTLE HONOUR: *South Africa 1899-1902*

71ST (CITY OF BALLARAT) INFANTRY

This regiment descended from part of the 3rd Battalion, Victorian Militia Infantry Brigade, raised in 1884, and headquartered at Ballarat, Victoria.

BATTLE HONOUR: *South Africa 1899-1902*

72ND Infantry—Vacant in 1914, allotted to Victoria

73RD INFANTRY (VICTORIAN RANGERS)

This regiment descended from part of the Victorian Rangers, raised in 1889, and headquartered at Ararat, Victoria.

BATTLE HONOUR: *South Africa 1899-1902*

MELBOURNE UNIVERSITY RIFLES

This unnumbered regiment was raised in 1910 and headquartered at Melbourne University, Melbourne, Victoria.

74TH (BOOTHBY) INFANTRY

This regiment descended from part of the 1st Regiment, South Australian Infantry, raised in 1885, and headquartered at Unley, South Australia.

BATTLE HONOUR: *South Africa 1899-1902*

75TH Infantry—Vacant in 1914, allotted to South Australia

76TH (HINDMARSH) INFANTRY

This regiment descended from part of the 1st Regiment, South Australian Infantry, raised in 1885, from the South Australian Scottish Regiment, raised in 1903, and from the Scottish Company of the 2nd Regiment, South Australian Infantry raised in 1885. This regiment was headquartered at Adelaide West, South Australia.

77TH Infantry—Vacant in 1914, allotted to South Australia

78TH INFANTRY (ADELAIDE RIFLES)

This regiment descended from part of the 1st Regiment, South Australian Infantry, raised in 1885, and headquartered at Adelaide, South Australia.

BATTLE HONOUR: *South Africa 1899-1902*

79TH (TORRENS) INFANTRY

This regiment descended from part of the 1st Regiment, South Australian Infantry, raised in 1885, and headquartered at Norwood, South Australia.

BATTLE HONOUR: *South Africa 1899-1902*

80TH Infantry—Vacant in 1914, allotted to South Australia

81ST (WAKEFIELD) INFANTRY

This regiment descended from the 1st and 2nd Battalions, 2nd Regiment, South Australian Infantry, raised in 1885, and headquartered at Wallaroo, South Australia.

BATTLE HONOUR: *South Africa 1899-1902*

82ND Infantry—Vacant in 1914, allotted to South Australia

83RD Infantry—Vacant in 1914, allotted to South Australia

84TH INFANTRY (GOLDFIELDS REGIMENT)

This regiment descended from the Goldfields Infantry Battalion, raised in 1900, and headquartered at Kalgoorie, Western Australia.

BATTLE HONOUR: *South Africa 1902*

85TH Infantry—Vacant in 1914, allotted to Western Australia

86TH INFANTRY (WESTERN AUSTRALIAN RIFLES)

This regiment descended from the 3rd and 4th Battalions, Western Australian Infantry Regiment, consolidated as a regiment from existing militia units in 1900 and headquartered at Fremantle, Western Australia.

BATTLE HONOUR: *South Africa 1899-1902*

87TH Infantry—Vacant in 1914, allotted to Western Australia

88TH (PERTH) INFANTRY

This regiment descended from the 1st and 2nd Battalions, Western Australian Infantry Regiment, consolidated as a regiment from existing militia units in 1900 and headquartered at Perth, Western Australia.

BATTLE HONOUR: *South Africa 1899-1902*

89TH Infantry—Vacant in 1914, allotted to Western Australia

90TH Infantry—Vacant in 1914, allotted to Tasmania

91ST INFANTRY (TASMANIAN RANGERS)

This regiment descended from the 3rd Battalion, Tasmanian Infantry Regiment, raised in 1898, and headquartered at Devonport, Tasmania.

BATTLE HONOUR: *South Africa 1900-1902*

92ND (LAUNCESTON) INFANTRY

This regiment descended from the 2nd Battalion, Tasmanian Infantry Regiment, raised in 1898, and headquartered at Launceston, Tasmania.

BATTLE HONOUR: *South Africa 1899-1902*

93RD (DERWENT) INFANTRY

This regiment descended from the 1st Battalion, Tasmanian Infantry Regiment, raised in 1898, and headquartered at Hobart, Tasmania.

BATTLE HONOUR: *South Africa 1899-1902*

Note: The following Australian infantry regiments had an English, Scottish or Irish connection.

25th Infantry (City of Sydney) was known as the New South Wales Scottish Rifles from 1903 to 1912 and maintained Scottish dress until 1912. However, a 1913 photograph shows some of the officers and men still in Scottish dress wearing khaki doublets with kilts of Black Watch or Government tartan. The headdress varied; some wore slouch hats or glengarry caps. Others wore khaki helmets. The officers and men in the photograph are probably those who had served in the New South Wales Scottish Rifles prior to 1912. The New South Wales Scottish Regiment was reformed in 1921 and uniformed in Scottish dress

31st (Leichardt) Infantry was known as St. George's English Rifle Regiment from 1903 to 1912.

33rd Infantry was known as the New South Wales Irish Rifle Regiment from 1903 to 1912.

52nd (Hobson's Bay) Infantry was formed in 1912 from the Victorian Scottish Regiment. Headquarters Company, Machine Gun Section and Companies A, B, C, and D (all volunteers) continued to wear kilts of Gordon tartan. Companies E, F, G, and H were universal trainees under the compulsory service plan and wore the khaki infantry uniform. The Victorian Scottish Regiment was reformed in 1929 and uniformed in Scottish dress.

76th (Hindmarsh) Infantry was a 1912 amalgamation of the 1st Regiment, South Australian Infantry, the South Australian Scottish Regiment, and the Scottish Company of the 2nd Regiment, South Australian Infantry. Evidently, Scottish dress was not worn after amalgamation. The South Australian Scottish Regiment was reformed in 1938 and uniformed in Scottish dress.

DEPARTMENTAL CORPS OF THE AUSTRALIAN CITIZEN MILITARY FORCES

AUSTRALIAN ARMY SERVICE CORPS

In 1914, personnel of this corps were in each of the six military districts of Australia, with headquarters at Melbourne.

1881	New South Wales organized the first Commissariat and Transport Corps
1903	The Australian Army Service Corps, Citizen Military Forces

The uniform included a khaki slouch hat with a blue band piped white on the top and bottom, a khaki tunic or woolen shirt, and khaki trousers and puttees. Mounted personnel wore khaki breeches and leather leggings.

AUSTRALIAN ARMY MEDICAL CORPS

In 1914, personnel of this corps were in each of the six military districts of Australia, with headquarters at Melbourne.

1888	New South Wales organized the first Volunteer Army Medical Corps
1903	The Australian Army Medical Corps, Citizen Military Forces

The uniform included a khaki slouch hat with a chocolate-brown band, a khaki tunic or woolen shirt, and khaki trousers with khaki puttees.

AUSTRALIAN ARMY VETERINARY CORPS

In 1914, personnel of this corp were in each of the six military districts of Australia, with headquarters at Melbourne.

1895	New South Wales organized the first Veterinary Department
1903	The Australian Army Veterinary Corps, Citizen Military Forces

The uniform included a khaki slouch hat with a maroon band, a khaki tunic or woolen shirt, and khaki breeches and puttees. Mounted personnel wore khaki breeches and leather leggings.

AUSTRALIAN NURSING SERVICE

In 1914, personnel of the nursing service were in each of the six military districts of Australia, with headquarters at Melbourne.

1899	First organized in New South Wales in connection with the Volunteer Army Medical Corps
1903	The Australian Nursing Service

Other than the badge, the uniform was essentially the same as Queen Alexandra's Imperial Military Nursing Service of Great Britain from which it was copied. (See Queen Alexandra's Imperial Military Nursing Service.)

CHAPTER FIVE

Land Forces of the Dominion of New Zealand, 1914

In 1914, the Permanent Force of New Zealand included the New Zealand Staff Corps (officers), the New Zealand Permanent Staff (noncommissioned officers), and the Royal New Zealand Artillery. The Permanent Force totaled around 1,600 men.

The majority of New Zealand's land forces were in a part-time volunteer force known as the Territorial Force. All cavalry (known as mounted rifles), all infantry, engineers, departmental corps, and the greater part of the artillery were in the Territorial Force.

A militia had been raised in New Zealand as early as 1845. In 1862, a colonial defence force was raised for the Maori War (1861-71), an intermittent conflict against certain Maori tribes (New Zealand natives of Polynesian descent) on the North Island of New Zealand. Since many Maori chiefs and tribesmen were on the side of the settlers, this war was by no means full scale. However, a number of sharp actions did take place, and the battle honour *New Zealand* was granted to the British regiments involved and to one New Zealand regiment descended from a participating volunteer unit.

After the Maori War, the majority of the volunteer units were disbanded. An armed constabulary had been formed in 1867 as a permanent formation. In 1886, the constabulary transferred to the Permanent Militia, a force organized for defence within New Zealand, thus allowing the last British battalion to leave New Zealand in 1870. The Royal Navy guarded against any possible invasion from overseas.

The 1880s saw a renewed interest in the volunteer corps and the formation of new volunteer units. New Zealand sent contingents raised from the volunteer forces to the South African War (1899-1902), a service recognized by the granting of the battle honour *South Africa* to most of the Territorial Force regiments when they were formed in 1911.

In 1903, the designation Permanent Militia was changed to the New Zealand Permanent Force. No. 1 Service Company became the Royal New Zealand Artillery, and No. 2 Service Company became the Royal New Zealand Engineers. In 1907, the permanent engineers were absorbed by the permanent artillery since both formations were involved in port defence. There were, of course, engineers in the volunteer formations.

New Zealand remained a British colony until 1907 when it became a Dominion consisting of the North Island and the South Island. The need for a revised system of national defence came under consideration by the new government. A defence act was passed in 1909 and implemented in 1911, replacing the volunteer system with the Territorial Force. The new Territorial Force regiments were raised in March 1911 from volunteer units already in existence.

New Zealand was divided into four military districts for administrative purposes. Auckland and Wellington Military Districts were on the North Island; Canterbury and Otago Military Districts were on the South Island. The central military administration was at Wellington, the capital.

In 1914, New Zealand's small population numbered just over one million. In spite of this number 42 percent of the male population (including Maoris) volunteered for active service in World War I. No other part of the British Empire showed a higher proportional rate of voluntary enlistment. In the first month of

World War I, New Zealand forces seized Germany's Pacific island colony, Samoa. All Territorial Force units provided service companies for the New Zealand Expeditionary Force.

UNIFORMS

The permanent forces of New Zealand are described and illustrated in full dress. A list of the Territorial Force units follows.

Some early formations of volunteers wore uniforms similar to the *full dress* of the British Army. By 1914, however, this uniform gave way to a *service dress* of khaki serge with puggarees (scarfs wound around the hat in place of a hat band) and piping of various colors to denote the branch of the army in which the wearer served. Badges were worn by all units. Officers wore leather leggings, rather than puttees, when on duty, together with swords, sword belts, and slings. Boots were worn off duty.

New Zealand forces wore the khaki slouch hat looped up on the left side in the Australian fashion, except for the 11th (Taranaki Rifles) Regiment of the Territorial Force. About 1911, this regiment reshaped the slouch hat into the *lemon squeezer* by turning the top of the hat to a peak and leaving the brim turned down on the left side. The regiment received permission to wear the hat in this manner as a regimental distinction.

During World War I, this method of wearing the slouch hat was adopted by all New Zealand forces to distinguish themselves from the Australians.

BANNERS, GUIDONS, AND COLOURS

In 1907, the King's Banner, a Union flag with a gold fringe, was presented to those units descended from the New Zealand contingents that had served in the South African War (1899-1902). These flags were considered honorary banners for service in South Africa.

Following a reorganization in 1911, mounted rifle regiments carried crimson guidons, including the regiment with *hussar* in the title. Infantry carried a King's Colour (the Union flag) and a Regimental Colour, including those regiments with *rifle* in the title. Information on pre-World War I colours is vague. However, it appears that many Regimental Colours used the facing colour of the volunteer units that formed the regiment. For example, the volunteers that formed the 6th (Hauraki) Regiment wore khaki with maroon facings. By 1914, the facings were gone but the maroon colour appeared on the Regimental Colour in the form of a maroon St. George's Cross on a white field. Heraldic devices and battle honours were embroidered on the colour within a wreath of silver fern, which is unique to New Zealand.

NEW ZEALAND PERMANENT FORCES

Both the New Zealand Staff Corps and the New Zealand Permanent Staff wore the fern leaf badge.

THE NEW ZEALAND STAFF CORPS

In 1914, officers of this corps were assigned to each of the four military districts in New Zealand as cadres. This corps was headquartered at Wellington.

1911 Raised as a corps of officers to assist in the administration and instruction of the Territorial Force

The uniform included a blue forage cap with a scarlet band, a scarlet tunic with blue facings, and blue trousers with red piping. The khaki *service dress* was worn when an officer was serving with the Territorial Forces.

THE NEW ZEALAND PERMANENT STAFF

In 1914, noncommissioned officers on this staff were assigned to each of the four military districts in New Zealand as cadres. This corps was headquartered at Wellington

1911 Raised as a corps of noncommissioned officers to assist in the administration and instruction of the Territorial Force.

The uniform included a blue forage cap with a black band, scarlet tunic with blue facings, gold on scarlet chevrons, and blue trousers with red piping. The khaki *service dress* was worn by those serving with the Territorial Force.

The uniforms of both these corps, for an officer and a sergeant, are illustrated by figure 140.

ROYAL NEW ZEALAND ARTILLERY

In 1914, companies of the Royal New Zealand Artillery, organized as garrison artillery, were stationed at defended ports in each of the four military districts of New Zealand. The Royal New Zealand Artillery was headquartered at Wellington.

1903 The New Zealand Permanent Militia redesignated as the New Zealand Permanent Force (No.1 Service Company became the Royal New Zealand Artillery. No.2 Service Company became the Royal New Zealand Engineers.)

1907 The Royal New Zealand Engineers absorbed into the Royal New Zealand Artillery (The engineers were mostly torpedo engineers. The torpedo corps was responsible for submarine mining in the harbors of Auckland and Wellington. In 1907, responsibility for submarine mining was taken over by the Royal Navy. There were other engineer formations in the New Zealand Territorial Force. The Royal New Zealand Artillery was mainly concerned with port defence.)

The uniform included a *full dress* blue helmet with a brass ball. Other than buttons and badges, the uniform was essentially the same as the Royal Garrison Artillery of the British Army. This uniform is illustrated by figure 141.

NEW ZEALAND TERRITORIAL FORCES

MOUNTED RIFLE REGIMENTS OF THE NEW ZEALAND TERRITORIAL FORCE

In 1914, the uniform for all mounted rifle regiments included a khaki slouch hat with a khaki-green-khaki puggaree, a khaki serge tunic with green piping on the shoulder straps, khaki breeches with green piping, and leather leggings. Badges identified the regiment and were worn on the front of the hat and on the collar.

1ST MOUNTED RIFLES (CANTERBURY YEOMANRY CAVALRY)

This South Island regiment was formed in 1911 with the amalgamation of the 1st Regiment, North Canterbury Mounted Rifles, and the 2nd Regiment, Canterbury Mounted Rifles. Both units had been consolidated as regiments from existing volunteer squadrons in 1901. This regiment was headquartered at Christchurch.

BATTLE HONOUR: *South Africa 1899-1902*

QUEEN ALEXANDRA'S 2ND (WELLINGTON WEST COAST) MOUNTED RIFLES

This North Island regiment was formed in 1911 with a change in title of the 1st Regiment, Wellington (West Coast) Mounted Rifles, consolidated as a regiment from existing volunteer squadrons in 1901. This regiment was headquartered at Wanganui.

BATTLE HONOUR: *South Africa 1899-1902*

3RD (AUCKLAND) MOUNTED RIFLES

This North Island regiment was formed in 1911 with a change in title of the 1st Regiment, Auckland Mounted Rifles, consolidated as a regiment from existing volunteer squadrons in 1901. This regiment was headquartered at Auckland.

BATTLE HONOUR: *South Africa 1901-02*

4TH (WAIKATO) MOUNTED RIFLES

This North Island regiment was formed in 1911 with the amalgamation of the 2nd Regiment, Auckland Mounted Rifles and the 4th Regiment, Auckland Mounted Rifles. Both units were consolidated as regiments from existing volunteer squadrons in 1901 and 1902, respectively. This regiment was headquartered at Hamilton.

BATTLE HONOUR: *South Africa 1900-1902*

5TH MOUNTED RIFLES (OTAGO HUSSARS)

This South Island regiment was formed in 1911 with a change in title of the 1st Regiment, Otago Mounted Rifles, consolidated as a regiment from existing volunteer squadrons in 1901. This regiment was headquartered at Dunedin.

BATTLE HONOUR: *South Africa 1899-1902*

6TH (MANAWATU) MOUNTED RIFLES

This North Island regiment was formed in 1911 with a change in title of the 3rd Regiment, Wellington (Manawatu) Mounted Rifles, consolidated as a regiment from existing volunteer squadrons in 1901. This regiment was headquartered at Palmerston North.

BATTLE HONOUR: *South Africa 1902*

7TH (SOUTHLAND) MOUNTED RIFLES

This South Island regiment was formed in 1911 with a change in title of the 2nd Regiment, Otago Mounted Rifles, consolidated as a regiment from existing volunteer squadrons in 1901. This regiment was headquartered at Invercargill.

BATTLE HONOUR: *South Africa 1902*

8TH (SOUTH CANTERBURY) MOUNTED RIFLES

This South Island regiment was formed in 1911 with a change in title of the 1st Regiment, South Canterbury Mounted Rifles, consolidated as a regiment from existing volunteer squadrons in 1901. This regiment was headquartered at Timaru.

BATTLE HONOUR: *South Africa 1902*

9TH (WELLINGTON EAST COAST) MOUNTED RIFLES

This North Island regiment was formed in 1911 with the amalgamation of the 2nd Regiment, Wellington (Wairarapa) Mounted Rifles and the 4th Regiment, Wellington (East Coast) Mounted Rifles. Both units had been consolidated as regiments in 1901. This regiment was headquartered at Napier.

BATTLE HONOUR: *South Africa 1900-02*

10TH (NELSON) MOUNTED RIFLES

This South Island regiment was formed in 1911 with a change in title of the 1st Regiment, Nelson Mounted Rifles, consolidated as a regiment from existing volunteer squadrons in 1901. This regiment was headquartered at Nelson.

BATTLE HONOUR: *South Africa 1900-02*

11TH (NORTH AUCKLAND) MOUNTED RIFLES

This North Island regiment was formed in 1911 with a change in title of the 3rd Regiment, Auckland Mounted Rifles, consolidated as a regiment from existing volunteer squadrons in 1902. This regiment was headquartered at Whangarei.

BATTLE HONOUR: *South Africa 1902*

12TH (OTAGO MOUNTED RIFLES)

This South Island regiment was raised in 1911 and headquartered at Dunedin.

Note: There was one New Zealand mounted rifle regiment with a Scottish connection. The Scottish Horse Mounted Volunteers, raised in 1906, were one of the volunteer squadrons that formed the 3rd Regiment, Auckland Mounted Rifles in 1902 and redesignated the 11th (North Auckland) Mounted Rifles in 1911. This squadron lost its Scottish identity when the volunteers transferred to the Territorial Force.

ARTILLERY OF THE NEW ZEALAND TERRITORIAL FORCE

FIELD ARTILLERY

In 1903, the New Zealand Field Artillery was organized from existing volunteer batteries and headquartered at Wellington. In 1914, the New Zealand Field Artillery was formed into four field artillery brigades, one for each of the four military districts in New Zealand.

Batteries A, G, and K were in the Auckland Field Artillery Brigade. Batteries E and H were in the Canterbury Field Artillery Brigade. Batteries B and C were in the Otago Field Artillery Brigade. Batteries D and F were in the Wellington Field Artillery Brigade.

The uniform included a khaki slouch hat with a dark blue-scarlet-dark blue puggaree, a khaki serge tunic with scarlet piping on the shoulder straps, khaki breeches with scarlet piping, and leather leggings. The artillery badge was worn on the front of the slouch hat and on the collar.

GARRISON ARTILLERY

In 1902, the New Zealand Garrison Artillery was organized from existing volunteer companies and headquartered at Wellington. In 1914, the New Zealand Garrison Artillery was organized into eight companies.

Companies 1, 6, and 7 were in the Auckland Division; Companies 3, 5, and 9 were in the Wellington Division. Company 4 was in the Canterbury Division, and Company 8 was at Port Chalmers. Evidently No. 2 Company was vacant.

The uniform included a khaki slouch hat with a dark blue-scarlet-dark blue puggaree, a khaki serge tunic with scarlet piping on the shoulder straps, khaki trousers with scarlet piping, and khaki puttees. The artillery badge was worn on the front of the slouch hat and on the collar.

ENGINEERS OF THE NEW ZEALAND TERRITORIAL FORCE

In 1914, the New Zealand Engineers were organized into four distinct branches and headquartered at Wellington.

In 1903, the New Zealand Engineers Volunteers Regiment was organized from existing volunteer companies. In 1911, this regiment was taken into the Territorial Force. There were four field companies, one for each of the four military districts of New Zealand. No. 1 Company was at Christchurch; No. 2 Company was at Dunedin; No. 3 Company was at Auckland; and No. 4 Company was at Wellington.

In 1911, the New Zealand Railway Corps was reorganized as part of the New Zealand Engineers. One battalion of eight companies was on the North Island, and one battalion of eight companies was on the South Island. In 1913, this corps was redesignated the New Zealand Railway Battalions, Corps of New Zealand Engineers.

In 1911, the New Zealand Post and Telegraph Corps consisting of trained signallers was reorganized as part of the New Zealand Engineers. One battalion of seven companies was on the North Island, and one battalion of five companies on the South Island.

In 1911, the New Zealand Signal Corps was reorganized as part of the New Zealand Engineers. In 1913, this corps was redesignated Mounted Signal Companies and Divisional Signal Companies. There were four Mounted Brigade Signal Companies and four Infantry Brigade Signal Companies, one of each for the four military districts of New Zealand.

The uniform included a khaki slouch hat with a khaki-dark blue-khaki puggarree (the signaller's puggaree was khaki-light blue-khaki), a khaki serge tunic with blue piping on the shoulder straps, and khaki trousers with blue piping. Mounted personnel wore khaki breeches with blue piping. The four branches had distinctive badges worn on the front of the slouch hat. The engineers and railway battalions wore a *flaming grenade* badge on the collar. The post and telegraph corps had distinctive collar badges as did the signal companies.

INFANTRY REGIMENTS OF THE NEW ZEALAND TERRITORIAL FORCE

In 1914, the uniform for all infantry regiments included a khaki slouch hat with a khaki-scarlet-khaki puggaree, a khaki serge tunic with scarlet piping on the shoulder straps, khaki trousers with scarlet piping, and khaki puttees. Badges denoted the regiment and were worn on the front of the slouch hat and the collar. New Zealand infantry regiments comprised only one battalion.

1ST (CANTERBURY) REGIMENT

This South Island regiment was formed in 1911 with a change in title of the 1st North Canterbury Battalion of Infantry. It was consolidated as a battalion from existing volunteer companies in 1895. This regiment was headquartered at Christchurch.

BATTLE HONOUR: *South Africa 1902*

2ND (SOUTH CANTERBURY) REGIMENT

This South Island regiment was formed in 1911 with a change in title of the South Canterbury Battalion of Infantry. It was consolidated as a battalion from existing volunteer companies in 1897. This regiment was headquartered at Timaru.

BATTLE HONOUR: *South Africa 1900-02*

3RD (AUCKLAND) REGIMENT (COUNTESS OF RANFURLY'S OWN)

This North Island regiment was formed in 1911 with a change in title of the 1st Battalion, Auckland Infantry (Countess of Ranfurly's Own). It was consolidated as a battalion from existing volunteer companies in 1898. This regiment was headquartered at Auckland.

BATTLE HONOUR: *South Africa 1900-02*

4TH (OTAGO RIFLES) REGIMENT

This South Island regiment was formed in 1911 with a change in title of the 1st Battalion, Otago Rifles. It was consolidated as a battalion from existing volunteer companies in 1898. This regiment was headquartered at Dunedin.

BATTLE HONOUR: *South Africa 1901-02*

5TH (WELLINGTON RIFLES) REGIMENT

This North Island regiment was formed in 1911 with a change in title of the 1st Battalion, Wellington Rifles. It was consolidated as a battalion from existing volunteer companies in 1898. This regiment was headquartered at Wellington.

BATTLE HONOUR: *South Africa 1901-02*

6TH (HAURAKI) REGIMENT

This North Island regiment was formed in 1911 with a change in title of the 2nd Battalion, Auckland (Hauraki) Infantry. It was consolidated as a battalion from existing volunteer companies in 1898. This regiment was headquartered at Tauranga.

BATTLE HONOUR: *South Africa 1900-02*

7TH (WELLINGTON WEST COAST RIFLES) REGIMENT

This North Island regiment was formed in 1911 with a change in title of the 2nd Battalion, Wellington (West Coast) Rifles. It was consolidated as a battalion from existing volunteer companies in 1901. This regiment was headquartered at Wanganui.

BATTLE HONOUR: *South Africa 1900-02*

8TH (SOUTHLAND RIFLES) REGIMENT

This South Island regiment was formed in 1911 with a change in title of the 2nd Battalion, Otago Rifles. It was consolidated as a battalion from existing volunteer companies in 1901. This regiment was headquartered at Invercargill.

BATTLE HONOUR: *South Africa 1901-02.*

9TH (HAWKES BAY) REGIMENT

This North Island regiment was formed in 1911 from the amalgamation of the 3rd Battalion, Wellington (East Coast) Rifles, and the 5th Battalion, Wellington (Centre or Ruahine) Rifles. Both battalions had been consolidated as battalions from existing volunteer companies in 1901. The new regiment was designated the 9th (Wellington East Coast Rifles) Regiment, a two-battalion regiment. In 1914, the 1st Battalion was redesignated the 9th (Hawkes Bay) Regiment, and the 2nd Battalion became the 17th (Ruahine) Regiment. This regiment was headquartered at Napier.

BATTLE HONOUR: *South Africa 1900-02.*

10TH (NORTH OTAGO RIFLES) REGIMENT

This South Island regiment was formed in 1911 with a change in title of the 3rd Battalion, Otago Rifles. It was consolidated as a battalion from existing volunteer companies in 1901. This regiment was headquartered at Oamaru.

BATTLE HONOUR: *South Africa 1901-02.*

11TH (TARANAKI RIFLES) REGIMENT

This North Island regiment was formed in 1911 with a change in title of the 4th Battalion, Wellington (Taranaki) Rifles. It was consolidated as a battalion from existing volunteer companies in 1901. This regiment was headquartered at New Plymouth. The battle honour *New Zealand* was inherited from a predecessor volunteer unit, the Taranaki Battalion of Militia, raised in 1859. The battle honour was granted for the Maori War (1861-71) and is shared only with certain British regular infantry regiments. This regiment wore the slouch hat in a unique way. (See New Zealand: Uniforms, at the beginning of this chapter.)

BATTLE HONOURS: *New Zealand, South Africa 1902*

12TH (NELSON) REGIMENT

This South Island regiment was formed in 1911 with the amalgamation of the 1st Battalion, Nelson Infantry and the 2nd Battalion, Nelson Infantry. Both battalions were consolidated as battalions from existing volunteer companies in 1901. This regiment was headquartered at Nelson.

BATTLE HONOUR: *South Africa 1900-02*

13TH (NORTH CANTERBURY AND WESTLAND) REGIMENT

This South Island regiment was formed in 1911 as the 13th (North Canterbury) Regiment with a change in title of the 2nd North Canterbury Battalion of Infantry. It was consolidated as a battalion from existing volunteer companies in 1903. Redesignated the 13th (North Canterbury and Westland) Regiment in 1912. This regiment was headquartered at Christchurch.

14TH (SOUTH OTAGO RIFLES) REGIMENT

This South Island regiment was formed in 1911 with a change in title of the 4th Battalion, Otago Rifles. It was consolidated as a battalion from existing volunteer companies in 1904. This regiment was headquartered at Dunedin.

15TH (NORTH AUCKLAND) REGIMENT

This North Island regiment was raised in 1911 and headquartered at Whangarei.

16TH (WAIKATO) REGIMENT

This North Island regiment was raised in 1911 and headquartered at Hamilton.

17TH (RUAHINE) REGIMENT

This North Island regiment was formed in 1914 from the 2nd Battalion of the then 9th (Wellington East Coast Rifles) Regiment. (See 9th (Hawkes Bay) Regiment.) This regiment was headquartered at Dannevirke.

Note: In 1911, when the volunteers transferred to the Territorial Force, the Scottish and Irish volunteer companies lost their identities. In 1939, the New Zealand Scots were successful in forming a new regiment, the New Zealand Scottish. The following list identifies those New Zealand infantry regiments that had a Scottish or Irish connection.

C Company, 1st (Canterbury) Regiment, was descended in part from the Canterbury Irish Rifle Volunteers raised in 1885.

C Company, 4th (Otago) Regiment, was descended from the Dunedin Highland Rifle Volunteers raised in 1871.

H Company, 5th (Wellington Rifles) Regiment, was descended from the Wellington Highland Volunteers raised in 1871.

F Company, 7th (Wellington West Coast Rifles) Regiment, was descended from the Wanganui Highland Rifle Volunteers raised in 1900.

H Company, 7th (Wellington West Coast Rifles) Regiment, was descended from the Irish Rifle Volunteers raised in 1900.

D Company, 13th (North Canterbury) Regiment, was descended from the Canterbury Highland Volunteers raised in 1900.

DEPARTMENTAL CORPS OF THE NEW ZEALAND TERRITORIAL FORCE

NEW ZEALAND VETERINARY CORPS

This corps was raised in 1907 and headquartered at Wellington. The uniform included a khaki slouch hat with a khaki-maroon-khaki puggaree, a khaki serge tunic with maroon piping on the shoulder straps, and khaki trousers with maroon piping. Mounted personnel wore khaki breeches with maroon piping. The corps badge was worn on the front of the slouch hat and the collar.

NEW ZEALAND ARMY MEDICAL CORPS

This corps was raised in 1908 from existing volunteer medical formations and headquartered at Wellington. The uniform included a khaki slouch hat with a khaki-dull cherry red-khaki puggarree, a khaki serge tunic with dull cherry red piping on the shoulder straps, and khaki trousers with dull cherry red piping. The corps badge was worn on the front of the slouch hat and the collar. In 1914, there were eight field ambulance companies.

NEW ZEALAND MEDICAL CORPS NURSING RESERVE

The Nursing Reserve was raised in 1908 and headquartered at Wellington. The uniform included a plain dark grey bonnet, a dark grey ankle-length dress with scarlet piping on the collar and cuffs, and a long dark grey cloak buttoned down the front with brass buttons and scarlet piping down the front seam.

NEW ZEALAND ARMY SERVICE CORPS

This corps was raised in 1910; however, it did not function until four British noncommissioned officers of the Army Service Corps arrived as advisors in 1913. This corps was headquartered in Wellington. The uniform included a khaki slouch hat with a khaki-white-khaki puggaree, a khaki serge tunic with white piping on the shoulder straps, and khaki trousers with white piping. Mounted personnel wore khaki breeches with white piping. The corps badge was worn on the front of the slouch hat and the collar.

NEW ZEALAND CHAPLAINS DEPARTMENT

This department was raised in 1911 and headquartered at Wellington. The uniform included a khaki slouch hat with a khaki puggarree edged in black, a khaki serge tunic with black piping on the shoulder straps, and khaki trousers with black piping. The department badge was worn on the front of the slouch hat and the collar.

CHAPTER SIX
Land Forces of the Union of South Africa, 1914

In 1914, the Permanent Force of the Union of South Africa consisted of five regiments of mounted rifles, known as the 1st to the 5th South African Mounted Riflemen, with attached field artillery. The attached artillery brigade was to consist of one battery of field artillery for each mounted rifle regiment; however, by 1914, only three batteries had been raised. Although the entire force, including the artillery, numbered just over 800 men, it was backed by considerable formations of the British Army still stationed in South Africa.

The majority of South Africa's land forces, as in other dominions, was a part-time militia known as the Active Citizen Force. The senior regiments of this force were descended from earlier volunteer corps of the British coastal colonies of the Cape of Good Hope and Natal Colony. These senior regiments had seen considerable active service, as attested to by their battle honours, starting with the Gaika-Galeka War (1877).

During the latter half of the 19th century, a great amount of friction developed between the British South African colonies and the Boers, South African settlers of Dutch and Huguenot descent, who had established themselves in the inland republics of the Transvaal and the Orange Free State. This friction led to the South African War (1899-1902), which ended in victory for the Imperial Forces. The Transvaal and Orange Free State became British colonies. In 1907, the four South African colonies became self-governing. In 1910, the Act of Union resulted in the four colonies (now provinces) becoming the self-governing Union of South Africa.

The South African Defence Act of 1912 established a permanent force, the South African Mounted Riflemen and attached artillery brigade, and an Active Citizen Force consisting of the old British colonial units and the new units raised in 1913.

With the outbreak of World War I, the majority of British forces were withdrawn from South Africa for service in Europe. South Africans, Briton and Boer together, raised an army to invade and occupy German South West Africa. The foundation of this army was the South African Mounted Rifles and units of the Active Citizen Force.

UNIFORMS

The South African Mounted Riflemen are described and illustrated in full dress. A list of the units of the Active Citizen Force follows. The older units of the Active Citizen Force retained a *full dress* uniform in many cases. Newer units were dressed in khaki.

The 1910 Act of Union recognized two languages in South Africa: English and Dutch, the language of the Boers. South African Dutch is the forerunner of modern Afrikaans, which became, together with English, an official language in 1922. The South African Mounted Rifles as a permanent force had both British and Boer personnel. Thus, the titles of the five regiments are written in both languages.

BANNERS, GUIDONS, AND COLOURS

The five regiments of South African Mounted Riflemen that formed the Permanent Force had only been raised in 1913 from mounted police units; therefore, proper guidons had not been presented by 1914.

In 1904 and 1905, King's Banners, a Union flag with a gold fringe, was presented to those South African units that had served in the South African War (1899-1902), including the Cape Medical Corps. These flags were considered honorary banners for service rendered in the war.

Mounted Rifle regiments of the Active Citizen Force had not yet been presented with proper guidons by 1914, although the 4th Mounted Rifles (Umvoti Mounted Rifles) is recorded to have had one.

In 1914, most of the infantry regiments of the Active Citizen Force had both King's Colours and Regimental Colours, which conformed to British regulations in using the facing colour for the background of the Regimental Colour. The 1st, 2nd, 3rd, 5th, 6th, and 7th Infantry Regiments had both King's and Regimental Colours. The 4th Infantry (First Eastern Rifles), a 1912 amalgamation of the Queenstown Rifle Volunteers and the First City of Grahamstown Volunteers, had two sets of colours. As of 1914, there was no resolution on which set of colours to use or if new ones were necessary. Some regiments with *rifle* in the title had colours but they were not uniformed as *rifles*. Two regiments, the 9th and 10th Infantry, were uniformed in rifle green but followed tradition in not having colours. In 1914, the 8th, 11th, and 12th Infantry Regiments had not yet been presented with colours.

Note: The following words will translate titles:
Ruiters = *Horse as in a regiment of horse*
Bereden = *Mounted*
Schutters = *Rifles or riflemen*
Other words in South African Dutch are place names or individual names.

SOUTH AFRICAN PERMANENT FORCES

1ST SOUTH AFRICAN MOUNTED RIFLEMEN
1E ZUID AFRIKAANSE BEREDEN SCHUTTERS

This regiment was formed in 1913 from the Cape Mounted Riflemen raised in 1878. It was headquartered at King William's Town, Cape of Good Hope.

2ND SOUTH AFRICAN MOUNTED RIFLEMEN
2E ZUID AFRIKAANSE BEREDEN SCHUTTERS

This regiment was formed in 1913 from part of the Natal Police, raised in 1874, and the Orange Free State Police, raised in 1908. The regiment was headquartered at Pietermaritzburg, Natal.

3RD SOUTH AFRICAN MOUNTED RIFLEMEN
3E ZUID AFRIKAANSE BEREDEN SCHUTTERS

This regiment was formed in 1913 from part of the Natal Police raised in 1874. It was headquartered at Dundee, Natal.

INDIA

Fig. 173. 26th King George's Own Light Cavalry

Fig. 174. 27th Light Cavalry

Fig. 175. 28th Light Cavalry

Fig. 176. 29th Lancers (Deccan Horse)

Fig. 177. 30th Lancers (Gordon's Horse)

Fig. 178. 31st Duke of Connaught's Own Lancers

INDIA

Fig. 179. 32nd Lancers

Fig. 180. 33rd Queen Victoria's Own Light Cavalry

Fig. 181. 34th Prince Albert Victor's Own Poona Horse

Fig. 182. 35th Scinde Horse

Fig. 183. 36th Jacob's Horse

Fig. 184. 37th Lancers (Baluch Horse)

INDIA

Fig. 185. 38th King George's Own Central India Horse

Fig. 186. 39th King George's Own Central India Horse

Fig. 187. The Aden Troop

Fig. 188. Indian Mountain Artillery

INDIA

Fig. 189. Heavy Battery, Royal Artillery

SAPPERS AND MINERS

Fig. 190. 1st King George's Own Sappers and Miners

Fig. 191. 2nd Queen Victoria's Own Sappers and Miners

Fig. 192. 3rd Sappers and Miners

INDIA
INFANTRY

Fig. 193. 1st Brahmans

Fig. 194. 2nd Queen Victoria's Own Rajput Light Infantry

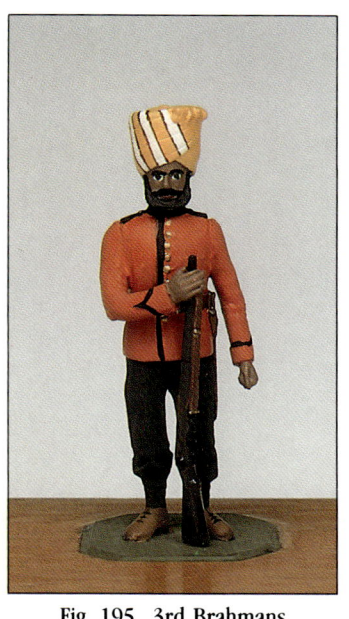

Fig. 195. 3rd Brahmans

Fig. 196. 4th Prince Albert Victor's Own Rajputs

Fig. 197. 5th Light Infantry

Fig. 198. 6th Jat Light Infantry

Fig. 199. 7th Duke of Connaught's Own Rajputs

Fig. 200. 8th Rajputs

INDIA

Fig. 201. 9th Bhopal Infantry

Fig. 202. 10th Jats

Fig. 203. 11th Rajputs

Fig. 204. 12th Pioneers (Khelat-i-Gilzie Regiment)

Fig. 205. 13th Rajputs (Shekhawati Regiment)

Fig. 206. 14th King George's Own Ferozepore Sikhs

Fig. 207. 15th Ludhiana Sikhs

Fig. 208. 16th Rajputs (The Lucknow Regiment)

INDIA

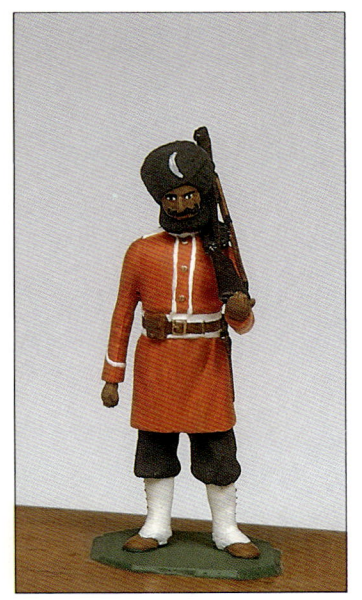

Fig. 209. 17th The Loyal Regiment

Fig. 210. 18th Infantry

Fig. 211. 19th Punjabis

Fig. 212. 20th (Duke of Cambridge's Own) Brownlow's Punjabis

Fig. 213. 21st Punjabis

Fig. 214. 22nd Punjabis

Fig. 215. 23rd Sikh Pioneers

Fig. 216. 24th Punjabis

INDIA

Fig. 217. 25th Punjabis

Fig. 218. 26th Punjabis

Fig. 219. 27th Punjabis

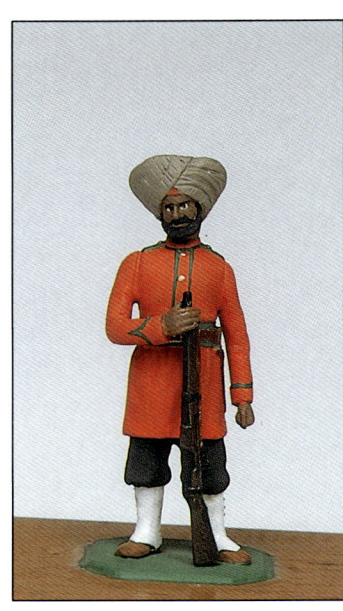

Fig. 220. 28th Punjabis

Fig. 221. 29th Punjabis

Fig. 222. 30th Punjabis

Fig. 223. 31st Punjabis

Fig. 224. 32nd Sikh Pioneers

INDIA

Fig. 225. 33rd Punjabis

Fig. 226. 34th Sikh Pioneers

Fig. 227. 35th Sikhs

Fig. 228. 36th Sikhs

Fig. 229. 37th Dogras

Fig. 230. 38th Dogras

Fig. 231. 39th Garhwal Rifles

Fig. 232. 40th Pathans

170 FORCES OF THE BRITISH EMPIRE—1914

INDIA

Fig. 233. 41st Dogras

Fig. 234. 42nd Deoli Regiment

Fig. 235. 43rd Erinpura Regiment

Fig. 236. 44th Mharwara Regiment

Fig. 237. 45th Rattray's Sikhs

Fig. 238. 46th Punjabis

Fig. 239. 47th Sikhs

Fig. 240. 48th Pioneers

INDIA

Fig. 241. 51st Sikhs
(Frontier Force)

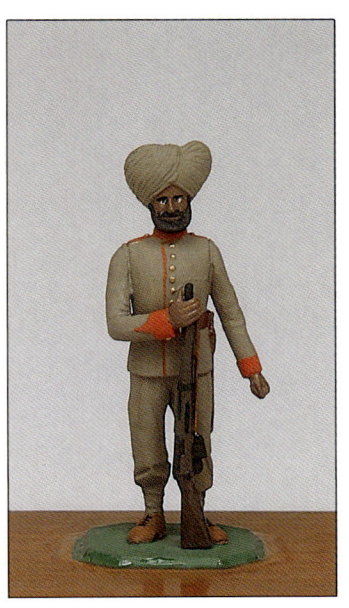

Fig. 242. 52nd Sikhs
(Frontier Force)

Fig. 243. 53rd Sikhs
(Frontier Force)

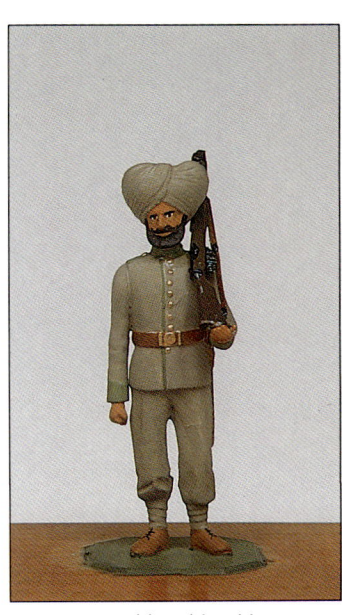

Fig. 244. 54th Sikhs
(Frontier Force)

Fig. 245. 55th Coke's Rifles
(Frontier Force)

Fig. 246. 56th Punjabi Rifles
(Frontier Force)

Fig. 247. 57th Wilde's Rifles
(Frontier Force)

Fig. 248. 58th Vaughn's Rifles
(Frontier Force)

172 FORCES OF THE BRITISH EMPIRE—1914

INDIA

Fig. 249. 59th Scinde Rifles (Frontier Force)

Fig. 250. 61st King George's Own Pioneers

Fig. 251. 62nd Punjabis

Fig. 252. 63rd Palamcottah Light Infantry

Fig. 253. 64th Pioneers

Fig. 254. 66th Punjabis

Fig. 255. 67th Punjabis

Fig. 256. 69th Punjabis

INDIA

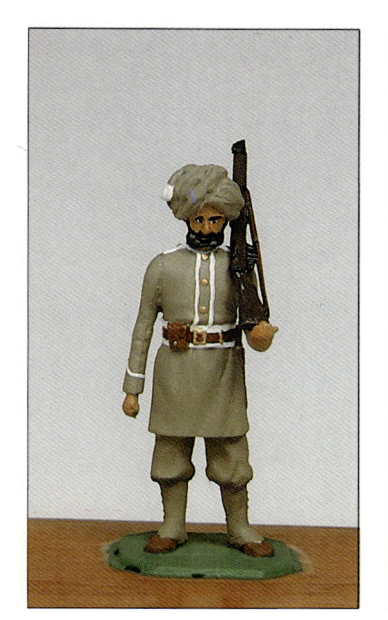

Fig. 257. 72nd Punjabis

Fig. 258. 73rd Carnatic Infantry

Fig. 259. 74th Punjabis

Fig. 260. 75th Carnatic Infantry

Fig. 261. 76th Punjabis

Fig. 262. 79th Carnatic Infantry

Fig. 263. 80th Carnatic Infantry

Fig. 264. 81st Pioneers

INDIA

Fig. 265. 82nd Punjabis

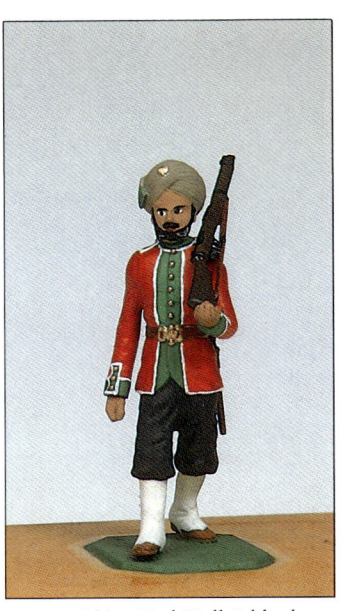

Fig. 266. 83rd Wallajahbad Light Infantry

Fig. 267. 84th Punjabis

Fig. 268. 86th Carnatic Infantry

Fig. 269. 87th Punjabis

Fig. 270. 88th Carnatic Infantry

Fig. 271. 89th Punjabis

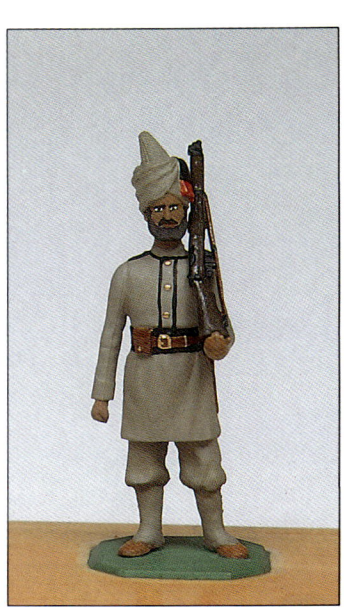

Fig. 272. 90th Punjabis

INDIA

Fig. 273. 91st Punjabis (Light Infantry)

Fig. 274. 92nd Punjabis

Fig. 275. 93rd Burma Infantry

Fig. 276. 94th Russell's Infantry

Fig. 277. 95th Russell's Infantry

Fig. 278. 96th Berar Infantry

Fig. 279. 97th Deccan Infantry

Fig. 280. 98th Infantry

INDIA

Fig. 281. 99th Deccan Infantry

Fig. 282. 101st Grenadiers

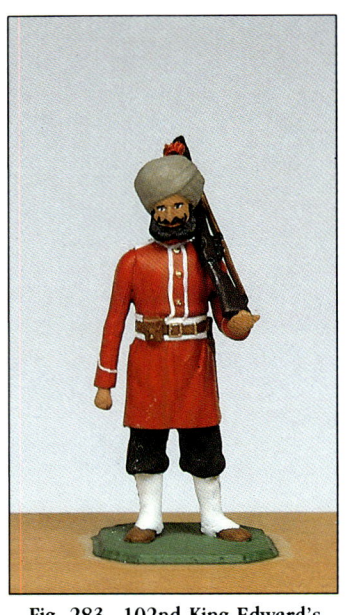

Fig. 283. 102nd King Edward's Own Grenadiers

Fig. 284. 103rd Mahratta Light Infantry

Fig. 285. 104th Wellesley's Rifles

Fig. 286. 105th Mahratta Light Infantry

Fig. 287. 106th Hazara Pioneers

Fig. 288. 107th Pioneers

FORCES OF THE BRITISH EMPIRE—1914   177

INDIA

Fig. 289. 108th Infantry

Fig. 290. 109th Infantry

Fig. 291. 110th Mahratta Light Infantry

Fig. 292. 112th Infantry

Fig. 293. 113th Infantry

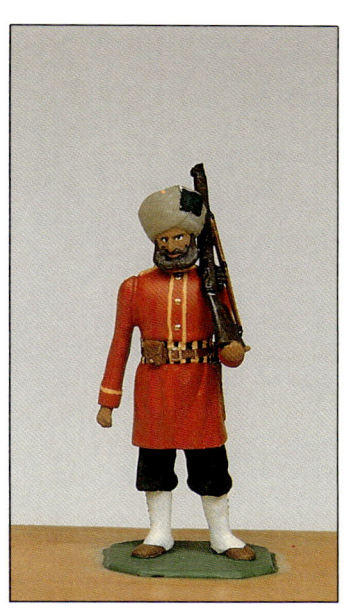

Fig. 294. 114th Mahrattas

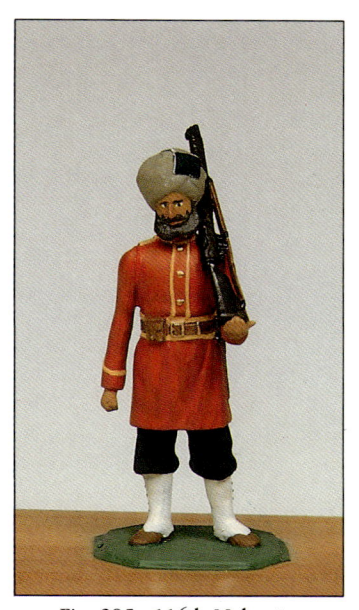

Fig. 295. 116th Mahrattas

Fig. 296. 117th Mahrattas

INDIA

Fig. 297. 119th Infantry (The Mooltan Regiment)

Fig. 298. 120th Rajputana Infantry

Fig. 299. 121st Pioneers

Fig. 300. 122nd Rajputana Infantry

Fig. 301. 123rd Outram's Rifles

Fig. 302. 124th Duchess of Connaught's Own Baluchistan Infantry

Fig. 303. 125th Napier's Rifles

Fig. 304. 126th Baluchistan Infantry

FORCES OF THE BRITISH EMPIRE—1914 179

INDIA

Fig. 305. 127th Queen Mary's Own Baluch Light Infantry

Fig. 306. 128th Pioneers

Fig. 307. 129th Duke of Connaught's Own Baluchis

Fig. 308. 130th King George's Own Baluchis (Jacob's Rifles)

BRIGADE OF GURKHAS

Fig. 309. 1st King George's Own Gurkha Rifles (The Malaun Regiment)

Fig. 310. 2nd King Edward's Own Gurkha Rifles (The Sirmoor Regiment)

Fig. 311. 3rd Queen Alexandra's Own Gurkha Rifles

Fig. 312. 4th Gurkha Rifles

INDIA

Fig. 313. 5th Gurkha Rifles (Frontier Force)

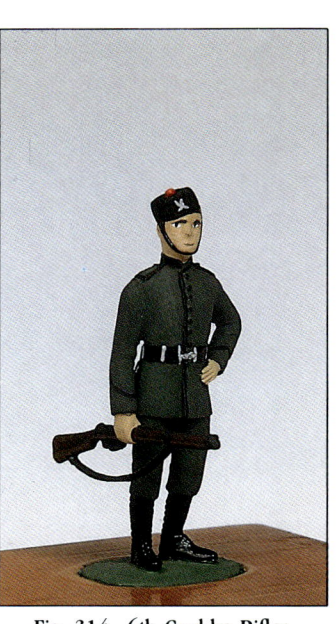

Fig. 314. 6th Gurkha Rifles

Fig. 315. 7th Gurkha Rifles

Fig. 316. 8th Gurkha Rifles

Fig. 317. 9th Gurkha Rifles

Fig. 318. 10th Gurkha Rifles

INDIA
DEPARTMENTAL CORPS

Fig. 319. Supply and Transport Corps

Fig. 320. Army Remount Department

Fig. 321. Army Clothing Department

Fig. 322. Indian Medical Department

INDIA

Fig. 323. **Army Hospital** Corps

Fig. 324. Army Bearer Corps

Fig. 325. Army Veterinary Service

Fig. 326. Indian Ordnance Department

Fig. 327. Military Farms Department

Fig. 328. Indian Army Corps of Clerks

FORCES OF THE BRITISH EMPIRE—1914 183

INDIA
IMPERIAL SERVICE TROOPS

Fig. 329. The Alwar Lancers

Fig. 330. The Alwar Infantry

Fig. 331. The Bahawalpur Mounted Escort

Fig. 332. The Bahawalpur Camel Transport Corps

Fig. 333. The Bharatpur Infantry

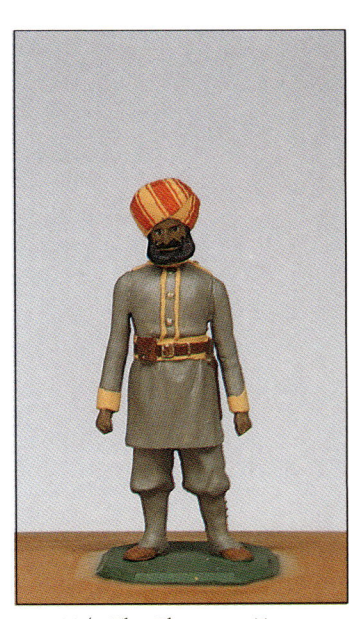

Fig. 334. The Bharatpur Transport Corps

184   FORCES OF THE BRITISH EMPIRE—1914

INDIA

Fig. 335. The Bhavanagar Lancers

Fig. 336. The Bhopal (Victoria) Lancers

Fig. 337. The Bikaner Camel Corps

Fig. 338. The Bikaner Sadul Light Infantry

Fig. 339. The Faridkot Sappers and Miners

Fig. 340. The Gwalior Lancers

INDIA

Fig. 341. 3rd Maharajah Scindia's Own Battalion (Gwalior)

Fig. 342. 4th Maharajah Bahadour Battalion (Gwalior)

Fig. 343. The Gwalior Transport Corps

Fig. 344. The Hyderabad Lancers

Fig. 345. The Indore Mounted Escort

Fig. 346. The Indore Transport Corps

INDIA

Fig. 347. The Jaipur Transport Corps

Fig. 348. The Jind Infantry

Fig. 349. The Jodhpur (Sardar Rissalah) Lancers

Fig. 350. The Junagarh Lancers

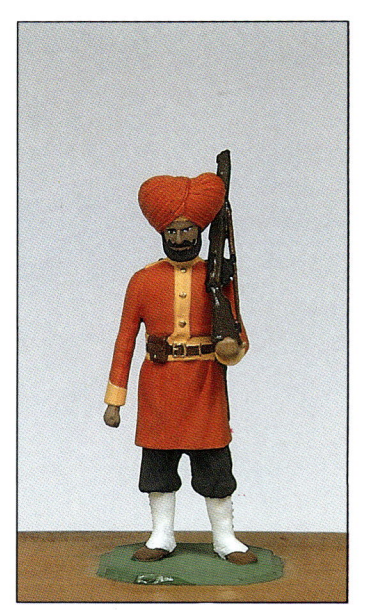

Fig. 351. The Karpurthala (Jagjit) Infantry

Fig. 352. The Kashmir Lancers

INDIA

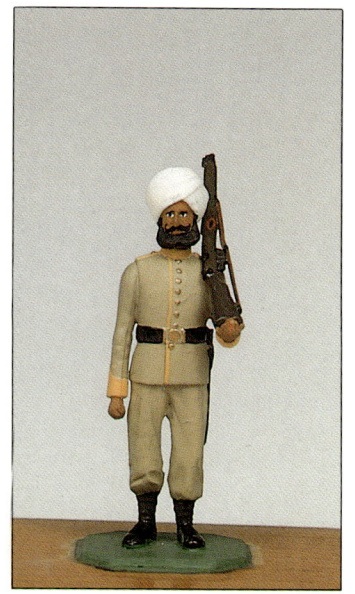

Fig. 353. The Kashmir Infantry

Fig. 354. The Kashmir Rifles

Fig. 355. The Kashmir Artillery

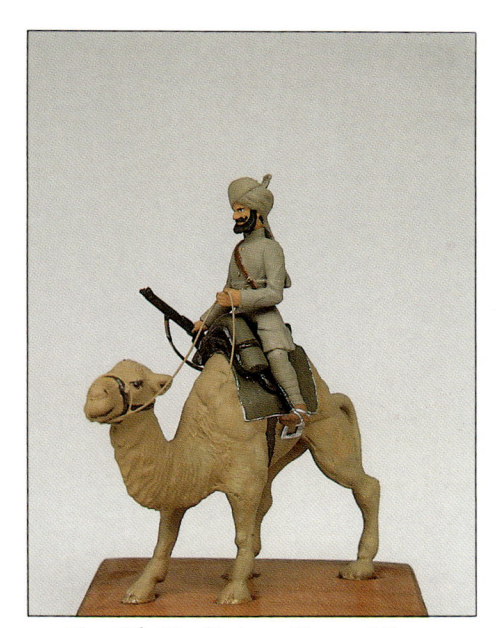

Fig. 356. The Khairpur Mounted Escort

Fig. 357. The Khairpur Camel Transport Corps

Fig. 358. The Malerkotla Sappers and Miners

INDIA

Fig. 359. The Mysore Lancers

Fig. 360. The Mysore Transport Corps

Fig. 361. The Nabha Infantry

Fig. 362. The Navanagar (Choti Khas) Lancers

Fig. 363. The Patiala (Rajinder) Lancers

Fig. 364. 1st Patiala Infantry

INDIA

Fig. 365. 2nd Patiala Infantry

Fig. 366. The Rampur (Rohilla) Lancers

Fig. 367. The Rampur Infantry

Fig. 368. The Simur Sappers and Miners

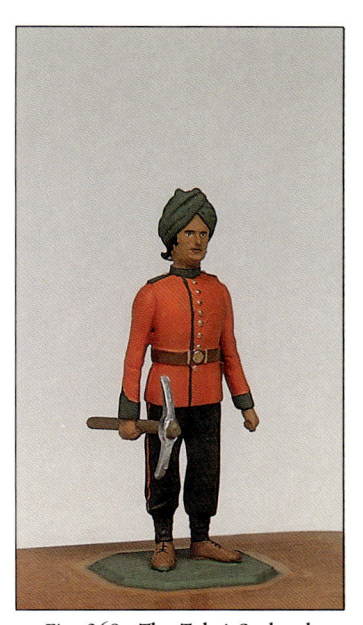

Fig. 369. The Tehri-Garhwal Sappers and Miners

Fig. 370. The Udaipur Lancers

COLONIAL

MALTA

Fig. 371. Royal Malta Artillery

WEST INDIES

Fig. 372. The West India Regiment

AFRICA

Fig. 373. The West Africa Regiment

Fig. 374. The West African Frontier Force, Infantry

Fig. 375. The West African Frontier Force, Artillery

COLONIAL

Fig. 376. The West African Frontier Force, Engineers

Fig. 377. The King's African Rifles

Fig. 378. The Somaliland Camel Corps

Fig. 379. The Northern Rhodesia Police (Military Wing)

COLONIAL

MALAY STATES

Fig. 380. The Malay States Guides

NORTH BORNEO

Fig. 381. The Armed Constabulary of North Borneo

SARAWAK

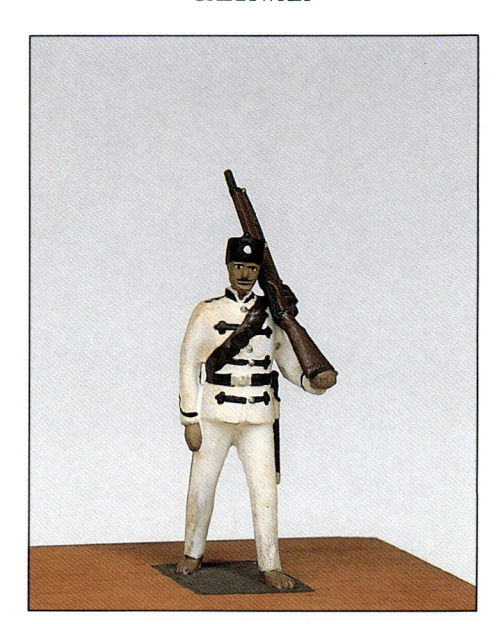

Fig. 382. The Sarawak Rangers

JOHORE

Fig. 383. The Johore Military Force Infantry & Artillery

4TH SOUTH AFRICAN MOUNTED RIFLEMEN
4E ZUID AFRIKAANSE BEREDEN SCHUTTERS

This regiment was formed in 1913 from the Transvaal Police raised in 1908. It was headquartered at Pretoria, Transvaal.

5TH SOUTH AFRICAN MOUNTED RIFLEMEN
5E ZUID AFRIKAANSE BEREDEN SCHUTTERS

This regiment was formed in 1913 from the Cape Mounted Police raised in 1904. It was headquartered at Kimberley, Cape of Good Hope Province.

The uniform for all five regiments of the South African Mounted Riflemen included a white helmet with a brass spike and a white puggarree edged red on the top. A brass numeral on the left side of the helmet denoted the number of the regiment. The blue tunic had brass numerals on the shoulder straps. The blue pantaloons had red piping, and there were brown leather belts, gauntlets, and boots. This uniform is illustrated by figure 142.

PERMANENT FORCE ARTILLERY BRIGADE

Each of the five regiments of Mounted Riflemen was to have a battery of field artillery attached. In 1914, the 1st, 2nd, and 4th batteries had been raised. The 3rd and 5th batteries had not yet been formed.

PERMANENT FORCE MEDICAL SECTION

This small formation was formed in 1913 from the regular staff of the Cape Medical Corps, originally raised as the Cape Medical Volunteer Staff Corps in 1890. Personnel were attached to the South African Mounted Rifle regiments.

SOUTH AFRICAN ACTIVE CITIZEN FORCES

MOUNTED RIFLE REGIMENTS OF THE SOUTH AFRICAN ACTIVE CITIZEN FORCE

1ST MOUNTED RIFLES (1ST NATAL CARABINEERS)

This regiment was formed in 1913 from part of the Natal Carabineers. It was consolidated as a regiment in 1885 from existing volunteer units. The regiment was headquartered at Pietermaritzburg, Natal. Field Marshal Kitchener of Khartoum was Colonel-in-Chief. The uniform included a white helmet with a brass spike, a blue tunic with white facings, and blue pantaloons with white piping.

BATTLE HONOURS: *South Africa 1879,* (inherited from an earlier volunteer unit) *South Africa 1899-1902, Defence of Ladysmith, Natal 1906*

2ND MOUNTED RIFLES (2ND NATAL CARABINEERS)

This regiment was formed in 1913 from part of the Natal Carabineers. It was consolidated as a regiment in 1885 from existing volunteer units. The regiment was headquartered at Ladysmith, Natal. Field Marshal Kitchener of Khartoum was Colonel-in-Chief. The uniform included a white helmet with a brass spike, a blue tunic with white facings, and blue pantaloons with white piping.

BATTLE HONOURS: *South Africa 1879,* (inherited from an earlier volunteer unit) *South Africa 1899-1902, Defence of Ladysmith, Natal 1906*

3RD MOUNTED RIFLES (NATAL MOUNTED RIFLES)

This regiment was formed in 1913 from the Natal Mounted Rifles. It was consolidated as a regiment in 1888 from existing volunteer units and the Border Mounted Rifles formed in 1894 from the Natal Mounted Rifles. The two units were reunited in 1913. The regiment was headquartered at Durban, Natal. The uniform included a grey slouch hat with a plume of blackcock's feathers, a khaki tunic with no facings, and khaki breeches.

BATTLE HONOURS: *South Africa 1879,* (inherited from an earlier volunteer unit) *South Africa 1899-1902, Defence of Ladysmith, Natal 1906*

4TH MOUNTED RIFLES (UMVOTI MOUNTED RIFLES)

This regiment was formed in 1913 from the Umvoti Mounted Rifles. It was consolidated as a regiment in 1893 from existing volunteer units, from part of the Border Mounted Rifles formed in 1894 from the Natal Mounted Rifles, and from the Zululand Mounted Rifles. The regiment was headquartered at Greytown, Natal. The uniform included a khaki slouch hat, a khaki tunic with maroon facings, and khaki breeches with maroon piping.

BATTLE HONOURS: *South Africa 1879*, (inherited from an earlier volunteer unit) *South Africa 1899-1902, Relief of Ladysmith, Natal 1906*

5TH MOUNTED RIFLES (IMPERIAL LIGHT HORSE)

This regiment was formed in 1913 from the Imperial Light Horse raised in 1899. The regiment was headquartered at Johannesburg, Transvaal. King George V was Colonel-in-Chief. The uniform included a khaki slouch hat, a khaki tunic with no facings, and khaki breeches.

BATTLE HONOURS: *South Africa 1899-1902, Defence of Ladysmith, Relief of Ladysmith, Natal 1906*

6TH MOUNTED RIFLES (CAPE LIGHT HORSE)

This regiment was formed in 1913 from the Cape Light Horse formed in 1909 from the Border Light Horse, the Transkei Mounted Rifles, and the Tembuland Light Horse. The regiment was headquartered at East London, Cape of Good Hope. The uniform included a khaki slouch hat, a khaki tunic with blue facings, and khaki breeches with blue piping.

The following mounted rifle regiments were all raised in 1913. Other than badges, their uniforms were the same: khaki slouch hat with a dark green puggarree, khaki tunic with dark green facings (for officers) and dark green piping for other ranks, and khaki breeches with green piping. Officers wore peaked caps with a dark green band.

7TH MOUNTED RIFLES (SOUTHERN MOUNTED RIFLES)

This regiment was headquartered at Oudtshoorn, Cape of Good Hope.

8TH MOUNTED RIFLES (MIDLANDSE RUITERS)

This regiment was headquartered at Middelburg, Cape of Good Hope.

9TH MOUNTED RIFLES (HOGEVELD RUITERS)

This regiment was headquartered at Ermelo, Transvaal.

10TH MOUNTED RIFLES (BOTHA RUITERS)

This regiment was headquartered at Standerton, Transvaal.

11TH MOUNTED RIFLES (POTECHEFSTROOM RUITERS)

This regiment was headquartered at Potechefstroom, Transvaal.

12TH MOUNTED RIFLES (KRUGERSDORP RUITERS)

This regiment was headquartered at Zeerust, Transvaal.

13TH MOUNTED RIFLES (NOORDELIKE TRANSVAAL BEREDENSCHUTTERS)

This regiment was headquartered at Pretoria, Transvaal.

14TH MOUNTED RIFLES (STEYN'S BEREDEN SCHUTTERS)

This regiment was headquartered at Kroonstad, Orange Free State.

15TH Mounted Rifles—Vacant in 1914

16TH MOUNTED RIFLES (RESTE VRIJSTAATSE REGIMENT)

This regiment was headquartered at Bloemfontein, Orange Free State.

17TH MOUNTED RIFLES (WESTERN PROVINCE MOUNTED RIFLES)

This regiment was headquartered at Worcester, Cape of Good Hope.

18TH MOUNTED RIFLES (GRIQUALAND WEST RUITERS)

This regiment was headquartered at Douglas, Cape of Good Hope.

19TH MOUNTED RIFLES (TRANSKEI MOUNTED RIFLES)

This regiment was headquartered at Umtata, Cape of Good Hope.

20TH MOUNTED RIFLES (GRAAF REINET RUITERS)

This regiment was headquartered at Graaf-Reinet, Cape of Good Hope.

BOESMANLAND INDEPENDENT MOUNTED RIFLE SQUADRONS

There were three independent mounted rifle squadrons organized from the sparsely inhabited northwestern district of the Cape of Good Hope Province.

DISMOUNTED RIFLE REGIMENTS OF THE SOUTH AFRICAN ACTIVE CITIZEN FORCE

Men liable for service who could not produce a horse or saddlery were formed into regiments of Dismounted Rifles all raised in 1913. These regiments could be converted to Mounted Rifles when two-thirds of the personnel could provide their own horses and saddlery. In 1914, the Dismounted Rifles acted as a reserve for the Mounted Rifles. The uniform was the same as the Mounted Rifles.

1ST DISMOUNTED RIFLES (1ST WESTERN PROVINCE RIFLES)

This regiment was headquartered at Worcester, Cape of Good Hope.

2ND DISMOUNTED RIFLES (2ND WESTERN PROVINCE RIFLES)

This regiment was headquartered at Malmesbury, Cape of Good Hope.

3RD DISMOUNTED RIFLES (3RD WESTERN PROVINCE RIFLES)

This regiment was headquartered at Stellenbosch, Cape of Good Hope.

4TH DISMOUNTED RIFLES (1ST SOUTHERN RIFLES)

This regiment was headquartered at Port Elizabeth, Cape of Good Hope.

5TH DISMOUNTED RIFLES (2ND SOUTHERN RIFLES)

This regiment was headquartered at Oudtshoorn, Cape of Good Hope.

6TH DISMOUNTED RIFLES (MIDLANDS SCHUTTERS)

This regiment was headquartered at Somerset East, Cape of Good Hope.

7TH DISMOUNTED RIFLES (HOEVELD SCHUTTERS)

This regiment was headquartered at Volksrust, Orange Free State.

8TH DISMOUNTED RIFLES (DE LA REY'S RUITERS)

This regiment was headquartered at Potchefstroom, Transvaal.

9TH DISMOUNTED RIFLES (BECHUANALAND RIFLES)

This regiment was headquartered at Mafeking, Cape of Good Hope.

10TH DISMOUNTED RIFLES (NOORDELIKE TRANSVAAL GRENS WAG)

This regiment was headquartered at Pretoria, Transvaal.

11TH DISMOUNTED RIFLES (ORANJE SKERPSCHUTTERS)

This regiment was headquartered at Kroonstad, Orange Free State.

12TH DISMOUNTED RIFLES (PRESIDENT BRAND'S REGIMENT)

This regiment was headquartered at Bloemfontein, Orange Free State.

13TH DISMOUNTED RIFLES (LICHTENBURG RUITERS)

This regiment was headquartered at Lichtenburg, Transvaal.

14TH DISMOUNTED RIFLES (KAROO SCHUTTERS)

This regiment was headquartered at De Aar, Transvaal.

BOESMANLAND INDEPENDENT DISMOUNTED RIFLE SQUADRONS

There were four independent Dismounted Rifle Squadrons organized from the sparsely inhabited northwestern district of the Cape of Good Hope Province.

ARTILLERY OF THE SOUTH AFRICAN ACTIVE CITIZEN FORCE

FIELD ARTILLERY

The 1st to the 5th field artillery batteries were in the Permanent Force.

6TH BATTERY (CAPE FIELD ARTILLERY, PRINCE ALFRED'S OWN)

This battery was raised in 1857 and headquartered at Capetown, Cape of Good Hope. The uniform included a khaki slouch hat, a khaki tunic with no facings, and khaki breeches.

7TH BATTERY (NATAL FIELD ARTILLERY)

This battery was raised in 1862 as the Natal Field Artillery. It was headquartered at Pietermaritzburg, Natal. The uniform included a *full dress* white helmet. Other than the white helmet, badges, and buttons, the uniform was essentially the same as the Royal Horse Artillery of the British Army.

8TH BATTERY (TRANSVAAL HORSE ARTILLERY)

This battery was raised in 1904 and headquartered at Johannesburg, Transvaal. The uniform included a white helmet, a blue tunic with scarlet facings, and blue breeches with wide scarlet stripes.

GARRISON ARTILLERY

CAPE GARRISON ARTILLERY

This unit was raised in 1891 and headquartered at Capetown, Cape of Good Hope. The uniform included a white helmet, a blue tunic with scarlet facings, and blue trousers with wide scarlet stripes.

DURBAN GARRISON ARTILLERY

This unit was formed in 1912 from part of the Natal Field Artillery raised in 1862. It was headquartered at Durban, Natal. The uniform included a khaki slouch hat, a khaki tunic with no facings, and khaki trousers with khaki puttees.

ENGINEERS OF THE SOUTH AFRICAN ACTIVE CITIZEN FORCE

CAPE FORTRESS ENGINEERS

This company-size unit was raised in July 1914 and headquartered at Capetown, Cape of Good Hope. This formation assisted and later took over the duties of the Corps of Royal Engineers in maintaining the coast defenses at Capetown as well as the telephone, signal and searchlight stations at the Simons Bay naval base. The uniform included a khaki slouch hat, a khaki tunic with no facings, and khaki trousers with khaki puttees.

INFANTRY REGIMENTS OF THE SOUTH AFRICAN ACTIVE CITIZEN FORCE

1ST INFANTRY (DURBAN LIGHT INFANTRY)

This regiment was raised in 1854 and headquartered at Durban, Natal. Field Marshal Arthur, Duke of Connaught and Strathearn, was Colonel-in-Chief. The uniform included a grey helmet, a grey tunic with white facings, and grey trousers with white piping.

BATTLE HONOURS: *South Africa 1879, South Africa 1899-1902, Relief of Ladysmith, Natal 1906*

2ND INFANTRY (DUKE OF EDINBURGH'S OWN RIFLES)

This regiment was raised in 1855 and headquartered at Capetown, Cape of Good Hope. The uniform included a white helmet, a scarlet tunic with yellow facings, and blue trousers with red piping.

BATTLE HONOURS: *Gaika-Galeka 1877, Transkei 1879, Basutoland 1880-81, Bechuanaland 1897, South Africa 1899-1902*

3RD INFANTRY (PRINCE ALFRED'S GUARD)

This regiment was raised in 1856 and headquartered at Port Elizabeth, Cape of Good Hope. The uniform included a khaki slouch hat, a khaki tunic with no facings, and khaki trousers with khaki puttees.

BATTLE HONOURS: *Gaika-Galeka 1877-78, Transkei 1877-78, Basutoland 1880-81, Bechuanaland 1897, Umzintzani, South Africa 1899-1902*

4TH INFANTRY (FIRST EASTERN RIFLES)

This regiment was formed in 1912 with the amalgamation of the Queenstown Volunteers, raised in 1860, and the First City of Grahamstown Volunteers, raised in 1875. The regiment was headquartered at Queenstown, Cape of Good Hope. The uniform included a khaki slouch hat, a brown tunic with green facings, and brown trousers with green piping.

BATTLE HONOURS: *Gaika-Galeka 1877-78, Basutoland 1880-81, Bechuanaland 1897, South Africa 1899-1902*

5TH INFANTRY (KAFFRARIAN RIFLES)

This regiment was formed in 1883 from existing volunteer units and headquartered at East London, Cape of Good Hope. The uniform included a grey helmet with a large green over red hackle, a grey tunic with green facings and red piping, and grey trousers with red piping.

BATTLE HONOURS: *Gaika-Galeka 1878*, (inherited from an earlier volunteer unit) *Bechuanaland 1897, South Africa 1899-1902*

6TH INFANTRY (DUKE OF CONNAUGHT AND STRATHEARN'S OWN CAPETOWN HIGHLANDERS)

This regiment was raised in 1885 and headquartered at Capetown, Cape of Good Hope. Field Marshal Arthur, Duke of Connaught and Strathearn, was Colonel-in-Chief. The uniform included a white helmet, a scarlet doublet with yellow facings, and a kilt of Gordon tartan. The black sporran had six white tassels and the hose was scarlet and white. The pipers wore blue glengarry caps with a red-white-blue diced border and blue doublets.

BATTLE HONOURS: *Bechuanaland 1896-97, South Africa 1899-1902*

7TH INFANTRY (KIMBERLEY REGIMENT)

This regiment was formed in 1899 from the Diamond Fields Horse raised in 1876, and the Kimberley Rifles, raised in 1887. In 1907, this regiment absorbed the Kimberley Light Horse raised in 1879, the Diamond Fields Artillery raised in 1890, and the Kimberley Mounted Corps raised in 1900. The regiment was headquartered at Kimberley, Cape of Good Hope. The uniform included a white helmet, a scarlet tunic with buff facings, and blue trousers with red piping.

BATTLE HONOURS: *Gaika-Galeka 1877-78, Griqualand West 1878, Bastutoland 1880-81, Transkei 1880-81, Bechuanaland 1896-97, South Africa 1899-1902, Defence of Kimberley*

8TH INFANTRY (TRANSVAAL SCOTTISH)

This regiment was raised in 1902 as the Transvaal Scottish Volunteer Regiment and headquartered at Johannesburg, Transvaal. The Duke of Atholl was Colonel-in-Chief. In 1912, it was redesignated the 8th Infantry (Transvaal Scottish). The uniform included a khaki helmet, a khaki doublet with no facings, and a kilt of Murray of Atholl tartan. The brown sporran had six white tassels, and the hose was scarlet and black. The pipers had the same uniform except for their kilts of Murray of Tullibardine tartan.

9TH INFANTRY (PRINCE OF WALES'S OWN REGIMENT OF PENINSULA RIFLES)

This regiment was raised in 1902 as a *town guard* in Capetown. In 1903, it became a regiment with the above title and was headquartered at Capetown, Cape of Good Hope. King George V was Colonel-in-Chief. The uniform included a black rifle busby with a scarlet and black plume, a rifle green tunic with scarlet facings and piping, and rifle green trousers. The uniform was essentially the same as the King's Royal Rifle Corps of the British Army, except for badges and buttons.

10TH INFANTRY (WITWATERSRAND RIFLES)

This regiment was raised in 1899 as the Railway Pioneer Regiment and headquartered at Johannesburg, Transvaal. In 1907, it was converted to infantry with the above title. The uniform included a black rifle busby with a black plume, a rifle green tunic with light green facings and piping, and rifle green trousers.

11TH INFANTRY (RAND LIGHT INFANTRY)

This regiment was raised in 1905 as the Transvaal Cycle Corps and headquartered at Johannesburg, Transvaal. In 1913, it was converted to infantry with the above title. Field Marshal Arthur, Duke of Connaught and Strathearn, was Colonel-in-Chief. The uniform included a khaki helmet with blue feathers, a khaki tunic with no facings, and khaki trousers with khaki puttees.

12TH INFANTRY (PRETORIA REGIMENT)

This regiment was formed in 1913 from the Pretoria company of the Transvaal Scottish (the company ceased to wear Scottish dress), the Central South African Railway Volunteers raised in 1901, the Northern Mounted Rifles raised in 1903, and the Transvaal Cycle and Motor Corps raised in 1909. The regiment was headquartered at Pretoria, Transvaal. The uniform included a khaki helmet, a khaki tunic with no facings, and khaki trousers with khaki puttees.

DEPARTMENTAL CORPS OF THE SOUTH AFRICAN ACTIVE CITIZEN FORCE

SOUTH AFRICAN ORDNANCE DEPARTMENT

This department was raised in 1912. In 1914, small detachments maintained the ordnance stores and ammunition magazines in Pretoria, Capetown, and Bloemfontein. The uniform included a khaki slouch hat, khaki, tunic with no facings, and khaki trousers with khaki puttees.

SOUTH AFRICAN SERVICE CORPS

This corps was raised in 1913. In 1914, there was one mounted brigade train headquartered at Pietermaritzburg, with three others being formed. In addition, there were three dismounted brigade trains being formed. There were two infantry brigade trains headquartered at Capetown and Durban, with a third being formed. The uniform included a khaki slouch hat, khaki tunic with no facings, and khaki trousers with khaki puttees. Mounted personnel wore khaki breeches and leather leggings.

SOUTH AFRICAN MEDICAL CORPS

This corps was formed in 1913 from existing volunteer medical units: the Cape Medical Corps originally known as the Cape Medical Volunteer Staff Corps raised in 1890, the Natal Volunteer Medical Corps raised in 1899, and the Transvaal Medical Volunteers raised in 1903. By 1914, the corps had expanded and comprised six mounted brigade field ambulance companies headquartered at King William's Town, Pietermaritzburg, Worcester, Port Elizabeth, Ladysmith, and Pretoria, with a seventh being formed. One divisional field ambulance company was headquartered at Johannesburg, with a second being formed. The uniform included a khaki slouch hat, a khaki tunic with no facings, and khaki trousers with khaki puttees.

CHAPTER SEVEN
The Armies of India, 1914

In 1914, the Indian Army was the most organized and suitable military force available outside the United Kingdom. The Indian Army was organized mainly to keep internal order and defend India from external aggression. However, many units had served overseas in Africa and Asia, and almost all of the others had seen extensive service within India. It must be remembered that the India of 1914 was much larger than the India of today. The territory of the Indian Empire included what is now India, Pakistan, Bangladesh, and Burma. There was usually some military activity going on somewhere along the frontiers of this vast empire.

The Indian Army of 1914 consisted of some 160,000 men trained and commanded by British and Indian officers and noncommissioned officers. By the end of World War I (1914-18), over 1,300,000 Indians of all races and creeds had volunteered for military service. The Indian Army had not served in the South African War (1899-1902) because it was not thought proper at the time to have colored men fight against white men. By 1914, attitudes had changed. Indian troops served in France and East Africa. They carried the main burden in Mesopotamia and made up a large part of the last great cavalry formations that served in Palestine. The record of the Indian Army was magnificent.

The Indian Army had its origins in the military forces of the Honourable East India Company founded at the end of the 16th century to exploit the trade with India and the Far East. From a simple trading company, the East India Company grew to be a great chartered organization with many functions, including raising its own regiments. These forces were eventually divided into three armies of the Bombay, Madras, and Bengal Presidencies. Many grievances under the East India Company led to the mutiny of 1857. The armies of Bombay and Madras, although not without problems, were little affected by the mutiny. The mutiny was by no means a national uprising. The majority of the Bombay and Madras regiments remained loyal as well as some of the Bengal regiments. A great number of the Indian princes and their forces actively aided in putting down the mutiny. After the upheaval of the mutiny, all military forces in India were transferred to the crown and reorganized. Regiments of Europeans became part of the British Army.

In 1895, the old presidency system was abolished and the entire army was placed under one command. By 1904, all the regiments of cavalry and infantry were renumbered consecutively. The cavalry regiments were numbered 1 to 39, not counting the bodyguards and the Aden Troop, with one vacant number. The infantry regiments were numbered 1 to 130 with 14 vacant numbers. The Brigade of Gurkhas, recruited from the independent Kingdom of Nepal, added another ten rifle regiments of two battalions each. Regiments of infantry in the Indian Army consisted of only one battalion except for the Gurkha regiments and the 39th Garhwal Rifles, which had two battalions.

In addition to the Indian Army that was controlled by the Government of India, smaller armies were maintained by the Indian princes (maharajahs, nizams, etc.), who were independent rulers of the Native Feudatory States. It should be remembered that these states covered almost as large a portion of India as that part under direct British rule. These states were linked to British India by treaty. The Government of India felt that these states should contribute towards the defence of India as a whole. To mark the jubilee of Victoria, the Queen-Empress (1887), a number of these states contributed formations of cavalry, infantry, transport, and, in the case of one state, two batteries of mountain artillery. These formations made up the Imperial Service Troops of the Native States. The Imperial Service Troops were financed by their rulers, while training and equipment were brought up to the standard of the Indian Army.

The Imperial Service Troops were regular units in every sense of the word. They were available for service within or outside of India. In many cases, units were commanded by the rulers themselves or their sons. In some cases, new formations were raised especially for the Imperial Service Troops. Remaining state forces were usually bodyguard formations for ceremonial purposes armed with outdated weapons.

UNIFORMS

The regiments and corps of the Indian Army, the Brigade of Gurkhas, and the units of the Imperial Service Corps are listed on the following pages and illustrated on the color plates. Formations of the Volunteer Forces, the Frontier Militia, and the Indian State forces are listed but not illustrated. The uniforms described and illustrated are that of a *sowar* or *sepoy*, unless otherwise indicated, in *full dress*. *Service dress* was the usual khaki, although some units used khaki with various facing colors as *full dress*. British officers of most cavalry regiments wore Indian *full dress*, including the turban; basically, it was the same uniform as the Indian men but more elaborate. British infantry officers wore a British-style uniform, (scarlet, green, khaki, etc.) with regimental facings. A topi (a light helmet made of pith), either white or khaki, was the usual headdress for infantry officers. Indian officers wore the regimental turban, which was usually more elaborate than those of the other ranks. Both British and Indian officers wore boots rather than the puttees of the other ranks.

STANDARDS AND COLOURS

Indian infantry regiments had King's and Regimental Colours. The ten Gurkha regiments, being *rifles,* did not have colours. The King's Colour was the Union flag and the Regimental Colour conformed to British regulations using the facings colour as the colour of the field. All Indian cavalry were lancers and, therefore, did not have standards or guidons. There were some exceptions; those with honorary standards are noted.

A GLOSSARY OF INDIAN TERMS

Alkhalak: A long coat worn by horsemen with a circular front

Khaki: Originally a Persian word meaning dust or earth; first adopted by certain units of the Indian Army

Kummerband: Waist sash

Kullah: A pointed cap worn by various racial groups of Indians; the turban was tied around the kullah

Kurta: A loose-fitting frock worn by cavalry

Sowar: Cavalry trooper

Sepoy: Infantry soldier

Turban: Many words were used for the Indian soldier's headdress, depending on the style or the way it was tied. The turban was determined by the class or religion of the wearer. In mixed regiments, that is, those regiments having companies of Hindus, Muslims, Sikhs, etc., there would be a uniform turban. Within the same regiment, however, there could be more than one or two ways that it was tied. For the sake of simplicity, the word, turban, will be used in this book.

Note: Indian names were taken from original sources. Contemporary spellings may be different.

BODYGUARDS

THE GOVERNOR GENERAL'S BODYGUARD

In 1914, this bodyguard was stationed at Dehra Dun and comprised two squadrons.

- 1774 Raised as the Governor General's Troop of Bodyguard
- 1781 The Governor General's Bodyguard

BATTLE HONOURS: *Java, Ava, Maharajpore, Ferozeshah, Aliwal, Sobraon*

The uniform included a blue and yellow turban with dark blue and light blue stripes, a scarlet knee-length tunic with double rows of brass buttons and blue facings and piping, a scarlet and gold girdle, and white breeches with black jackboots. This uniform is illustrated by figure 143.

THE GOVERNOR'S BODYGUARD, MADRAS

In 1914, this bodyguard was stationed at Madras and comprised one squadron.

- 1778 Raised with a European troop
- 1781 An Indian troop added
- 1784 The European troop disbanded
- 1820 The bodyguard consisted of details from Madras cavalry regiments
- 1897 Became a separate formation, the Governor's Bodyguard, Madras

BATTLE HONOUR: *Seetabuldee*

The uniform included a blue and yellow turban with red stripes on the yellow part and white stripes on the blue part, a scarlet alkhalak reaching to the knees with yellow piping on the circular front, a blue kummerband with red and yellow stripes on the hanging end, a white belt, white breeches, and black boots. It appears that there was no badge, but the letters G.B.G. were embroidered in gold on the blue shabracque. This uniform is illustrated by figure 144.

THE GOVERNOR'S BODYGUARD, BOMBAY

In 1914, this bodyguard was stationed at Ganeshkhind and comprised one squadron.

- 1865 When the Southern Mahratta Horse was disbanded, a section was retained to provide a bodyguard for the Governor of Bombay.

The uniform included a yellow and purple turban with red stripes on the yellow part, a scarlet kurta worn with a blue panel on the front, a yellow aiguillette worn on the left with the ends hooked in front on the blue panel, a blue kummerband, a white belt, white breeches, and black boots. It appears there was no badge, but the letters B.B.G. with the crown above were embroidered in gold on the blue shabracque. This uniform is illustrated by figure 145.

THE GOVERNOR'S BODYGUARD, BENGAL

In 1914, this bodyguard was stationed at Calcutta and comprised one squadron.

- 1912 Raised at Calcutta from selected volunteers from Indian cavalry regiments

The uniform included a light blue turban with dark blue stripes, a scarlet alkhalak worn reaching to the knees with yellow piping on the circular front, a blue kummerband, a white belt, white breeches, and black boots. It appears that there was no badge. This uniform is illustrated by figure 146.

ESCORT TO THE BRITISH RESIDENT, NEPAL

In 1914, this escort was stationed at Katmandu, Nepal.

1816 Raised as a small infantry escort

1908 A small mounted escort added. The mounted section escorted the British Resident; the infantry section, a company-size unit comprised of Brahmans and Rajputs, provided the guard at the legation and the treasury.

The cavalry uniform included a blue and yellow turban with dark blue and white stripes on the yellow part and white stripes on the dark blue part, a scarlet kurta was worn with blue facings and yellow piping, a scarlet kummerband, white breeches, and blue puttees.

The infantry uniform included the same turban as the cavalry. A long, scarlet collarless tunic was worn with blue facings and piping. There was yellow piping on the cuffs, a blue kummerband, and blue trousers with red piping. It appears that there was no badge. These uniforms are illustrated by figure 147.

CORPS OF GUIDES, CAVALRY AND INFANTRY

QUEEN VICTORIA'S OWN CORPS OF GUIDES (FRONTIER FORCE) (LUMSDEN'S)

GUIDES

In 1914, this corps was stationed at Mardan with a detachment at Abazi. This corps was always stationed on the North-West Frontier of India and was considered an elite unit. The cavalry comprised one squadron of Sikhs, one of Pathans, one half-squadron of Dogras and Punjabi Hindus, and one half-squadron of Punjabi Muslims. The infantry comprised two companies of Sikhs, one of Dogras, one of Gurkhas, two of Pathans, one of Punjabi Muslims, and one mixed company.

1847 Raised as the Corps of Guides by Sir Harry Lumsden (1821-1896)

1857 The Corps of Guides, Punjab Frontier Force

1876 The Queen's Own Corps of Guides, Punjab Frontier Force

1904 The Queen's Own Corps of Guides (Lumsden's)

1911 Queen Victoria's Own Corps of Guides (Frontier Force) (Lumsden's)

BATTLE HONOURS: *Punjab, Mooltan, Goojerat, Delhi, Ali Masjid, Kabul 1879, Afghanistan 1878-80, Chitral, Punjab Frontier, Malakand*

The cavalry uniform included a dark and light blue turban with dark blue stripes on the light blue part and a scarlet kullah. A khaki kurta was worn with scarlet facings and piping, a scarlet kummerband, and khaki breeches with khaki puttees.

The infantry uniform included a khaki turban with a scarlet kullah, a long, khaki collarless tunic with scarlet piping, and khaki trousers with khaki puttees. These uniforms are illustrated by figure 148.

CAVALRY

1ST DUKE OF YORK'S OWN LANCERS (SKINNER'S HORSE)

In 1914, this regiment was stationed at Peshawar. King George V was Colonel-in-Chief. Major General Sir Madho Rao Scindia, Maharaja of Gwalior, was the Honorary Colonel. The regiment comprised four squadrons of Hindustani Muslims.

1803	Raised as Captain James Skinner's (1778-1841) Corps of Irregular Horse
1823	1st Regiment of Local Cavalry
1840	1st Bengal Cavalry
1861	1st Regiment of Bengal Cavalry
1896	1st Regiment of Bengal Lancers
1899	1st (Duke of York's Own) Regiment of Bengal Lancers (Skinner's Horse)
1901	1st (Duke of York's Own) Bengal Lancers (Skinner's Horse)
1903	1st Duke of York's Own Lancers (Skinner's Horse)

BATTLE HONOURS: *Bhurtpore, Kandahar 1842, Afghanistan 1879-80, Pekin 1900*

The uniform included a light blue and yellow turban with yellow stripes on the light blue part and black stripes on the yellow part. A deep yellow kurta was worn with black facings and red piping on the collar, cuffs, and front panel; a black kummerband and white breeches with blue puttees completed the uniform. This uniform is illustrated by figure 149.

2ND LANCERS (GARDNER'S HORSE)

In 1914, this regiment was stationed at Saugor and comprised one squadron of Sikhs, one of Rajputs, one of Jats, and one of Hindustani Muslims.

1809	Raised as Lieutenant Colonel Gardner's Corps of Irregular Horse
1823	2nd Regiment of Local Horse
1840	2nd Bengal Irregular Cavalry
1861	2nd Regiment of Bengal Cavalry
1890	2nd Regiment of Bengal Lancers
1901	2nd Bengal Lancers
1903	2nd Lancers (Gardners's Horse)

BATTLE HONOURS: *Arracan, Sobraon, Punjab, Egypt 1882, Tel el Kebir*

The uniform included a dark blue and light blue-grey turban with dark blue stripes on the lighter part. Officers wore a blue kurta with light blue facings; other ranks wore a blue kurta with no facings or piping. A red kummerband, white breeches, and blue puttees completed the uniform. This uniform is illustrated by figure 150.

3RD SKINNER'S HORSE

In 1914, this regiment was stationed at Meerut and comprised one squadron of Sikhs, one of Jats, one of Rajputs, and one of Mohammedan Rajputs.

1814	Raised as the Second Corps of Skinner's Irregular Horse
1821	Baddeley's Frontier Horse
1823	4th Regiment of Local Horse
1840	4th Bengal Irregular Cavalry
1861	3rd Regiment of Bengal Cavalry
1901	3rd Bengal Cavalry
1903	3rd Skinner's Horse

BATTLE HONOURS: *Afghanistan, Ghuznee 1839, Majarajpore, Khelat, Moodkee, Ferozeshah, Aliwal, Kandahar 1880, Afghanistan 1897-80, Punjab Frontier*

The uniform included a dark and light blue turban with dark blue stripes on the lighter part. Officers wore a blue kurta with yellow facings; other ranks wore a blue kurta with no facings or piping. A red kummerband, white breeches, and blue puttees completed the uniform. The lance pennons were blue over yellow instead of the usual red over white. This uniform is illustrated by figure 151.

4TH CAVALRY

In 1914, this regiment was stationed at Bareilly and comprised one squadron of Sikhs, one of Jats, one of Mohammedan Rajputs, and one of Hindustani Muslims.

1838	Raised as the cavalry regiment of the Oudh Auxiliary Force
1840	6th Regiment of Bengal Irregular Cavalry
1861	4th Regiment of Bengal Cavalry
1900	4th Regiment of Bengal Lancers
1903	4th Lancers
1904	4th Cavalry

BATTLE HONOUR: *Afghanistan 1879-80*

This regiment was granted an honorary standard for service in Sind, 1844. The standard bore the image of a lion.

The uniform included a blue and yellow turban with dark blue and light blue stripes on the yellow part. Officers wore a scarlet kurta with blue facings; other ranks wore a scarlet kurta with blue piping. A blue kummerband, white breeches, and blue puttees completed the uniform. This uniform is illustrated by figure 152.

5TH CAVALRY

In 1914, this regiment was stationed at Rawalpindi and comprised two squadrons of Hindustani Muslims, one of Rajputs, and one of Jats.

1841	Raised as the 7th Regiment of Bengal Irregular Cavalry
1861	5th Regiment of Bengal Cavalry
1901	5th Bengal Cavalry
1903	5th Cavalry

BATTLE HONOURS: *Punjab, Mooltan, Afghanistan 1879-80*

The uniform included a light blue turban with white stripes edged dark blue and a red kullah. Officers wore a scarlet kurta with blue facings; other ranks wore a scarlet kurta with blue piping. A blue kummerband, white breeches, and blue puttees completed the uniform. This uniform is illustrated by figure 153.

6TH KING EDWARD'S OWN CAVALRY

In 1914, this regiment was stationed at Sialkot. King George V was Colonel-in-Chief. This regiment comprised one squadron of Jat Sikhs, one of Sikhs other than Jats, one of Jats, and one of Hindustani Muslims.

1842	Raised as the 8th Regiment of Bengal Irregular Cavalry
1861	6th Regiment of Bengal Cavalry
1883	6th (Prince of Wales's) Regiment of Bengal Cavalry
1901	6th (Prince of Wales's) Bengal Cavalry
1903	6th Prince of Wales's Cavalry
1906	6th King Edward's Own Cavalry

BATTLE HONOURS: *Punniah, Moodkee, Ferozeshah, Sobraon, Egypt 1882, Tel el Kebir, Punjab Frontier*

The uniform included a dark and light blue turban with white stripes on the light blue part, edged in dark blue with a thin dark blue stripe in the middle, and a red kullah. Officers wore a blue kurta with scarlet facings; other ranks wore a blue kurta with scarlet piping. A red kummerband, white breeches, and blue puttees completed the uniform. This uniform is illustrated by figure 154.

7TH HARIANA LANCERS

In 1914, this regiment was stationed at Ferozepore and comprised one squadron of Sikhs, one of Jats, one of Dogras, and one of Hindustani Muslims.

1846	Raised as the 16th Regiment of Bengal Irregular Cavalry
1847	17th Regiment of Bengal Irregular Cavalry
1861	7th Regiment of Bengal Cavalry
1900	7th Regiment of Bengal Lancers
1903	7th Lancers
1904	7th Hariana Lancers

BATTLE HONOURS: *Punjab, Burma 1885-87*

The uniform included a dark and light blue turban with dark blue stripes on the lighter part and a red kullah. Officers wore a scarlet kurta with blue facings; other ranks wore a scarlet kurta with blue piping. A scarlet kummerband, white breeches, and blue puttees completed the uniform. This uniform is illustrated by figure 155.

8TH CAVALRY

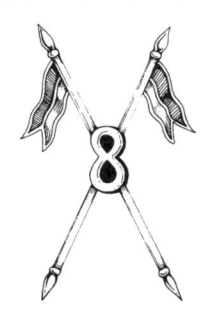

In 1914, this regiment was stationed at Jhansi and comprised two squadrons of Hindustani Muslims, one of Rajputs, and one of Jats.

1846	Raised as the 17th Regiment of Bengal Irregular Cavalry
1847	18th Regiment of Bengal Irregular Cavalry
1861	8th Regiment of Bengal Cavalry
1900	8th Regiment of Bengal Lancers
1903	8th Lancers
1904	8th Cavalry

BATTLE HONOUR: *Afghanistan 1878-80*

The uniform included a dark and light blue turban with dark blue stripes on the lighter part, a red kullah, and a white fringe on the stand-up end of the turban. A blue kurta was worn with a scarlet collar and piping, a scarlet kummerband, white breeches, and blue puttees. This uniform is illustrated by figure 156.

9TH HODSON'S HORSE

In 1914, this regiment was stationed at Ambala and comprised one and one-half squadrons of Sikhs, one-half squadron of Dogras, one and one-half squadrons of Punjabi Muslims, and one half-squadron of Pathans.

1857	Raised as Hodson's Horse by Major William S.R. Hodson (1821-1858)
1858	1st Regiment of Hodson's Horse
1861	9th Regiment of Bengal Cavalry
1886	9th Regiment of Bengal Lancers
1901	9th Bengal Lancers (Hodson's Horse)
1903	9th Hodson's Horse

BATTLE HONOURS: *Delhi, Lucknow, Suakin 1885, Chitral, Punjab Frontier*

The uniform included a blue turban with yellow stripes. Officers wore a blue kurta with white facings; other ranks wore a blue kurta with white piping. A scarlet kummerband, white breeches, and blue puttees completed the uniform. This uniform is illustrated by figure 157.

10TH DUKE OF CAMBRIDGE'S OWN LANCERS (HODSON'S HORSE)

In 1914, this regiment was stationed at Loralai and comprised one squadron of Dogras, one of Punjabi Muslims, one and one-half squadrons of Sikhs, and one-half squadron of Pathans.

1857	Raised as Hodson's Horse by Major William S.R. Hodson (1821-1858)
1858	2nd Regiment of Hodson's Horse
1861	10th Regiment of Bengal Cavalry
1864	10th Regiment of Bengal Cavalry (Lancers)
1874	10th Regiment of Bengal Lancers
1878	10th (Duke of Cambridge's Own) Bengal Lancers
1901	10th (Duke of Cambridge's Own) Bengal Lancers (Hodson's Horse)
1903	10th Duke of Cambridge's Own Lancers (Hodson's Horse)

BATTLE HONOURS: *Delhi, Lucknow, Abyssinia, Afghanistan 1878-80.*

The uniform included a dark and light blue turban with white stripes on the light blue part edged in dark blue with a thin blue stripe in the middle of each white stripe. Officers wore a blue kurta with scarlet facings; other ranks wore a blue kurta with scarlet piping. A scarlet kummerband, white breeches, and blue puttees completed the uniform. The lance pennon was red over blue instead of the usual red over white. This uniform is illustrated by figure 158.

11TH KING EDWARD'S OWN LANCERS (PROBYN'S HORSE)

In 1914, this regiment was stationed at Delhi. King George V was Colonel-in-Chief. This regiment comprised two squadrons of Sikhs, one of Dogras, one-half squadron of Punjabi Muslims, and one-half squadron of Pathans.

1857	Raised as Wales's Horse, later the same year became the 1st Regiment of Sikh Irregular Cavalry
1860	Probyn's Horse
1861	11th Regiment of Bengal Cavalry
1864	11th Regiment of Bengal Cavalry (Lancers)
1874	11th Regiment of Bengal Lancers
1901	11th (The Prince of Wales's Own) Regiment of Bengal Lancers
1903	11th Prince of Wales's Own Lancers
1904	11th Prince of Wales's Own Lancers (Probyn's Horse)
1906	11th King Edward's Own Lancers (Probyn's Horse)

BATTLE HONOURS: *Delhi, Lucknow, Taku Forts, Pekin, Ali Masjid, Afghanistan 1878-79, Chitral, Punjab Frontier, Malakand*

The uniform included a blue and white turban with wide dark blue stripes on the white part. Officers wore a blue kurta with scarlet facings; other ranks wore a blue kurta with no facings or piping. A scarlet kummerband, white breeches, and blue puttees completed the uniform. The lance pennon was red over blue instead of the usual red over white. This uniform is illustrated by figure 159.

12TH CAVALRY

In 1914, this regiment was stationed at Fyzabad and comprised two squadrons of Sikhs, one of Dogras, and one of Punjabi Muslims.

1857	Raised as the 2nd Regiment of Sikh Irregular Cavalry
1861	12th Regiment of Bengal Cavalry
1901	12th Bengal Cavalry
1903	12th Cavalry

BATTLE HONOURS: *Abyssinia, Peiwar, Kotal, Charasiah, Kabul 1879, Afghanistan 1878-80*

The uniform included a blue turban with white stripes. A blue kurta was worn with a low yellow collar and one line of yellow piping down the front of the kurta. There was no piping on the cuffs and no visible buttons on the front of the kurta. The shoulder chains of this regiment were cut square rather than coming to a point. A scarlet kummerband, white breeches, and blue puttees completed the uniform. This uniform is illustrated by figure 160.

13TH DUKE OF CONNAUGHT'S LANCERS (WATSON'S HORSE)

In 1914, this regiment was stationed at Risalpur. Field Marshal Arthur, Duke of Connaught and Strathearn, was Colonel-in-Chief. This regiment comprised two squadrons of Punjabi Muslims, one of Sikhs, and one of Dogras.

1858	Raised as the 4th Regiment of Sikh Irregular Cavalry
1861	13th Regiment of Bengal Cavalry
1864	13th Regiment of Bengal Cavalry (Lancers)
1874	13th Regiment of Bengal Lancers
1884	13th (Duke of Connaught's) Regiment of Bengal Lancers
1901	13th Duke of Connaught's Bengal Lancers
1903	13th Duke of Connaught's Lancers
1904	13th Duke of Connaught's Lancers (Watson's Horse)

BATTLE HONOURS: *Afghanistan 1878-80, Egypt 1882, Tel el Kebir, Punjab Frontier*

The uniform included a blue and yellow turban with white stripes edged red on the yellow part. Officers wore a blue kurta with scarlet facings; other ranks wore a blue kurta with scarlet piping on the front of the kurta but no piping on the cuffs. A scarlet kummerband, khaki breeches, and blue puttees completed the uniform. The lance pennon was red over blue instead of the usual red over white. This uniform illustrated by figure 161.

14TH MURRAY'S JAT LANCERS

In 1914, this regiment was stationed at Risalpur and comprised four squadrons of Jats.

1857	Raised as the Jat Horse Yeomanry
1859	Murray's Jat Horse
1861	14th Regiment of Bengal Cavalry
1864	14th Regiment of Bengal Cavalry (Lancers)
1874	14th Regiment of Bengal Lancers
1901	14th Regiment of Bengal Lancers (Murray's Jat Horse)
1903	14th Murray's Jat Lancers

BATTLE HONOURS: *Charasiah, Kabul 1879, Afghanistan 1878-80*

The uniform included a red turban. A blue kurta was worn with scarlet facings and yellow piping on the collar, the front panel of the kurta, and the cuffs. A scarlet kummerband, white breeches, and blue puttees completed the uniform. This uniform is illustrated by figure 162.

15TH LANCERS (CURETON'S MULTANIS)

In 1914, this regiment was stationed at Jullundur and comprised four squadrons of Muslims (Multani Pathans and Muslims of the Derajat and Cis-Indus).

1858	Raised as the Multani Regiment of Cavalry
1860	Cureton's Multani Regiment of Cavalry
1861	15th Regiment of Bengal Cavalry
1871	15th (Cureton's Multani) Regiment of Bengal Cavalry
1890	15th (Cureton's Multani) Regiment of Bengal Lancers
1901	15th (Cureton's Multani) Bengal Lancers
1903	15th Lancers (Cureton's Multanis)

BATTLE HONOUR: *Afghanistan 1879-80*

The uniform included a blue and white turban with blue stripes in sets of two on the white part. Officers wore a blue kurta with scarlet facings; other ranks wore a blue kurta with no facings or piping. A scarlet kummerband, white breeches, and blue puttees completed the uniform. This uniform is illustrated by figure 163.

16TH CAVALRY

In 1914, this regiment was stationed at Lucknow and comprised two squadrons of Sikhs, one of Dogras, and one of Jats.

1857	Raised as the Rohilkand Horse
1862	16th Bengal Cavalry
1882	Disbanded
1885	Reraised as the 16th Regiment of Bengal Cavalry
1900	16th Regiment of Bengal Lancers
1901	16th Bengal Lancers
1903	16th Cavalry

BATTLE HONOUR: *China 1900*

The uniform included a dark and light blue turban. There were white stripes edged in dark blue with a thin dark blue stripe in the middle of the white stripes, all on the light blue part of the turban. A blue kurta without facings or piping, a scarlet kummerband, white breeches, and blue puttees completed the uniform. This uniform is illustrated by figure 164.

17TH CAVALRY

In 1914, this regiment was stationed at Allahabad and comprised two squadrons of Punjabi Muslims and two squadrons of Pathans.

1857	Raised as the Muttra Horse, later the same year known as the Muttra Police Corps
1858	Rohilkand Auxiliary Police Levy, also known as Robart's Horse
1861	17th Regiment of Bengal Cavalry
1882	Disbanded
1885	Reraised as the 17th Regiment of Bengal Cavalry
1900	17th Regiment of Bengal Lancers
1901	17th Bengal Lancers
1903	17th Cavalry

BATTLE HONOUR: *Afghanistan 1879-80*

The uniform included a light blue and white turban with dark blue stripes in sets of two on the white part and a white kullah. Officers wore a blue kurta with white facings; other ranks wore a blue kurta with no facings or piping. A light blue kummerband, white breeches, and blue puttees completed the uniform. This regiment maintained a mounted pipe band! There were no uniform distinctions for the pipe band. This uniform is illustrated by figure 165.

18TH KING GEORGE'S OWN LANCERS

In 1914, this regiment was stationed at Meerut. King George V was Colonel-in-Chief. This regiment comprised three squadrons of Punjabi Muslims and one squadron of Sikhs.

1858	Raised as the 2nd Regiment of Mahratta Horse
1861	18th Regiment of Bengal Cavalry
1886	18th Regiment of Bengal Lancers
1901	18th Bengal Lancers
1903	18th Tiwana Lancers
1906	18th Prince of Wales's Own Tiwana Lancers
1910	18th King George's Own Lancers

BATTLE HONOURS: *Afghanistan 1878-80, Punjab Frontier, Tirah*

The uniform included a dark blue and white turban with dark blue stripes in sets of twos on the white part. The ends of the turban were white, and the kullah was red. Officers wore a scarlet kurta with white facings; other ranks wore a scarlet kurta with blue piping. A blue kummerband, white breeches, and blue puttees completed the uniform. This uniform is illustrated by figure 166.

19TH LANCERS (FANE'S HORSE)

In 1914, this regiment was stationed at Sialkot and comprised one and one-half squadrons of Sikhs, one half-squadron of Dogras, one squadron of Punjabi Muslims, and one of Pathans.

1860	Raised as Fane's Horse
1861	19th Regiment of Bengal Cavalry
1864	19th Regiment of Bengal Cavalry (Lancers)
1874	19th Regiment of Bengal Lancers
1901	19th Bengal Lancers (Fane's Horse)
1903	19th Lancers (Fanes's Horse)

BATTLE HONOURS: *Taku Forts, Pekin, Ahmed Khel, Afghanistan 1878-80*

The uniform included a dark blue and white turban with dark blue stripes on the white part and a red kullah. Officers wore a blue kurta with French grey facings; other ranks wore a blue kurta with no facings or piping. A scarlet kummerband, white breeches, and light blue puttees completed the uniform. The lance pennon was blue over white instead of the usual red over white. This uniform is illustrated by figure 167.

20TH DECCAN HORSE

In 1914, this regiment was stationed at Bolarum. Colonel Sir Usman Ali Khan, Nizam of Hyderabad, was the Honorary Colonel. This regiment was comprised of one squadron of Sikhs, one of Jats, and two of Dekhani Muslims.

1826	Raised as the 1st Regiment, Nizam of Hyderabad's Cavalry
1854	1st Cavalry, Hyderabad Contingent
1890	1st Lancers, Hyderabad Contingent
1903	20th Deccan Horse

BATTLE HONOUR: *Central India*

The uniform included a rifle green and light blue turban with white and dark blue stripes on the light blue part and a red kullah. Officers wore a rifle green kurta with white facings; other ranks wore a rifle green kurta with no facings or piping. A scarlet kummerband, white breeches, and rifle green puttees completed the uniform. This uniform is illustrated by figure 168.

21ST PRINCE ALBERT VICTOR'S OWN CAVALRY (FRONTIER FORCE) (DALY'S HORSE)

In 1914, this regiment was stationed at Jhelum and comprised one and one-half squadrons of Sikhs, one half-squadron of Dogras, one squadron of Hindustani Muslims, and one of Pathans.

1849	Raised as the 1st Regiment of Punjab Cavalry
1851	1st Regiment of Cavalry, Punjab Irregular Force
1865	1st Regiment of Cavalry, Punjab Frontier Force
1890	1st (Prince Albert Victor's Own) Regiment of Punjab Cavalry
1901	1st (Prince Albert Victor's Own) Punjab Cavalry
1903	21st Prince Albert Victor's Own Cavalry (Frontier Force)
1904	21st Prince Albert Victor's Own Cavalry (Frontier Force) (Daly's Horse)

BATTLE HONOURS: *Delhi, Lucknow, Ahmad Khel, Afghanistan 1878-80*

The uniform included a dark blue and white turban with wide and narrow dark blue stripes on the white part and a red kullah. Officers wore a blue kurta with scarlet facings; other ranks wore a blue kurta with scarlet piping. A scarlet kummerband, khaki breeches, and blue puttees completed the uniform. This uniform is illustrated by figure 169.

22ND SAM BROWNE'S CAVALRY (FRONTIER FORCE)

In 1914, this regiment was stationed at Jacobabad and comprised one and one-half squadrons of Sikhs, one half-squadron of Hindustani Hindus, one squadron of Punjabi Muslims, one half-squadron of Pathans, and one half-squadron of Hindustani Muslims.

1849	Raised as the 2nd Regiment of Punjab Cavalry
1851	2nd Regiment of Cavalry, Punjab Irregular Force
1865	2nd Regiment of Cavalry, Punjab Frontier Force
1901	2nd Punjab Cavalry
1903	22nd Cavalry (Frontier Force)
1904	22nd Sam Browne's Cavalry (Frontier Force)

BATTLE HONOURS: *Delhi, Lucknow, Ahmed Khel, Afghanistan 1878-80*

The uniform included a yellow turban with wide white stripes edged in dark blue with narrow dark blue stripes within the white stripes. Officers wore a scarlet kurta with blue facings; other ranks wore a scarlet kurta with yellow piping on the collar, front panel, and lower edge of the cuffs. A blue kummerband, white breeches, and blue puttees completed the uniform. This uniform is illustrated by figure 170.

23RD CAVALRY (FRONTIER FORCE)

In 1914, this regiment was stationed at Lahore and comprised one and one-half squadrons of Sikhs, one half-squadron of Dogras, one squadron of Hindustani Muslims, one half-squadron of Punjabi Muslims, and one half-squadron of Pathans.

1849	Raised as the 3rd Regiment of Punjab Cavalry
1851	3rd Regiment of Cavalry, Punjab Irregular Force
1865	3rd Regiment of Cavalry, Punjab Frontier Force
1901	3rd Punjab Cavalry
1903	23rd Cavalry (Frontier Force)

BATTLE HONOURS: *Kandahar 1880, Afghanistan 1878-80*

The uniform included a dark blue and white turban with wide and narrow dark blue stripes on the white part and a red kullah. Officers wore a blue kurta with scarlet facings; other ranks wore a blue kurta with scarlet piping. A scarlet kummerband, white breeches, and blue puttees completed the uniform. This uniform is illustrated by figure 171.

24TH Cavalry—Vacant in 1914

25TH CAVALRY (FRONTIER FORCE)

In 1914, this regiment was stationed at Bannu and comprised one squadron of Sikhs, one of Dogras, one of Punjabi Muslims, one half-squadron of Hindustani Muslims and one half-squadron of Pathans.

1849	Raised as the 5th Regiment of Punjab Cavalry
1851	5th Regiment of Cavalry, Punjab Irregular Force
1865	5th Regiment of Cavalry, Punjab Frontier Force
1901	5th Punjab Cavalry
1903	25th Cavalry (Frontier Force)

BATTLE HONOURS: *Delhi, Lucknow, Charasiah, Kabul 1879, Afghanistan 1878-80*

The uniform included a red turban with black stripes. Regulations record the kurta as very dark green; in fact, it was black. Officers wore red facings on the kurta; other ranks wore a red collar, a red panel on the front of the kurta, and red piping on the cuffs. A red kummerband, white breeches, and blue puttees completed the uniform. This uniform is illustrated by figure 172.

26TH KING GEORGE'S OWN LIGHT CAVALRY

In 1914, this regiment was stationed at Bangalore. King George V was Colonel-in-Chief. Sir Sri Krishnaraja Wadia, Maharaja of Mysore, was the Honorary Colonel. The regiment comprised one squadron of Madras and Dekhani Muslims, one of Punjabi Muslims, one of Rajputana Rajputs, and one of Jats.

1787	Raised as the 5th Regiment of Madras Native Cavalry
1788	1st Regiment of Madras Native Cavalry
1819	1st Regiment of Madras Light Cavalry
1886	1st Regiment of Madras Lancers
1901	1st Madras Lancers
1903	26th Light Cavalry
1906	26th Prince of Wales's Own Light Cavalry
1910	26th King George's Own Light Cavalry

BATTLE HONOURS: *Mysore, Seringapatam, Ava, Central India, Afghanistan 1879-80*

The uniform included a blue turban with red, white, and yellow stripes and a red and white fringe at the end of the turban. Officers wore a French grey, single-breasted kurta with buff facings; other ranks wore a French grey single-breasted kurta with no facings or piping. A scarlet kummerband, blue breeches with French grey stripes, and blue puttees completed the uniform. This uniform is illustrated by figure 173.

27TH LIGHT CAVALRY

In 1914, this regiment was stationed at Neemuch with detachments at Nasirabad, Jaipur and Baroda. The regiment comprised one squadron of Madras and Dekhani Muslims, one of Punjabi Muslims, one of Rathore Rajputs, and one of Jats.

?	Date of this regiment's raising is unknown. Before being received into the service of the East India Company in 1784, it was known to have been in the service of the Nawab of Arcot prior to 1780.
1784	3rd Regiment of Madras Native Cavalry; regiment number changed to 1st in the same year
1786	4th Regiment of Madras Native Cavalry
1788	2nd Regiment of Madras Native Cavalry
1819	2nd Regiment of Light Cavalry
1886	2nd Regiment of Madras Lancers
1901	2nd Madras Lancers
1903	27th Light Cavalry

BATTLE HONOURS: *Sholinghur, Carnatic, Mysore, Seringapatam, Burma 1885-87*

The uniform included a dark blue and light blue turban with dark blue and white stripes on the light blue part. Officers wore a French grey, single-breasted kurta with buff facings; other ranks wore a French grey single-breasted kurta with no facings or piping. A blue kummerband, blue breeches with French grey stripes, and blue puttees completed the uniform. This uniform is illustrated by figure 174.

28TH LIGHT CAVALRY

In 1914, this regiment was stationed at Quetta and comprised one squadron of Madras and Dekhani Muslims, one of Punjabi Muslims, one of Rajputana Rajputs, and one of Jats.

1784	Raised as the 2nd Regiment of Madras Native Cavalry
1786	1st Regiment of Madras Native Cavalry
1788	3rd Regiment of Madras Native Cavalry
1819	3rd Regiment of Madras Light Cavalry
1891	3rd Regiment of Madras Lancers
1901	3rd Madras Lancers
1903	28th Light Cavalry

BATTLE HONOURS: *Mysore, Seringapatam, Mahidpore*

The uniform included a dark blue and white turban with dark blue stripes on the white part and a red kullah. Officers wore a French grey, single-breasted kurta with buff facings; other ranks wore a French grey single-breasted kurta with no facings or piping. A blue kummerband, blue breeches with French grey stripes, and blue puttees completed the uniform. This uniform is illustrated by figure 175.

29TH LANCERS (DECCAN HORSE)

In 1914, this regiment was stationed at Poona and comprised two squadrons of Jats, one of Sikhs, and one of Dekhani Muslims.

1826	Raised as the 2nd Regiment, Nizam of Hyderabad's Cavalry
1854	2nd Cavalry, Hyderabad Contingent
1890	2nd Lancers, Hyderabad Contingent
1903	29th Lancers (Deccan Horse)

BATTLE HONOUR: *Poona*

The uniform included a rifle green and light blue turban with white and dark blue stripes on the light blue part and a white kullah. Officers wore a rifle green kurta with white facings; other ranks wore a rifle green kurta with no facings or piping. A scarlet kummerband, white breeches, and rifle green puttees completed the uniform. This uniform is illustrated by figure 176.

30TH LANCERS (GORDON'S HORSE)

In 1914, this regiment was stationed at Ambala and comprised two squadrons of Sikhs, one of Jats, and one of Hindustani Muslims.

1826	Raised as the 4th Regiment, Nizam of Hyderabad's Cavalry
1854	4th Cavalry, Hyderabad Contingent
1890	4th Lancers, Hyderabad Contingent
1903	30th Lancers (Gordon's Horse)

BATTLE HONOUR: *Central India*

The uniform included a rifle green and light blue turban with white and dark blue stripes on the light blue part and a white kullah. Officers wore a rifle green kurta with white facings; other ranks wore a rifle green kurta with no facings or piping. A scarlet kummerband, white breeches, and rifle green puttees completed the uniform. This uniform is illustrated by figure 177.

31ST DUKE OF CONNAUGHT'S OWN LANCERS

In 1914, this regiment was stationed at Kohat. Field Marshal Arthur, Duke of Connaught and Strathearn, was Colonel-in-Chief. The regiment comprised one squadron of Dekhani Mahrattas, one of Jats, one of Sikhs, and one of Pathans.

1817	Raised as the 1st Regiment of Bombay Light Cavalry
1842	1st Regiment of Bombay Light Cavalry (Lancers)
1862	1st Regiment of Bombay Light Cavalry
1880	1st Bombay Lancers
1890	1st (Duke of Connaught's Own) Bombay Lancers
1903	31st Duke of Connaught's Own Lancers

BATTLE HONOURS: *Afghanistan, Ghuznee 1839, Punjab, Mooltan, Central India, Burma 1885-87*

The uniform included a dark blue and light blue turban with white stripes edged in dark blue on the light blue part. Officers wore a blue kurta with scarlet facings; other ranks wore a blue kurta with scarlet piping. A scarlet kummerband, white breeches, and blue puttees completed the uniform. This uniform is illustrated by figure 178.

32ND LANCERS

In 1914, this regiment was stationed at Jubbulpore and comprised two squadrons of Mohammedan Rajputs, one of Rajputs, and one of Sikhs.

1817	Raised as the 2nd Regiment of Bombay Light Cavalry
1883	2nd Bombay Lancers
1903	32nd Lancers

BATTLE HONOURS: *Central India, Afghanistan 1879-80*

The uniform included a blue and yellow turban with blue stripes edged red on the yellow part and a red kullah. Officers wore a blue kurta with white facings; other ranks wore a blue kurta with no facings or piping. A scarlet kummerband, white breeches, and blue puttees completed the uniform. This uniform is illustrated by figure 179.

33RD QUEEN VICTORIA'S OWN LIGHT CAVALRY

In 1914, this regiment was stationed at Aurangabad and comprised one squadron of Sikhs, one of Jats, one of Kaimkhanis, and one of Mohammedan Rajputs.

1820	Raised as the 3rd Regiment of Bombay Light Cavalry
1875	3rd (The Queen's Own) Regiment of Bombay Light Cavalry
1901	3rd (Queen's Own) Bombay Light Cavalry
1903	33rd Queen's Own Light Cavalry
1911	33rd Queen Victoria's Own Light Cavalry

BATTLE HONOURS: *Ghuznee 1842, Cabul 1842, Hyderabad, Persia, Reshire, Bushire, Koosh-ab, Central India, Abyssinia, Kandahar 1880, Afghanistan 1879-80, China 1900*

The uniform included a dark blue and red turban with white stripes edged in dark blue on the red part and a red kullah. A blue kurta was worn with scarlet collar and cuffs. There was scarlet piping on the front panel and yellow piping on the collar and cuffs. Scarlet padding under the shoulder chains, a scarlet kummerband, white breeches, and blue puttees completed the uniform. This uniform is illustrated by figure 180.

34TH PRINCE ALBERT VICTOR'S OWN POONA HORSE

In 1914, this regiment was stationed at Secunderabad. Major General Sir Pratap Singh, Maharaja of Idar and Regent of Jodhpur, was the Honorary Colonel. The regiment comprised two squadrons of Rathore Rajputs, one of Kaimkhanis, and one of Punjabi Muslims.

1817	Raised as the Auxiliary Horse
1818	Poona Auxiliary Horse
1847	Poona Irregular Horse
1861	1st Regiment Poona Horse
1862	The Poona Horse
1885	4th Bombay Cavalry (Poona Horse)
1890	4th (Prince Albert Victor's Own) Bombay Cavalry (Poona Horse)
1903	34th Prince Albert Victor's Own Poona Horse

BATTLE HONOURS: *Corygaum, Ghuznee 1839, Afghanistan, Kandahar 1842, Meeanee, Hyderabad, Persia, Reshire, Koosh-ab, Kandahar 1880, Afghanistan 1879-80*

This regiment also carried a standard captured at the Battle of Koosh-ab in 1857. The standard bore a Persian inscription and the staff was surmounted by a silver hand.

The uniform included a dark and light blue turban with white and dark blue stripes on the light blue part and a red kullah. Officers wore a blue kurta with French grey facings; other ranks wore a blue kurta with French grey piping. A scarlet kummerband, white breeches, and blue puttees completed the uniform. This uniform is illustrated by figure 181.

35TH SCINDE HORSE

In 1914, this regiment was stationed at Dera Ismail Khan and comprised two squadrons of Derajat Muslims, one of Pathans, and one of Sikhs.

1839	Raised as the Scinde Irregular Horse
1860	1st Regiment, Scinde Horse
1885	5th Bombay Cavalry (Jacob-ka-Rissallah)
1888	5th Bombay Cavalry (Scinde Horse)
1903	35th Scinde Horse

BATTLE HONOURS: *Cutchee, Meeanee, Hyderabad, Punjab, Mooltan, Goojerat, Persia, Central India, Afghanistan 1878-79*

This regiment was granted an honorary standard for service in Sind, 1843. The standard bore the device of a native horseman with a lance. The regiment also carried a standard captured at *Meeanee*. The staff was surmounted by an open hand.

The uniform included red kullah and a dark and light blue turban with dark blue stripes and yellow stripes edged in dark blue, all on the light blue part. Officers wore a blue kurta with white facings; other ranks wore a blue kurta with no facings or piping. Scarlet padding under the shoulder chains, a scarlet kummerband, white breeches, and blue puttees completed the uniform. This uniform is illustrated by figure 182.

36TH JACOB'S HORSE

In 1914, this regiment was stationed at Cawnpore and comprised two squadrons of Derajat Muslims and Baluchis, one of Pathans, and one of Sikhs.

1846	Raised as the 2nd Regiment, Scinde Irregular Horse
1860	2nd Regiment of Scinde Horse
1885	6th Bombay Cavalry. (Jacob-ka-Rissallah)

1888   6th Bombay Cavalry (Jacob's Horse)
1903   36th Jacob's Horse

BATTLE HONOURS: *Cutchee, Meeanee, Hyderabad, Punjab, Mooltan, Goojerat, Afghanistan 1879-80*

This regiment was granted an honorary standard for service in Sind, 1843. This standard bore the device of a native horseman with a lance.

The uniform included a red kullah and a blue, white, and yellow turban with blue stripes within the white part and red stripes within the yellow part. Officers wore a blue kurta with primrose yellow facings; other ranks wore a blue kurta with no facings or piping. A scarlet kummerband, white breeches, and blue puttees completed the uniform. This uniform is illustrated by figure 183.

37TH LANCERS (BALUCH HORSE)

In 1914, this regiment was stationed at Multan and comprised two squadrons of Derajat Muslims and Baluchis, one of Pathans, and one of Sikhs.

1885   Raised as the 7th Bombay Cavalry (Jacob-ka-Rissallah)
1886   7th Bombay Cavalry (Baluch Horse)
1890   7th Bombay Lancers (Baluch Horse)
1903   37th Lancers (Baluch Horse)

The uniform included a khaki turban with white stripes edged dark blue and a khaki kullah. Officers wore a khaki kurta with a salmon shade of buff facings; other ranks wore a khaki kurta with no facings or piping. A scarlet kummerband, blue padding under the shoulder chains, khaki breeches, and khaki puttees completed the uniform. When not on parade with their men, officers wore a blue kurta with salmon buff facings. This uniform is illustrated by figure 184.

38TH KING GEORGE'S OWN CENTRAL INDIA HORSE

In 1914, this regiment was stationed at Guna. King George V was Colonel-in-Chief. This regiment comprised two squadrons of Sikhs, one of Pathans, and one of Mohammedan Rajputs.

1858   Raised as Mayne's Horse
1860   1st Regiment of Central India Horse
1903   38th Central India Horse
1906   38th Prince of Wales's Own Central India Horse
1910   38th King George's Own Central India Horse

BATTLE HONOURS: *Kandahar 1880, Afghanistan 1879-80, Punjab Frontier 1897-98*

The uniform included a dark and light blue turban with white stripes edged in dark blue on the light blue part and a red kullah. Officers wore a khaki kurta with maroon facings; other ranks wore a khaki kurta with red piping. A red kummerband, red padding under the shoulder chains, white breeches, and blue puttees completed the uniform. This uniform is illustrated by figure 185.

39TH KING GEORGE'S OWN CENTRAL INDIA HORSE

In 1914, this regiment was stationed at Agar. King George V was Colonel-in-Chief. This regiment comprised two squadrons of Sikhs, one of Punjabi Muslims, and one of Mohammedan Rajputs.

1858   Raised as Beatson's Horse
1860   2nd Regiment of Mayne's Horse, renamed in the same year; 2nd Regiment of Central India Horse

1903 39th Central India Horse
1905 39th Prince of Wales's Own Central India Horse
1910 39th King George's Own Central India Horse

BATTLE HONOURS: *Kandahar 1880, Afghanistan 1879-80, Punjab Frontier 1897-98*

The uniform and badges were the same as the 38th King George's Own Central India Horse. This uniform is illustrated by figure 186.

ADEN TROOP

In 1914, the Aden Troop provided the cavalry arm for the Aden Brigade of British and Indian troops stationed at Aden. The troop numbered around 100 of all ranks. At the time, Aden was administered as part of India under the Governor of Bombay.

1855 A troop of cavalry raised for service in Aden, formed with volunteers from the Scinde Horse

1867 The troop was reformed with volunteers from the Poona Horse and the 1st and 2nd Scinde Horse

The uniform included a khaki turban, kurta, kummerband, and breeches with khaki puttees. Research has failed to uncover any record of a badge for this formation. This uniform is illustrated by figure 187.

ARTILLERY

THE ROYAL REGIMENT OF ARTILLERY, IN INDIA

The Royal Artillery maintained a number of field and mountain batteries in India. There were garrison artillery companies at defended ports. The officers and men of these artillery formations were British, although some field batteries had Indian drivers.

In addition, there were batteries of Indian Mountain Artillery and the Frontier Garrison Artillery. These batteries had British officers. The composition of each battery was one-half Punjabi Muslims and one-half Sikhs and other Hindus. The Indian Mountain batteries were armed with the light 10-pounder, breech-loading, quick-firing guns that could be broken down and transported on the backs of mules. The Frontier Garrison Artillery manned the guns at various forts along the northwest frontier of India.

The batteries of the Indian Mountain Artillery received battle honours, unlike their British counterparts.

INDIAN MOUNTAIN ARTILLERY

21st KOHAT MOUNTAIN BATTERY (FRONTIER FORCE)

This battery was raised in 1851. In 1914, it was stationed at Dehra Dun.

BATTLE HONOURS: *Peiwar Kotal, Kabul 1879, Afghanistan 1887-80, Punjab Frontier, Tirah*

22ND DERAJAT MOUNTAIN BATTERY (FRONTIER FORCE)

This battery was raised in 1849. In 1914, it was stationed at Maymyo, Burma.

BATTLE HONOURS: *Charasiah, Kabul 1879, Kandahar 1880, Afghanistan 1878-80, Chitral, Punjab Frontier, Tirah*

23RD PESHAWAR MOUNTAIN BATTERY (FRONTIER FORCE)

This battery was raised in 1853. In 1914, it was stationed at Abbotabad.

BATTLE HONOUR: *Afghanistan 1878-79*

24TH HAZARA MOUNTAIN BATTERY (FRONTIER FORCE)

This battery was raised in 1851. In 1914, it was stationed at Hong Kong.
BATTLE HONOURS: *Ali Masjid, Kabul 1879, Afghanistan 1878-80, Burma 1885-87, Chitral*

25TH MOUNTAIN BATTERY (FRONTIER FORCE)

This battery was raised in 1827. In 1914, it was stationed at Nowshera.
BATTLE HONOURS: *Punjaub, Mooltan, Abyssinia, Burma 1885-87, Punjab Frontier, Tirah*

26TH JACOB'S MOUNTAIN BATTERY

This battery was raised in 1843. In 1914, it was stationed at Dehra Dun.
BATTLE HONOUR: *Afghanistan 1878-80*

27TH MOUNTAIN BATTERY

This battery was raised in 1886. In 1914, it was stationed at Abbottabad.
BATTLE HONOUR: *Burma 1885-87*

28TH MOUNTAIN BATTERY

This battery was raised in 1886. In 1914, it was stationed at Abbottabad.
BATTLE HONOURS: *Burma 1885-87, Punjab Frontier, Malakand*

29TH MOUNTAIN BATTERY

This battery was raised in 1898. In 1914, it was stationed at Bannu.

30TH MOUNTAIN BATTERY

This battery was raised in 1900. In 1914, it was stationed at Abbottabad.

31ST MOUNTAIN BATTERY

This battery was raised in 1907. In 1914, it was stationed at Kohat.

32ND MOUNTAIN BATTERY

This battery was raised in 1907. In 1914, it was stationed at Dera Ismail Khan.

THE FRONTIER GARRISON ARTILLERY

This formation was raised in 1851 as a garrison company from a Sikh detachment of artillery. In 1914, headquarters was at Kohat with detachments at Malakand, Chakdara, Peshawar, Jamrud, Samana, Fort Lockhart and Bannu.

UNIFORM

The Indian Mountain Batteries and the Frontier Garrison Artillery were uniformed alike. The uniform included a red turban, except for the 21st Kohat Battery (Frontier Force) who wore a khaki turban. A blue tunic was worn with red tabs on the collar, brown leather belts, blue trousers with wide red stripes, and blue puttees completed the uniform. This uniform, together with the mules and gun of a 10-pounder mountain battery, is illustrated by figure 188.

HEAVY BATTERIES, ROYAL GARRISON ARTILLERY (INDIA)

The heavy batteries of the Royal Garrison Artillery in India consisted of 40-pounder guns and 5-inch howitzers. The guns with their limbers were pulled by elephants as illustrated. Alternately the guns could be disassembled and packed on the elephant's backs when passing through rough country. The officers and men of the battery were British; the mahouts (elephant drivers and keepers) were Indian. An illustration of the early 1900s shows the mahouts dressed in khaki with red turbans and kummerbands. The mahout's uniform is illustrated by figure 189.

SAPPERS AND MINERS

1ST KING GEORGE'S OWN SAPPERS AND MINERS

In 1914, this corps was headquartered at Rurki. It consisted of six field companies, a depot company with a mounted detachment, two electric lights sections, a printing section, and a photo-litho section. King George V was Colonel-in-Chief. The Corps of Royal Engineers furnished the Officers for this corps. This corps comprised Sikhs, Hindustanis, Punjabi Muslims, and Pathans.

1803	Raised as the Bengal Pioneers
1819	The Corps of Bengal Sappers and Miners
1903	1st Sappers and Miners
1906	1st Prince of Wales's Own Sappers and Miners
1910	1st King George's Own Sappers and Miners

BATTLE HONOURS: *Bhurtpore, Cabool 1842, Ferozeshah, Sobraon, Punjab, Mooltan, Goojerat, Delhi, Lucknow, Ali Masjid, Charasiah, Kabul 1879, Ahmad Kheyl, Afghanistan 1878-80, Burma 1885-87, Chitral, Punjab Frontier, Tirah, China 1900*

The uniform included a blue turban with a red end and yellow fringe. The scarlet tunic had blue facings and piping with yellow piping on the cuffs. The blue trousers had wide scarlet stripes, and the puttees were blue. Mounted personnel wore blue breeches with wide scarlet stripes. This uniform is illustrated by figure 190.

2ND QUEEN VICTORIA'S OWN SAPPERS AND MINERS

In 1914, this corps was headquartered at Bangalore. It comprised seven field companies, a depot company including printing and photo-litho sections, and an electric lights section stationed at Rangoon, Burma. The Corps of Royal Engineers furnished the officers for this corps. This corps was mixed; it comprised Madrasis of all classes.

1780	Two companies of pioneers raised at Madras
1793	The Madras Pioneer Battalion
1803	1st and 2nd Battalions of Madras Pioneers
1831	The Corps of Madras Sappers and Miners
1876	Queen's Own Corps of Madras Sappers and Miners
1903	2nd Queen's Own Sappers and Miners
1911	2nd Queen Victoria's Own Sappers and Miners

BATTLE HONOURS: *Egypt (with the Sphinx), Carnatic, Sholinghur, Mysore, Seringapatam, Assaye, Java, Nagpore, Maheidpoor, Ava, Meeanee, Hyderabad, Pegu, Persia, Lucknow, Central India, Taku Forts, Pekin, Abyssinia, Afghanistan 1878-80, Egypt 1882, Tel el Kebir, Suakin 1885, Tofrek, Burma 1885-87, Chitral, Punjab Frontier, Malakand, Tirah, China 1900*

This corps had a very distinctive headdress: a blue fez with a narrow red turban at the base. Indian officers wore a turban with alternating gold and blue stripes. The scarlet tunic had blue facings with yellow piping on the cuffs. The blue trousers had wide red stripes, and there were blue puttees. This uniform is illustrated by figure 191.

3RD SAPPERS AND MINERS

In 1914, this corps was headquartered at Kirkee. It comprised six field companies, a fortress company at Aden including an electric lights section, a depot company including printing and photo-litho sections, two railway companies, two signal companies, and a wireless company. The Corps of Royal Engineers furnished the officers for this corps. Half of this corps were Muslims; one-fourth were Mahrattas, and one-fourth were Sikhs.

1820	Raised as a company and known as the Bombay Sappers and Miners
1829	Referred to as *Engineers*
1840	Bombay Sappers and Miners
1903	3rd Sappers and Miners

BATTLE HONOURS: *Beni Boo Ali, Ghuznee 1839, Afghanistan, Khelat, Punjab, Mooltan, Goojerat, Persia, Reshire, Bushire, Koosh-ab, Central India, Abyssinia, Kandahar 1880, Afghanistan 1878-80, Burma 1885-87, Punjab Frontier, Tirah, China 1900*

The uniform included a khaki turban with red stripes in sets of twos and a red kullah. The scarlet tunic had blue facings with yellow piping on the cuffs. The blue trousers had wide red stripes, and there were blue puttees. This uniform is illustrated by figure 192.

INFANTRY

1ST BRAHMANS

In 1914, this regiment was stationed at Trimulgherry and comprised eight companies of Brahmans.

1776	Raised as part of a force in service of the Nawab Wazir
1777	Entered the East India Company's service as the 30th Battalion, Bengal Native Infantry
1857	21st Bengal Native Infantry
1861	1st Regiment of Bengal Native Infantry
1901	1st Brahman Infantry
1903	1st Brahmans

BATTLE HONOURS: *Laswaree, Bhurtpore, Burma 1885-87*

The uniform included a khaki turban with a red fringe, a scarlet tunic with white facings, blue trousers with red piping, and blue puttees. This uniform is illustrated by figure 193.

2ND QUEEN VICTORIA'S OWN RAJPUT LIGHT INFANTRY

In 1914, this regiment was stationed at Bombay and comprised eight companies of Rajputs.

1798	Raised as the 2nd Battalion, 15th Regiment, Bengal Native Infantry
1857	31st Light Infantry, Bengal Native Infantry
1861	2nd Bengal Light Infantry
1876	2nd (The Queen's Own) Bengal Native Light Infantry
1897	2nd (Queen's Own) Rajput Bengal Light Native Infantry
1901	2nd (Queen's Own) Rajput Light Infantry
1911	2nd Queen Victoria's Own Rajput Light Infantry

BATTLE HONOURS: *Delhi, Laswaree, Deig, Bhurtpore, Khelet, Afghanistan, Maharajpore, Punjab, Chillianwallah, Goojerat, Central India, Afghanistan 1879-80, Burma 1885-87, China 1900*

This regiment carried a third or honorary colour granted in 1803 for distinguished service.

The uniform included a blue turban with a red fringe, a long-skirted scarlet tunic with black facings, a black kummerband, blue trousers with red piping, and white gaiters. This uniform is illustrated by figure 194.

3RD BRAHMANS

In 1914, this regiment was stationed at Nowgong and comprised eight companies of Brahmans.

1798	Raised as the 1st Battalion, 16th Regiment, Bengal Native Infantry
1824	32nd Regiment of Bengal Native Infantry
1861	3rd Regiment of Bengal Native Infantry
1885	3rd Regiment of Bengal Infantry
1901	3rd Brahman Infantry
1903	3rd Brahmans

BATTLE HONOURS: *Bhurtpore, Afghanistan 1879-80*

The uniform included a yellow turban with white stripes edged in maroon. The scarlet tunic had black facings, blue trousers with red piping, and blue puttees. This uniform is illustrated by figure 195.

4TH PRINCE ALBERT VICTOR'S OWN RAJPUTS

In 1914, this regiment was stationed at Multan and comprised eight companies of Rajputs.

1798	Raised as the 2nd Battalion, 16th Regiment, Bengal Native Infantry
1824	33rd Regiment of Bengal Native Infantry
1861	4th Regiment of Bengal Native Infantry
1890	4th (Prince Albert Victor's) Bengal Infantry
1897	4th (Prince Albert Victor's) Rajput Regiment, Bengal Infantry
1901	4th (Prince Albert Victor's) Rajput Infantry
1903	4th Prince Albert Victor's Rajputs

BATTLE HONOURS: *Laswaree, Bhurtpore, Cabul 1842, Ferozeshah, Sobraon, Afghanistan 1878-80, Burma 1885-87*

The uniform included a blue turban, a long-skirted scarlet tunic with black facings, a black kummerband, blue trousers with red piping, and white gaiters. This uniform is illustrated by figure 196.

5TH LIGHT INFANTRY

In 1914, this regiment was stationed at Singapore and comprised eight companies of Muslims of the Eastern Punjab and Hindustan.

1803	Raised as the 2nd Battalion, 21st Regiment, Bengal Native Infantry
1824	42nd Regiment of Bengal Native Infantry
1842	42nd Regiment of Bengal Native (Light) Infantry
1861	5th Regiment of Bengal Native (Light) Infantry
1885	5th Regiment of Bengal (Light) Infantry
1903	5th Light Infantry

BATTLE HONOURS: *Arracan, Afghanistan, Kandahar, Ghuznee, Cabul 1842, Moodkee, Ferozeshah, Sobraon, Afghanistan 1878-80, Burma 1885-87*

The uniform included a blue turban, a long-skirted scarlet tunic with yellow facings, a yellow kummerband, blue trousers with red piping, and white gaiters. This uniform is illustrated by figure 197.

6TH JAT LIGHT INFANTRY

In 1914, this regiment was stationed at Secunderbad and comprised eight companies of Jats.

1803	Raised as the 1st Battalion, 22nd Regiment, Bengal Native Infantry
1824	43rd Regiment of Bengal Native Infantry
1842	43rd Regiment of Bengal Native (Light) Infantry
1861	6th Regiment of Bengal Native (Light) Infantry
1897	6th (Jat) Regiment of Bengal (Light) Infantry
1901	6th Jat Light Infantry

BATTLE HONOURS: *Nagpore, Afghanistan, Kandahar 1842, Ghuznee, Cabul 1842, Maharapore, Sobraon, Ali Masjid, Afghanistan 1878-80, China 1900*

The uniform included a blue turban with a red kullah, a scarlet tunic with white facings, blue trousers with red piping, and blue puttees. This uniform is illustrated by figure 198.

7TH DUKE OF CONNAUGHT'S OWN RAJPUTS

In 1914, this regiment was stationed at Ahmedabad. Field Marshal Arthur, Duke of Connaught and Strathearn, was Colonel-in-Chief. The regiment comprised eight companies of Rajputs.

1804	Raised as the 1st Battalion, 24th Native Infantry
1824	47th Native Infantry. Disbanded. Reraised in the same year as the 69th Native Infantry
1828	Restored as 47th Native Infantry
1861	7th Regiment of Bengal Native Infantry
1883	7th (Duke of Connaught's Own) Bengal Native Infantry
1893	7th (Duke of Connaught's Own) Rajput Regiment of Bengal Native Infantry
1903	7th Duke of Connaught's Own Rajputs

BATTLE HONOURS: *Moodkee, Ferozeshah, Aliwal, Sobraon, China 1858-59, Egypt 1882, Tel el Kebir, Pekin 1900*

The uniform included a blue turban with a red fringe and a red kullah, a long-skirted scarlet tunic with yellow facings, a yellow kummerband, blue trousers with red piping, and white gaiters. This uniform is illustrated by figure 199.

8TH RAJPUTS

In 1914, this regiment was stationed at Jubbulpore and comprised eight companies of Rajputs.

1814	Raised as the 1st Battalion, 30th Regiment, Bengal Native Infantry
1824	59th Regiment of Bengal Native Infantry
1861	8th Regiment of Bengal Native Infantry
1897	8th (Rajput) Regiment of Bengal Infantry
1901	8th Rajput Infantry
1903	8th Rajputs

BATTLE HONOURS: *Sobraon, Afghanistan*

The uniform included a dark blue and light blue turban with white and dark blue stripes, a long-skirted scarlet tunic with yellow facings, a yellow kummerband, blue trousers with red piping, and white gaiters. This uniform is illustrated by figure 200.

9TH BHOPAL INFANTRY

In 1914, this regiment was stationed at Fyzabad and comprised two companies of Sikhs, two of Rajputs, two of Brahmans, and two of Muslims.

1859   Raised as the Bhopal Levy
1865   The Bhopal Battalion
1903   9th Bhopal Infantry

BATTLE HONOUR: *Afghanistan 1878-80*

The uniform included a khaki turban with a chocolate brown fringe, a khaki tunic with chocolate brown facings, khaki trousers, and khaki puttees. This uniform is illustrated by figure 201.

10TH JATS

In 1914, this regiment was stationed at Jhansi and comprised eight companies of Jats.

1823   Raised as the 1st Battalion, 33rd Regiment, Bengal Native Infantry
1824   65th Regiment of Bengal Native Infantry
1861   10th Regiment of Bengal Native Infantry
1885   10th Regiment of Bengal Infantry
1897   10th (Jat) Regiment, Bengal Infantry
1901   10th Jat Infantry
1903   10th Jats

BATTLE HONOURS: *China 1858-59, Burma 1885-87*

The uniform included a blue turban with a yellow kullah, a scarlet tunic with yellow facings, blue trousers with red piping, and blue puttees. This uniform is illustrated by figure 202.

11TH RAJPUTS

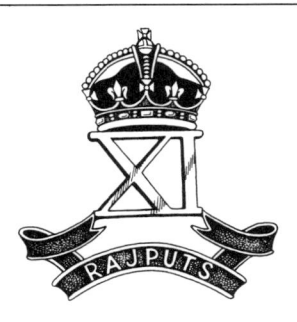

In 1914, this regiment was stationed at Dacca and comprised eight companies of Rajputs.

1825   Raised as the 2nd Extra Regiment, Bengal Native Infantry
1828   70th Regiment of Bengal Native Infantry
1861   11th Regiment of Bengal Native Infantry
1885   11th Regiment of Bengal Infantry
1897   11th (Rajput) Regiment of Bengal Infantry
1901   11th Rajput Infantry
1903   11th Rajputs

BATTLE HONOURS: *Punjab, Chillianwallah, Goojerat, China 1858-59, Afghanistan 1878-80, Burma 1885-87*

The uniform included a dark blue and light blue turban with white and dark blue stripes on the light blue part, a long-skirted scarlet tunic with yellow facings, a yellow kummerband, blue trousers with red piping, and white gaiters. This uniform is illustrated by figure 203.

12TH PIONEERS (KHELAT-I-GHILZIE REGIMENT)

In 1914, this regiment was stationed at Quetta and comprised four companies of Jats and four of Lobana Sikhs.

1838   Raised as the 3rd Regiment of Infantry, Shah Shujah's Force
1842   The Regiment of Khelat-i-Ghilzie
1861   12th Regiment of Bengal Native Infantry
1864   12th (Khelat-i-Ghilzie) Regiment of Bengal Native Infantry
1903   12th Pioneers (Khelat-i-Ghilzie Regiment)

BATTLE HONOURS: *Khelat-i-Ghilzie, Kandahar, Ghuznee, Cabul 1842, Maharajpore, Afghanistan 1878-80, Burma 1885-87, Punjab Frontier*

This regiment carried a unique regimental colour of red, yellow, and blue.

The uniform included a dark blue and light blue turban with white stripes edged in dark blue on the light blue part, a long-skirted scarlet tunic with black facings, a black kummerband, blue trousers with red piping, and blue puttees. Leather belts crossed in the back supported the pioneer equipment, including a shovel, ax, or pickax. This uniform is illustrated by figure 204.

13TH RAJPUTS (THE SHEKHAWATI REGIMENT)

In 1914, this regiment was stationed at Agra. Major General Sir Sawai Madho Singh, Maharaja of Jaipur, was the Honorary Colonel. The regiment comprised eight companies of Rajputana Rajputs.

1835	Raised as the Infantry of the Shekhawati Brigade
1847	The Shekhawati Battalion
1861	13th Regiment of Bengal Native Infantry
1884	13th (Shekhawati) Regiment of Bengal Native Infantry
1897	13th (Shekhawati) Rajput Regiment of Bengal Infantry
1901	13th (Shekhawati) Rajput Infantry
1903	13th Rajputs (The Shekhawati Regiment)

BATTLE HONOURS: *Aliwal, Afghanistan 1878-80, Chitral*

The uniform included a blue turban with a red fringe, a long-skirted scarlet tunic with blue facings, a blue kummerband, blue trousers with red piping, and white gaiters. This uniform is illustrated by figure 205.

14TH KING GEORGE'S OWN FEROZEPORE SIKHS

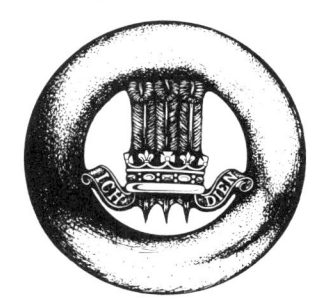

In 1914, this regiment was stationed at Peshawar. King George V was Colonel-in-Chief. The regiment comprised eight companies of Sikhs.

1846	Raised as the Regiment of Ferozepore
1861	14th Regiment of Bengal Native Infantry
1864	14th (The Ferozepore) Regiment of Bengal Native Infantry
1885	14th Regiment of Bengal Native Infantry (Ferozepore Sikhs)
1901	14th (Ferozepore) Sikh Infantry
1903	14th Ferozepore Sikhs
1906	14th Prince of Wales's Own Ferozepore Sikhs
1910	14th King George's Own Ferozepore Sikhs

BATTLE HONOURS: *Lucknow, Ali Masjid, Afghanistan 1878-79, Defence of Chitral, China 1900*

The uniform included a blue turban, a long-skirted scarlet tunic with yellow facings, a yellow kummerband, blue trousers with red piping, and white gaiters. This uniform is illustrated by figure 206.

15TH LUDHIANA SIKHS

In 1914, this regiment was stationed at Loralai with detachments at Musa Khel, Drug, Sargandai, Ghurlama, and Zarrozai. This regiment comprised eight companies of Sikhs.

1846	Raised as the Regiment of Ludhiana
1861	15th Regiment of Bengal Native Infantry
1864	15th (Ludhiana) Regiment of Bengal Native Infantry
1885	15th Regiment of Bengal Native Infantry (Ludhiana Sikhs)
1901	15th (Ludhiana) Sikhs Infantry
1903	15th Ludhiana Sikhs

BATTLE HONOURS: *China 1861-62, Ahmed Khel, Kandahar 1880, Afghanistan 1878-80, Suakin 1885, Tofrek, Chitral, Punjab Frontier, Tirah*

The uniform included a yellow turban with red stripes, a long-skirted scarlet tunic with emerald green facings, an emerald green kummerband, blue trousers with red piping, and white gaiters. The name was spelled *Loodianah* on the badge. This uniform is illustrated by figure 207.

16TH RAJPUTS (THE LUCKNOW REGIMENT)

In 1914, this regiment was stationed at Fort William and comprised eight companies of Rajputs.

- 1857 Formed as the Regiment of Lucknow from loyal elements of the 13th, 48th, and 71st Bengal Native Infantry
- 1861 16th Regiment of Bengal Native Infantry
- 1864 16th (The Lucknow) Regiment of Bengal Native Infantry
- 1885 16th (The Lucknow) Regiment of Bengal Infantry
- 1897 16th (The Lucknow) Rajput Regiment, Bengal Native Infantry
- 1901 16th (Lucknow) Rajput Infantry
- 1903 16th Rajputs (The Lucknow Regiment)

BATTLE HONOURS: *Lucknow, Afghanistan 1878-80, Burma 1885-87*

The uniform included a yellow turban with green stripes, a long-skirted scarlet tunic with white facings, a white kummerband, blue trousers with red piping, and white gaiters. This uniform is illustrated by figure 208.

17TH THE LOYAL REGIMENT

In 1914, this regiment was stationed at Lucknow and comprised eight companies of Muslims of the Eastern Punjab and Hindustan.

- 1858 Formed as the Loyal Purbiah Regiment from loyal elements of the 3rd, 36th, and 61st Bengal Native Infantry
- 1861 17th Regiment of Bengal Native Infantry
- 1864 17th (Loyal Purbiah) Regiment of Bengal Native Infantry
- 1898 17th (The Loyal) Regiment of Bengal Native Infantry
- 1902 17th Musulman Rajput Infantry (The Loyal Regiment)
- 1903 17th The Loyal Regiment

BATTLE HONOURS: *Afghanistan 1879-80, Suakin 1885, Tofrek*

The uniform included a blue turban with a distinctive crescent moon badge worn on the front, a long-skirted scarlet tunic with white facings, white kummerband, blue trousers with red piping, and white gaiters. This uniform is illustrated by figure 209.

18TH INFANTRY

In 1914, this regiment was stationed at Dera Ismail Khan and comprised eight companies of Muslims of the Eastern Punjab and Hindustan.

- 1795 Raised as the Calcutta Native Militia
- 1859 The Alipore Regiment
- 1861 The 18th Regiment of Bengal Native Infantry
- 1864 18th (Alipore) Regiment of Bengal Native Infantry
- 1885 18th Regiment of Bengal Native Infantry
- 1902 18th Musulman Rajput Infantry
- 1903 18th Infantry

BATTLE HONOUR: *Burma 1885-87*

The uniform included a purple turban, a long-skirted scarlet tunic with black facings, a black kummerband, blue trousers with red piping, and white gaiters. This uniform is illustrated by figure 210.

19TH PUNJABIS

In 1914, this regiment was stationed at Quetta and comprised four companies of Sikhs, two of Punjabi Muslims, and two of Pathans.

1857	Formed from companies of the 2nd and 7th Punjab Police Battalions and known as the 7th Regiment of Punjab Infantry
1861	19th Regiment of Bengal Native Infantry
1864	19th (Punjab) Regiment of Bengal Native Infantry
1885	19th (Punjab) Regiment of Bengal Infantry
1901	19th Punjab Infantry
1903	19th Punjabis

BATTLE HONOURS: *Ahmed Khel, Afghanistan 1878-80*

The uniform included a blue turban with a gold fringe and a red kullah, a long-skirted scarlet tunic with blue facings, blue kummerband, blue trousers with red piping, and white gaiters. This uniform is illustrated by figure 211.

20TH (DUKE OF CAMBRIDGE'S OWN) BROWNLOW'S PUNJABIS

In 1914, this regiment was stationed at Poona with a detachment at Mahableshwar. The regiment comprised four companies of Pathans, two of Sikhs, and two of Dogras.

1857	Formed as the 8th Regiment of Punjab Infantry from the 4th and 5th Punjab Infantry
1861	20th Regiment of Bengal Native Infantry
1864	20th (Punjab) Regiment of Bengal Native Infantry
1883	20th (Duke of Cambridge's Own Punjab) Regiment of Bengal Native Infantry
1901	20th (Duke of Cambridge's Own) Punjab Infantry
1904	20th (Duke of Cambridge's Own) Brownlow's Punjabis

BATTLE HONOURS: *Taku Forts, Pekin, Ali Masjid, Afghanistan 1878-80, Egypt 1882, Tel el Kebir, Punjab Frontier, China 1900*

The uniform included a khaki turban with an emerald green fringe and an emerald green kullah, a long-skirted khaki tunic with emerald green facings, an emerald green kummerband, khaki trousers, and khaki gaiters. This uniform is illustrated by figure 212.

21ST PUNJABIS

In 1914, this regiment was stationed at Peshawar and comprised three companies of Pathans, three of Sikhs, one of Dogras, and one of Punjabi Muslims.

1857	Formed as the 9th Regiment of Punjab Infantry from the 3rd and 6th Punjab Infantry
1861	21st Regiment of Bengal Native Infantry
1864	21st (Punjab) Regiment of Bengal Native Infantry
1885	21st (Punjab) Regiment of Bengal Infantry
1901	21st Punjab Infantry
1903	21st Punjabis

BATTLE HONOURS: *Abyssinia, Afghanistan 1878-80*

The uniform included a khaki turban with a red fringe and a red kullah, a long-skirted khaki tunic with red facings, a red kummerband, khaki trousers, and khaki gaiters. This uniform is illustrated by figure 213.

22ND PUNJABIS

In 1914, this regiment was stationed at Dacca and comprised four companies of Sikhs, three of Punjabi Muslims, and one of Pathans.

1857	Formed as the 11th Punjab Infantry from the 1st Sikh Infantry and the 3rd Punjab Police Battalion
1861	22nd Regiment of Bengal Native Infantry
1864	22nd (Punjab) Regiment of Bengal Native Infantry
1885	22nd (Punjab) Regiment of Bengal Infantry
1901	22nd Punjab Infantry
1903	22nd Punjabis

BATTLE HONOURS: *China 1860-62, Afghanistan 1879-80, Punjab Frontier*

The uniform included a red turban with blue stripes edged in white with a blue fringe and a red kullah, a long-skirted scarlet tunic with blue facings, blue kummerband, blue trousers with red piping, and white gaiters. This uniform is illustrated by figure 214.

23RD SIKH PIONEERS

In 1914, this regiment was stationed at Lahore and comprised eight companies of Mazbi and Ramdasia Sikhs.

1857	Raised as the 15th (Pioneer) Regiment of Punjab Infantry
1861	23rd Regiment of Bengal Native Infantry
1864	23rd (Punjab) Regiment of Bengal Native Infantry (Pioneers)
1885	23rd (Punjab) Regiment of Bengal Infantry (Pioneers)
1901	23rd Punjab Pioneers
1903	23rd Sikh Pioneers

BATTLE HONOURS: *Taku Forts, Pekin, Abyssinia, Peiwar Kotal, Charasiah, Kabul 1897, Afghanistan 1878-80, Chitral*

The uniform included a chocolate brown turban, a long-skirted khaki tunic with chocolate brown facings, khaki trousers, and khaki puttees. The leather belts crossed in back supported the pioneer equipment, including a shovel, ax, or pickax. This uniform is illustrated by figure 215.

24TH PUNJABIS

In 1914, this regiment was stationed at Nowshera and comprised four companies of Sikhs, two of Afridis, one of Dogras, and one of Punjabi Muslims.

1857	Raised as the 16th Punjab Infantry
1861	24th Regiment of Bengal Native Infantry
1864	24th (Punjab) Regiment of Bengal Native Infantry
1885	24th (Punjab) Regiment of Bengal Infantry
1901	24th Punjab Infantry
1903	24th Punjabis

BATTLE HONOURS: *Kandahar 1880, Afghanistan 1878-80, Punjab Frontier, Malakand, Pekin 1900*

The uniform included a blue turban, a long-skirted scarlet tunic with white facings, a white kummerband, blue trousers with red piping, and white gaiters. This uniform is illustrated by figure 216.

25TH PUNJABIS

In 1914, this regiment was stationed at Hong Kong and comprised three companies of Sikhs, two of Dogras, two of Punjabi Muslims, and one of Pathans.

1857	Raised as the Lahore Punjab Battalion and numbered the 17th Punjab Infantry
1861	25th Regiment of Bengal Native Infantry
1864	25th (Punjab) Regiment of Bengal Native Infantry
1885	25th (Punjab) Regiment of Bengal Infantry
1901	25th Punjab Infantry
1903	25th Punjabis

BATTLE HONOURS: *Ahmed Khel, Kandahar, Afghanistan 1878-80, Chitral*

The uniform included a blue turban with a white fringe, a long-skirted scarlet tunic with white facings, a white kummerband, blue trousers with red piping, and white gaiters. This uniform is illustrated by figure 217.

26TH PUNJABIS

In 1914, this regiment was stationed at Hong Kong and comprised four companies of Sikhs, two of Afridi Pathans, and two of Punjabi Muslims.

1857	Raised as the 18th Punjab Infantry
1861	26th Regiment of Bengal Native Infantry
1864	26th (Punjab) Regiment of Bengal Native Infantry
1885	26th (Punjab) Regiment of Bengal Infantry
1901	26th Punjab Infantry
1903	26th Punjabis

BATTLE HONOURS: *Afghanistan 1878-79, Burma 1885-87*

The uniform included a khaki turban with a red fringe, a red kullah, a long-skirted khaki tunic with scarlet facings, a scarlet kummerband, khaki trousers, and khaki gaiters. This uniform is illustrated by figure 218.

27TH PUNJABIS

In 1914, this regiment was stationed at Dera Ismail Khan and comprised three companies of Sikhs, two of Punjabi Muslims, two of Pathans, and one of Dogras.

1857	Raised as the Regiment of Rawal Pindi and numbered the 19th Regiment of Punjab Infantry
1861	27th Regiment of Bengal Native Infantry
1864	27th (Punjab) Regiment of Bengal Native Infantry
1885	27th (Punjab) Regiment of Bengal Infantry
1901	27th Punjab Infantry
1903	27th Punjabis

BATTLE HONOURS: *China 1860-62, Ali Masjid, Afghanistan 1878-80, Burma 1885-87*

The uniform included a black turban with a red fringe, a long-skirted khaki tunic with scarlet facings, a scarlet kummerband, khaki trousers, and khaki gaiters. This uniform is illustrated by figure 219.

28TH PUNJABIS

In 1914, this regiment was stationed at Colombo, Ceylon, and comprised three companies of Sikhs, three of Pathans, one of Dogras, and one of Punjabi Muslims.

1857	Raised as the Ferozepore Punjab Battalion and numbered 20th Regiment of Punjab Infantry
1861	28th Regiment of Bengal Native Infantry
1864	28th (Punjab) Regiment of Bengal Native Infantry
1885	28th (Punjab) Regiment of Bengal Infantry
1901	28th Punjab Infantry
1903	28th Punjabis

BATTLE HONOURS: *Charasiah, Kabul 1879, Afghanistan 1878-80*

The uniform included a khaki turban, a long-skirted scarlet tunic with emerald green facings, an emerald green kummerband, blue trousers with red piping, and white gaiters. This uniform is illustrated by figure 220.

29TH PUNJABIS

In 1914, this regiment was stationed at Hyderabad (Sind) with a detachment at Chaman. The regiment comprised four companies of Sikhs, two of Dogras, and two of Punjabi Muslims.

1857	Raised as the 21st Regiment of Punjab Infantry
1861	29th Regiment of Bengal Native Infantry
1864	29th (Punjab) Regiment of Bengal Native Infantry
1885	29th (Punjab) Regiment of Bengal Infantry
1901	29th Punjab Infantry
1903	29th Punjabis

BATTLE HONOURS: *Peiwar Kotal, Afghanistan 1878-80, Chitral*

The uniform included a khaki turban with a red kullah, a long-skirted scarlet tunic with blue facings, a dark blue kummerband, blue trousers with red piping, and white gaiters. This uniform is illustrated by figure 221.

30TH PUNJABIS

In 1914, this regiment was stationed at Delhi and comprised four companies of Sikhs, two of Dogras, and two of Punjabi Muslims.

1857	Raised as the 22nd Regiment of Punjab Infantry
1861	30th Regiment of Bengal Native Infantry
1864	30th (Punjab) Regiment of Bengal Native Infantry
1885	30th (Punjab) Regiment of Bengal Infantry
1901	30th Punjab Infantry
1903	30th Punjabis

BATTLE HONOURS: *Afghanistan 1878-80, Chitral, Punjab Frontier*

This uniform included a blue and white turban with dark blue stripes on the white part, a long-skirted scarlet tunic with white facings, a white kummerband, blue trousers with red piping, and white gaiters. This uniform is illustrated by figure 222.

31ST PUNJABIS

In 1914, this regiment was stationed at Fort Sandeman and comprised four companies of Sikhs, two of Dogras, and two of Punjabi Muslims.

1857	Raised as Cortlandt's Levy and numbered 23rd Punjab Infantry
1861	31st Regiment of Bengal Native Infantry
1864	31st (Punjab) Regiment of Bengal Native Infantry
1901	31st Punjab Infantry
1903	31st Punjabis

BATTLE HONOURS: *Afghanistan 1879-80, Punjab Frontier, Malakand*

The uniform included a blue turban with gold stripes, a long-skirted scarlet tunic with white facings, a white kummerband, blue trousers with red piping, and white gaiters. This uniform is illustrated by figure 223.

32ND SIKH PIONEERS

In 1914, this regiment was stationed at Sialkot and comprised eight companies of Mazbi and Ramdasia Sikhs.

1857	Raised and known as the Punjab Sappers or Punjab Pioneers
1858	24th (Pioneer) Regiment of Punjab Infantry
1861	32nd Regiment of Bengal Native Infantry
1864	32nd (Punjab) Regiment of Bengal Native Infantry (Pioneers)
1885	32nd (Punjab) Regiment of Bengal Infantry
1901	32nd Punjab Pioneers
1903	32nd Sikh Pioneers

BATTLE HONOURS: *Delhi, Lucknow, Afghanistan 1878-80, Chitral*

The uniform included a red turban, a long-skirted scarlet tunic with blue facings, a blue kummerband, blue trousers with red piping, and blue puttees. The leather belts crossed in back supported the pioneer equipment, including a shovel, ax, or pickax. This uniform is illustrated by figure 224.

33RD PUNJABIS

In 1914, this regiment was stationed at Bannu and comprised four companies of Punjabi Muslims, two of Pathans, and two of Sikhs.

1857 Raised as the Allahabad Levy
1861 33rd Regiment of Bengal Native Infantry
1864 33rd (Allahabad) Regiment of Bengal Native Infantry
1885 33rd Regiment of Bengal Infantry
1890 33rd (Punjabi Mahomedan) Regiment of Bengal Infantry
1901 33rd Punjab Infantry
1903 33rd Punjabis

BATTLE HONOUR: *Burma 1885*

The uniform included a khaki turban with a green fringe, a green kullah, a long-skirted khaki tunic with green facings, a green kummerband, khaki trousers, and khaki gaiters. This uniform is illustrated by figure 225.

34TH SIKH PIONEERS

In 1914, this regiment was stationed at Ambala and comprised eight companies of Mazbi and Ramdasia Sikhs.

1887 Raised as the 34th (Punjab) Regiment of Bengal Infantry (Pioneers)
1901 34th Punjab Pioneers
1903 34th Sikh Pioneers

BATTLE HONOURS: *Chitral, Punjab Frontier, China 1900*

The uniform included a red turban, a long-skirted scarlet tunic with blue facings, a blue kummerband, blue trousers with red piping, and blue puttees. The leather belts crossed in back supported the pioneer equipment, including a shovel, ax, or pickax. This uniform is illustrated by figure 226.

35TH SIKHS

In 1914, this regiment was stationed at Rawalpindi and comprised eight companies of Sikhs.

1887 Raised as the 35th (Sikh) Regiment of Bengal Infantry
1901 35th Sikh Infantry
1903 35th Sikhs

BATTLE HONOURS: *Punjab Frontier, Malakand*

The uniform included a yellow turban with red stripes, a long-skirted scarlet tunic with yellow facings, a yellow kummerband, blue trousers with red piping, and white gaiters. This uniform is illustrated by figure 227.

36TH SIKHS

In 1914, this regiment was stationed at Tientsin, North China, and comprised eight companies of Sikhs.

1887 Raised as the 36th (Sikh) Regiment of Bengal Infantry
1901 36th Sikh Infantry
1903 36th Sikhs

BATTLE HONOURS: *Punjab Frontier, Samana, Tirah*

The uniform included a red turban, a long-skirted scarlet tunic with yellow facings, a yellow kummerband, blue trousers with red piping, and white gaiters. This uniform is illustrated by figure 228.

37TH DOGRAS

In 1914, this regiment was stationed at Jhelum. Major General Sir Partab Singh, Maharaja of Jammu and Kashmir, was the Honorary Colonel. The regiment comprised eight companies of Dogras.

1887	Raised as the 37th (Dogra) Regiment of Bengal Infantry
1901	37th Dogra Infantry
1903	37th Dogras

BATTLE HONOURS: *Chitral, Punjab Frontier*

The uniform included a khaki turban with a yellow fringe, a long-skirted scarlet tunic with yellow facings, a yellow kummerband, blue trousers with red piping, and white gaiters. This uniform is illustrated by figure 229.

38TH DOGRAS

In 1914, this regiment was stationed at Malakand and comprised eight companies of Dogras.

1858	Raised as the Agra Levy
1861	38th Regiment of Bengal Native Infantry
1864	38th (Agra) Regiment of Bengal Native Infantry
1890	38th (Dogra) Regiment of Bengal Infantry
1891	38th Dogra Infantry
1903	38th Dogras

BATTLE HONOURS: *Punjab Frontier, Malakand*

The uniform included a blue turban, a long-skirted scarlet tunic with yellow facings, a yellow kummerband, blue trousers with red piping, and white gaiters. This uniform is illustrated by figure 230.

39TH GARHWAL RIFLES

In 1914, both battalions of this regiment were stationed at Lansdowne. Each battalion comprised eight companies of Garhwalis. The Garhwalis were similar to the Gurkhas but were usually taller. Their home was the Himalayan foothills west of Nepal.

1887	Raised as the 2nd Battalion, 3rd (Kamaon) Gurkha Regiment
1890	39th (Garhwali) Regiment of Bengal Infantry
1892	39th (Garhwal Rifles) Regiment of Bengal Infantry
1901	39th Garhwal Rifles. The 2nd Battalion raised.

BATTLE HONOUR: *Punjab Frontier.*

The uniform included a black round cap, a rifle green tunic with black facings, rifle green trousers, and black puttees. This uniform was the same as the Gurkha regiments. This uniform is illustrated by figure 231.

40TH PATHANS

In 1914, this regiment was stationed at Hong Kong and comprised two companies of Orakzais, two of Punjabi Muslims, two of Dogras, one of Afridi Pathans, and one of Yusufzais.

1858	Raised as the Shahjehanpur Levy
1861	40th Regiment of Bengal Native Infantry
1864	40th (Shahjehanpur) Regiment of Bengal Native Infantry

1885 40th (Shahjehanpur) Regiment of Bengal Infantry
1890 40th (Baluch) Regiment of Bengal Infantry
1892 40th (Pathan) Regiment of Bengal Infantry
1901 40th Pathan Infantry
1903 40th Pathans

The uniform included a khaki turban with a green kullah, a long-skirted khaki tunic with green facings, a green kummerband, khaki trousers, and khaki gaiters. This uniform is illustrated by figure 232.

41ST DOGRAS

In 1914, this regiment was stationed at Bareilly and comprised eight companies of Dogras.

1900 Raised as the 41st (Dogra) Regiment of Bengal Infantry
1901 41st Dogra Infantry
1903 41st Dogras

The uniform included a khaki turban with a red end and a yellow fringe, a long-skirted scarlet tunic with yellow facings, a yellow kummerband, blue trousers with red piping, and white gaiters. This uniform is illustrated by figure 233.

42ND DEOLI REGIMENT

In 1914, this regiment was stationed at Deoli with detachments at Jaipur and Kotah. The regiment comprised four companies of Rajputana Hindus and four of Rajputana Muslims

1857 Raised as the Meena Battalion
1860 Infantry of the Deoli Irregular Force
1903 42nd Deoli Regiment

BATTLE HONOURS: *Central India, Afghanistan 1879-80*

The uniform included a khaki turban with a red fringe, a long-skirted rifle green tunic with red facings, a red kummerband, rifle green trousers with red piping, and white gaiters. This uniform is illustrated by figure 234.

43RD ERINPURA REGIMENT

In 1914, this regiment was stationed at Erinpura and comprised four companies of Rajputana Hindus and four of Rajputana Muslims.

1860 Raised as the Infantry of the Erinpura Irregular Force
1903 43rd Erinpura Regiment

The uniform included a yellow turban with red stripes and a red fringe, a rifle green tunic with red facings, red trousers, and white gaiters. This uniform is illustrated by figure 235.

44TH MHARWARA REGIMENT

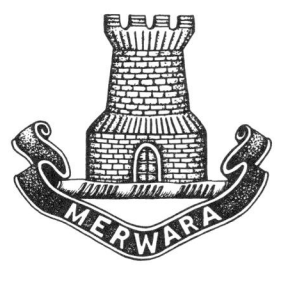

In 1914, this regiment was stationed at Ajmer with detachments at Rajkot and Deesa. This regiment comprised four companies of Mers and four of Mohammedan Merats.

1822 Raised as the 14th (Mhairwara) Local Battalion
1826 9th (Mhairwara) Local Battalion
1843 The Mhairwara Battalion
1861 The Ajmer and Mhairwara Police Corps
1871 The Mhairwara Battalion
1903 44th Mharwara Regiment (spelling changed)

BATTLE HONOURS: *Central India, Afghanistan 1878-80*

The uniform included a light blue turban with yellow and dark blue stripes, a long-skirted scarlet tunic with gosling green facings, a gosling green kummerband, blue trousers with red piping, and white gaiters. The spelling of the name differed on the badge. This uniform is illustrated by figure 236.

45TH RATTRAY'S SIKHS

In 1914, this regiment was stationed at Tank and comprised eight companies of Sikhs.

1856	Raised as the Bengal Military Police Battalion
1858	1st Bengal Military Police Battalion
1861	Bengal Military Police Battalion
1864	45th (Rattray's Sikh) Regiment of Bengal Native Infantry
1885	45th (Rattray's Sikh) Regiment of Bengal Infantry
1901	45th (Rattray's) Sikh Infantry
1903	45th Rattray's Sikhs

BATTLE HONOURS: *Defence of Arrah, Ali Masjid, Afghanistan 1879-80, Punjab Frontier, Malakand*

The uniform included a dark blue turban with light blue stripes, a long-skirted scarlet tunic with white facings, a white kummerband, blue trousers with red piping, and white gaiters. This uniform is illustrated by figure 237.

46TH PUNJABIS

In 1914, this regiment was stationed at Nowshera and comprised four companies of Punjabi Muslims, two of Labana Sikhs, one of Afridi Pathans, and one of Orakzais.

1900	Raised as the 46th (Punjab) Regiment of Bengal Infantry
1901	46th Punjab Infantry
1903	46th Punjabis

The uniform included a khaki turban with an emerald green fringe with a khaki kullah, a long-skirted khaki tunic with emerald green facings, an emerald green kummerband, khaki trousers, and khaki gaiters. This uniform is illustrated by figure 238.

47TH SIKHS

In 1914, this regiment was stationed at Jullundur and comprised eight companies of Sikhs.

1901	Raised as the 47th (Sikh) Regiment of Bengal Infantry and became the 47th Sikh Infantry in the same year
1903	47th Sikhs

The uniform included a khaki turban, a long-skirted scarlet tunic with yellow facings, a yellow kummerband, blue trousers with red piping, and white gaiters. This uniform is illustrated by figure 239.

48TH PIONEERS

In 1914, this regiment was stationed at Kirkee and comprised four companies of Jats and four of Labana Sikhs.

1901	Raised as the 48th Regiment of Bengal Infantry (Pioneers) and became the 48th Bengal Pioneers in the same year
1903	48th Pioneers

The uniform included a blue and orange-red turban with blue stripes on the orange-red part, a long-skirted scarlet tunic with black facings, a black kummerband, blue trousers with red piping, and blue puttees. The leather belts, crossed in the back, supported the pioneer equipment, including a shovel, ax, or pickax. This uniform is illustrated by figure 240.

49TH Regiment—Vacant in 1914

50TH Regiment—Vacant in 1914

51ST SIKHS (FRONTIER FORCE)

In 1914, this regiment was stationed at Dargai with a detachment at Chakdara. This regiment comprised four companies of Sikhs, two of Pathans, one of Dogras, and one of Punjabi Muslims.

1846	Raised as the 1st Regiment of Infantry of the Frontier Brigade
1847	1st Regiment of Sikh Local Infantry
1857	1st Sikh Infantry, Punjab Irregular Force
1865	1st Sikh Infantry, Punjab Frontier Force
1901	1st Sikh Infantry
1903	51st Sikhs (Frontier Force)

BATTLE HONOURS: *Punjab, Ali Masjid, Afghanistan 1878-79, Pekin 1900*

The uniform included a khaki turban, khaki tunic with yellow facings, khaki trousers, and khaki puttees. This uniform is illustrated by figure 241.

52ND SIKHS (FRONTIER FORCE)

In 1914, this regiment was stationed at Bannu and comprised three companies of Dogras, two of Sikhs, two of Punjabi Muslims, and one of Pathans.

1846	Raised as the 2nd Regiment of Infantry of the Frontier Brigade
1847	2nd (or Hill) Regiment of Sikh Infantry
1857	2nd (or Hill) Regiment of Sikh Infantry, Punjab Irregular Force
1865	2nd (or Hill) Regiment, Sikh Infantry, Punjab Frontier Force
1901	2nd (or Hill) Sikh Infantry
1903	52nd Sikhs (Frontier Force)

BATTLE HONOURS: *Punjab, Ahmed Khel, Kandahar 1880, Afghanistan 1879-80*

The uniform included a khaki turban, khaki tunic with scarlet facings, khaki trousers, and khaki puttees. This uniform is illustrated by figure 242.

53RD SIKHS (FRONTIER FORCE)

In 1914, this regiment was stationed at Kohat and comprised four companies of Sikhs, two of Khattaks, one of Dogras, and one of Punjabi Muslims.

1846	Raised as the 3rd Regiment of Infantry of the Frontier Brigade
1847	3rd Regiment of Sikh Local Infantry
1857	3rd Regiment of Sikh Infantry, Punjab Irregular Force
1865	3rd Regiment of Sikh Infantry, Punjab Frontier Force
1901	3rd Sikh Infantry
1903	53rd Sikhs (Frontier Force)

BATTLE HONOURS: *Kabul 1879, Kandahar 1880, Afghanistan 1879-80, Punjab Frontier, Tirah*

The uniform included a khaki turban, khaki tunic with black facings, khaki trousers, and khaki puttees. This uniform is illustrated by figure 243.

54TH SIKHS (FRONTIER FORCE)

In 1914, this regiment was stationed at Kohat and comprised four companies of Sikhs, two of Punjabi Muslims, one of Dogras, and one of Pathans

1846	Raised as the 4th Regiment of Infantry of the Frontier Brigade
1847	4th Regiment of Sikh Local Infantry
1857	4th Sikh Infantry, Punjab Irregular Force
1865	4th Sikh Infantry, Punjab Frontier Force
1901	4th Sikh Infantry
1903	54th Sikhs (Frontier Force)

BATTLE HONOURS: *Pegu, Delhi, Chitral*

The uniform included a khaki turban, a khaki tunic with emerald green facings, khaki trousers, and khaki puttees. This uniform is illustrated by figure 244.

55TH COKE'S RIFLES (FRONTIER FORCE)

In 1914, this regiment was stationed at Bannu with detachments at Idak, Saidgi, Thal, Jani Khel, and Kurram Garhi. The regiment comprised two companies of Sikhs, two of Afridis, one of Yusufzais, one of Punjabi Muslims, and one of Dogras.

1849	Raised as the 1st Regiment of Punjab Infantry
1851	1st Regiment of Punjab Infantry, Punjab Irregular Force
1865	1st Regiment of Infantry, Punjab Frontier Force
1901	1st Punjab Infantry, Punjab Frontier Force
1903	55th Coke's Rifles (Frontier Force)

BATTLE HONOURS: *Delhi, Afghanistan 1878-79*

The uniform included a rifle green turban, a long-skirted rifle green tunic with scarlet facings, a scarlet kummerband, rifle green trousers, and khaki gaiters. This uniform is illustrated by figure 245.

56TH PUNJAB RIFLES (FRONTIER FORCE)

In 1914, this regiment was stationed at Hangu with a detachment at Thal. This regiment comprised two companies of Sikhs, two of Dogras, two of Punjabi Muslims, and two of Khattak Pathans.

1849	Raised as the 2nd Regiment of Punjab Infantry
1851	2nd Regiment of Infantry, Punjab Irregular Force
1865	2nd Regiment of Infantry, Punjab Frontier Force
1901	2nd Punjab Infantry
1903	56th Infantry (Frontier Force)
1906	56th Punjab Rifles. (Frontier Force)

BATTLE HONOURS: *Delhi, Lucknow, Peiwar Kotal, Afghanistan 1878-79, Punjab Frontier, Tirah*

The uniform included a khaki turban with a black end, a red kullah, a khaki tunic with black facings, khaki trousers, and black puttees. This uniform is illustrated by figure 246.

57TH WILDE'S RIFLES (FRONTIER FORCE)

In 1914, this regiment was stationed at Ferozepore and comprised two companies of Sikhs, two of Dogras, two of Punjabi Muslims, and two of Afridi Pathans.

1849	Raised as the 4th Regiment of Punjab Infantry
1851	4th Regiment of Infantry, Punjab Irregular Force
1865	4th Regiment of Infantry, Punjab Frontier Force
1901	4th Punjab Infantry
1903	57th Wilde's Rifles (Frontier Force)

BATTLE HONOURS: *Delhi, Lucknow, Afghanistan 1879-80, China 1900*

The uniform included a khaki turban with a Prussian blue end, a khaki kullah, a khaki tunic with Prussian blue facings, khaki trousers, and khaki puttees. This uniform is illustrated by figure 247.

58TH VAUGHN'S RIFLES (FRONTIER FORCE)

In 1914, this regiment was stationed at Chaman and comprised three companies of Sikhs, three of Pathans, one of Dogras, and one of Punjabi Muslims.

1849	Raised as the 5th Regiment of Punjab Infantry
1851	5th Regiment of Infantry, Punjab Irregular Force
1865	5th Regiment of Infantry, Punjab Frontier Force
1901	5th Punjab Infantry
1903	58th Vaughn's Rifles (Frontier Force)

BATTLE HONOURS: *Peiwar Kotal, Charasiah, Kabul 1879, Afghanistan 1878-80*

The uniform included a khaki turban with an emerald green end, a khaki kullah, a khaki tunic with emerald green facings, khaki trousers, and khaki puttees. This uniform is illustrated by figure 248.

59TH SCINDE RIFLES (FRONTIER FORCE)

In 1914, this regiment was stationed at Jullundur with a detachment at Amritsar. This regiment comprised three companies of Pathans, two of Sikhs, two of Dogras, and one of Punjabi Muslims.

1843	Raised as the Scinde Camel Corps
1853	6th Regiment of Infantry, Punjab Irregular Force or the Scinde Rifle Corps
1856	6th Regiment of Punjab Infantry
1865	6th Regiment of Infantry, Punjab Frontier Force
1901	6th Punjab Infantry
1903	59th Scinde Rifles (Frontier Force)

The uniform included a khaki turban with a scarlet end, a scarlet kullah, a khaki tunic with scarlet facings, khaki trousers, and khaki puttees. This uniform is illustrated by figure 249.

60TH Regiment—Vacant in 1914

61ST KING GEORGE'S OWN PIONEERS

In 1914, this regiment was stationed at Bangalore. King George V was Colonel-in-Chief. This regiment comprised four companies of Tamils, two of Madrasi Muslims, and two of Paraiyans and Christians.

1758	Formed from independent companies as the 1st Battalion, Coast Sepoys
1769	1st Carnatic Battalion
1784	1st Madras Battalion
1796	1st Battalion, 1st Regiment of Madras Native Infantry
1824	1st Regiment of Madras Native Infantry
1883	1st Regiment of Madras Native Infantry (Pioneers)
1885	1st Regiment Madras Infantry (Pioneers)
1901	1st Madras Pioneers
1903	61st Pioneers
1906	61st Prince of Wales Own Pioneers
1910	61st King George's Own Pioneers

BATTLE HONOURS: *Carnatic, Mysore, Seringapatam, Seetabuldee, Nagpore, Ava, Pegu, Central India, Afghanistan 1878-80, Burma 1885-87, China 1900*

The uniform included a blue turban with a red end, a blue kullah, a scarlet tunic with white facings, blue trousers with red piping, and white gaiters. This regiment continued to wear the pre-1903 tunic with a front panel of the facing color and distinctive cuffs. This uniform is illustrated by figure 250.

62ND PUNJABIS

In 1914, this regiment was stationed at Cawnpore and comprised four companies of Punjabi Muslims, two of Sikhs, and two of Rajputs from Western Rajputana and the Eastern Punjab.

1759	Formed from independent companies as the 3rd Battalion, Coast Sepoys
1769	2nd Carnatic Battalion
1784	2nd Madras Battalion
1796	1st Battalion, 2nd Regiment of Madras Native Infantry
1824	2nd Regiment of Madras Native Infantry
1885	2nd Regiment of Madras Infantry
1901	2nd Madras Infantry
1903	62nd Punjabis

BATTLE HONOURS: *Carnatic, Mysore, Assaye, Nagpore, China*

The uniform included a khaki turban with an emerald green fringe, a khaki kullah, a long-skirted scarlet tunic with emerald green facings, an emerald green kummerband, blue trousers with red piping, and white gaiters. This uniform is illustrated by figure 251.

63RD PALAMCOTTAH LIGHT INFANTRY

In 1914, this regiment was stationed at Kamptee and comprised four companies of Madrasi Muslims, two of Tamils, and two of Paraiyans and Christians.

1759	Formed from independent companies as the 4th Battalion, Coast Sepoys
1769	4th Carnatic Battalion
1770	3rd Carnatic Battalion
1784	3rd Madras Battalion
1796	1st Battalion, 3rd Regiment of Madras Native Infantry
1812	3rd Regiment of Madras Native Infantry (Palamcottah Light Infantry)
1885	3rd (or Palamcottah) Regiment of Madras Native Light Infantry
1901	63rd (Palamcottah) Madras Light Infantry
1903	63rd Palamcottah Light Infantry

BATTLE HONOURS: *Carnatic, Sholinghur, Mysore, Mahidpoor, Ava, Burma 1885-87, China 1900*

The uniform included a khaki turban with an emerald green fringe, a red kullah, a scarlet tunic with emerald green facings and white piping, blue trousers with red piping, and white gaiters. This regiment continued to wear the pre-1903 tunic with a front panel of the facing color and distinctive cuffs. This uniform is illustrated by figure 252.

64TH PIONEERS

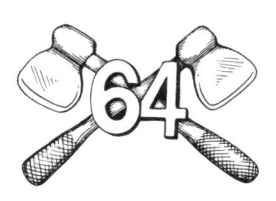

In 1914, this regiment was stationed at Mandalay, Burma, and comprised four companies of Tamils, two of Madrasi Muslims, and two of Paraiyans and Christians.

1759	Formed from independent companies as the 5th Battalion, Coast Sepoys
1769	5th Carnatic Battalion
1770	4th Carnatic Battalion
1784	4th Madras Battalion
1796	1st Battalion, 4th Regiment of Madras Native Infantry
1824	4th Regiment of Madras Native Infantry
1883	4th Regiment of Madras Native Infantry (Pioneers)
1901	4th Regiment of Madras Infantry (Pioneers)
1903	64th Pioneers

BATTLE HONOURS: *Carnatic, Sholinghur, Mysore, Assaye, Afghanistan 1879-80*

The uniform included a khaki turban with a red end and a white fringe, a red kullah, a scarlet tunic with white facings, blue trousers with red piping, and white gaiters. This regiment continued to wear the pre-1903 tunic with a front panel of the facing color and distinctive cuffs. This uniform is illustrated by figure 253.

65TH Regiment—Vacant in 1914

66TH PUNJABIS

In 1914, this regiment was stationed at Rangoon, Burma, and comprised four companies of Punjabi Muslims, two of Sikhs, and two of Rajputs from Western Rajputana and Eastern Punjab.

1761	Raised as the 7th Battalion, Coast Sepoys
1769	7th Carnatic Battalion
1770	6th Carnatic Battalion
1784	6th Madras Battalion
1796	1st Battalion, 6th Regiment of Madras Native Infantry
1824	6th Regiment of Madras Native Infantry
1885	6th Regiment of Madras Infantry
1901	6th Madras Infantry
1903	66th Punjabis

BATTLE HONOURS: *Carnatic, Sholinghur, Mysore, Seringapatem, Bourbon, China*

The uniform included a khaki turban with a green fringe, a khaki kullah, a long-skirted scarlet tunic with emerald green facings, an emerald green kummerband, blue trousers with red piping, and white gaiters. This uniform is illustrated by figure 254.

67TH PUNJABIS

In 1914, this regiment was stationed at Quetta and comprised four companies of Punjabi Muslims, two of Sikhs, and two of Punjabi Hindus.

1761	Raised as the 8th Battalion, Coast Sepoys
1769	8th Carnatic Battalion
1770	7th Carnatic Battalion
1784	7th Madras Battalion
1796	1st Battalion, 7th Regiment of Madras Native Infantry
1824	7th Regiment of Madras Native Infantry
1885	7th Regiment of Madras Infantry
1901	7th Madras Infantry
1903	67th Punjabis

BATTLE HONOURS: *Carnatic, Mysore, Ava*

The uniform included a khaki turban, a long-skirted scarlet tunic with emerald green facings, an emerald green kummerband, blue trousers with red piping, and white gaiters. This uniform is illustrated by figure 255.

68TH Regiment—Vacant in 1914

69TH PUNJABIS

In 1914, this regiment was stationed at Jhelum and comprised four companies of Punjabi Muslims, two of Sikhs, and two of Punjabi Hindus.

1762	Raised as the 10th Battalion, Coast Sepoys
1769	10th Carnatic Battalion
1770	9th Carnatic Battalion
1784	9th Madras Battalion
1796	1st Battalion, 9th Regiment of Madras Native Infantry
1824	9th Regiment of Madras Native Infantry
1885	9th Regiment of Madras Infantry
1901	9th Madras Infantry
1903	69th Punjabis

BATTLE HONOURS: *Carnatic, Sholinghur, Mysore, Ava, Pegu*

The uniform included a khaki turban, a long-skirted scarlet tunic with emerald green facings, an emerald green kummerband, blue trousers with red piping, and white gaiters. This uniform is illustrated by figure 256.

70TH Regiment—Vacant in 1914

71ST Regiment—Vacant in 1914

72ND PUNJABIS

In 1914, this regiment was stationed at Peshawar and comprised four companies of Sikhs, two of Punjabi Muslims, and two of Pathans.

1767	Raised as the 16th Battalion, Coast Sepoys
1769	13th Carnatic Battalion
1770	12th Carnatic Battalion
1784	12th Madras Battalion
1796	2nd Battalion, 8th Regiment of Madras Native Infantry
1824	12th Regiment of Madras Native Infantry
1890	2nd Regiment of Burma Infantry
1891	12th Regiment (2nd Burma Battalion) Madras Infantry
1901	12th Burma Infantry
1903	72nd Punjabis

BATTLE HONOURS: *Carnatic, Sholinghur, Ava, Burma 1885-87*

This uniform included a khaki turban with a white fringe, a long-skirted khaki tunic with white facings, a white kummerband, khaki trousers. and white gaiters. This uniform is illustrated by figure 257.

73RD CARNATIC INFANTRY

In 1914, this regiment was stationed at Trichinopoly with detachments at Ootacamund and Berbera. This regiment comprised four companies of Madrasi Muslims, two of Tamils, and two of Paraiyans and Christians.

1776	Formed from drafts from the 4th, 7th, and 11th Carnatic Battalions as the 13th Carnatic Battalion
1784	13th Madras Battalion
1796	2nd Battalion, 3rd Regiment of Madras Native Infantry
1824	13th Regiment of Madras Native Infantry
1885	13th Regiment of Madras Infantry
1901	13th Madras Infantry
1903	73rd Carnatic Infantry

BATTLE HONOURS: *Carnatic, Sholinghur, Mysore, Seringapatam, Burma 1885-87*

This uniform included a khaki turban with a white fringe, a khaki kullah, a scarlet tunic with white facings, blue trousers with red piping, and white gaiters. This regiment continued to wear the pre-1903 tunic with a front panel of the facing color and distinctive cuffs. This uniform is illustrated by figure 258.

74TH PUNJABIS

In 1914, this regiment was stationed at Hong Kong and comprised four companies of Punjabi Muslims, two of Sikhs, and two of Punjabi Hindus.

1776	Formed from drafts from the 5th, 9th, and 10th Carnatic Battalions as the 14th Carnatic Battalion
1784	14th Madras Battalion
1796	2nd Battalion, 6th Regiment of Madras Native Infantry
1824	14th Regiment of Madras Native Infantry
1885	14th Regiment of Madras Infantry
1901	14th Madras Infantry
1903	74th Punjabis

BATTLE HONOURS: *Carnatic, Sholinghur, Mysore, Mahidpoor, China, Burma 1885-87*

The uniform included a blue turban with a red end, a long-skirted scarlet tunic with emerald green facings, an emerald green kummerband, blue trousers with red piping, and white gaiters. This uniform is illustrated by figure 259.

75TH CARNATIC INFANTRY

In 1914, this regiment was stationed at Cannanore with a detachment at Trivandrum. This regiment comprised four companies of Madrasi Muslims, two of Tamils, and two of Paraiyans and Christians.

1776	Formed from drafts from the 2nd, 6th, and 12th Carnatic Battalions as the 15th Carnatic Battalion
1784	15th Madras Battalion
1796	2nd Battalion, 4th Regiment of Madras Native Infantry
1824	15th Regiment of Madras Native Infantry
1885	15th Regiment of Madras Infantry
1901	15th Madras Infantry
1903	75th Carnatic Infantry

BATTLE HONOURS: *Carnatic, Sholinghur, Mysore, Afghanistan 1879-80, Burma 1885-87*

The uniform included a khaki turban with a yellow fringe, a scarlet tunic with yellow facings, blue trousers with red piping, and white gaiters. This regiment continued to wear the pre-1903 tunic with a front panel of the facing color and distinctive cuffs. This uniform is illustrated by figure 260.

76TH PUNJABIS

In 1914, this regiment was stationed at Jhelum and comprised four companies of Punjabi Muslims, two of Sikhs, and two of Jats.

1776	Formed from drafts from the 1st, 3rd, and 8th Carnatic Battalions as the 16th Carnatic Battalion
1784	16th Madras Battalion
1796	2nd Battalion, 5th Regiment of Madras Native Infantry
1824	16th Regiment of Madras Native Infantry
1885	16th Regiment of Madras Infantry
1901	16th Madras Infantry
1903	76th Punjabis

BATTLE HONOURS: *Carnatic, Sholinghur, Mysore, Seringapatam, Ava, Burma 1885-87*

The uniform included a khaki turban with a green fringe, a khaki kullah, a long-skirted scarlet tunic with emerald green facings, an emerald green kummerband, blue trousers with red piping, and white gaiters. This uniform is illustrated by figure 261.

77TH Regiment—Vacant in 1914

78TH Regiment—Vacant in 1914

79TH CARNATIC INFANTRY

In 1914, this regiment was stationed at Rangoon, Burma, with a detachment at Port Blair. This regiment comprised four companies of Madrasi Muslims, two of Tamils, and two of Paraiyans and Christians.

1777	Formed from drafts from the 1st, 3rd, 8th, and 16th Carnatic Battalions as the 20th Carnatic Battalion
1784	20th Madras Battalion
1796	2nd Battalion, 7th Regiment of Madras Native Infantry
1824	19th Regiment of Madras Native Infantry
1885	19th Regiment of Madras Infantry
1901	19th Madras Infantry
1903	79th Carnatic Infantry

BATTLE HONOURS: *Carnatic, Sholinghur, Mysore, Seringapatam, Pegu, Central India*

The uniform included a khaki turban with a yellow fringe, a scarlet tunic with yellow facings, blue trousers with red piping, and white gaiters. This regiment continued to wear the pre-1903 tunic with a front panel of the facing color and distinctive cuffs. This uniform is illustrated by figure 262.

80TH CARNATIC INFANTRY

In 1914, this regiment was stationed at Bhamo, Burma, and comprised four companies of Madrasi Muslims, two of Tamils, and two of Paraiyans and Christians.

1777	Formed from drafts from the 2nd, 6th, 12th, and 15th Carnatic Battalions as the 21st Carnatic Battalion
1784	21st Madras Battalion
1796	2nd Battalion, 2nd Regiment of Madras Native Infantry
1824	20th Regiment of Madras Native Infantry
1885	20th Regiment of Madras Infantry
1901	20th Madras Infantry
1903	80th Carnatic Infantry

BATTLE HONOURS: *Carnatic, Sholinghur, Mysore, Seringapatam*

This regiment carried a third honorary colour with the inscription *Hyder Ally, Sholinghur, Hejira 1195*

The uniform included a khaki turban with a green fringe, a scarlet tunic with emerald green facings, blue trousers with red piping, and white gaiters. This regiment continued to wear the pre-1903 tunic with a front panel of the facing color and distinctive cuffs. This uniform is illustrated by figure 263.

81ST PIONEERS

In 1914, this regiment was stationed at Belgaum and comprised four companies of Tamils, two of Madrasi Muslims, and two of Paraiyans and Christians.

1786	Formed from the Ganjam Sebundy Corps and drafts from the 11th and 18th Madras Battalions as the 28th Madras Battalion
1796	1st Battalion, 11th Regiment of Madras Native Infantry
1824	21st Regiment of Madras Native Infantry
1885	21st Regiment of Madras Infantry
1891	21st Regiment of Madras Infantry (Pioneers)
1901	21st Madras Pioneers
1903	81st Pioneers

BATTLE HONOURS: *Mysore, Seringapatam, Nagpore, Afghanistan 1878-80, Burma 1885-87, Punjab Frontier, Tirah*

The uniform included a khaki turban with a white fringe, a scarlet tunic with white facings, blue trousers with red piping, and white gaiters. This regiment continued to wear the pre-1903 tunic with a front panel of the facing color and distinctive cuffs. This uniform is illustrated by figure 264.

82ND PUNJABIS

In 1914, this regiment was stationed at Nowshera and comprised four companies of Punjabi Muslims, two of Sikhs, and two of Jats.

1788	Raised as the 29th Madras Battalion
1796	2nd Battalion, 11th Regiment of Madras Native Infantry
1824	22nd Regiment of Madras Native Infantry
1885	22nd Regiment of Madras Infantry
1901	22nd Madras Infantry
1903	82nd Punjabis

BATTLE HONOURS: *Mysore, Seringapatam, Ava*

The uniform included a khaki turban with a green fringe, a red kullah, a long-skirted scarlet tunic with emerald green facings, an emerald green kummerband, blue trousers with red piping, and white gaiters. This uniform is illustrated by figure 265.

83RD WALLAJAHBAD LIGHT INFANTRY

In 1914, this regiment was stationed at Secunderabad and comprised four companies of Madrasi Muslims, two of Tamils, and two of Paraiyans and Christians.

1794	Raised as the 33rd Madras Battalion
1797	1st Battalion, 12th Regiment of Madras Native Infantry
1824	23rd Regiment of Madras Native Infantry or Wallajahbad Light Infantry
1885	23rd (Wallajahbad) Regiment of Madras (Light Infantry)
1901	23rd (Wallajahbad) Madras Light Infantry
1903	83rd Wallajahbad Light Infantry

BATTLE HONOURS: *Seringapatam, Nagpore, Burma 1885-87*

The uniform included a khaki turban with a green fringe, a scarlet tunic with emerald green facings, blue trousers with red piping, and white gaiters. This regiment continued to wear the pre-1903 tunic with a front panel of the facings color and distinctive cuffs. This uniform is illustrated by figure 266.

84TH PUNJABIS

In 1914, this regiment was stationed at Rawalpindi and comprised four companies of Punjabi Muslims, two of Sikhs, and two of Rajputs from Western Rajputana and Eastern Punjab.

1794	Raised as the 34th Battalion of Madras Native Infantry
1797	2nd Battalion, 12th Regiment of Madras Native Infantry
1824	24th Regiment of Madras Native Infantry
1885	24th Regiment of Madras Infantry
1901	24th Madras Infantry
1903	84th Punjabis

BATTLE HONOURS: *Seringapatam, Assaye, Bourbon*

The uniform included a khaki turban with a green fringe, an emerald green kullah, a long-skirted scarlet tunic with emerald green facings, an emerald green kummerband, blue trousers with red piping, and white gaiters. This uniform is illustrated by figure 267.

85TH Regiment—Vacant in 1914

86TH CARNATIC INFANTRY

In 1914, this regiment was stationed at St. Thomas' Mount and comprised four companies of Madrasi Muslims, two of Tamils, and two of Paraiyans and Christians.

1794	Raised as the 36th Battalion of Madras Native Infantry
1798	2nd Battalion, 13th Regiment of Madras Native Infantry
1824	26th Regiment of Madras Native Infantry
1885	26th Regiment of Madras Infantry
1901	26th Madras Infantry
1903	86th Carnatic Infantry

BATTLE HONOURS: *Nagpore, Kemendine, Ava, Pegu, Burma 1885-87*

The uniform included a dark green turban with a long hanging end, a khaki kullah, a scarlet tunic with emerald green facings, blue trousers with red piping, and white gaiters. This regiment continued to wear the pre-1903 tunic with a front panel of the facing color and distinctive cuffs. This uniform is illustrated by figure 268.

87TH PUNJABIS

In 1914, this regiment was stationed at Jhelum and comprised four companies of Punjabi Muslims, two of Sikhs, and two of Jats.

1798	Raised as the 1st Extra Battalion of Madras Native Infantry, and became the 1st Battalion, 14th Regiment of Madras Native Infantry, in the same year
1824	27th Regiment of Madras Native Infantry
1885	27th Regiment of Madras Infantry
1901	27th Madras Infantry
1903	87th Punjabis

BATTLE HONOURS: *Mahidpore, Lucknow, Burma 1885-87*

The uniform included a khaki turban with a red-yellow-blue striped end and a yellow fringe, a long-skirted scarlet tunic with emerald green facings, and emerald green kummerband, blue trousers with red piping, and white gaiters. This uniform is illustrated by figure 269.

88TH CARNATIC INFANTRY

In 1914, this regiment was stationed at Secunderabad and comprised four companies of Madrasi Muslims, two of Tamils, and two of Paraiyans and Christians.

1798	Raised as the 2nd Extra Battalion of Madras Native Infantry became 1st Battalion, 14th Regiment of Madras Native Infantry in the same year
1824	28th Regiment of Madras Native Infantry
1885	28th Regiment of Madras Infantry
1901	28th Madras Infantry
1903	88th Carnatic Infantry

BATTLE HONOURS: *Mahidpore, Nagpore, Ava, China 1900*

The uniform included a khaki turban with a yellow end and a red fringe, a scarlet tunic with yellow facings, blue trousers with red piping, and white gaiters. This regiment continued to wear the pre-1903 tunic with a front panel of the facing color and distinctive cuffs. This uniform is illustrated by figure 270.

89TH PUNJABIS

In 1914, this regiment was stationed at Dinapore and comprised three companies of Sikhs, three of Punjabi Muslims, one of Brahmans, and one of Rajputs.

1798	Raised as the 3rd Extra Battalion of Madras Native Infantry and became the 1st Battalion, 15th Regiment of Madras Native Infantry in the same year
1824	29th Regiment of Madras Native Infantry
1885	29th Regiment of Madras Infantry
1893	29th Regiment (7th Burma Battalion) Madras Infantry
1901	29th Burma Infantry
1903	89th Punjabis

The uniform included a khaki turban with a blue fringe, a long-skirted khaki tunic with blue facings, a blue kummerband, khaki trousers, and khaki gaiters. This uniform is illustrated by figure 271.

90TH PUNJABIS

In 1914, this regiment was stationed at Nasirabad and comprised four companies of Sikhs, two of Punjabi Muslims, one of Brahmans, and one of Rajputs.

1799	Raised as the Masulipatam Battalion

1800   2nd Battalion, 15th Regiment of Madras Native Infantry
1824   30th Regiment of Madras Native Infantry
1885   30th Regiment of Madras Infantry
1892   30th Regiment (5th Burma Battalion) Madras Infantry
1901   30th Infantry (5th Burma Battalion)
1903   90th Punjabis

BATTLE HONOURS: *Ava, Afghanistan 1878-80, Burma 1885-87*

The uniform included a khaki turban with a black end and a red fringe, a long-skirted khaki tunic with black facings, a black kummerband, khaki trousers, and khaki gaiters. This uniform is illustrated by figure 272.

91ST PUNJABIS (LIGHT INFANTRY)

In 1914, this regiment was stationed at Mandalay, Burma, and comprised three companies of Punjabi Muslims, two of Sikhs, two of Dogras, and one of Hindustani Muslims.

1800   Raised as the 1st Battalion, 16th Regiment, Madras Native Infantry
1824   31st Regiment of Madras Native Infantry or Trichinopoly Light Infantry
1885   31st (Trichinopoly) Regiment of Madras Light Infantry
1892   31st Regiment (6th Burma Battalion) Madras Light Infantry
1901   31st Burma Light Infantry
1903   91st Punjabis (Light Infantry)

BATTLE HONOURS: *Mahidpoor, China 1900*

The uniform included a khaki turban with a red fringe, a red kullah, a long-skirted khaki tunic with cherry-red facings, a cherry-red kummerband, khaki trousers, and khaki gaiters. This uniform is illustrated by figure 273.

92ND PUNJABIS

In 1914, this regiment was stationed at Benares and comprised four companies of Sikhs and four of Punjabi Muslims.

1800   Raised as the 2nd Battalion, 16th Regiment, Madras Native Infantry
1824   32nd Regiment of Madras Native Infantry
1885   32nd Regiment of Madras Infantry
1890   4th Regiment of Burma Infantry
1891   32nd Regiment (4th Burma Battalion) Madras Infantry
1901   32nd Burma Infantry
1903   92nd Punjabis

BATTLE HONOUR: *Ava*

The uniform included a blue turban with a red end and a white fringe, a white kullah, a long-skirted khaki tunic with white facings, a white kummerband, khaki trousers, and khaki gaiters. This uniform is illustrated by figure 274.

93RD BURMA INFANTRY

In 1914, this regiment was stationed at Barrackpore and comprised four companies of Sikhs and four of Punjabi Muslims.

1800   Raised as the 1st Battalion, 17th Regiment, Madras Native Infantry
1824   33rd Regiment of Madras Native Infantry
1885   33rd Regiment of Madras Infantry
1890   3rd Regiment of Burma Infantry
1891   33rd Regiment (3rd Burma Battalion) Madras Infantry
1901   33rd Burma Infantry
1903   93rd Burma Infantry

The uniform included a khaki turban with a yellow fringe, a long-skirted khaki tunic with yellow facings, a yellow kummerband, khaki trousers, and khaki gaiters. This uniform is illustrated by figure 275.

94TH RUSSELL'S INFANTRY

In 1914, this regiment was stationed at Bolarum and comprised three companies of Rajputs, three of Dekhani Muslims, and two of Jats.

1813	Raised as the 1st Battalion of the Russell Brigade
1826	1st Regiment of Infantry, Nizam's Army
1854	1st Infantry, Hyderabad Contingent
1903	94th Russell's Infantry

BATTLE HONOURS: *Mahidpoor, Nowah*

This uniform included a dark green turban with a dark green kullah, a long-skirted scarlet tunic with dark green facings, a dark green kummerband with a hanging end on the right side, blue trousers with red piping, and white gaiters. This uniform is illustrated by figure 276.

95TH RUSSELL'S INFANTRY

In 1914, this regiment was stationed at Bombay with detachments in the Persian Gulf. This regiment comprised three companies of Rajputs, three of Hindustani Muslims, and two of Ahirs of the Eastern Punjab.

1813	Raised as the 2nd Battalion of the Russell Brigade
1826	2nd Regiment of Infantry, Nizam's Army
1854	2nd Infantry, Hyderabad Contingent
1903	95th Russell's Infantry

BATTLE HONOURS: *Mahidpoor, Nowah, Burma 1885-87*

The uniform included a dark green turban with a yellow kullah, a long-skirted scarlet tunic with dark green facings, a dark green kummerband with a dark green hanging end and yellow stripes in sets of four and a yellow fringe on the right side, blue trousers with red piping, and white gaiters. This uniform is illustrated by figure 277.

96TH BERAR INFANTRY

In 1914, this regiment was stationed at Mhow and comprised three companies of Rajputs, three of Hindustani Muslims, and two of Jats.

1797	Raised as the 2nd Battalion, Aurangabad Division
1826	3rd Regiment of Infantry, Nizam's Army
1854	3rd Infantry, Hyderabad Contingent
1903	96th Berar Infantry

BATTLE HONOURS: *Nowah, Central India, Burma 1885-87*

The uniform included a dark green turban with yellow stripes, a long-skirted scarlet tunic with dark green facings, dark green kummerband with a dark green hanging end with evenly spaced yellow stripes on the right side, blue trousers with red piping, and white gaiters. This uniform is illustrated by figure 278.

97TH DECCAN INFANTRY

In 1914, this regiment was stationed at Jubbulpore with a detachment at Sutna. This regiment comprised three companies of Rajputs, three of Dekhani Muslims, and two of Jats.

1794	Raised as the 3rd Battalion, Aurangabad Division
1826	4th Regiment of Infantry, Nizam's Army

1854   4th Infantry, Hyderabad Contingent
1903   97th Deccan Infantry

BATTLE HONOUR: *Nagpore*

The uniform included a dark green turban with a red fringe, a long-skirted scarlet tunic with dark green facings, a dark green kummerband with a dark green hanging end with pink-white-pink evenly spaced stripes on the left side, blue trousers with red piping, and white gaiters. This uniform is illustrated by figure 279.

98TH INFANTRY

In 1914, this regiment was stationed at Saugor and comprised three companies of Rajputs, three of Hindustani Muslims, and two of Ahirs of the Eastern Punjab.

1788   Raised as Salabat Khan's Regiment and also known as the 1st Battalion, Ellichpur Brigade
1826   7th Regiment of Infantry, Nizam's Army
1854   5th Infantry, Hyderabad Contingent
1903   98th Infantry

BATTLE HONOURS: *Central India, China 1900*

This uniform included a dark green turban, a long-skirted scarlet tunic with dark green facings, a dark green kummerband with a plain dark green hanging end on the left side, blue trousers with red piping, and white gaiters. This uniform is illustrated by figure 280.

99TH DECCAN INFANTRY

In 1914, this regiment was stationed at Sehore and comprised three companies of Rajputs, three of Hindustani Muslims, and two of Jats.

1788   Raised as the 2nd Battalion, Ellichpur Brigade
1826   8th Regiment of Infantry, Nizam's Army
1854   6th Infantry, Hyderabad Contingent
1903   99th Deccan Infantry

This uniform included a dark green turban, a long-skirted scarlet tunic with dark green facings, a dark green kummerband with a plain dark green hanging end on the left side, blue trousers with red piping, and white gaiters. This uniform is illustrated by figure 281.

100TH Regiment—Vacant in 1914

101ST GRENADIERS

In 1914, this regiment was stationed at Bangalore and comprised two companies of Dekhani Mahrattas, two of Konkani Mahrattas, two of Rajputana Muslims, and two of Punjabi Muslims.

1778   Raised from the Grenadier Companies of other regiments and designated the 8th Battalion, Bombay Sepoys
1783   Bombay Grenadiers
1784   Bombay Grenadier Battalion
1788   1st Bombay Battalion or Bombay Grenadiers
1796   1st or Grenadier Battalion, 1st Regiment of Bombay Native Infantry
1824   1st or Grenadier Regiment of Bombay Native Infantry
1885   1st Regiment of Bombay Infantry (Grenadiers)
1901   1st Bombay Grenadiers
1903   101st Grenadiers

BATTLE HONOURS: *Mangalore, Mysore, Hyderabad, Kandahar 1880, Afghanistan 1878-80, Burma 1885-87*

The uniform included a khaki turban with a blue and white striped fringe, a red kullah, a long-skirted scarlet tunic with white facings, a white kummerband with red stripes in sets of twos with a hanging end on the right side, blue trousers with red piping, and white gaiters. This uniform is illustrated by figure 282.

102ND KING EDWARD'S OWN GRENADIERS

In 1914, this regiment was stationed at Muscat, Oman, with detachments at Bushire and Baghdad. King George V was Colonel-in-Chief. This regiment comprised two companies of Western Rajputana Jats, two of Bagri Jats and Jats from Eastern Rajputana, two of Rajputana Gujars, and two of Punjabi Muslims.

1796	Raised as the 13th Battalion, Bombay Native Infantry
1797	1st Battalion, 5th Regiment of Bombay Native Infantry
1798	2nd Battalion, 1st Regiment of Bombay Native Infantry
1818	2nd Battalion, 1st or Grenadier Regiment of Bombay Native Infantry
1824	2nd or Grenadier Regiment of Bombay Native Infantry
1876	2nd (Prince of Wales's Own) Regiment of Bombay Native Infantry (Grenadiers)
1885	2nd (Prince of Wales's Own) Regiment of Bombay Infantry (Grenadiers)
1901	2nd (Prince of Wales's Own) Bombay Grenadiers
1903	102nd Prince of Wales's Own Grenadiers
1906	102nd King Edward's Own Grenadiers

BATTLE HONOURS: *Egypt (with the Sphinx), Kirkee, Corygaum, Abyssinia*

The uniform included a khaki turban with an upright red fringe, a long-skirted scarlet tunic with white facings, a white kummerband, blue trousers with red piping, and white gaiters. This uniform is illustrated by figure 283.

103RD MAHRATTA LIGHT INFANTRY

In 1914, this regiment was stationed at Ahmednagar and comprised four companies of Dekhani Mahrattas, two of Konkani Mahrattas, and two of Dekhani Muslims.

1768	Raised as the 2nd Battalion of Bombay Sepoys
1796	1st Battalion, 2nd Regiment of Bombay Native Infantry
1824	3rd Regiment of Bombay Native Infantry
1871	3rd Bombay Native (Light) Infantry
1901	3rd Bombay Light Infantry
1903	103rd Mahratta Light Infantry

BATTLE HONOURS: *Mysore, Seedaseer, Seringapatam, Beni Boo Ali, Punjab, Mooltan, Goojerat, Abyssinia*

The uniform included a khaki turban with a red fringe, a black kullah, a long-skirted scarlet tunic with black facings, a black kummerband, blue trousers with red piping, and white gaiters. This uniform is illustrated by figure 284.

104TH WELLESLEY'S RIFLES

In 1914, this regiment was stationed at Baroda and comprised four companies of Rajputana Jats, two of Rajputana Rajputs, and two of Punjabi Muslims.

1775	Raised as the 5th Battalion of Bombay Sepoys
1778	9th Battalion of Bombay Sepoys
1796	2nd Battalion, 2nd Regiment of Bombay Native Infantry
1824	4th Regiment of Bombay Native Infantry
1885	4th Regiment of Bombay Infantry, or Rifle Corps
1889	4th Regiment (1st Battalion Rifle Corps) Bombay Infantry
1901	4th Bombay Rifles
1903	104th Wellesley's Rifles

BATTLE HONOURS: *Mysore, Seringapatam, Bourbon, Beni Boo Ali, Punjab, Mooltan, Persia, Reshire, Bushire, Kooshab, Central India, Kandahar 1881, Afghanistan 1878-80, British East Africa 1898*

The uniform included a rifle green turban, a long-skirted rifle green tunic with red facings, a red kummerband, rifle green trousers, and rifle green puttees. This uniform is illustrated by figure 285.

105TH MAHRATTA LIGHT INFANTRY

In 1914, this regiment was stationed at Poona with a detachment at Satara. This regiment comprised four companies of Dekhani Mahrattas, two of Konkani Mahrattas, and two of Dekhani Muslims.

1788	Raised as the 3rd Battalion of Bombay Sepoys
1796	1st Battalion, 3rd Regiment of Bombay Native Infantry
1824	5th Regiment of Bombay Native Infantry
1841	5th Regiment of Bombay Native (Light) Infantry
1885	5th Regiment of Bombay (Light) Infantry
1901	5th Bombay Light Infantry
1903	105th Mahratta Light Infantry

BATTLE HONOURS: *Mysore, Seedaseer, Seringapatam, Beni Boo Ali, Kahun, China 1860-62, Afghanistan 1879-80, Burma 1885-87*

The uniform included a khaki turban with a red fringe, a black kullah, a long-skirted scarlet tunic with black facings, a black kummerband, blue trousers with red piping, and white gaiters. This uniform is illustrated by figure 286.

106TH HAZARA PIONEERS

In 1914, this regiment was stationed at Quetta with detachments at Kacha, Kila Saifulla, Manzai, Hirok, Hindubag, and Ziarat. This regiment comprised eight companies of Hazaras.

1904	Formed from drafts from the 124th Duchess of Connaught's Own, and the 126th Baluchistan Infantry Regiments as the 106th Hazara Pioneers

The uniform included a khaki turban, a long-skirted khaki tunic with red facings, a red kummerband, khaki trousers, and khaki puttees. The leather belts crossed in back supported the pioneer equipment, including a shovel, ax, or pickax. This uniform is illustrated by figure 287.

107TH PIONEERS

In 1914, this regiment was stationed at Meerut and comprised two companies of Pathans, two of Rajputana Muslims, two of Sikhs, and two of Dekhani Mahrattas.

1788	Raised as the 4th Battalion, Bombay Sepoys
1796	1st Battalion, 4th Regiment of Bombay Native Infantry
1824	7th Regiment of Bombay Native Infantry
1885	7th Regiment of Bombay Infantry
1900	7th Bombay Infantry (Pioneers)
1903	107th Pioneers

BATTLE HONOURS: *Mysore, Seedaseer, Seringapatam, Beni Boo Ali, Burma 1885-87*

The uniform included a khaki turban with a red fringe, a long-skirted scarlet tunic with white facings, a white kummerband, blue trousers with red piping, and blue puttees. The leather belts crossed in back supported the pioneer equipment, including a shovel, ax, or pickax. This uniform is illustrated by figure 288.

108TH INFANTRY

In 1914, this regiment was stationed at Bangalore and comprised two companies of Dekhani Mahrattas, two of Konkani Mahrattas, two of Punjabi Muslims, and two of Rajputana Muslims.

1768	Raised as the 1st Battalion, Bombay Sepoys
1796	2nd Battalion, 4th Regiment of Bombay Native Infantry
1824	8th Regiment of Bombay Native Infantry
1885	8th Regiment of Bombay Infantry
1901	8th Bombay Infantry
1903	108th Infantry

BATTLE HONOURS: *Mysore, Hyderabad, Afghanistan 1879-80*

The uniform included a khaki turban with a white fringe, a long-skirted scarlet tunic with white facings, a white kummerband, blue trousers with red piping, and white gaiters. This uniform is illustrated by figure 289.

109TH INFANTRY

In 1914, this regiment was stationed at Aden with detachments at Perim, Sheik Othman, and Berbera. This regiment comprised two companies of Dekhani Mahrattas, two of Konkani Mahrattas, two of Rajputana Muslims, and two of Punjabi Muslims.

1788	Raised as the 5th Battalion, Bombay Sepoys
1796	2nd Battalion, 1st Regiment of Bombay Native Infantry
1824	9th Regiment of Bombay Native Infantry
1885	9th Regiment of Bombay Infantry
1901	9th Bombay Infantry
1903	109th Infantry

BATTLE HONOURS: *Mysore, Seringapatam, Punjab, Mooltan, Afghanistan 1879-80*

The uniform included a blue turban with a white fringe, a red kullah, a long-skirted scarlet tunic with black facings, a black kummerband with a hanging end with white stripes in sets of three on the right side, blue trousers with red piping, and white gaiters. This uniform is illustrated by figure 290.

110TH MAHRATTA LIGHT INFANTRY

In 1914, this regiment was stationed at Belgaum and comprised four companies of Dekhani Mahrattas, two of Konkani Mahrattas, and two of Dekhani Muslims.

1797	Raised as the 2nd Battalion, 5th (Travancore) Regiment of Bombay Native Infantry
1824	10th Regiment of Bombay Native Infantry
1871	10th Regiment of Bombay Native (Light) Infantry
1885	10th Regiment of Bombay (Light) Infantry
1901	10th Bombay Light Infantry
1903	110th Mahratta Light Infantry

BATTLE HONOURS: *Central India, Abyssinia, Afghanistan 1879-80*

The uniform included a khaki turban with red edging, a black kullah, a long-skirted scarlet tunic with black facings, a black kummerband, blue trousers with red piping, and white gaiters. This uniform is illustrated by figure 291.

111TH Regiment—Vacant in 1914

112TH INFANTRY

In 1914, this regiment was stationed at Nowshera and comprised two companies of Western Rajputana Jats, two of Bagri Jats and Jats from Eastern Rajputana, two of Rajputana Gujars, and two of Punjabi Muslims.

1798	Raised as the 2nd Battalion, 6th Regiment of Bombay Native Infantry
1824	12th Regiment of Bombay Native Infantry
1885	12th Regiment of Bombay Infantry
1901	12th Bombay Infantry
1903	112th Infantry

BATTLE HONOURS: *Kirkee, Meanee, Hyderabad, Central India*

The uniform included a khaki turban with a red fringe, a white kullah, a long-skirted scarlet tunic with yellow facings, a yellow kummerband, blue trousers with red piping, and white gaiters. This uniform is illustrated by figure 292.

113TH INFANTRY

In 1914, this regiment was stationed at Dibrugarh with detachments at Buksa Duar, Gangtok, Gyantse, and Yatung. This regiment comprised two companies of Western Rajputana Jats, two of Bagri Jats and Jats from Eastern Rajputana, two of Rajputana Gujars, and two of Punjabi Muslims.

1800	Raised as the 1st Battalion, 7th Regiment of Bombay Native Infantry
1824	13th Regiment of Bombay Native Infantry
1885	13th Regiment of Bombay Infantry
1901	13th Bombay Infantry
1903	113th Infantry

BATTLE HONOURS: *Egypt, (with the Sphinx), Kirkee, Beni Boo Ali, Central India, Afghanistan 1878-80*

The uniform included a khaki turban with a red fringe, a long-skirted scarlet tunic with yellow facings, a yellow kummerband, blue trousers with red piping, and white gaiters. This uniform is illustrated by figure 293.

114TH MAHRATTAS

In 1914, this regiment was stationed at (Alipore) Calcutta and comprised four companies of Konkani Mahrattas, two of Dekhani Mahrattas, and two of Dekhani Muslims.

1800	Raised as the 2nd Battalion, 7th Regiment of Bombay Native Infantry
1824	14th Regiment of Bombay Native Infantry
1885	14th Regiment of Bombay Infantry
1901	14th Bombay Infantry
1903	114th Mahrattas

The uniform included a khaki turban with a dark blue end, a khaki kullah, a long-skirted scarlet tunic with yellow facings, a yellow kummerband, blue trousers with red piping, and white gaiters. This uniform is illustrated by figure 294.

115TH Regiment—Vacant in 1914

116TH MAHRATTAS

In 1914, this regiment was stationed at Jhansi and comprised four companies of Konkani Mahrattas, two of Dekhani Mahrattas, and two of Dekhani Muslims.

1800	Raised as the 2nd Battalion, 8th Regiment of Bombay Native Infantry or Gore's Regiment
1824	16th Regiment of Bombay Native Infantry
1885	16th Regiment of Bombay Infantry
1901	16th Bombay Infantry
1903	116th Mahrattas

BATTLE HONOURS: *Afghanistan 1879-80, British East Africa 1901*

The uniform included a khaki turban with a dark blue end, a red kullah, a long-skirted scarlet tunic with yellow facings, a yellow kummerband. blue trousers with red piping, and white gaiters. This uniform is illustrated by figure 295.

117TH MAHRATTAS

In 1914, this regiment was stationed at Poona with a detachment at Satara. This regiment comprised four companies of

Konkani Mahrattas, two of Dekhani Mahrattas, and two of Dekhani Muslims.

1800	Raised as the Bombay Fencible Regiment
1803	1st Battalion, 9th Regiment of Bombay Native Infantry
1824	17th Regiment of Bombay Native Infantry
1885	17th Regiment of Bombay Infantry
1901	17th Bombay Infantry
1903	117th Mahrattas

The uniform included a khaki turban with evenly spaced blue stripes, a red kullah, a long-skirted scarlet tunic with yellow facings, a yellow kummerband, blue trousers with red piping, and white gaiters. This uniform is illustrated by figure 296.

118TH Regiment—Vacant in 1914

119TH INFANTRY (THE MOOLTAN REGIMENT)

In 1914, this regiment was stationed at Ahmednagar and comprised two companies of Rajputana Gujars, two of Mers, two of Rajputana Rajputs, and two of Hindustani Muslims.

1817	Raised as the 1st Battalion, 10th Regiment of Bombay Native Infantry
1824	19th Regiment of Bombay Native Infantry
1885	19th Regiment of Bombay Infantry
1901	19th Bombay Infantry
1903	119th Infantry (The Mooltan Regiment)

BATTLE HONOURS: *Ghuznee 1839, Afghanistan, Punjab, Mooltan, Goojerat, Kandahar 1880, Afghanistan 1878-80*

The uniform included a khaki turban with a wide white stripe on the end, a yellow kullah, a long-skirted scarlet tunic with yellow facings, a yellow kummerband, blue trousers with red piping, and white gaiters. This uniform is illustrated by figure 297.

120TH RAJPUTANA INFANTRY

In 1914, this regiment was stationed at Belgaum and comprised two companies of Rajputana Gujars, two of Mers, two of Rajputana Rajputs, and two of Hindustani Muslims.

1817	Raised as the 2nd Battalion, 10th Regiment of Bombay Native Infantry
1824	20th Regiment of Bombay Native Infantry
1885	20th Regiment of Bombay Infantry
1901	20th Bombay Infantry
1903	120th Rajputana Infantry

BATTLE HONOURS: *Persia, Reshire, Bushire, Koosh-ab*

The uniform included a khaki turban, a yellow kullah, a long-skirted scarlet tunic with yellow facings, a yellow kummerband, blue trousers with red piping, and white gaiters. This uniform is illustrated by figure 298.

121ST PIONEERS

In 1914, this regiment was stationed at Jhansi and comprised two companies of Dekhani Mahrattas, two of Rajputana Muslims, two of Western Rajputana Jats, and two of Pathans.

1777	Raised as the Marine Battalion
1818	1st (or Marine) Battalion, 11th Regiment of Bombay Native Infantry
1824	21st or Marine Battalion
1861	21st Regiment of Bombay Native Infantry (The Marine Battalion)
1885	21st Regiment of Bombay Infantry (The Marine Battalion)
1901	21st Bombay Infantry (The Marine Battalion)
1903	121st Pioneers

BATTLE HONOURS: *Persian Gulf, Beni Boo Ali, Burma, Aden, Hyderabad, Punjab, Abyssinia*

The uniform included a blue turban with a white end and fringe, a long-skirted scarlet tunic with white facings, a white kummerband, blue trousers with red piping, and blue puttees. The leather belts crossed in back supported the pioneer equipment, including a shovel, ax, or pickax. This uniform is illustrated by figure 299.

122ND RAJPUTANA INFANTRY

In 1914, this regiment was stationed at Kohat and comprised two companies of Rajputana Gujars, two of Mers, two of Rajputana Rajputs, and two of Hindustani Muslims.

1818	Raised as the 2nd Battalion, 11th Regiment of Bombay Native Infantry
1824	22nd Regiment of Bombay Native Infantry
1885	22nd Regiment of Bombay Infantry
1901	22nd Bombay Infantry
1903	122nd Rajputana Infantry

BATTLE HONOUR: *China 1900*

The uniform included a khaki turban, a yellow kullah, a long-skirted scarlet tunic with emerald green facings, an emerald green kummerband with a hanging end with crimson-yellow-crimson stripes in sets of three on the left side, blue trousers with red piping, and white gaiters. This uniform is illustrated by figure 300.

123RD OUTRAM'S RIFLES

In 1914, this regiment was stationed at Manipur with a detachment at Kohima. This regiment comprised four companies of Rajputana Jats, two of Rajputana Rajputs, and two of Punjabi Muslims.

1820	Raised as the 1st Battalion, 12th Regiment of Bombay Native Infantry
1824	23rd Regiment of Bombay Native Infantry
1841	23rd Regiment of Bombay Native (Light) Infantry
1889	23rd Regiment (2nd Battalion Rifle Regiment) of Bombay Infantry
1901	23rd Bombay Rifles
1903	123rd Outram's Rifles

BATTLE HONOURS: *Kirkee, Persia, Afghanistan 1879-80, Burma 1885-87*

The uniform included a rifle green turban, a red kullah, a long-skirted rifle green tunic with red facings, a red kummerband with dark green vertical stripes, rifle green trousers, and rifle green puttees. This uniform is illustrated by figure 301.

124TH DUCHESS OF CONNAUGHT'S OWN BALUCHISTAN INFANTRY

In 1914, this regiment was stationed at Quetta and comprised two companies of Hazaras, two of Punjabi Muslims, two of Sikhs, one of Khattaks, and one of Wazirs.

1820	Raised as the 2nd (Marine) Battalion, 12th Regiment of Bombay Native Infantry
1823	2nd Battalion, 12th Regiment of Bombay Native Infantry
1824	24th Regiment of Bombay Native Infantry
1885	24th Regiment of Bombay Infantry
1891	24th (Baluchistan) Regiment of Bombay Infantry
1895	24th (Duchess of Connaught's Own Baluchistan) Regiment of Bombay Infantry
1901	24th (Duchess of Connaught's Own Baluchistan) Infantry
1903	124th Duchess of Connaught's Own Baluchistan Infantry

BATTLE HONOURS: *Aden, Central India, Afghanistan 1879-80, British East Africa 1896*

The uniform included a khaki turban, a red kullah, a long-skirted khaki tunic with red facings, a red kummerband with vertical green stripes in sets of two, red trousers, and white gaiters. This uniform is illustrated by figure 302.

125TH NAPIER'S RIFLES

In 1914, this regiment was stationed at Mhow and comprised four companies of Rajputana Jats, two of Rajputana Rajputs, and two of Punjabi Muslims.

1820	Raised as the 1st Extra Battalion of Bombay Native Infantry
1826	25th Regiment of Bombay Native (Light) Infantry
1889	25th Regiment (3rd Battalion Rifle Regiment) of Bombay Infantry
1901	25th Bombay Rifles
1903	125th Napier's Rifles

BATTLE HONOURS: *Meanee, Hyderabad, Central India, Abyssinia, Burma 1885-87*

The uniform included a rifle green turban, a long-skirted rifle green tunic with red facings, a red kummerband, red trousers, and white gaiters. A black metal badge on a red cloth background was worn on the front of the turban. This uniform is illustrated by figure 303.

126TH BALUCHISTAN INFANTRY

In 1914, this regiment was stationed at Fort Sandeman and comprised two companies of Hazaras, two of Sikhs, two of Baluchis and Brahuis, one of Khattaks, and one of Wazirs.

1825	Raised as the 2nd Extra Battalion of Bombay Native Infantry
1826	26th Regiment of Bombay Native Infantry
1885	26th Regiment of Bombay Native Infantry
1892	26th (Baluchistan) Regiment of Bombay Infantry
1901	26th Baluchistan Infantry
1903	126th Baluchistan Infantry

BATTLE HONOURS: *Persia, Koosh-ab, China 1900*

This uniform included a khaki turban, a red kullah, a long-skirted khaki tunic with red facings, a red kummerband, red trousers, and white gaiters. This uniform is illustrated by figure 304.

127TH QUEEN MARY'S OWN BALUCH LIGHT INFANTRY

In 1914, this regiment was stationed at Karachi and comprised three companies of Pathans, three of Mahsuds, and two of Punjabi Muslims.

1844	Raised as the Balooch Battalion or Scinde Baluchi Corps
1846	1st Baluch Battalion
1858	1st Baluch Extra Battalion of Bombay Native Infantry
1859	1st Baluch Regiment
1871	27th Bombay Native (Light) Infantry or 1st Baluch Regiment
1888	27th (1st Baluch Battalion) Bombay Light Infantry
1901	27th Baluch Light Infantry
1903	127th Baluch Light Infantry
1909	127th Princess of Wales's Own Baluch Light Infantry
1910	127th Queen Mary's Own Baluch Light Infantry

BATTLE HONOURS: *Delhi, Abyssinia, Afghanistan 1879-80, Burma 1885-87, British East Africa 1897-99*

The uniform included a rifle green turban, a red kullah, a long-skirted rifle green tunic with red facings, a red kummerband, red trousers, and white gaiters. This uniform is illustrated by figure 305.

128TH PIONEERS

In 1914, this regiment was stationed at Sitapur and comprised two companies of Yusufzais, two of Rajputana Muslims, two of Sikhs, and two of Dekhani Mahrattas.

1846	Raised as the 28th Regiment of Bombay Native Infantry
1885	28th Regiment of Bombay Infantry
1888	28th (Pioneer) Regiment of Bombay Infantry
1901	28th Bombay Pioneers
1903	128th Pioneers

BATTLE HONOURS: *Kandahar 1880, Afghanistan 1878-80, Suakin 1885, Tofrek, Punjab Frontier, Tirah*

The uniform included a blue turban with a white end and fringe, a long-skirted scarlet tunic with white facings, a white kummerband, blue trousers with red piping, and blue puttees. The leather belts crossed in the back supported the pioneer equipment, including a shovel, ax, or pickax. This uniform is illustrated by figure 306.

129TH DUKE OF CONNAUGHT'S OWN BALUCHIS

In 1914, this regiment was stationed at Karachi with a detachment at Sirola. Field Marshal Arthur, Duke of Connaught and Strathearn, was Colonel-in-Chief. This regiment comprised three companies of Pathans, three of Mahsuds, and two of Punjabi Muslims.

1846	Raised as the 2nd Baluch Battalion
1858	2nd Baluch Extra Battalion of Bombay Native Infantry
1859	2nd Bombay Baluch Regiment
1861	29th Regiment of Bombay Native Infantry or 2nd Baluch Regiment
1883	29th (Duke of Connaught's Own) Regiment of Bombay Native Infantry or 2nd Baluch Regiment
1888	29th (Duke of Connaught's Own) Regiment of Bombay Infantry
1903	129th Duke of Connaught's Own Baluchis

BATTLE HONOURS: *Persia, Reshire, Bushire, Kandahar 1880, Afghanistan 1878-80, Egypt 1882, Tel el Kebir*

The uniform included a rifle green turban, a red kullah, a long-skirted rifle green tunic with red facings, a red kummerband, red trousers, and white gaiters. This uniform is illustrated by figure 307.

130TH KING GEORGE'S OWN BALUCHIS (JACOB'S RIFLES)

In 1914, this regiment was stationed at Aurangabad. King George V was Colonel-in-Chief. This regiment comprised three companies of Pathans, three of Mahsuds, and two of Punjabi Muslims.

1858	Raised as the 1st Regiment, Jacob's Rifles
1861	30th Regiment of Bombay Native Infantry or Jacob's Rifles
1881	30th Regiment of Bombay Native Infantry or 3rd Baluch Battalion
1885	30th Regiment of Bombay Infantry
1901	30th Bombay Infantry
1903	130th Baluchis
1906	130th Prince of Wales's Own Baluchis
1909	130th Prince of Wales's Own Baluchis (Jacob's Rifles)
1910	130th King George's Own Baluchis (Jacob's Rifles)

BATTLE HONOURS: *Afghanistan 1878-80, China 1900*

The uniform included a rifle green turban, a red kullah, a long-skirted rifle green tunic with red facings, a red kummerband, red trousers, and white gaiters. This uniform is illustrated by figure 308.

THE BRIGADE OF GURKHAS

1ST KING GEORGE'S OWN GURKHA RIFLES (THE MALAUN REGIMENT)

In 1914, the 1st Battalion was stationed at Dharmsala; the 2nd Battalion was stationed at Chitral. King George V was Colonel-in-Chief.

1815	Raised as the 1st Nasiri Battalion
1823	1st Nasiri Local Battalion
1850	66th or Gurkha Regiment
1858	66th or Gurkha Light Infantry Regiment
1861	1st Gurkha Regiment (Light Infantry)
1886	The 2nd Battalion raised
1891	1st Gurkha (Rifle) Regiment
1901	1st Gurkha Rifles
1903	1st Gurkha Rifles (The Malaun Regiment)
1906	1st Prince of Wales's Own Gurkha Rifles (The Malaun Regiment)
1910	1st King George's Own Gurkha Rifles (The Malaun Regiment)

BATTLE HONOURS: *Bhurtpore, Aliwal, Sobraon, Afghanistan 1878-80, Punjab Frontier, Tirah*

The uniform included a black round cap, a rifle green tunic with scarlet facings, rifle green trousers, and black puttees. This uniform is illustrated by figure 309.

2ND KING EDWARD'S OWN GURKHA RIFLES (THE SIRMOOR REGIMENT)

In 1914, the 1st and 2nd Battalions were both stationed at Dehra Dun. King George V was Colonel-in-Chief.

1815	Raised as the Sirmoor Battalion
1823	8th (or Sirmoor) Local Battalion
1826	6th (or Sirmoor) Local Battalion
1850	Sirmoor Battalion
1858	Sirmoor Rifle Regiment
1861	17th Regiment of Bengal Native Infantry
1864	2nd Gurkha (Sirmoor Rifle) Regiment
1876	2nd (Prince of Wales's Own) Gurkha Regiment (The Sirmoor Rifles)
1886	The 2nd Battalion raised
1906	2nd King Edward's Own Gurkha Rifles (The Sirmoor Regiment)

BATTLE HONOURS: *Bhurtpore, Aliwal, Sobraon, Delhi, Kabul 1879, Kandahar 1880, Afghanistan 1878-80, Punjab Frontier, Tirah*

The uniform included a black round cap with a red and black diced border, a rifle green tunic with scarlet facings, rifle green trousers, and black puttees. This uniform is illustrated by figure 310.

3RD QUEEN ALEXANDRA'S OWN GURKHA RIFLES

In 1914, the 1st Battalion was stationed at Almora; the 2nd Battalion was stationed at Lansdowne.

1815	Raised as the Kamaon Battalion
1826	7th Kamaon Local Battalion
1860	Kamaon Battalion
1861	18th Regiment of Bengal Native Infantry
1864	3rd (The Kamaon) Gurkha Regiment
1887	3rd Gurkha Regiment, a second battalion is raised
1890	The 2nd Battalion becomes the 39th Garhwal Rifles
1891	3rd Gurkha (Rifle) Regiment, a new 2nd Battalion raised
1901	3rd Gurkha Rifles
1907	3rd The Queen's Own Gurkha Rifles
1908	3rd Queen Alexandra's Own Gurkha Rifles

BATTLE HONOURS: *Delhi, Ahmed Khel, Afghanistan 1878-80, Burma 1885-87, Chitral, Punjab Frontier, Tirah*

The uniform included a black round cap, a rifle green tunic with black facings, rifle green trousers, and black puttees. This uniform is illustrated by figure 311.

4TH GURKHA RIFLES

In 1914, the 1st and 2nd Battalions were both stationed at Bakloh.

1857	Raised as the Extra Gurkha Regiment
1861	19th Regiment of Bengal Native Infantry; later in the same year, designated the 4th Gurkha Regiment
1886	The 2nd Battalion raised
1891	4th Gurkha (Rifle) Regiment
1901	4th Gurkha Rifles

BATTLE HONOURS: *Ali Masjid, Kabul 1879, Kandahar 1880, Afghanistan 1878-80, Chitral, Punjab Frontier, Tirah, China 1900*

The uniform included a black round cap, a rifle green tunic with black facings, rifle green trousers, and black puttees. This uniform is illustrated by figure 312.

5TH GURKHA RIFLES (FRONTIER FORCE)

In 1914, the 1st and 2nd Battalions were both stationed at Abbotabad.

1858	Raised as the 25th Punjab Infantry or Hazara Gurkha Battalion
1861	5th Gurkha Regiment or Hazara Gurkha Battalion, Punjab Irregular Force
1886	The 2nd Battalion raised
1887	5th Gurkha Regiment
1891	5th Gurkha (Rifle) Regiment
1901	5th Gurkha Rifles
1903	5th Gurkha Rifles (Frontier Force)

BATTLE HONOURS: *Peiwar, Kotal, Charasiah, Kabul 1879, Kandahar 1880, Afghanistan 1878-80, Punjab Frontier*

The uniform included a black round cap, a rifle green tunic with black facings, rifle green trousers, and black puttees. This uniform is illustrated by figure 313.

6TH GURKHA RIFLES

In 1914, the 1st and 2nd Battalions were both stationed at Abbottabad.

1817	Raised as the Cuttack Legion
1823	Rangpur Light Infantry Battalion
1826	8th (or Rangpur) Local Light Infantry
1844	1st Assam Light Infantry
1861	42nd Regiment of Bengal Native Infantry
1864	42nd (Assam) Regiment of Bengal Native (Light) Infantry
1885	42nd (Assam) Regiment of Bengal (Light) Infantry
1886	42nd (Gurkha) Light Infantry
1891	42nd Gurkha (Rifle) Regiment of Bengal Infantry
1901	42nd Gurkha Rifles
1903	6th Gurkha Rifles
1904	The 2nd Battalion raised

BATTLE HONOUR: *Burma 1885-87*

The uniform included a black round cap with a red pom-pom on the top, a rifle green tunic with black facings, rifle green trousers, and black puttees. This uniform is illustrated by figure 314.

7TH GURKHA RIFLES

In 1914, the 1st and 2nd Battalions were both stationed at Quetta.

1907	The 2nd Battalion of the 10th Gurkha Rifles became the 1st and 2nd Battalions of the 7th Gurkha Rifles. A previous 7th Gurkha Rifles became the 2nd Battalion, 8th Gurkha Rifles, in 1903.

The uniform included a black round cap, a rifle green tunic with black facings, rifle green trousers, and black puttees. This uniform is illustrated by figure 315.

8TH GURKHA RIFLES

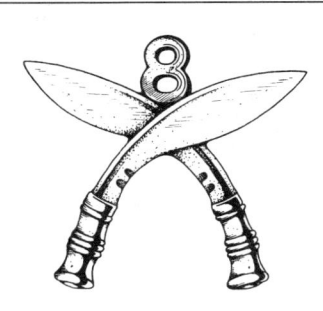

In 1914, the 1st Battalion was stationed at Shillong; the 2nd Battalion was stationed at Lansdowne.

1ST BATTALION

1824	Raised as the Sylhet Local Battalion
1826	11th Sylhet Local (Light) Infantry
1861	44th Bengal Native Infantry
1864	44th (Sylhet) Regiment of Bengal Native (Light) Infantry
1885	44th (Sylhet) Regiment of Bengal (Light) Infantry
1886	44th Gurkha (Light) Infantry
1891	44th Gurkha (Rifle) Regiment of Bengal Infantry
1901	44th Gurkha Rifles
1903	1st Battalion, 8th Gurkha Rifles

2ND BATTALION

1835	Raised as the Assam Sebundy Corps
1844	2nd Assam Light Infantry
1861	43rd Regiment of Bengal Native Infantry
1864	43rd (Assam) Regiment of Bengal Native Infantry
1885	43rd (Assam) Regiment of Bengal Infantry
1886	43rd Regiment, Gurkha Light Infantry
1891	43rd Gurkha (Rifle) Regiment of Bengal Infantry
1901	43rd Gurkha Rifles
1903	7th Gurkha Rifles
1907	2nd Battalion, 8th Gurkha Rifles

BATTLE HONOUR: *Burma 1885-87*

The uniform included a black round cap, a rifle green tunic with black facings, rifle green trousers, and black puttees. This uniform is illustrated by figure 316.

9TH GURKHA RIFLES

In 1914, the 1st and 2nd Battalions were both stationed at Dehra Dun.

1817	Raised as the Fatagarh Levy
1891	Mianpuri Levy
1824	63rd Regiment of Bengal Native Infantry
1861	9th Regiment of Bengal Native Infantry
1885	9th Regiment of Bengal Infantry
1894	9th (Gurkha Rifle) Regiment of Bengal Infantry
1901	9th Gurkha Rifles
1904	The 2nd Battalion raised

BATTLE HONOURS: *Bhurtpore, Sobraon, Afghanistan 1878-80, Punjab Frontier*

The uniform included a black round cap, a rifle green tunic with black facings, rifle green trousers, and black puttees. This uniform is illustrated by figure 317.

10TH GURKHA RIFLES

In 1914, the 1st Battalion was stationed at Maymyo, Burma; the 2nd Battalion was stationed at Darjeeling.

1890	Raised as the 1st Regiment of Burma Infantry from the Kubo Valley Police Battalion
1891	10th Regiment (1st Burma Battalion), Madras Infantry
1892	10th Regiment (1st Burma Rifles), Madras Infantry
1895	10th Regiment (1st Burma Gurkha Rifles), Madras Infantry
1901	10th Gurkha Rifles; a second battalion raised
1907	The 2nd Battalion of the 10th Gurkha Rifles became the 1st and 2nd Battalions of the 7th Gurkha Rifles
1908	A new 2nd Battalion raised

The uniform included a black round cap, a rifle green tunic with black facings, rifle green trousers, and black puttees. Illustration 318 is a rear view showing the kukri, the famous curved knife of the Gurkhas.

DEPARTMENTAL CORPS

SUPPLY AND TRANSPORT CORPS

This corps was raised in 1810 and was known as the Commissariat and Transport Department. In 1895, it became the Supply and Transport Corps.

The Supply and Transport Corps bore the tremendous responsibility of feeding and supplying both men and animals in the Indian Army. In addition, it was responsible for the transport of rations, forage, ammunition, and all other sorts of needed equipment. This corps operated both wheeled and pack transport. Illustrated is a two-wheeled cart in common use in 1914. Wheeled transport was usually drawn by ponies, mules, or bullocks. In 1914, there was no mechanical transport in India. Pack transport used mules or camels. During World War I (1914-18), the Supply and Transport Corps expanded many times over. The mule corps alone was expanded into more than 50 trains.

The uniform for officers included a white helmet or turban, a blue tunic with white facings, and blue trousers with white stripes. Other ranks wore a khaki turban with a white fringe, a long-skirted khaki tunic, khaki trousers, and khaki puttees. A British officer and an Indian driver, together with a two-wheeled cart, are illustrated by figure 319.

ARMY REMOUNT DEPARTMENT

Organized in 1808, this department was responsible for purchasing, rearing, training, and issuance of horses to British and Indian cavalry regiments. It also issued mules for pack and wheeled transport. The department operated breeding farms for horses and mules in northern India. In 1828, a remount depot for southern India was established at Hosur, a town near Madras. Horses from Australia were brought there to be acclimatized and trained.

The uniform for officers included a white helmet or turban, a blue tunic with yellow facings, and blue trousers. Other ranks wore a khaki turban and a khaki uniform. An Indian officer's uniform is illustrated by figure 320.

ARMY CLOTHING DEPARTMENT

This department was probably organized around 1912. It was responsible for the clothing requirements of the Indian Army.

The uniform for officers included a white helmet or turban, a blue tunic with light blue facings, and blue trousers. Other ranks wore a khaki turban and a khaki uniform. It appears that this department did not have a badge in 1914. An Indian officer's uniform is illustrated by figure 321.

INDIAN MEDICAL SERVICE AND DEPARTMENT

The Indian Medical Service included both British and Indian commissioned medical officers (doctors). British medical officers were furnished by the Royal Army Medical Corps. The equivalent of warrant and noncommissioned officers of the Royal Army Medical Corps were found in the Indian Medical Department. Members of this department (all Indians) were called assistant surgeons; they received three years of medical training and were able to deal with most medical procedures except for the most serious cases. In 1914, female nurses were not employed by the Indian Army.

The uniform of an Indian medical officer included a blue turban, a blue tunic with black velvet facings, and blue trousers. This uniform is illustrated by figure 322.

ARMY HOSPITAL CORPS

Although medical officers of the Royal Army Medical Corps were assigned to Indian medical establishments, hospital personnel were not. The Army Hospital Corps replaced them. This corps provided ward servants, cooks, water carriers, sweepers, and washermen. The Indian caste system made this division of labor necessary. In 1914, there were 11 companies of the Army Hospital Corps, all stationed in India, except for one at Aden. The uniform included a khaki turban and a khaki uniform. This uniform is illustrated by figure 323.

ARMY BEARER CORPS

The personnel of this corps were members of a separate and distinct caste. They served as bearers of the sick and wounded. The ambulance wagons of this corps were the typical two-wheeled carts drawn by bullocks or mules. In 1914, there were 11 companies of the Army Bearer Corps, all stationed in India, except for one at Aden. The uniform included a khaki turban with a purple fringe and a khaki uniform. This uniform is illustrated by figure 324.

ARMY VETERINARY SERVICE

A farrier and veterinary service was first organized in India in 1821. Veterinary officers in the Indian Army wore the uniform of the regiment or corps to which they were attached. The uniform of unattached veterinary officers included a blue turban, a blue tunic with maroon facings, and blue trousers with maroon stripes. Mounted personnel wore blue breeches with maroon stripes. An unattached Indian veterinary officer's uniform is illustrated by figure 325.

INDIAN ORDNANCE DEPARTMENT

This department was organized in 1884 and was responsible for the purchase, manufacture, repair and distribution of ammunition, weapons and equipment.

The uniform for officers included a white helmet or turban, a blue tunic with scarlet facings, and blue trousers with wide scarlet stripes. Other ranks wore a khaki turban and a khaki uniform. It appears that there was no badge for this formation in 1914. An Indian officer's uniform is illustrated by figure 326.

MILITARY FARMS DEPARTMENT

This unique department was organized in 1912. It was responsible for maintaining military farms that produced the dairy products consumed by the Indian Army and the tremendous amount of forage required by the animals.

The uniform for officers included a white helmet or turban, a scarlet tunic with green facings, and blue trousers. Other ranks wore a khaki turban and a khaki uniform. An Indian officer's uniform is illustrated by figure 327.

INDIAN ARMY CORPS OF CLERKS

This corps was organized in 1912. It was responsible for clerical and administrative duties at brigade and higher levels.

The uniform included a blue turban, a scarlet tunic with blue facings, blue trousers with red piping, and khaki puttees. It appears that there was no badge for this corps in 1914. This uniform is illustrated by figure 328.

IMPERIAL SERVICE TROOPS

THE ALWAR LANCERS

This regiment was raised in 1884. The uniform included a dark blue and light blue turban with dark blue stripes on the lighter part, a scarlet kurta with white facings, a blue kummerband, white breeches, and blue puttees. The lance pennon was dark blue over yellow. This uniform is illustrated by figure 329.

THE ALWAR INFANTRY

This regiment was raised in 1889. The uniform included a red over white over blue turban, a long-skirted scarlet tunic with white facings including the cuffs and front panel, a scarlet kummerband. blue trousers with red piping, and white gaiters. This uniform is illustrated by figure 330.

THE BAHAWALPUR MOUNTED ESCORT

This unit was originally raised as lancers in 1885. In 1901, it was partially converted to a camelry escort for the Transport Corps. The uniform included a khaki turban with green stripes, a khaki kurta with green facings, a green kummerband, khaki breeches, and khaki puttees. This uniform is illustrated by figure 331.

THE BAHAWALPUR CAMEL TRANSPORT CORPS

This unit was originally raised as lancers in 1885. In 1901, it was partially converted to a camel transport corps. In 1914, this corps consisted of a train of over 900 pack camels.

The uniform included a khaki turban with green stripes, a long-skirted khaki tunic with green facings, a green kummerband, khaki trousers, and khaki puttees. This uniform is illustrated by figure 332.

THE BHARATPUR INFANTRY

The year that this regiment was raised could not be determined. The uniform included a yellow turban with red and white stripes, a long-skirted scarlet tunic with yellow facings, a scarlet kummerband, blue trousers with red piping, and khaki gaiters. This uniform is illustrated by figure 333.

THE BHARATPUR TRANSPORT CORPS

The year that this corps was raised could not be determined. In 1914, this corps consisted of a train of ponies and carts. The uniform included a yellow turban with red and white stripes, a long-skirted khaki tunic with yellow facings, a yellow kummerband, khaki trousers, and khaki gaiters. This uniform is illustrated by figure 334.

THE BHAVANAGAR LANCERS

This regiment was raised in 1892. In 1914, the regiment consisted of only two squadrons. The uniform included a blue and yellow turban with red, white, and blue stripes on the yellow part, a blue kurta with scarlet facings, a scarlet kummerband, white breeches, and blue puttees. This uniform is illustrated by figure 335.

THE BHOPAL (VICTORIA) LANCERS

This regiment was raised in 1902. The uniform included a blue and yellow turban with wide blue stripes on the yellow part, a blue tunic with yellow facings and plastron, white breeches, and blue puttees. This uniform is illustrated by figure 336.

THE BIKANER CAMEL CORPS

This corps was raised in 1884. In 1914, it was personally commanded by the Maharajah of Bikaner. The uniform included a yellow turban with red stripes, a white kurta with red facings, a red kummerband, white breeches, and blue puttees. This uniform is illustrated by figure 337.
BATTLE HONOURS: *China 1900, Somaliland 1901-04*

THE BIKANER SADUL LIGHT INFANTRY

This regiment was raised in 1839. The uniform included a long-skirted scarlet tunic with yellow facings, a yellow kummerband, blue trousers with red piping, and white gaiters. The turban appears to have been very similar to that of the Camel Corps. This uniform is illustrated by figure 338.

THE FARIDKOT SAPPERS AND MINERS

This company-size unit was raised in 1900. The uniform included a dark green turban, a scarlet tunic with dark green facings, blue trousers with red piping, and blue puttees. The spelling of Faridkot varied (see shoulder title above). This uniform is illustrated by figure 339.

THE GWALIOR LANCERS

1ST GWALIOR (JAYAJI) LANCERS

This regiment was raised in 1833.

2ND GWALIOR (ALIJAH) LANCERS

This regiment was raised in 1852.

3RD GWALIOR (MAHARAJAH RAO SCINDIA'S OWN) LANCERS

This regiment was raised in 1868.

The three regiments of Gwalior lancers appear to have been uniformed alike. A numeral within the badge indicated the regiment. The uniform included a blue and yellow turban with blue stripes in sets of two on the yellow part, a blue kurta with scarlet facings and plastron, yellow piping on the collar and cuffs, white breeches, and blue puttees. This uniform is illustrated by figure 340.

THE GWALIOR INFANTRY

3RD MAHARAJAH SCINDIA'S OWN BATTALION, GWALIOR INFANTRY

This battalion was raised in 1885. The uniform included a black turban, a long-skirted scarlet tunic with black facings, a black kummerband, blue trousers with red piping, and white gaiters. This uniform is illustrated by figure 341.

4TH MAHARAJAH BAHADOUR BATTALION, GWALIOR INFANTRY

This battalion was raised in 1822. The uniform included a dark green turban, a red kullah, a long-skirted dark green tunic with red facings, a red kummerband, dark green trousers, and white gaiters. This uniform is illustrated by figure 342.

(Note: A numeral within the badge indicated the battalion. The 1st and 2nd Battalions of the Gwalior Infantry remained in the Gwalior State Forces.)

THE GWALIOR TRANSPORT CORPS

This corps was raised in 1890. In 1914, it consisted of a train of over 300 carts. The uniform included a red turban, a long-skirted blue tunic with red facings, a red kummerband, blue trousers with red piping, and khaki gaiters. This uniform is illustrated by figure 343.

BATTLE HONOURS: *Chitral, Tirah*

THE HYDERABAD LANCERS

1ST (NIZAM'S OWN) HYDERABAD LANCERS

This regiment was raised in 1864.

2ND (NIZAM'S OWN) HYDERABAD LANCERS

This regiment was raised in 1893.

Except for the badges, both regiments of the Hyderabad Lancers appear to have been uniformed alike. The uniform included a dark green and white turban with yellow stripes on the white part, a dark green kurta with buff facings, a buff kummerband, white breeches, and dark green puttees. This uniform is illustrated by figure 344.

THE INDORE MOUNTED ESCORT

Raised in 1904, this unit was a cavalry escort to the Indore Transport Corps. The uniform included a khaki turban; a khaki kurta with gold brocade on the collar, cuffs, and front panel; a khaki kummerband; khaki breeches; and blue puttees. The Indore Mounted Escort consisted of only one squadron. This uniform is illustrated by figure 345.

THE INDORE TRANSPORT CORPS

This corps was raised in 1904 and consisted of a train of ponies and carts. The uniform included a buff-colored turban with brown stripes in sets of three, a long dark green tunic with buff facings, buff trousers, and khaki gaiters. This uniform is illustrated by figure 346

THE JAIPUR TRANSPORT CORPS

This corps was raised in 1889. In 1914, it consisted of a train of 550 carts. The uniform included a dark green and yellow turban with dark green stripes in sets of four on the yellow part, a dark green tunic, khaki trousers, and khaki puttees. This uniform is illustrated by figure 347.

BATTLE HONOURS: *Chitral, Tirah*

THE JIND INFANTRY

This regiment was raised in 1839. The uniform included a dark green turban, a long dark green tunic with white facings, dark green trousers, and khaki gaiters. This uniform is illustrated by figure 348.

BATTLE HONOUR: *Tirah*

THE JODHPUR (SARDAR RISSALAH) LANCERS

1ST JODHPUR (SARDAR RISSALAH) LANCERS

This regiment was raised in 1888.
BATTLE HONOURS: *Tirah, China 1900*

2ND JODHPUR (SARDAR RISSALAH) LANCERS

This regiment was raised in 1888.
BATTLE HONOURS: *Tirah, China 1900*

Both regiments appear to have been uniformed alike. The uniform included a blue turban with a band of red and yellow stripes and an upright white fringe on top of the turban, a white kurta, a rust-colored kummerband, white breeches, and blue puttees. The lance pennons were orange. This uniform is illustrated by figure 349

THE JUNAGARH LANCERS

This regiment was raised in 1891. In 1914, it consisted of only one squadron. The uniform included a blue turban, a blue kurta with red facings, a red kummerband, white breeches, and blue puttees. This uniform is illustrated by figure 350.

THE KARPURTHALA (JAGJIT) INFANTRY

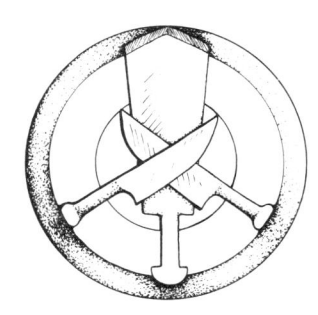

This regiment was formed in 1890 as Imperial Service infantry from an existing Karpurthala battalion that dated at least to 1857. The uniform included a scarlet turban, a long-skirted scarlet tunic with yellow facings, a yellow kummerband, blue trousers with red piping, and white gaiters. This uniform is illustrated by figure 351.

BATTLE HONOUR: *Tirah*

THE KASHMIR LANCERS

The year that this regiment was raised could not be determined. The uniform included a blue and yellow turban with thin black stripes in sets of three on the yellow part, a blue kurta with red facings, a red kummerband, white breeches, and blue puttees. This uniform is illustrated by figure 352.

BATTLE HONOUR: *Tirah*

THE KASHMIR INFANTRY

1ST KASHMIR INFANTRY

This battalion was raised in 1873. The uniform included a white turban, a khaki tunic with yellow facings, khaki trousers, and black puttees. This uniform is illustrated by figure 353.

BATTLE HONOUR: *Tirah*

2ND KASHMIR RIFLES

! This battalion was raised in 1869.

BATTLE HONOUR: *Tirah*

3RD KASHMIR RIFLES

This battalion was raised in 1856.

BATTLE HONOUR: *Tirah*

Both battalions of the Kashmir Rifles were uniformed alike. The uniform included a white turban, a khaki tunic with bottle green facings, khaki trousers, and black puttees. This uniform is illustrated by figure 354.

(NOTE: The badge of the Kashmir Infantry had a numeral between the handles of the kukri to indicate the battalion.)

THE KASHMIR MOUNTAIN ARTILLERY

The year that this unit was raised could not be determined. In 1914, the Kashmir Mountain Artillery consisted of two batteries.

The uniform included a khaki turban with a red fringe, a khaki tunic with blue facings, khaki trousers, and khaki puttees. A numeral worn above the shoulder title (illustrated above) indicated the 1st or 2nd Battery. This uniform is illustrated by figure 355.

BATTLE HONOUR: *Tirah*

THE KHAIRPUR MOUNTED ESCORT

This unit was raised in 1905 as a camelry escort for the Khairpur Camel Transport Corps. The uniform included a khaki turban, a khaki kurta, kummerband, breeches, and puttees. This uniform is illustrated by figure 356.

THE KHAIRPUR CAMEL TRANSPORT CORPS

This corps was raised in 1905 and consisted of a train of pack camels. The uniform included a khaki turban, a long-skirted khaki tunic, kummerband, trousers, and gaiters. This uniform is illustrated by figure 357.

THE MALERKOTLA SAPPERS AND MINERS

The year that this company-sized unit was raised could not be determined; however, it was in existence in 1878 (see battle honours). The uniform included a dark green turban, a scarlet tunic with dark green facings, blue trousers with red piping, and blue puttees. This uniform is illustrated by figure 358.

BATTLE HONOURS: *Afghanistan 1878-80, China 1900*

THE MYSORE LANCERS

This regiment was raised in 1799 as the Sillidar Horse of Mysore. The uniform included a dark blue and light blue turban with dark blue stripes in sets of twos on the lighter part, a blue kurta with white facings and plastron, blue breeches with double white stripes, and blue puttees. The lance pennons were dark blue over white. This uniform is illustrated by figure 359.

BATTLE HONOURS: *Assaye, Mahidopore, Argaum, Central India*

THE MYSORE TRANSPORT CORPS

This corps, consisting of ponies and carts, was probably raised around 1889. The uniform included a dark blue and yellow turban with white and dark blue stripes on the yellow part, a long-skirted khaki tunic, a red kummerband, khaki trousers, and khaki puttees. The officer's uniform was more elaborate. The uniform of a dismounted officer of this corps is illustrated by figure 360.

THE NABHA INFANTRY

This regiment was raised in 1889. The uniform included a scarlet turban, a long-skirted scarlet tunic with white facings, a white kummerband, blue trousers with red piping, and white gaiters. This uniform is illustrated by figure 361.

BATTLE HONOUR: *Tirah*

THE NAVANAGAR (CHOTI KHAS) LANCERS

The year that this regiment was raised could not be determined. In 1914, this regiment consisted of only one squadron. The uniform included a dark green turban, a dark green kurta with red facings, a red kummerband, white breeches, and dark green puttees. This uniform is illustrated by figure 362.

THE PATIALA (RAJINDER) LANCERS

This regiment was raised in 1824. The uniform included a dark green turban with primrose-yellow stripes, a dark green kurta with primrose-yellow facings, a primrose-yellow kummerband, white breeches, and dark green puttees. This uniform is illustrated by figure 363.

BATTLE HONOUR: *Tirah*

THE PATIALA INFANTRY

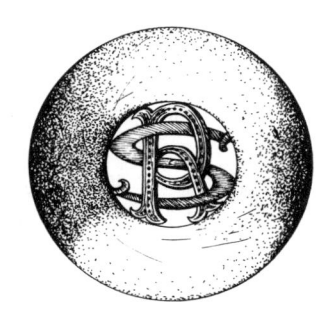

1ST PATIALA INFANTRY

This battalion was raised in 1700. The uniform included a khaki turban, a long-skirted scarlet tunic with white facings, a white kummerband, blue trousers with red piping, and white gaiters. This uniform is illustrated by figure 364.

BATTLE HONOUR: *Tirah*

2ND PATIALA INFANTRY

This battalion was raised in 1710. The uniform included a khaki turban, a long-skirted scarlet tunic with green facings, a green kummerband, blue trousers with red piping, and white gaiters. This uniform is illustrated by figure 365.

BATTLE HONOUR: *Tirah*

THE RAMPUR (ROHILLA) LANCERS

The year that this regiment was raised could not be determined. In 1914, the regiment consisted of only two squadrons. The uniform included a blue and yellow turban with dark blue stripes on the yellow part, a scarlet kurta with yellow piping on the collar, cuffs and front panel, a blue kummerband, white breeches, and blue puttees. This uniform is illustrated by figure 366.

THE RAMPUR INFANTRY

The year that this regiment was raised could not be determined. The uniform included a khaki turban, a long-skirted scarlet tunic with yellow facings, a yellow kummerband, blue trousers with red piping, and white gaiters. This uniform is illustrated by figure 367.

THE SIMUR SAPPERS AND MINERS

This company-sized unit was raised in 1890. The uniform included a blue and yellow turban with white and blue stripes on the yellow part, a scarlet tunic with blue facings, blue trousers with red piping, and blue puttees. This uniform is illustrated by figure 368.

BATTLE HONOUR: *Tirah*

THE TEHRI-GARHWAL SAPPERS AND MINERS

This company-sized unit was raised in 1907. The uniform included a dark green turban, a scarlet tunic with dark green facings, dark blue trousers with red piping, and blue puttees. This uniform is illustrated by figure 369.

THE UDAIPUR LANCERS

This regiment was raised in 1908. It consisted of only one squadron. It was also known as the Mewar Lancers. The uniform included a white turban with an upright crimson fringe, white kurta with crimson facings, a crimson kummerband, white breeches, and blue puttees. No badge could be found for this regiment. This uniform is illustrated by figure 370.

VOLUNTEER FORCES, INDIA, 1914.

The Volunteer Forces were part-time formations recruited from the British and Anglo-Indian communities in India. In many cases, these units numbered only 30 to 100 men. The uniform was khaki with a khaki helmet, unless otherwise noted.

LIGHT HORSE

THE ASSAM VALLEY LIGHT HORSE

This regiment was raised in 1891. The uniform was khaki.

THE BIHAR LIGHT HORSE

This regiment was raised in 1862. Officers wore a white helmet with a blue uniform; other ranks wore khaki.

THE BOMBAY LIGHT HORSE

This regiment was raised in 1885. Officers wore a white helmet with a blue uniform; other ranks wore khaki.

THE CALCUTTA LIGHT HORSE

This regiment was raised in 1881. The uniform was khaki.

THE CHOTA-NAGPUR LIGHT HORSE

This regiment was raised in 1891. The uniform was khaki.

THE PUNJAB LIGHT HORSE

This regiment was raised in 1893. Officers and other ranks wore white helmets and blue uniforms.

THE SURMA VALLEY LIGHT HORSE

This regiment was raised in 1883. The uniform included a white helmet, a blue tunic, and white breeches. The officer's tunic had white facings; other ranks had no facings.

1ST UNITED PROVINCES HORSE

This regiment was raised in 1904. The uniform was khaki.

2ND UNITED PROVINCES HORSE

This regiment was raised in 1909. The uniform was khaki.

MOUNTED RIFLES

THE NORTHERN BENGAL MOUNTED RIFLES

This regiment was raised in 1873. The uniform included a white helmet, a scarlet tunic with white facings, and white breeches.

THE SOUTHERN PROVINCES MOUNTED RIFLES

This regiment was raised in 1904. The uniform was khaki.

ARTILLERY

THE BOMBAY VOLUNTEER ARTILLERY

This volunteer force was raised in 1887. The uniform was khaki.

THE CALCUTTA PORT DEFENCE VOLUNTEERS, ARTILLERY

This volunteer force was raised in 1899. The uniform included a white helmet, a blue tunic with scarlet facings, and blue trousers with wide scarlet stripes.

THE COSSIPORE ARTILLERY VOLUNTEERS

This volunteer force was raised in 1884. The uniform was blue with white helmets.

THE KARACHI ARTILLERY VOLUNTEERS

This volunteer force was raised in 1892. The uniform was khaki.

THE MADRAS ARTILLERY VOLUNTEERS (THE DUKE'S OWN)

This volunteer force was raised in 1879. The uniform was blue with white helmets.

THE MOULMEIN VOLUNTEER ARTILLERY

This volunteer force was raised in 1885. The uniform was khaki.

RANGOON PORT DEFENCE VOLUNTEERS (THE DUKE'S OWN) ARTILLERY

This volunteer force was raised in 1879. The uniform was blue with white helmets.

ENGINEERS

THE BOMBAY VOLUNTEER ARTILLERY (ELECTRICAL ENGINEER COMPANY)

This company was raised in 1902. The uniform was khaki.

THE CALCUTTA PORT DEFENCE VOLUNTEER CORPS (ELECTRICAL ENGINEER COMPANY)

This company was raised in 1902. The uniform included a white helmet, a scarlet tunic with blue facings, and blue trousers with wide scarlet stripes.

THE EAST INDIAN RAILWAY VOLUNTEER RIFLES (ENGINEER COMPANY)

This company was raised in 1892. The uniform was khaki.

THE KARACHI ARTILLERY VOLUNTEERS (ELECTRICAL ENGINEER COMPANY)

This company was raised in 1902. The uniform was khaki.

THE MADRAS ARTILLERY VOLUNTEERS (ELECTRICAL ENGINEER COMPANY)

This company was raised in 1902. The uniform was khaki.

THE RANGOON PORT DEFENCE VOLUNTEER CORPS (ELECTRICAL ENGINEER COMPANY)

This company was raised in 1902. The uniform was khaki.

RIFLES

THE AGRA VOLUNTEER RIFLES

This regiment was raised in 1878. The uniform was khaki with grass-green facings.

THE ALLAHABAD VOLUNTEER RIFLES

This regiment was raised in 1871. The uniform was khaki.

THE ASSAM-BENGAL RAILWAY VOLUNTEER RIFLES

This regiment was raised in 1901 and included a troop of mounted rifles. The uniform was khaki with dark green facings.

THE BALUCHISTAN VOLUNTEER RIFLES

This regiment was raised in 1883. The uniform was khaki.

THE BANGALORE RIFLE VOLUNTEERS

This regiment was raised in 1868 and included one section of mounted rifles. The uniform included a white helmet, a scarlet tunic with green facings, and blue trousers with red piping.

THE BENGAL AND NORTH-WESTERN RAILWAY VOLUNTEER RIFLES

This regiment was raised 1879. The uniform was khaki.

THE BENGAL-NAGPUR RAILWAY VOLUNTEER RIFLE CORPS

This regiment was raised in 1888. In 1914, there were two battalions. The uniform was khaki.

THE BOMBAY, BARODA AND CENTRAL INDIA RAILWAY VOLUNTEER RIFLES

This regiment was raised in 1877 and included a mounted troop. The uniform was khaki.

THE BOMBAY VOLUNTEER RIFLES

This regiment was raised in 1877. The uniform was khaki.

THE BURMA RAILWAYS VOLUNTEER CORPS

This regiment was raised in 1879. The uniform was khaki with maroon facings.

THE CALCUTTA SCOTTISH VOLUNTEERS

This regiment was raised in 1911. The uniform included a white helmet and a scarlet doublet with white facings. The kilt was of Hunting Stewart tartan. The sporran was white with six black tassels. The hose was green and white, and the green glengarry cap had a green and white diced border.

1ST BATTALION, CALCUTTA VOLUNTEER RIFLES

This battalion was raised in 1863. The uniform was khaki.

2ND (PRESIDENCY BATTALION), CALCUTTA VOLUNTEER RIFLES

This battalion was raised in 1888. The uniform was khaki.

THE CAWNPORE VOLUNTEER RIFLES

This regiment was raised in 1877 and included a half troop of mounted rifles. The uniform was khaki.

THE COORG AND MYSORE RIFLES

This regiment was raised in 1884. The uniform was khaki.

THE EAST COAST VOLUNTEER RIFLES

This regiment was raised in 1885. The uniform was khaki.

THE EAST INDIAN RAILWAY VOLUNTEER RIFLES

This regiment was raised in 1869. The uniform was khaki.

THE EASTERN BENGAL STATE RAILWAY VOLUNTEER RIFLES

This regiment was raised in 1873. The uniform was khaki.

THE EASTERN BENGAL VOLUNTEER RIFLES

This regiment was raised in 1901 and included a mounted troop originally raised in 1885. The uniform was khaki with green facings.

THE GREAT INDIAN PENINSULA RAILWAY VOLUNTEER RIFLE CORPS

This regiment was raised in 1875. The uniform was khaki.

THE HYDERABAD VOLUNTEER RIFLES

This regiment was raised in 1882 and included a mounted troop. The uniform was khaki.

THE KOLAR GOLD FIELDS RIFLE VOLUNTEERS

This regiment was raised in 1903 and included a mounted troop. The uniform was khaki.

THE LUCKNOW VOLUNTEER RIFLES

This regiment was raised in 1872. The uniform was khaki.

THE MADRAS AND SOUTHERN MAHRATTA RAILWAY RIFLES

The 1st Battalion was raised in 1885; the 2nd Battalion was raised in 1886. The uniform was khaki.

THE MADRAS VOLUNTEER GUARDS

This regiment was raised in 1857 and included a mounted troop, originally raised in 1885. The uniform included a white helmet, a blue tunic with scarlet facings, and blue trousers with red piping.

THE MALABAR VOLUNTEER RIFLES

This regiment was raised in 1885. The uniform was khaki.

THE MOULMEIN VOLUNTEER RIFLES

This regiment was raised in 1877. The uniform was khaki.

THE MUSSOORIE VOLUNTEER RIFLES

This regiment was raised in 1871. The uniform was khaki.

THE NAGPUR VOLUNTEER RIFLES

This regiment was raised in 1861 and included a mounted troop. The uniform was khaki.

THE NAINI TAL VOLUNTEER RIFLES

This regiment was raised in 1871. The uniform was khaki.

THE NILGIRI VOLUNTEER RIFLES

This regiment was raised in 1878. The uniform was khaki.

THE NORTH-WESTERN RAILWAY VOLUNTEER RIFLES

This regiment was raised in 1880. The uniform was khaki.

THE OUDH AND ROHILKHAND RAILWAY VOLUNTEER RIFLES

This regiment was raised in 1903. The uniform was khaki.

THE POONA VOLUNTEER RIFLES

This regiment was raised in 1887 and included one section of mounted rifles. The uniform was khaki.

THE PUNJAB VOLUNTEER RIFLES

This regiment was raised in 1861. The uniform was khaki.

THE RANGOON VOLUNTEER RIFLES

This regiment was raised in 1877 and included a mounted troop originally raised in 1884. The uniform was khaki.

THE SIMLA VOLUNTEER RIFLES

This regiment was raised in 1861. The uniform was khaki with green facings.

THE SIND VOLUNTEER RIFLES

This regiment was raised in 1879. The uniform was khaki.

THE SOUTH ANDAMAN VOLUNTEER RIFLES

This regiment was raised in 1884. The uniform was khaki.

THE SOUTH INDIAN RAILWAY VOLUNTEER RIFLES

This regiment was raised in 1884. The uniform was khaki.

THE UPPER BURMA VOLUNTEER RIFLES

This regiment was raised in 1888 and included a mounted troop. The uniform was khaki.

THE YERCAUD RIFLES VOLUNTEERS

This regiment was raised in 1886. The uniform was khaki.

FRONTIER MILITIA FORCES, INDIA

The Frontier Militia Forces were recruited from friendly tribes in the remote North-West Frontier Province in India. The tribes involved received a subsidy from the Indian Government for their services. The Frontier Militia patrolled designated areas and provided intelligence on the movement of any hostile forces. Uniforms were khaki with khaki turbans and other dress. Most likely, various items of tribal dress were worn as well. The Khyber Rifles had green facings.

THE KHYBER RIFLES
Raised in 1878

THE ZHOB MILITIA
Raised in 1894

THE SEMANA RIFLES
Raised in 1897

THE NORTH WAZIRISTAN MILITIA
Raised in 1899

THE SOUTH WAZIRISTAN MILITIA
Raised in 1899

THE KURRAM MILITIA
Raised in 1900

THE NORTHERN SCOUTS
Raised in 1900

THE GILGIT SCOUTS
Probably raised around 1900

THE MAKRAN LEVIES
Probably raised around 1900

THE PESHIN SCOUTS
Probably raised around 1900

THE THAL SCOUTS
Probably raised around 1900

THE TOCHI SCOUTS
Probably raised around 1900

INDIAN STATE FORCES

For many centuries, the Indian Feudal States under their rulers (maharajahs, nizams, etc.), maintained their own armies. There were 610 Feudal States ranging in size from Jammu and Kashmir (85,885 square miles) down to the smallest of only a few square miles. When the Imperial Service Troops plan was initiated, many states that contributed units reduced their state forces in order to maintain their Imperial Service units up to the standards of the Indian Army. State forces that remained served as household guards, ceremonial troops, etc. They also served to maintain order within the state and enhance the ruler's prestige. Even the smallest states maintained a few men as a bodyguard. For the most part, state forces were armed with outdated weapons of the Victorian era. In 1914, some states still maintained sizable forces of cavalry, infantry, and artillery.

The uniforms of the state forces are not well documented. It is likely that some records remain in the hands of various princes or their descendants. It is known that some of the bodyguard and ceremonial type units were very elaborately uniformed. The Nizam of Hyderabad even imported Arabs and African Negroes to serve in his forces.

The following list names the states that still maintained substantial military forces apart from the Imperial Service Troops in 1914. Some states had contributed their entire military force to the Imperial Service Troops. Some states contributed to the Imperial Service Troops and maintained some forces. Others maintained state forces only.

FATEH PALTAN

This Alwar infantry regiment was raised in 1825

THE BARIA RANJIT INFANTRY

Raised in 1909

THE BARODA CAVALRY

There were two regiments raised in 1886.

THE BARODA GUARDS

An infantry regiment raised in 1886

THE BARODA ARTILLERY

One battery of field artillery raised in 1886

1ST BARODA INFANTRY

Raised in 1862

2ND BARODA INFANTRY

Raised in 1860

THE BENARES INFANTRY

Raised in 1826

THE BAHAWALPUR INFANTRY

Raised in 1827

THE CHAURAS BODYGUARD

The year that this Bharatpur bodyguard was raised could not be determined.

THE BHAVAANAGAR INFANTRY

Raised in 1872

THE BHOPAL SULTANA INFANTRY

The year that this regiment was raised could not be determined.

THE BIKANER DUNGAR LANCERS

Raised in 1455

A camel pack artillery battery was raised in 1906.

THE CHAMBA INFANTRY

Raised in 1881

THE COCHIN INFANTRY

The year that this regiment was raised could not be determined.

THE COOCH BEHAR INFANTRY

This regiment was raised in the 16th Century.

THE MAHARAJAH KUMARI KAMLA RAJE'S OWN LIGHT HORSE

Raised in Dhar in 1864

THE DHARANGADA MAKHWAN INFANTRY

Raised in 1909

THE DHOLPUR MAKHUAN INFANTRY

Raised in 1909

THE FARIDKOT INFANTRY

Raised in 1892

1ST MAHARAJAH SAKHYA BATTALION

This Gwalior infantry battalion was raised in 1858.

2ND MAHARAJAH JAYAJIRAO'S BATTALION

This Gwalior infantry battalion was raised in 1822.

Gwalior also maintained three batteries of horse artillery raised in 1861, 1863, and 1898, respectively.

THE GOLCONDA LANCERS

This Hyderabad lancer regiment was raised in 1873.

THE HYDERABAD INFANTRY

There were three battalions raised between 1859 and 1864.

THE RAJENDRA HAZARI GUARDS

This Jaipur cavalry regiment was raised in the 15th century.

THE SAWAI MAN GUARDS

This Jaipur infantry regiment was raised in the 16th century.

THE KALAT INFANTRY

The date that this regiment was raised could not be determined.

THE KARPURTHALA PARAMJIT INFANTRY

Raised in 1800

THE FAIZ LIGHT INFANTRY

The date that this Khairpur regiment was raised could not be determined.

THE KOLHAPUR INFANTRY

The date that this regiment was raised could not be determined.

THE MYSORE CAVALRY

There were two regiments of cavalry. The dates that these regiments were raised could not be determined.

THE MYSORE INFANTRY

There were three battalions of infantry. The dates that these battalions were raised could not be determined.

THE NAVANAGAR SHATRUSHALYA INFANTRY

Raised in 1876

THE RAJPIPLA STATE INFANTRY

The date that this regiment was raised could not be determined.

THE SUKET INFANTRY

The date that this regiment was raised could not be determined.

1ST TRAVANCORE INFANTRY

Raised in 1740

2ND TRAVANCORE INFANTRY

Raised in 1819

Travancore also maintained a small force of cavalry (60 men) and a battery of artillery (30 men).

THE MEWAR INFANTRY

This regiment was raised in Udaipur (Mewar) in 1880.

CHAPTER EIGHT
Land Forces of the Colonies and Protectorates of the British Empire, 1914

The colonies and protectorates of the British Empire stretched around the globe in 1914, including tropical and frigid islands, desert coastlines, a large portion of Africa, and a scattering of ports and outposts in all parts of the world. This colonial empire was never really planned. Through conquest and treaty, the British Empire controlled most of the vital gates of the world: Gibraltar, Suez, Aden, and others. These gates gave the Royal Navy command of the world's sea-lanes, vital to the Empire's existence. Important areas of the Empire were garrisoned by British and Indian troops. Small detachments of infantry and artillery were provided for the lesser, more remote colonies.

Some colonies and protectorates raised regular forces from the native populations. All colonies and protectorates maintained a police or constabulary force. Civilian rifle clubs acted as a sort of reserve. Most colonies had a volunteer or militia force in being or at least an ordinance enacted by the colonial government for some sort of a defence force. In many cases, however, the unit had not yet been raised.

UNIFORMS

The regular regiments of the colonies and protectorates are listed on the following pages and illustrated on the color plates. Colonial militia and volunteer formations are listed but are not illustrated. The uniforms illustrated are those of a private in *full dress*. *Service dress* consisted of the usual khaki, with modifications depending on the weather and local conditions.

PERMANENT FORCES OF THE COLONIES AND PROTECTORATES

ROYAL MALTA ARTILLERY

1800	Raised as the Maltese Light Infantry
1803	The Maltese Light Infantry provided 300 men to form the Maltese Coast Artillery
1861	The Maltese Light Infantry and the Maltese Coast Artillery amalgamated to form the Royal Malta Fencibile Artillery
1889	The word, fencible, dropped from the title
1914	The Royal Malta Artillery consisted of three garrison artillery companies

BATTLE HONOUR: *Egypt 1882*

The uniform included a white Wolseley helmet with a brass ball and a blue tunic with a scarlet collar and piping down the front. There were yellow shoulder cords and piping around the collar and on the cuffs. Blue trousers had wide scarlet stripes. This uniform is illustrated by figure 371.

THE WEST INDIA REGIMENT

In 1914, the 1st Battalion was stationed at Sierra Leone, West Africa; the 2nd Battalion was stationed at Kingston, Jamaica.

1ST BATTALION

1778   Raised in North America as the South Carolina Regiment (Blacks). In 1914, the 1st Battalion was recruited in Jamaica.

2ND BATTALION

1792   Raised as St. Vincent's Black Rangers. In 1914, the 2nd Battalion was recruited in Barbados.

BATTLE HONOURS: *Dominica, Martinique, Guadaloupe, Ashantee, West Africa 1887, 1892,93,94, Sierra Leone 1898*

The uniform included a red skull cap with a wraparound white turban with a hanging end at the back, a white shirt with yellow piping on the cuffs, a scarlet zouave, vest-type jacket with yellow piping, blue trousers with yellow stripes, and white gaiters with leather tops. This uniform is illustrated by figure 372.

British officers wore a white Wolseley helmet with a brass spike, a scarlet tunic with white facings, and blue trousers with scarlet stripes.

The colours of the West India Regiment conformed to British regulations for an infantry regiment with white facings. The King's Colour was the Union. The Regimental Colour was white with a red St. George's Cross. The West India regiment was administered as part of the British Army.

THE WEST AFRICA REGIMENT

1896   Raised for the defence of Sierra Leone and the port of Freetown, a naval base and headquarters for all military forces in West Africa.

BATTLE HONOURS: *Sierra Leone 1897-98, Ashanti 1900*

The uniform included a red fez with a black tassel, a khaki tunic, a red kummerband, khaki shorts, and khaki puttees. This uniform is illustrated by figure 373.

(NOTE: The West Africa Regiment should not be confused with the Sierra Leone Battalion of the West African Frontier Force.)

THE WEST AFRICAN FRONTIER FORCE

1897   Organized from existing native colonial formations in West Africa

In 1914, the West African Frontier Force (W.A.F.F.) consisted of the Nigeria Regiment with five infantry battalions. One battalion was mounted infantry. The Gold Coast Regiment had two infantry battalions: the Sierra Leone Battalion of infantry and the Gambia Company of infantry. In addition to the infantry formations, there were three batteries of pack artillery and three companies of engineers.

BATTLE HONOURS: *Ashantee 1873-74* (inherited from earlier units)

Ashanti 1900 (The spelling of the earlier and later battle honours differs.)

Except for brass shoulder titles denoting the battalion or company and colored vests denoting the arm, units of the West African Frontier Force wore the same uniform. The uniform included a red fez with a black tassel, a khaki tunic, a red kummerband, khaki shorts, and khaki puttees. In addition, a vest of various colors and piping indicated the arm of service. Infantry wore a red vest with yellow piping and a blue collar. Artillery wore a blue vest with yellow piping and a red collar. Engineers wore a red vest with blue piping. These uniforms are illustrated by figures 374, 375 and 376.

THE KING'S AFRICAN RIFLES

1895   The Central Africa Rifles raised from native levies around the nucleus of an Indian contingent

1895   The Uganda Rifles raised from native levies around the nucleus of Sudanese troops formerly of the army of the Khedive of Egypt

1895   The East Africa Rifles raised from private forces maintained by the Imperial British East Africa Company

1902   The Central Africa Rifles, the Uganda Rifles, and the East Africa Rifles amalgamated to form the King's African Rifles

BATTLE HONOURS: *Ashanti 1900* (inherited from the earlier units) *Somaliland 1901-04*

In 1914, there were three active battalions of the King's African Rifles. The 1st (Central African) Battalion was stationed in Nyasaland. The 2nd battalion was disbanded in 1912. The 3rd (East African) Battalion was in Kenya, and the 4th (Uganda) Battalion was in Uganda.

The uniform included a red fez with a black tassel, a khaki tunic, khaki shorts, and khaki puttees. This uniform is illustrated by figure 377.

THE SOMALILAND CAMEL CORPS

1912   Raised as a camel constabulary
1914   The Somaliland Camel Corps, a military force

The uniform included a khaki turban with a blue flash and the letters *S C C* sewn on the turban, a greenish-brown pullover, khaki shorts, and blue puttees. This uniform is illustrated by figure 378.

THE NORTHERN RHODESIA POLICE (MILITARY WING)

This force was formed in 1912 from the North-Eastern Rhodesia Constabulary, raised in 1898, and from the Barotseland Police, raised in 1900. The word *police* in the title is misleading since this force was indeed a military unit with officers on loan from the British Army. In 1933, the Northern Rhodesia Police was re-designated the Northern Rhodesia Regiment.

The uniform included a black fez with a red tassel, a khaki tunic, khaki shorts, and khaki puttees. It appears that there was no badge for this unit until it became a regiment in 1933. This uniform is illustrated by figure 379.

THE MALAY STATES GUIDES

This formation was raised in 1875 and maintained by the sultans of the Federated Malay States of Perak, Selangor, and the confederation of nine small states known as Negri Sembilan. The Malay States Guides were recruited in India.

In 1914, the Malay States Guides were an infantry formation consisting of four companies of Sikhs, two companies of Punjabi Muslims and Pathans, and an attached battery of mountain artillery.

The uniform included a dark blue and yellow turban with light blue stripes on the dark blue part and dark blue stripes on the yellow part, a scarlet tunic with green facings and white piping, blue trousers with red piping, and white gaiters. This uniform is illustrated by figure 380.

THE ARMED CONSTABULARY OF NORTH BORNEO

1897 Raised as the British North Borneo Dyak Police
1903 Redesignated the Armed Constabulary of North Borneo

Even though the word *constabulary* appears in the title, this unit was liable for service as a military force outside the colony of North Borneo.

Besides Dyaks (natives of North Borneo), Malays, Sikhs, and Punjabi Muslims were recruited for this unit.

The uniform varied according to the race of the wearer. Dyaks and Malays wore a round red cap. Sikhs and Punjabis wore turbans. A khaki tunic and khaki trousers or shorts were worn by all. The Dyaks were barefoot; the others wore boots and khaki puttees. A Dyak uniform is illustrated by figure 381.

Note: The illustration shows a Dyak constable on patrol riding on a carabao, a type of water buffalo found in Borneo. This animal had no trouble carrying its rider through the swampy jungles found in this remote area.

THE SARAWAK RANGERS

This unit was raised in 1872 as a private force by Sir Charles Johnson Brooke, nephew of James Brooke, founder of Sarawak and known as the White Raja of Sarawak. When Sarawak became a British protectorate in 1888, the Sarawak Rangers continued as the military force. Sarawak formed part of the Island of Borneo. In 1914, the Sarawak Rangers numbered some 250 men, mostly Dyak natives and some Sikhs recruited from India, under a British commandant.

The government of Sarawak also maintained a small naval force to patrol the coastline and the swampy estuaries of this remote protectorate. The naval force comprised one paddle steamer (1884), mounting one gun, and two schooners (1881 and 1875), each mounting two guns. Naval officers and crews were issued uniforms of white drill and blue serge. The badge was an anchor and a crown.

The military uniform of the Sarawak Rangers included a short black fez with a black pom-pom on top and a white tunic with black brandenbergs in a set of three on the front of the tunic. There was black piping on the cuffs and the trousers were white. The Dyaks were barefoot. The Sikhs, of course, wore a turban. The uniform of a Dyak ranger is illustrated by figure 382.

THE JOHORE MILITARY FORCE

1878 Raised as a bodyguard by the Sultan of Johore. Johore was an independent Malay state under British protection.
1910 The Johore Military Force had grown from a bodyguard unit into a full battalion of Malay infantry with an attached battery of pack artillery manned by Pathans recruited in India.

In 1914, the Johore Military Force was under the personal command of the Sultan of Johore.

The infantry uniform included a blue cap without a brim. A brass badge was centered within a white semicircular front above the hat band. The uniform also included a khaki tunic, khaki shorts, and khaki puttees. The Pathans of the artillery battery wore a khaki turban, a khaki tunic, trousers, and puttees. These uniforms are illustrated by figure 383.

The infantry battalion carried the flag of Johore with a gold fringe and tassels as its colour. It was a blue flag with a red canton in the upper left and, within the canton, a white crescent and star.

(NOTE: There had been three other regular colonial regiments, but these had been disbanded by 1914.)

The Ceylon Regiment—Disbanded in 1874, this regiment was made up of Malays and later Africans imported for the job. Military service did not appeal to the Sinhalese. From 1874, Ceylon was garrisoned by British and Indian troops.

The Hong Kong Regiment—Raised in 1891 and disbanded in 1909, this regiment had been manned by Sikhs recruited in India. From 1909, Hong Kong was strongly garrisoned by British and Indian troops.

The Chinese Regiment—Raised in 1898 and disbanded in 1902, this regiment had been raised for the defence of Wei-Hai-Wei, a British naval station on the coast of the Shangtung Peninsula of China. The regiment consisted of Chinese troops with British officers and noncommissioned officers. In 1914, Wei-Hai-Wei was defended by the Royal Navy.

MILITIA, VOLUNTEERS AND YEOMANRY OF THE COLONIES

THE ANTIGUA DEFENCE FORCE

This defence force was raised in 1897 and consisted of a company of mounted infantry. The uniform was khaki.

THE BARBADOS VOLUNTEER FORCE

This volunteer force was raised in 1902 and consisted of a company of mounted infantry, a company of garrison artillery, and two companies of infantry. The uniform was khaki.

THE BERMUDA VOLUNTEER RIFLE CORPS

This corps was raised in 1895 and consisted of four companies of infantry. The uniform included a black rifle busby, a rifle green tunic with green facings, and rifle green trousers.

THE BERMUDA MILITIA ARTILLERY

This artillery formation was raised in 1902 and consisted of two companies of garrison artillery. The uniform included a white helmet, a blue tunic with scarlet facings, and blue trousers with wide scarlet stripes.

THE BRITISH GUIANA MILITIA

This militia formation was raised in 1891 and consisted of a company of infantry and a company of garrison artillery. The infantry uniform included a white Wolesley helmet, a scarlet tunic with white facings, and blue trousers with red piping. The artillery uniform included a white Wolesley helmet, a blue tunic with scarlet facings, and blue trousers with wide scarlet stripes.

THE BELIZE LIGHT INFANTRY VOLUNTEERS

This volunteer force was raised in British Honduras in 1897 and consisted of two companies of infantry. The uniform included a white Wolesley helmet, a scarlet tunic with green facings, and blue trousers with red piping.

THE BELIZE MOUNTED INFANTRY VOLUNTEERS

This volunteer force was raised in British Honduras in 1904 and consisted of a company of mounted infantry. The uniform was khaki.

THE CEYLON LIGHT INFANTRY

This regiment was raised in 1881 and consisted of a battalion of 14 companies. The uniform was khaki.

THE CEYLON VOLUNTEER MEDICAL CORPS

This corps was raised in 1881 and consisted of a medical company. The uniform was khaki.

THE CEYLON MOUNTED RIFLES

This unit was raised in 1887 and consisted of two squadrons of mounted rifles. The uniform was khaki.

THE CEYLON ARTILLERY VOLUNTEERS

This volunteer force was raised in 1888 and consisted of two companies of garrison artillery. The uniform was khaki.

THE CEYLON ENGINEER VOLUNTEERS

This volunteer force was raised in 1896 and consisted of a company of engineers. The uniform was khaki.

THE CEYLON PLANTERS RIFLE CORPS

This corps was raised in 1901 and consisted of an infantry battalion of eight companies. The uniform was khaki.

THE FALKLAND ISLANDS VOLUNTEER CORPS

This volunteer corps was raised in 1893 and consisted of a company of infantry. The uniform included a green wedge cap with scarlet piping, a dark grey tunic with green facings and scarlet piping, and dark grey trousers.

THE GAMBIA ARTILLERY VOLUNTEERS

This volunteer force was raised in 1907 consisted of a small formation of garrison artillery. The uniform was khaki.

THE GOLD COAST VOLUNTEERS

This volunteer force was raised in 1906 and consisted of a company of infantry. The uniform was khaki.

THE HONG KONG VOLUNTEER CORPS

This corps was raised in 1854 and consisted of a company of mounted rifles, four companies of garrison artillery, a company of engineers, and a company of infantry. The uniform was khaki.

THE JAMAICA MILITIA ARTILLERY

This militia force raised in 1879 consisted of a company of garrison artillery. The uniform included a khaki slouch hat, a blue tunic, trousers, and puttees.

THE JOHORE VOLUNTEER FORCE

This volunteer force was raised in 1904 by the Sultan of Johore. It was a battalion of infantry consisting wholly of Malays. The uniform was khaki.

THE KING'S OWN MALTA REGIMENT OF MILITIA

This regiment was raised in 1889 and consisted of two infantry battalions of eight companies each. The uniform included a white Wolesley helmet, a scarlet tunic with blue facings, and blue trousers with red piping.

CORPS OF ROYAL ENGINEERS (MILITIA) MALTA DIVISION

This militia formation was raised in 1901 and consisted of a company of engineers. The uniform included a white Wolesley helmet, a scarlet tunic with blue facings, and blue trousers with a wide red stripe.

THE PENANG VOLUNTEERS

This volunteer force was raised in 1889 and consisted of three companies of infantry, one each of Europeans, Malays, and Chinese. The uniform was khaki.

THE SINGAPORE VOLUNTEER CORPS

This corps was raised in 1854 and consisted of three companies of infantry, one each of Europeans, Malays, and Chinese. There were two companies of garrison artillery, a company of engineers, and a bearer company. The uniform was khaki.

THE SOUTHERN RHODESIA VOLUNTEERS

This volunteer force was raised in 1898, disbanded in 1901, and reraised in 1914. It originally consisted of two battalions of infantry. The uniform was khaki.

THE TRINIDAD LIGHT HORSE (YEOMANRY)

This yeomanry formation was raised in 1902 and perpetuated a volunteer unit originally raised in 1879. It consisted of three troops of light horse. The uniform was khaki.

THE TRINIDAD LIGHT INFANTRY (VOLUNTEERS)

This volunteer force was raised in 1902 and perpetuated a volunteer unit originally raised in 1879. It consisted of five companies of infantry. The uniform was khaki.

THE TRINIDAD BATTERY OF GARRISON ARTILLERY

This battery of garrison artillery was raised in 1879. The uniform was khaki.

EGYPT

In 1914, Egypt was a tributary state of the Turkish (Ottoman) Empire ruled by a hereditary prince known as a khedive, a title equivalent to a king. For various reasons, such as the strategic location of Egypt and the Suez Canal, Egypt had been under British occupation since 1882 with British officials assisting the government and British officers overseeing the command of the Egyptian Army. The badge illustrated above was worn by British officers attached to the Egyptian Army.

The Sudan was an Anglo-Egyptian condominium created by an agreement between Great Britain and Egypt in 1899 to share sovereignty in governing the Sudan. Defence of the Sudan was entrusted to the Egyptian Army, which included Sudanese units.

In 1914, the Egyptian Army was organized as follows: four squadrons of cavalry (one of which was Sudanese), four batteries of field artillery, three companies of garrison artillery, a camel corps of three camel companies and one mule company, nine Egyptian infantry battalions, and six Sudanese infantry battalions. In addition, there were small engineering and departmental corps units.

In 1914, the following British forces were stationed in Egypt and the Sudan:

3rd (Prince of Wales's) Dragoon Guards, Cairo, Egypt

2nd Battalion, Devonshire Regiment, Cairo, Egypt

1st Battalion, Worcestershire Regiment, Cairo, Egypt

2nd Battalion, Gordon Highlanders, Cairo, Egypt

2nd Battalion, Northamptonshire Regiment, Alexandria, Egypt.

1st Battalion, Suffolk Regiment, Khartoum, Anglo-Egyptian Sudan

Formations of the Royal Artillery, the Corps of Royal Engineers, a horse transport company of the Army Service Corps, and detachments of other departmental corps were also stationed in Egypt and the Sudan.

Due to the fact that the Turkish (Ottoman) Empire joined with Germany in World War I, Egypt was declared a British protectorate in December 1914.

BIBLIOGRAPHY

Barnes, R. Money, Major. *A History of the Regiments and Uniforms of the British Army.* London: Seeley Service & Co. 1950.

Barnes, R. Money, Major. *The Uniforms and History of the Scottish Regiments.* London: Seeley Service & Co. 1956.

Barnes, R. Money, Major. *Military Uniforms of Britain and the Empire.* London: Seeley Service & Co. 1960.

Barnes, R. Money, Major. *The British Army of 1914.* London: Seeley Service & Co. 1968.

Barthorp, Michael and Burns, Jeffrey. *Indian Infantry Regiments.* London: Osprey Publishing, Ltd. 1979.

Bowen, Frank C. *The King's Navy.* London: Methuen & Co. 1925.

Bowling, A.H. *Indian Cavalry Regiments.* London: Almark Publishing Co., Ltd. 1971.

"Butcher Watercolours, The". Unpublished paintings on cardboard of Indian and Imperial Service regiments circa 1914. Reference # 6803/10 (1-9). National Army Museum, London.

Campbell, D. Alistair, Major. *The Dress of the Royal Artillery.* London. Royal Artillery Institution. 1971. Cambridge, Marquess of. Unpublished letters, notes, etc. Reference # 8208-728-5. National Army Museum, London.

Carmen, W.Y. *Indian Army Uniforms Under the British from the 18th Century to 1947; Cavalry.* London: Leonard Hill (Books) Ltd. 1961.

Carmen, W.Y. *Indian Army Uniforms Under the British from the 18th Century to 1947; Infantry, Artillery, Engineers.* London: Morgan-Grampian. 1969.

Chichester, Henry Manners and Burges-Short, George. *Records and Badges of the British Army.* London: Gale and Polden, Ltd. 1900.

Corbett, D.A. *The Regimental Badges of New Zealand.* Auckland: Ray Richards Publishing. 1980.

Cox, Reginald H.W. *Military Badges of the British Empire, 1914-1918.* London: Ernest Benn, Ltd. 1982.

Dupuy, R. Ernest and Dupuy, Trevor N. *The Encyclopedia of Military History.* New York: Harper and Row. 1986.

Ellis, Chris and Bishop, Denis. *Military Transport of World War I Including Vintage Vehicles and Post War Models.* London: Blandford Press, Ltd. 1970.

Encyclopedia Brittanica, (various articles). Encyclopedia Britannica, Ltd. Chicago, London, Toronto, Geneva: 1910 Edition.

Encyclopedia Brittanica, (Various articles). Encyclopedia Britannica, Ltd. Chicago, London, Toronto, Geneva: 1961 Edition.

Festberg, Alfred. *Australian Army Lineage Book.* Historical Society of Australia. Melbourne, 1965.

Festberg, Alfred. *Australian Army Guidons and Colours.* Allara Publishing Co., Melbourne, 1972.

Fyfe, Christopher. *A History of Sierra Leone.* Oxford: Oxford University Press. 1962.

Harris, R.G. *Fifty Years of Yeomanry Uniforms.* London: Frederick Muller, Ltd. 1972.

Hering, P.G., Squadron Leader. *Customs and Traditions of the Royal Air Force.* Aldershot, Hants. Gale and Polden. 1961.

Hughes, B.P., Major General. *Honour Titles of the Royal Artillery.* Dorset: The Dorset Press. 1988.

Jackson, Donovan. *India's Army.* London: Sampson, Low, Marston & Co., Ltd. 1940.

Jaipur, H.H., the Maharajah of. *A History of the Indian State Forces.* New Delhi: Orient Longmans, Ltd. 1967.

Jane, Fred T. *Janes Fighting Ships, 1914.* London: Sampson, Low, Marston & Co., Ltd. 1914.

Land Forces of British Dominions, Colonies and Protectorates (Other than India): Part IV (1909), Part V (1910). London: Government Printing Office.

Lunt, C.B.E., James, Major General. *Imperial Sunset.* London: MacDonald. 1981.

MacMunn, G.B., Major and Lovett, A.C., Major. *The Armies of India.* London: A & C Black, Ltd. 1910.

Malcom, C.A. *The Piper in Peace and War.* London: John Murray. 1927.

Manchester, William. *The Last Lion: Winston Spencer Churchill; Visions of Glory.* Boston-Toronto: Little Brown & Company. 1983.

Mazeaz, Daniel. *Insignes Armee Canadienne, 1900-1914.* (Privately printed in France, date unknown).

Mollo, Boris. *The Indian Army.* Poole, Dorset: Blandford Press. 1981.

Quarterly Army List (United Kingdom) July 1914. London: Government Printing Office. 1914.

Quarterly Army List of the Dominion of Canada Corrected to June 1914. Ottawa: Government Printing Office. 1914.

Ross, David and Chartrand, Rene. *Canadian Militia Dress Regulations 1907,* illustrated with amendments to 1914. St. John, N.B. The New Brunswick Museum. 1977.

Seton, Bruce, Sir, Brevet Colonel and, Grant, John, Pipe Major. *The Pipes of War.* Glasgow: Maclehose, Jackson & Co. 1920.

Smith, D.J. *Discovering Horse Drawn Transport of the British Army.* Aylesbury, Bucks: Shire Publications. 1977.

Smith, Hugh H. *Army, Air Force and Naval Colours and Flags in South Africa, 1652-1978.* Documentation Service of the South African Defence Force. Grahamstown: 1980.

Stewart, Charles H. *The Concise Lineages of the Canadian Army.* Privately printed. Toronto: 1982.

Swinson, Arthur (edited by). *A Register of the Regiments and Corps of the British Army.* London: The Archive Press. 1972.

Sydenham, Lord of Combe. *India and the War.* London: Hodder and Stoughton. 1915.

Taylor, Arthur. *Discovering Military Traditions.* Aylesbury, Bucks. Shire Publications. 1969.

The State of Johore, Malaya. Singapore: The Advertising and Publicity Bureau, Ltd. 1939.

Tylden, G. Major. *The Armed Forces of South Africa.* Parow, Cape Province. Cape Times, Ltd. 1954.

Westlake, Ray. *The Territorial Force, 1914.* Newport, South Wales: Ray Westlake-Military Books. 1988.

Wicksteed, M.R., Major. *The New Zealand Army.* Wellington. P.D. Hasselberg, Government Printer. 1982.

The following books by Byron Farwell provide a valuable insight to attitudes and conditions of British and Empire military forces prior to 1914.

Queen Victoria's Little Wars. Harper & Row, New York, 1972. Allen Lane/The Penguin Press, London, 1973. Paperback: W.W. Norton, New York, 1985.

Mr. Kipling's Army. New York, W.W. Norton, 1981. Published in the United Kingdom under the title, *For Queen and Country,* by Allen Lane/The Penguin Press, London, 1981. Paperback: New York, W.W. Norton, 1987.

The Gurkhas. New York, W.W. Norton, 1984, London. Allen Lane/The Penguin Press, 1984. Paperback: Penguin, 1985 and Norton, 1990.

Armies of the Raj: From the Great Indian Mutiny to Independence, 1858-1947. New York, W.W. Norton, 1989. London, Viking, 1990.

INDEX

Numbers in italic type refer to illustration pages.

Abegweit Light Infantry, 133
Adelaide Rifles, 147
Aden Troop, *163,* 215
Administrative and Instructional Staff, Australia, *122,* 139
Agra Volunteer Rifles, 267
Albert Park Infantry, 146
Alberta Dragoons, 93
Alberta Hussars, 93
Alberta Rangers, 93
Alderney Artillery, 82
Alexandra, Princess of Wales's Own (Yorkshire Regiment), 55, *110*
Algonquin Rifles, 135
Allahabad Volunteer Rifles, 268
Alwar Infantry, *183,* 258
Alwar Lancers, *183,* 258
Angus and Dundee Battalion, 65
Annapolis Regiment, 132
Antigua Defence Force, 277
Ardeer Company, 56
Ardwick Battalion, 71
Argenteuil Rangers (Duke of York's Royal Canadian Hussars), 93
(Argyll and Sutherland Highlanders) Princess Louise's, 75, *116*
(Argyll Highlanders), Victoria Regiment, 134
Argyll Light Infantry, 129
Argyllshire Battalion, 75
Armagh Militia, 75
Armed Constabulary of North Borneo, *192,* 276
Army Bearer Corps, *182,* 257
Army Clothing Department, *181,* 256
Army Hospital Corps, *182,* 257
Army Ordnance Department and Corps, 83, *118*
Army Pay Corps and Department, 82, *117*
Army Remount Department, *181,* 256
Army Service Corps, 83, 84, *118*
Army Veterinary Corps, 83, *118*
Army Veterinary Service, *182,* 257
Artillery, Australia, Citizen Military Forces, 142
Artillery, Canada, Militia, 94, 95
Artillery, India, Volunteers, 267
Artillery, Royal Australian, Permanent Force, *122,* 139
Artillery, Royal Canadian, Permanent Force, 89, *120*
Artillery, Royal New Zealand, Permanent Force, *123,* 153

Artillery, Royal Regiment of, Great Britain, 45, 46, *105, 106, 107,* 215
Artillery, New Zealand Territorial Force, 154, 155
Artillery, South Africa, Active Citizen Force, 196
Artists Rifles, 80
Assam-Bengal Railway Volunteer Rifles, 268
Assam Valley Light Horse, 266
Auckland Mounted Rifles, 153
Auckland Regiment (Countess of Ranfurly's Own), 155
Australian Army Medical Corps, Citizen Force, 149
Australian Army Medical Corps, Permanent Section, *122,* 140
Australian Army Service Corps, Citizen Force, 149
Australian Army Service Corps, Permanent Section, *122,* 140
Australian Army Veterinary Corps, Citizen Force, 149
Australian Army Veterinary Corps, Permanent Section, *122,* 140
Australian Horse, 141
Australian Nursing Service, 149
Australian Rifles, 145
Ayrshire (Earl of Carrick's Own) Yeomanry, 40

Bahawalpur Camel Transport Corps, *183,* 258
Bahawalpur Infantry, 271
Bahawalpur Mounted Escort, *183,* 258
Ballarat Regiment, 147
Baluch Horse, *162,* 214
Baluchistan Infantry, *178,* 251
Baluchistan Volunteer Rifles, 268
Banff and Donside Battalion, 73
Bangalore Rifle Volunteers, 268
Barbados Volunteer Force, 277
Baria Ranjit Infantry, 271
Baroda Artillery, 271
Baroda Cavalry, 271
Baroda Guards (Infantry), 271
Baroda Infantry, 1st., 271
Baroda Infantry, 2nd., 271
Barossa Light Horse, 142
Bechuanaland Rifles, 195
Bedfordshire Militia, 54
Bedfordshire Regiment, 54, *110*
Bedfordshire Yeomanry, 43

Belize Light Infantry Volunteers, 277
Belize Mounted Infantry Volunteers, 277
Benares Infantry, 271
Bendigo Infantry, 147
Bengal and North-Western Railway Volunteer Rifles, 268
Bengal Lancers (1st-19th Cavalry, India), 203-208
Bengal-Nagpur Railway Volunteer Rifle Corps, 268
Berar Infantry, *175,* 243
Berkshire Yeomanry, 41
Bermuda Militia Artillery, 277
Bermuda Volunteer Rifle Corps, 277
Bharatpur Infantry, *183,* 259
Bharatpur Transport Corps, *183,* 259
Bhavanagar Infantry, 271
Bhavanagar Lancers, *184,* 259
Bhopal Infantry, 9th., *166,* 220
Bhopal Sultana Infantry, 271
Bhopal (Victoria) Lancers, *184,* 259
Bihar Light Horse, 266
Bikaner Camel Corps, *184,* 259
Bikaner Dungar Lancers, 271
Bikaner Sadul Light Infantry, *184,* 259
Black Watch (Royal Highland Regiment), 65, *113*
Blackheath and Woolwich Battalion, 79
Blue Mountains Infantry, 145
Blythswood Battalion, 72
Bodyguards, India, *124,* 201
Boesmanland Independent Dismounted Rifle Squadrons, 196
Boesmanland Independent Mounted Rifle Squadrons, 195
Bombay, Baroda and Central India Railway Volunteer Rifles, 268
Bombay Light Horse, 266
Bombay Volunteer Artillery, 267
Bombay Volunteer Artillery (Electrical Engineer Co.), 267
Bombay Volunteer Rifles, 268
Boothby Infantry, 147
Border Battalion, 57
Border Horse, 93
Border Light Horse, 194
Border Mounted Rifles, 193, 194
Border Regiment, 62, *112*
Botha Ruiters, 194
Brahmans, 1st., *165,* 218
Brahmans, 3rd., *165,* 219
Brant Dragoons, 93

Brecknockshire Battalion, 57
Brighton Rifles, 146
British Columbia Horse, 30th., 94
British Columbia Horse, 31st., 94
British Columbia Regiment, (Artillery), 95
British Guiana Militia, 277
Brockville Rifles, 130
Brownlow's Punjabis, *167,* 224
Bruce Regiment, 130
Buchan and Formartin Battalion, 73
Buckinghamshire Battalion, 65
Buckinghamshire Yeomanry (Royal Bucks Hussars), 41
Buffs, The, (East Kent Regiment), 50, *108*
Burma Infantry, *175,* 242
Burma Railways Volunteer Corps, 268

Calcutta Light Horse, 266
Calcutta Port Defence Volunteer Corps (Electrical Engineer Co.), 267
Calcutta Port Defence Volunteer Corps, Naval Division, 20
Calcutta Port Defense Volunteers, Artillery, 267
Calcutta Scottish Volunteers, 268
Calcutta Volunteer Rifles, 1st Battalion, 268
Calcutta Volunteer Rifles, 2nd (Presidency) Battalion, 268
Calgary Rifles, 135
Cambridgeshire Regiment, 81
Cameron Highlanders of Canada, 133
Cameron Highlanders, The Queen's Own, 74, *116*
Cameronians (Scottish Rifles), 58, *111*
Campaspie Light Horse, 142
Canadian Army Medical Corps, 90, *121*
Canadian Army Medical Corps (Militia), 136
Canadian Army Pay Corps, 91, *121*
Canadian Army Service Corps, 90, *121*
Canadian Army Service Corps (Militia), 136
Canadian Army Veterinary Corps, 91, *121*
Canadian Army Veterinary Corps (Militia), 136
Canadian Highlanders, 134
Canadian Ordnance Corps, 90, *121*
Canadian Ordnance Corps (Militia), 136
Canadian Postal Corps (Militia), 136
Canadian Signal Corps (Militia), 95
Canterbury Highland Rifle Volunteers, *Note* 157
Canterbury Irish Rifle Volunteers, *Note* 157
Canterbury Regiment, 155
Canterbury Yeomanry Cavalry, 153
Cape Field Artillery, Prince Alfred's Own, 196
Cape Fortress Engineers, 196
Cape Garrison Artillery, 196
Cape Light Horse, 194
Cape Medical Corps, 193, 198
Cape Medical Volunteer Staff Corps, 193, 198
Capetown Highlanders, Duke of Connaught and Strathearn's Own, 197
(Carabiniers) Dragoon Guards, 32, *101*
Carabiniers de Sherbrooke, 131
Carleton Light Infantry, 132
Carnarvonshire and Anglesey Battalion, 57
Carnatic Infantry, 73rd., *173,* 237
Carnatic Infantry, 75th., *173,* 238
Carnatic Infantry, 79th., *173,* 238
Carnatic Infantry, 80th., *173,* 239
Carnatic Infantry, 86th., *174,* 240
Carnatic Infantry, 88th., *174,* 241
Cavalry, 4th., *125,* 204
Cavalry, 5th., *125,* 204

Cavalry, 8th., *126,* 205
Cavalry, 12th., *126,* 206
Cavalry, 16th., 127, 207
Cavalry, 17th., 127, 208
Cavalry, Australia—see Light Horse
Cavalry, Canada, Militia, 91-94
Cavalry, Canada, Permanent Force, 88-89
Cavalry (Frontier Force), 23rd., 128, 210
Cavalry (Frontier Force), 25th., 128, 210
Cavalry, India, 203-215
Cavalry, New Zealand—see Mounted Rifles, New Zealand
Cavalry of the Line Regiments, Great Britain, 30-39
Cavalry, South Africa,—see Mounted Rifles, South Africa.
Cavalry, Special Reserve, Great Britain, 44
Cavalry regiments, Territorial Force, Great Britain—See Yeomanry regiments.
Cavan Militia, 75
Cawnpore Volunteer Rifles, 268
Central African Rifles, 275
Central Albert Horse, 94
Central Queensland Light Horse, 140
Central South African Railway Volunteers, 198
Ceylon Artillery Volunteers, 277
Ceylon Engineer Volunteers, 278
Ceylon Light Infantry, 277
Ceylon Mounted Rifles, 277
Ceylon Planters Rifle Corps, 278
Ceylon Regiment, 277
Ceylon Volunteer Medical Corps, 277
Chamba Infantry, 271
Channel Islands Militia, 82
Chaplains Department, 85
Chasseurs Canadiens, 96
Chateauguay and Beauharnois Regiment, 132
Chauras Bodyguard, 271
Cheshire Regiment, 56, *111*
Cheshire (The Earl of Chester's) Yeomanry, 40
Chinese Regiment, 277
Chota-Nagpur Light Horse, 266
Cinque Ports Battalion, 62
City of Ballarat Infantry, 147
City of Bristol Battalion, 59
City of Dundee Battalion, 65
City of Glasgow Battalion, 72
City of London Battalions, 78
(City of London Regiment), Royal Fusiliers, 51, 78, *109*
City of London Yeomanry (Rough Riders), 43
City of Melbourne Regiment, 147
(City of Sydney) 25th Infantry, 145, 148
Civil Service Rifles, 79
Cochin Infantry, 271
Coke's Rifles (Frontier Force), *171,* 233
Colchester and Hants Rifles, 133
Coldstream Guards, 48, *108*
Collingwood Infantry, 146
Colonial Forces, 273-278
Connaught Rangers, 75, *116*
Cooch Behar Infantry, 271
Coorg and Mysore Rifles, 268
Corangamite Light Horse, 142
Corps of Guides, Canada, Militia, 95
Corps of Guides, India, Queen Victoria's Own, *124,* 202
Corps of Military Police, 82, *117*
Corps of Military Staff Clerks, 91, *121*
Corps of Royal Engineers, 46, 47, *107,* 217, 218
Corps of Royal Engineers (Militia) Malta Division, 278

Cossipore Artillery Volunteers, 267
County of London Battalions, 78-80
Cumberland Battalion, 62
Cumberland and Westmorland Battalion, 62
Cumberland Regiment, 134
Cureton's Multanis, 127, 207

Daly's Horse, 128, 209
Darling Downs Light Horse, 141
Darling Downs Regiment, 144
Deccan Horse, 20th., 128, 209
Deccan Horse, 29th., *161,* 211
Deccan Infantry, 97th., *175,* 243
Deccan Infantry, 99th., *176,* 244
Deeside Highland Battalion, 73
De La Rey's Ruiters, 195
Denbighshire Battalion, 57
Denbighshire Yeomanry, 40
Deoli Regiment, *170,* 230
Departmental Corps, Australia, Citizen Military Forces, 149
Departmental Corps, Australia, Permanent Force, 140
Departmental Corps, Canada, Militia, 136
Departmental Corps, Canada, Permanent Force, 90, 91
Departmental Corps, Great Britain, 82-84
Departmental Corps, India, 256-258
Departmental Corps, New Zealand, Territorial Force, 157
Departmental Corps, South Africa, Active Citizen Force, 198
Derby Militia, 1st., 66
Derby Militia, 2nd., 66
Derbyshire Yeomanry, 41
Derwent Infantry, 148
Devon Militia, 52
Devonshire Regiment, 52, *109*
Dharangada Makhwan Infantry, 271
Dholpur Makhuan Infantry, 271
Diamond Fields Artillery, 197
Diamond Fields Horse, 197
Dismounted Rifles, South Africa, Active Citizen Force, 195-196
Dogras, 37th., *169,* 229
Dogras, 38th., *169,* 229
Dogras, 41st., *170,* 230
Dorchester Regiment, 134
Dorset Militia, 63
Dorset Yeomanry, The Queen's Own, 41
Dorsetshire Regiment, 63, *113*
Dragoons, 2nd (Canada), 92
Dublin County Militia, 77
Duchess of Connaught's Own Baluchistan Infantry, *178,* 250
Dufferin Rifles of Canada, 130
Duke of Cambridge's Hussars, 41
(Duke of Cambridge's Own) Lancers, 37, *104*
Duke of Cambridge's Own Lancers (Hodson's Horse), *126,* 205
Duke of Cambridge's Own (Middlesex Regiment), 69, *114*
Duke of Cambridge's Own Punjabis, *167,* 224
Duke of Connaught's Lancers (Watson's Horse), 127, 206
Duke of Connaught's Own Baluchis, *179,* 252
Duke of Connaught's Own Battalion, 62
Duke of Connaught's Own Lancers, *161,* 212
Duke of Connaught's Own Rajputs, *165,* 220
Duke of Connaught's Own Rifles, 96
Duke of Connaught's Royal Canadian Hussars, 92
Duke of Cornwall's Light Infantry, 61, *112*
Duke of Cornwall's Own Rifles, 131

INDEX 283

Duke of Edinburgh's Own Rifles, 197
Duke of Edinburgh's (Wiltshire Regiment), 70, *115*
Duke of Lancaster's Own Yeomanry, 40
Duke of Wellington's (West Riding Regiment), 61, *112*
Duke of York's Own Lancers (Skinner's Horse), *125,* 203
Duke of York's Own Loyal Suffolk Hussars, 42
Duke of York's Royal Canadian Hussars (Argenteuil Rangers), 93
Dumbartonshire Battalion, 75
Dumfries and Galloway Battalion, 57
Dunedin Highland Rifle Volunteers, *Note* 157
Durban Garrison Artillery, 196
Durban Light Infantry, 197
Durham Light Infantry, 72, *115*
Durham Militia, 1st., 72
Durham Militia, 2nd., 72
Durham Regiment, 131

Earl Grey's Own Rifles, 135
(Earl of Chester's) Battalion, 56
East Africa Rifles, 275
East Battalion, 82
East Coast Volunteer Rifles, 268
East Indian Railway Volunteer Rifles, 268
East Indian Railway Volunteer Rifles (Engineer Co.), 267
East Kent Militia, 50
(East Kent Regiment), The Buffs, 50, *108*
East Kootenay Regiment, 135
East Lancashire Regiment, 60, *112*
East Melbourne Regiment, 147
East Riding of Yorkshire Yeomanry, 44
East Surrey Regiment, 60, *112*
East Sydney Regiment, 145
East York Militia, 54
East Yorkshire Regiment, 54, *110*
Eastern Bengal State Railway Volunteer Rifles, 268
Eastern Bengal Volunteer Rifles, 268
Edinburgh Light Infantry Militia, 49
Edmonton Fusiliers, 135
Egypt-Egyptian Army, 279
(Empress of India's) Lancers, 39, *105*
Engineers, Australia, Citizen Military Forces, 143
Engineers, Canada, Militia, 95
Engineers, Corps of Royal, Great Britain, 46, 47, *107,* 217, 218
Engineers, India, Volunteers, 267
Engineers, New Zealand, Territorial Force, 155
Engineers, Royal Australian, Permanent Force, *122,* 139
Engineers, Royal Canadian, Permanent Force, 89, *120*
Engineers, South Africa, Active Citizen Force, 196
Erinpura Regiment, *170,* 230
Escort to the British Resident—Nepal, *124,* 202
Essendon Rifles, 146
Essex Fusiliers, 129
Essex Regiment, 66, *113*
Essex (Rifles) Militia, 66
Essex Yeomanry, 43

Faiz Light Infantry, 272
Falkland Islands Volunteer Corps, 278
Fane's Horse, 128, 208
Faridkot Infantry, 272
Faridkot Sappers and Miners, *184,* 260

Fateh Paltan, 271
Fermanagh Militia, 58
Fife and Forfar Yeomanry, 43
Fife Battalion, 65
Finsbury Rifles, 79
First Aid Nursing Yeomanry, *Note* 85
First City of Grahamstown Volunteers, 197
First Eastern Rifles, 197
First Surrey Rifles, 80
Flinders Light Horse, 142
Flintshire Battalion, 57
Foot, 1st., 49
Foot, 2nd., 49
Foot, 3rd., 50
Foot, 4th., 50
Foot, 5th., 50
Foot, 6th., 51
Foot, 7th., 51
Foot, 8th., 51
Foot, 9th., 52
Foot, 10th., 52
Foot, 11th., 52
Foot, 12th., 53
Foot, 13th., 53
Foot, 14th., 54
Foot, 15th., 54
Foot, 16th., 54
Foot, 17th., 54
Foot, 18th., 55
Foot, 19th., 55
Foot, 20th., 55
Foot, 21st., 56
Foot, 22nd., 56
Foot, 23rd., 57
Foot, 24th., 57
Foot, 25th., 57
Foot, 26th., 58
Foot, 27th., 58
Foot, 28th., 59
Foot, 29th., 59
Foot, 30th., 60
Foot, 31st., 60
Foot, 32nd., 61
Foot, 33rd., 61
Foot, 34th., 62
Foot, 35th., 62
Foot, 36th., 59
Foot, 37th., 62
Foot, 38th., 63
Foot, 39th., 63
Foot, 40th., 64
Foot, 41st., 64
Foot, 42nd., 65
Foot, 43rd., 65
Foot, 44th., 66
Foot, 45th., 66
Foot, 46th., 61
Foot, 47th., 67
Foot, 48th., 67
Foot, 49th., 67
Foot, 50th., 68
Foot, 51st., 68
Foot, 52nd., 65
Foot, 53rd., 69
Foot, 54th., 63
Foot, 55th., 62
Foot, 56th., 66
Foot, 57th., 69
Foot, 58th., 67
Foot, 59th., 60
Foot, 60th., 70
Foot, 61st., 59
Foot, 62nd., 70
Foot, 63rd., 70

Foot, 64th., 71
Foot, 65th., 71
Foot, 66th., 67
Foot, 67th., 62
Foot, 68th., 72
Foot, 69th., 64
Foot, 70th., 60
Foot, 71st., 72
Foot, 72nd., 73
Foot, 73rd., 65
Foot, 74th., 72
Foot, 75th., 73
Foot, 76th., 61
Foot, 77th., 69
Foot, 78th., 73
Foot, 79th., 74
Foot, 80th., 63
Foot, 81st., 67
Foot, 82nd., 64
Foot, 83rd., 74
Foot, 84th., 71
Foot, 85th., 69
Foot, 86th., 74
Foot, 87th., 74
Foot, 88th., 75
Foot, 89th., 74
Foot, 90th., 58
Foot, 91st., 75
Foot, 92nd., 73
Foot, 93rd., 75
Foot, 94th., 75
Foot, 95th., 66
Foot, 96th., 70
Foot, 97th., 68
Foot, 98th., 71
Foot, 99th., 70
Foot, 100th., 76
Foot, 101st., 76
Foot, 102nd., 77
Foot, 103rd., 77
Foot, 104th., 76
Foot, 105th., 68
Foot, 106th., 72
Foot, 107th., 62
Foot, 108th., 58
Foot, 109th., 76
Foot Guards, Great Britain, 47, 48
Fort Garry Horse, 94
Frontenac Regiment, 131
Frontier Garrison Artillery, 216
Frontier Militia, India, 270
Fusiliers, 7th, 96

Galway Militia, 75
Gambia Artillery Volunteers, 278
Gambia Company, 274
Gardner's Horse, *125,* 203
Garhwal Rifles, *169,* 229
Gilgit Scouts, 270
Gippsland Light Horse, 141
Glamorgan Battalion, 64
Glamorgan Yeomanry, 43
Glasgow Highlanders, 72
Gloucestershire Regiment, 59, *112*
Golconda Lancers, 272
Gold Coast Regiment, 274
Gold Coast Volunteers, 278
Goldfields Regiment, 148
Gordon Highlanders (Canada), 131
Gordon Highlanders (Great Britain), 73, *116*
Gordon's Horse, *161,* 212
Governor's Bodyguard, Bengal, *124,* 201
Governor's Bodyguard, Bombay, *124,* 201
Governor's Bodyguard, Madras, *124,* 201

Governor General's Bodyguard (Canada), 91
Governor General's Bodyguard (India), *124,* 201
Governor General's Foot Guards, 95
Graaf Reinet Ruiters, 195
Great Indian Peninsula Railway Volunteer Rifle Corps, 269
Grenadier Guards, 47, *108*
Grenadier Guards of Canada, 95
Grenadiers, 101st., *176,* 244
Grenville Regiment (Lisgar Rifles), 132
Grey Regiment, 130
Grey's Horse, 93
Griqualand West Ruiters, 195
Guernsey Artillery, 82
Guernsey Engineers, 82
Gurkha Rifles, 4th., *179,* 254
Gurkha Rifles, 6th., *179,* 254
Gurkha Rifles, 7th., *179,* 255
Gurkha Rifles, 8th., *179,* 255
Gurkha Rifles, 9th., *179,* 255
Gurkha Rifles, 10th., *179,* 256
Gurkha Rifles (Frontier Force), 5th., *179,* 254
Gurkhas, Brigade of, India, 179-180, 253-256
Gwalior Infantry (Imperial Service Troops), *185,* 260
Gwalior Infantry (State Force), 272
Gwalior Lancers, *184,* 260
Gwalior Transport Corps, *185,* 260

Hackney Battalion, 78
Haldimand Rifles, 130
Halifax Regiment (Artillery), 95
Halifax Rifles, 132
Hallamshire Battalion, 71
Halton Rifles, 129
Hampshire Carabiniers Yeomanry, 41
Hampshire Militia, 62
Hampshire Regiment, 62, *113*
Hants Regiment, 133
Hariana Lancers, *126,* 205
Hastings Rifles, 131
Hauraki Regiment, 156
Hawkes Bay Regiment, 156
Hazara Pioneers, *176,* 246
Herefordshire Regiment, 81
Hertfordshire Militia, 54
Hertfordshire Regiment, 81
Hertfordshire Yeomanry, 41
Highland Borderers Militia, 75
Highland Cyclist Battalion, 81
Highland Light Infantry, 72, *115*
Highland (Light Infantry) Militia, 74
Highland (Rifle) Militia, 73
Highlanders, 48th., 131
Hindmarsh Infantry, 147, 149
Hobson's Bay Infantry, 146, 149
Hodson's Horse, *126,* 205
Hoeveld Schutters, 195
Hogeveld Ruiters, 194
Hong Kong Regiment, 277
Hong Kong-Singapore Battalion, 46
Hong Kong Volunteer Corps, 278
Honourable Artillery Company, 80
Household Cavalry, Great Britain, 29-30, 100
Hunter River Infantry, 144
Hunter River Lancers, 141
Huntingdon Militia, 70
Huntingdonshire Cyclist Battalion, 81
Huron Regiment, 130
Hussars, 1st (Canada), 91
Hussars, 4th (Canada), 92
Hussars, 7th (Canada), 92
Hussars, 11th (Canada), 92

Hussars, 13th (Great Britain), 36, *103*
Hussars, 20th (Great Britain), 38, *104*
Hyderabad Infantry, 272
Hyderabad Lancers (Nizam's Own), *185,* 261
Hyderabad Volunteer Rifles, 269

Illawarra Infantry, 145
Illawarra Light Horse, 142
Imperial Light Horse, 194
Imperial Service Troops, India, 258-266
Indi Light Horse, 141
Indian Army Corps of Clerks, *182,* 258
Indian Medical Department, *181,* 257
Indian Medical Service, 257
Indian Mountain Artillery, *163,* 215-216
Indian Ordnance Department, *182,* 257
Indian State Forces, 270-272
Indore Mounted Escort, *185,* 261
Indore Transport Corps, *185,* 261
Infantry, 12th (Australia), 144
Infantry, 13th (Australia), 144
Infantry, 17th (Australia), 144
Infantry, 18th (India), *167,* 223
Infantry, 26th (Australia), 145
Infantry, 33rd (Australia), 145, 149
Infantry, 34th (Australia), 145
Infantry, 38th (Australia), 145
Infantry, 39th (Australia), 145
Infantry, 98th (India), *175,* 244
Infantry, 108th (India), *177,* 246
Infantry, 109th (India), *177,* 247
Infantry, 112th (India), *177,* 247
Infantry, 113th (India), *177,* 248
Infantry, 119th (The Mooltan Regiment), *178,* 249
Infantry regiments and Cyclist battalions, unaffiliated, of the Territorial Force, Great Britain, 78-81
Infantry, Australia, Citizen Military Forces, 143-148
Infantry, Canada, Militia, 95-96, 129-135
Infantry, Canada, Permanent Force, 90, *120*
Infantry, India, 218-252
Infantry, New Zealand, Territorial Force, 155-157
Infantry of the Line regiments with affiliated Militia and Territorial battalions, Great Britain, 49-77
Infantry, South Africa, Active Citizen Force, 197-198
(Inniskilling) Dragoons, 34, *102*
Inns of Court Officers Training Corps, 80
Intelligence Corps, Australia, 143
(Irish) Battalion, Liverpool Regiment, 51, 52
Irish Fusiliers of Canada, 96
Irish Guards, 48, *108*
Irish Rifle Volunteers, *Note* 157
Isle of Man Volunteer Battalion, 51
Isle of Wight Rifles, Princess Beatrice's, 62

Jacob's Horse, *162,* 213
Jacob's Rifles, *179,* 252
Jaipur Transport Corps, *186,* 261
Jamaica Militia Artillery, 278
Jat Light Infantry, *165,* 220
Jats, 10th., *166,* 221
Jersey Artillery, 82
Jind Infantry, *186,* 261
Jodhpur (Sardar Rissalah) Lancers, *186,* 262
Johore Military Force, *192,* 276
Johore Volunteer Force, 278
Joliette Regiment, 134
Junagarah Lancers, *186,* 262

Kaffarian Rifles, 197
Kalat Infantry, 272
Karachi Artillery Volunteers, 267
Karachi Artillery Volunteers (Electrical Engineer Co.) 267
Karoo Schutters, 196
Karpurthala (Jagjit) Infantry, *186,* 262
Karpurthala (Paramjit) Infantry, 272
Kashmir Infantry, *187,* 263
Kashmir Lancers, *186,* 262
Kashmir Mountain Artillery, *187,* 263
Kashmir Rifles, *187,* 263
Kennedy Regiment, 143
Kensington Battalion, 79
Kent Cyclist Battalion, 81
Kent Regiment, 129
Kerry Militia, 76
Khairpur Camel Transport Corps, *187,* 263
Khairpur Mounted Escort, *187,* 263
Khelat-i-Gilzie Regiment, *166,* 221
Khyber Rifles, 270
Kildare Militia, 77
Kilkenny Militia, 55
Kimberley Light Horse, 197
Kimberley Mounted Corps, 197
Kimberley Regiment, 197
Kimberley Rifles, 197
King Edward's Horse (The King's Overseas Dominions Regiment), 44
King Edward's Own Cavalry, *125,* 204
King Edward's Own Grenadiers, *176,* 245
King Edward's Own Gurkha Rifles (The Sirmoor Regiment), *179,* 253
King Edward's Own Lancers (Probyn's Horse), *126,* 206
King George's Own Baluchis (Jacob's Rifles), *179,* 252
King George's Own Central India Horse, 38th., *163,* 214
King George's Own Central India Horse, 39th., *163,* 214
King George's Own Ferozepore Sikhs, *166,* 222
King George's Own Gurkha Rifles (The Malaun Regiment), *179,* 253
King George's Own Lancers, 127, 208
King George's Own Light Cavalry, *161,* 210
King George's Own Pioneers, *172,* 234
King George's Own Sappers and Miners, *164,* 217
King's African Rifles, *191,* 275
King's Canadian Hussars, 93
King's County Militia, 76
(King's) Dragoon Guards, 30, 100
(King's) Hussars, 36, *103*
(King's Own) Hussars, 33, *102*
King's Own Malta Regiment of Militia, 278
King's Own (Royal Lancaster Regiment), 50, *108*
King's Own Scottish Borderers, 57, *111*
King's Own Stafford Militia, 1st., 63
King's Own Stafford Militia, 2nd., 71
King's Own Stafford Militia, 3rd., 71
King's Own Tower Hamlets Militia, 77
King's Own (Yorkshire Light Infantry), 68, *114*
(King's Royal Irish) Hussars, 35, *102*
King's Royal Rifle Corps, 70, *115*
King's, The (Shropshire Light Infantry), 69, *114*
(King's, The) Hussars, 37, *104*
King's, The (Liverpool Regiment), 51, *109*
Kolar Gold Fields Rifle Volunteers, 269
Kolhapur Infantry, 272

Kooyong Infantry, 146
Krugersdorp Ruiters, 194
Kuring-Gai Infantry, 144
Kurram Militia, 270

Lachlan Mac Quarie Infantry, 146
Lake Superior Regiment, 135
Lambton Regiment (St. Clair Borderers), 129
Lanark and Renfrew Regiment, 130
Lanark Battalion, 72
Lanarkshire Yeomanry, 40
Lancashire Fusiliers, 55, *110*
Lancashire Hussars Yeomanry, 43
Lancers, 32nd., *162,* 212
Launceston Infantry, 148
Leeds Rifles, 54
Leicestershire Militia, 54
Leicestershire Regiment, 54, *110*
Leicestershire Yeomanry (Prince Albert's Own), 40
Leichardt Infantry, 145, 148
Leinster Regiment (Royal Canadians), The Prince of Wales's, 76, *116*
Lichtenburg Ruiters, 196,
Life Guards, 1st., 29, 100
Life Guards, 2nd., 30, 100
Light Cavalry, 27th., *161,* 211
Light Cavalry, 28th., *161,* 211
Light Horse, 15th., 93
Light Horse, 16th., 93
Light Horse, 27th., 94
Light Horse, 29th., 94
Light Horse regiments, Australia, Citizen Military Forces, 140-142
Light Horse Volunteers, India, 266
Light Infantry, 5th, *165,* 219
Lincoln and Welland Regiment, 131
Lincoln Regiment, 129
Lincolnshire Regiment, 52, *109*
Lincolnshire Yeomanry, 43
(Lisgar Rifles) Grenville Regiment, 132
Liverpool Irish, 51, 52
(Liverpool Regiment), The King's, 51, *109*
Liverpool Scottish, 51, 52
Logan and Albert Infantry, 144
London Irish Rifles, 79
London Regiment, 78-80
London Rifle Brigade, 78
London Scottish, 79
Lord Strathcona's Horse (Royal Canadians), 89, *120*
(Lothian Regiment), The Royal Scots, 49, *108*
Lothians and Border Horse Yeomanry, 42
Lovat's Scouts Yeomanry, 1st., 44
Lovat's Scouts Yeomanry, 2nd., 44
Loyal North Lancashire Regiment, 67, *114*
Loyal Regiment, *167,* 223
Lucknow Regiment, *166,* 223
Lucknow Volunteer Rifles, 269
Ludhiana Sikhs, *166,* 222
Lunenburg Regiment, 133

Madras and Southern Mahratta Railway Rifles, 269
Madras Artillery Volunteers (Electrical Engineer Co.), 267
Madras Artillery Volunteers (The Duke's Own), 267
Madras Volunteer Guards, 269
Maharajah Jayajirao's Battalion, 272
Maharajah Kumari Kamla Raje's Own Light Horse, 271
Maharajah Sakhya Battalion, 272
Mahratta Light Infantry, 103rd., *176,* 245

Mahratta Light Infantry, 105th., *176,* 246
Mahratta Light Infantry, 110th., *177,* 247
Mahrattas, 114th., *177,* 248
Mahrattas, 116th., *177,* 248
Mahrattas, 117th., *177,* 248
Makran Levies, 270
Malabar Volunteer Rifles, 269
(Malaun Regiment, The) King George's Own Gurkha Rifles, *179,* 253
Malay States Guides, *192,* 275
Malerkotla Sappers and Miners, *187,* 263
Manawatu Mounted Rifles, 154
Manchester Regiment, 70, *115*
Manitoba Dragoons, 92
Manitoba Horse, 94
Manitoba Rangers, 135
Melbourne University Rifles, 147
Merioneth and Montgomery Battalion, 57
Mewar Infantry, 272
Mewar Lancers,—see Udaipur Lancers
Mharwara Regiment, *170,* 230
Middlesex Light Infantry, 129
(Middlesex Regiment), The Duke of Cambridge's Own, 69, *114*
Midland Schutters, 195
Midlandse Ruiters, 194
military bands, 86
Military Farms Department, *182,* 258
Mississauga Horse, 92
Monmouthshire Regiment, 81
Montgomeryshire Yeomanry, 42
Montmagny and L'Islet Regiment, 132
Montreal Siege Company (Artillery), 95
Mooltan Regiment, *178,* 249
Morayshire Battalion, 73
Moreton Regiment, 143
Moulmein Volunteer Artillery, 267
Moulmein Volunteer Rifles, 269
Mount Alexander Infantry, 147
Mount Royal Rifles, 132
Mounted Riflemen, South Africa, Permanent Force, *123,* 160-161
Mounted Rifles, 18th., 93
Mounted Rifles, India, Volunteers, 266-267
Mounted Rifles, New Zealand, Territorial Force, 153-154
Mounted Rifles, South Africa, Active Citizen Force, 193-195
Murray's Jat Lancers, 127, 207
Mussoorie Volunteer Rifles, 269
Mysore Cavalry, 272
Mysore Infantry, 272
Mysore Lancers, *188,* 264
Mysore Transport Corps, *188,* 264

Nabha Infantry, *188,* 264
Nagpur Volunteer Rifles, 269
Naini Tal Volunteer Rifles, 269
Napier's Rifles, *178,* 251
Natal Carabineers, 1st., 193
Natal Carabineers, 2nd., 193
Natal Field Artillery, 196
Natal Mounted Rifles, 193, 194
Natal Volunteer Medical Corps, 198
Navanagar (Choti-Khas) Lancers, *188,* 264
Navanagar (Shatrushalya) Infantry, 272
Nelson Mounted Rifles, 154
Nelson Regiment, 156
Nepal Escort, *124,* 202
New Brunswick Dragoons, 94
New Brunswick Rangers, 133
New Brunswick Regiment (Artillery), 95
Newcastle Regiment, 144
New England Light Horse, 141

New South Wales Irish Rifle Regiment, 145, *Note* 149
New South Wales Lancers, 141
New South Wales Mounted Rifles, 141
New South Wales Scottish Rifles, 145, *Note* 148
New Zealand Army Medical Corps, 157
New Zealand Army Service Corps, 157
New Zealand Chaplains Department, 157
New Zealand Engineers, 155
New Zealand Engineer Volunteers, 155
New Zealand Medical Corps Nursing Reserve, 157
New Zealand Permanent Staff, *123,* 152
New Zealand Post and Telegraph Corps, 155
New Zealand Railway Corps, 155
New Zealand Signal Corps, 155
New Zealand Staff Corps, *123,* 152
New Zealand Veterinary Corps, 157
Nicolet Regiment, 133
Nigeria Regiment, 274
Nilgiri Volunteer Rifles, 269
Noordelike Transvaal Bereden Schutters, 194
Noordelike Transvaal Grens Wag, 195
Norfolk Militia, 52
Norfolk Regiment, 52, *109*
Norfolk Rifles, 130
Norfolk Yeomanry Dragoons (The King's Own Royal Regiment), 43
North Auckland Mounted Rifles, 154
North Auckland Regiment, 157
North Canterbury Regiment and Westland Regiment, 156
North Irish Horse, 44
North Otago Rifles, 156
North Queensland Light Horse, 142
North Somerset Yeomanry, 40
(North Staffordshire Regiment), Prince of Wales's Own, 71, *115*
North Sydney Infantry, 144
North Tipperary Militia, 55
North Waziristan Militia, 270
North-Western Railway Volunteer Rifles, 269
Northampton and Rutland Militia, 67
Northamptonshire Regiment, 67, *114*
Northamptonshire Yeomanry, 44
Northern Bengal Mounted Rifles, 266
Northern Cyclist Battalion, 81
Northern Mounted Rifles, 198
Northern Pioneers, 129
Northern Rhodesia Police (Military Wing), *191,* 275
Northern River Lancers, 141
Northern Scouts, 270
Northumberland Fusiliers, 50, *109*
Northumberland Hussars, 40
Northumberland Militia, 50
Northumberland Regiment, 40th., 130
Northumberland Regiment, 73rd., 133
(Nottingham and Derbyshire Regiment), Sherwood Foresters, 66, *114*
Nottingham (Sherwood Rangers) Yeomanry, 39
Nurses, Canada—see Canadian Army Medical Corps Militia

Ontario Regiment, 130
Oranje Skerpschutters, 196
Otago Hussars, 154
Otago Mounted Rifles, 154
Otago Rifles, 155
Oudh and Rohilkhand Railway Volunteer Rifles, 269
Outram's Rifles, *178,* 250

286 FORCES OF THE BRITISH EMPIRE—1914

Oxford Militia, 65
Oxford Rifles, 129
Oxfordshire and Buckinghamshire Light Infantry, 65, *113*
Oxley Battalion, 144

Palamcottah Light Infantry, *172, 235*
Parramatta Infantry, 144
Pathans, 40th., *169,* 229
Patiala Infantry, 1st., *188,* 265
Patiala Infantry, 2nd., *189, 265*
Patiala (Rajinder) Lancers, *188,* 264
Peel Regiment, 130
Pembroke Yeomanry, 41
Penang Volunteers, 278
Perth Infantry, 148
Perth Regiment, 129
Perthshire Battalion, 65
Peshin Scouts, 270
Peterborough Rangers, 132
Pictou Regiment (Highlanders), 133
Pioneers, 12th (Khelat-i-Gilzie Regiment), *166,* 221
Pioneers, 48th, *170, 231*
Pioneers, 64th, *172, 235*
Pioneers, 81st, *173, 239*
Pioneers, 107th, *176, 240*
Pioneers, 121st, *178, 249*
Pioneers, 128th, *179, 252*
Poona Volunteer Rifles, 269
Poplar and Stepney Rifles, 79
Port Curtis Infantry, 143
Port Phillip Horse, 142
Post Office Rifles, 78
Potechefstroom Ruiters, 194
Prahan Infantry, 146
President Brand's Regiment, 196
Pretoria Regiment, 198
Prince Albert Volunteers, 131
(Prince Albert's Own) Hussars, 36, *103*
Prince Albert's (Somerset Light Infantry, 53, *110*
Prince Albert Victor's Own Cavalry (Frontier Force) (Daly's Horse), 128, 129
Prince Albert Victor's Own Poona Horse, *162,* 213
Prince Albert Victor's Rajputs, *165,* 219
Prince Alfred's Guard, 197
Prince Edward Island Light Horse, 94
Prince Edward Regiment, 129
Prince of Wales's Battalion, 53
(Prince of Wales's) Canadian Dragoons, 92
(Prince of Wales's) Dragoon Guards, 31, 100
Prince of Wales's Leinster Regiment (Royal Canadians), 76, *116*
Prince of Wales's (North Staffordshire Regiment), 71, *115*
Prince of Wales's Own Regiment of Peninsula Rifles, 198
(Prince of Wales's Own Royal) Hussars, 35, *103*
Prince of Wales's Own (West Yorkshire Regiment), 53, *110*
(Prince of Wales's Royal) Lancers, 36, *103*
Prince of Wales's Volunteers (South Lancashire Regiment), 64, *113*
Princes Hill Infantry, 146
(Princess Charlotte of Wales's) Dragoon Guards, 31, *101*
Princess Charlotte of Wales's (Royal Berkshire Regiment), 67, *114*
Princess Louise's (Argyll and Sutherland Highlanders), 75, *116*
Princess Louise's Dragoon Guards, 92

Princess Louise's Fusiliers, 132
Princess Louise's New Brunswick Hussars, 92
Princess of Wales's Own Rifles, 96
(Princess Royal's) Dragoon Guards, 32, *101*
Princess Victoria's (Royal Irish Fusiliers), 74, *116*
Probyn's Horse, *126,* 206
Punjab Light Horse, 266
Punjab Rifles (Frontier Force), *171,* 233
Punjab Volunteer Rifles, 269
Punjabis, 19th., *167,* 224
Punjabis, 21st., *167,* 224
Punjabis, 22nd., *167,* 224
Punjabis, 24th., *167,* 225
Punjabis, 25th., *168,* 225
Punjabis, 26th., *168,* 226
Punjabis, 27th., *168,* 226
Punjabis, 28th., *168,* 226
Punjabis, 29th., *168,* 226
Punjabis, 30th., *168,* 227
Punjabis, 31st., *168,* 227
Punjabis, 33rd., *169,* 228
Punjabis, 46th., *170,* 231
Punjabis, 62nd., *172,* 235
Punjabis, 66th., *172,* 236
Punjabis, 67th., *172,* 236
Punjabis, 69th., *172,* 236
Punjabis, 72nd., *173,* 237
Punjabis, 74th., *173,* 237
Punjabis, 76th., *173,* 238
Punjabis, 82nd., *174,* 239
Punjabis, 84th., *174,* 240
Punjabis, 87th., *174,* 241
Punjabis, 89th., *174,* 241
Punjabis, 90th., *174,* 241
Punjabis, 92nd., *175,* 242
Punjabis (Light Infantry), 91st, *175, 242*

Quebec and Levis Regiment (Artillery), 95
Quebec Regiment, 134
Queen Alexandra's Imperial Military Nursing Service, 85, *119*
Queen Alexandra's Own Gurkha Rifles, *179,* 253
(Queen Alexandra's Own Royal) Hussars, 38, *104*
Queen Alexandra's Royal Naval Nursing Service, 20
Queen Mary's Own Baluch Light Infantry, *179,* 251
(Queen Mary's Own) Hussars, 38, *104*
Queen Victoria's Own Corps of Guides (Frontier Force) (Lumsden's) 124, 202
Queen Victoria's Own Light Cavalry, *162,* 212
Queen Victoria's Own Rajput Light Infantry, *165,* 218
Queen Victoria's Rifles, 78
Queen Victoria's Own Sappers and Miners, *164,* 217
(Queen's Bays) Dragoon Guards, 31, 100
Queen's County Militia, 76
Queen's Edinburgh Rifles, 49
Queen's Own Cameron Highlanders, 74, *116*
Queen's Own Dorset Yeomanry, 41
(Queen's Own) Hussars, 4th., 33, *102*
(Queen's Own) Hussars, 7th., 34, *102*
Queen's Own Oxfordshire Hussars, 42
Queen's Own Rifles of Canada, 95
Queen's Own Royal Glasgow and Lower Ward of Lanarkshire Yeomanry, (Dragoons), 42
Queen's Own Royal Tower Hamlets Militia, 77

Queen's Own (Royal West Kent Regiment), 68, *114*
Queen's Own West Kent Yeomanry (Hussars), 42
Queen's Own Wocestershire Hussars, 42
Queen's Own Yorkshire Dragoons, 40
(Queen's Royal) Lancers, 35, *103*
(Queen's, The) County of London Battalion, 22nd., 80
(Queen's, The) County of London Battalion, 24th., 80
(Queen's, The) Lancers, 37, *104*
(Queen's, The) Royal West Surrey Regiment, 49, *108*
Queen's Westminster Rifles, 79
Queensland Mounted Infantry, 141
Queenstown Volunteers, 197

Railway Pioneer Regiment, 198,
Rajendra Hazari Guards, 272
Rajpipla State Infantry, 272
Rajputana Infantry, 120th., *178,* 249
Rajputana Infantry, 122nd., *178,* 250
Rajputs, 8th., *165,* 220
Rajputs, 11th., *166,* 221
Rajputs, 13th (The Shekhawati Regiment), *166,* 222
Rajputs, 16th (The Lucknow Regiment), *166,* 223
Rampur Infantry, *189,* 265
Rampur (Rohilla) Lancers, *189,* 265
Rand Light Infantry, 198
Rangers, The, 79
Rangoon Port Defence Volunteer Corps (Electrical Engineer Co.), 267
Rangoon Port Defence Volunteers (The Duke's Own) Artillery, 267
Rangoon Volunteer Rifles, 269
Rattray's Sikhs, *170,* 231
Regiment, 17th, 129
Regiment, 25th, 129
Regiment, 85th, 134
Regiment, 98th, 135
Renfrewshire Battalions, 75
Reste Vrijstaatse Regiment, 194
Rifle Brigade, (The Prince Consort's Own), 77, *117*
Rifles (City of London) Battalion, 78
Rifles, India, Volunteers, 267-270
Rifles of Canada, 60th., 132,
Riverina Infantry, 146
Robin Hood Battalion, 66
Rocky Mountain Rangers, 135
Roscommon Militia, 75
Ross Highland Battalion, 73
Rough Riders, Lancers, City of London Yeomanry, 43
Royal Aberdeenshire Militia, 73
Royal Antrim Militia, 74
Royal Army Medical Corps, 84, *119*
Royal Australian Engineers, *122,* 139
Royal Australian Field Artillery, *122,* 139
Royal Australian Garrison Artillery, *122,* 139
Royal Australian Navy, 23
Royal Ayr and Wigtown Militia, 56
Royal Berkshire Militia, 67
(Royal Berkshire Regiment), Princess Charlotte of Wales's, 67, *114*
Royal Canadian Dragoons, 88, *120*
Royal Canadian Engineers, 89, *120*
Royal Canadian Garrison Artillery, 89, *120*
Royal Canadian Horse Artillery, 89, *120*
Royal Canadian Navy, 23
Royal Canadian Regiment, 90, *120*

INDEX 287

Royal Cheshire Militia, 56
Royal Cornwall Rangers Militia, 61
Royal Cumberland Militia, 62
Royal Denbigh and Flint Militia, 57
(Royal) Dragoons, 32, *101*
Royal Dublin City Militia, 77
Royal Dublin Fusiliers, 77, *117*
Royal East Kent Yeomanry (The Duke of Connaught's Own), 41
Royal East Middlesex Militia, 69
Royal Elthorne Militia, 69
Royal Engineers, Corps of, 46, 47, *107,* 217, 218
Royal Engineers (Militia) Malta Division, 278
Royal Field Artillery, 45, 46, *106*
Royal First Devonshire Yeomanry, 42
Royal Fleet Reserve, 20
Royal Flying Corps, 86, *119*
Royal Fusiliers (City of London Regiment), 51, 78, *109*
Royal Garrison Artillery, 45, 46, *106,* 107, *164,* 216
Royal Glamorgan Militia, 64
Royal Gloucestershire Hussars, 41
Royal Grenadiers, 96
Royal Guernsey Light Infantry, 82
(Royal Highland Regiment) Black Watch, 65, *113*
Royal Highlanders of Canada, 96
Royal Horse Artillery, 45, *105*
Royal Horse Guards (The Blues), 30, 100
Royal Indian Marine, 23
Royal Inniskilling Fusiliers, 58, *111*
(Royal Irish) Dragoon Guards, 31, *101*
(Royal Irish Fusiliers), Princess Victoria's, 74, *116*
(Royal Irish) Lancers, 34, *102*
Royal Irish Regiment, 55, *110*
Royal Irish Rifles, 74, *116*
Royal Lanark Militia, 1st., 72
Royal Lanark Militia, 2nd., 58
Royal Lancashire Militia, 1st., 50
Royal Lancashire Militia, 2nd., 51
Royal Lancashire Militia, 3rd., 67
Royal Lancashire Militia, 4th., 64
Royal Lancashire Militia, 5th., 60
Royal Lancashire Militia, 6th., 71
Royal Lancashire Militia, 7th., 55
Royal Lancaster Regiment (King's Own), 50, *108*
Royal Limerick County Militia, 76
Royal London Militia, 51
Royal Malta Artillery, *190,* 273
Royal Marine Artillery, 24, *99*
Royal Marine Light Infantry, 24, *99*
Royal Meath Militia, 76
Royal Middlesex Militia, 70
Royal Militia of the Island of Jersey, 82
Royal Munster Fusiliers, 76, *116*
Royal Naval Air Service, 20, *119*
Royal Naval Reserve, 20
Royal Naval Volunteer Reserve, 20
Royal Navy, 20-23, *99*
Royal Newfoundland Naval Reserve, 20
Royal New Zealand Artillery, *123,* 153
Royal North Devon Yeomanry (Hussars), 42
Royal North Down Militia, 74
Royal North Lincolnshire Militia, 52
Royal Perth Militia, 65
Royal Regiment, 96
Royal Regiment of Artillery, 45, 215
Royal Renfrew Militia, 75
Royal Rifles, 96
Royal Scots Fusiliers, 56, *111*

(Royal Scots Greys) Dragoons, 33, *101*
Royal Scots (Lothian Regiment), 49, *108*
Royal Sherwood Foresters Militia, 66
Royal South Down Militia, 74
Royal South Gloucestershire Militia, 59
Royal South Middlesex Militia, 51
Royal South Wales's Borderers Militia, 57
Royal Surrey Militia, 1st., 60
Royal Surrey Militia, 2nd., 49
Royal Surrey Militia, 3rd., 60
Royal Sussex Militia, 62
Royal Sussex Regiment, 62, *112*
Royal Tyrone Militia, 58
Royal Warwickshire Regiment, 51, *109*
Royal Welsh Fusiliers, 57, *111*
(Royal West Kent Regiment), Queen's Own, 68, *114*
(Royal West Surrey Regiment), The Queen's, 49, *108*
Royal Westminster Militia, 51
Royal Wiltshire Militia, 70
Royal Wiltshire Yeomanry (Prince of Wales's Own Royal Regiment), 39 Ruahine Regiment, 157
Russell's Infantry, 94th., *175,* 243
Russell's Infantry, 95th., *175,* 243

Saguenay Regiment, 129
(St. Clair Borderers), Lambton Regiment, 129
St. George's English Rifle Regiment, 145, Note 148
St. Hyacinthe Regiment, 134
St. John Fusiliers, 132
St. Pancras Battalion, 79
Sam Browne's Cavalry (Frontier Force), 128, 209
Sappers and Miners, India, 217-218
Sappers and Miners, 3rd., 218
Saskatchewan Light Horse, 93
Saskatchewan Rifles, 135
Saskatoon Fusiliers, 135
Sarawak Naval Force, 276
Sarawak Rangers, *192,* 276
Sawai Man Guards, 272
Scinde Horse, *162,* 213
Scinde Rifles (Frontier Force), *172,* 234
Scots Guards, 48, *108*
(Scottish) Battalion, Liverpool Regiment, 51, 52
Scottish Borderers, (King's Own), 57, *111*
Scottish Borderers Militia, 57
Scottish Horse, 1st., 44
Scottish Horse, 2nd., 44
Scottish Horse Mounted Rifle Volunteers, Note 154
Scottish Light Dragoons, 92
(Scottish Rifles), The Cameronians, 58, *111*
Seaforth Highlanders of Canada, 133
Seaforth Highlanders (Ross-shire Buffs, The Duke of Albany's), 73, *115*
Semana Rifles, 270
Sharpshooters, 3rd County of London Yeomanry, 43
Shekhawati Regiment, *166,* 222
Sherbrooke Regiment, 131
Sherwood Foresters,(Nottingham and Derbyshire Regiment), 66, *114*
Shetland Islands Companies, 73
(Shropshire Light Infantry), King's The, 69, *114*
Shropshire Militia, 69
Shropshire Yeomanry (Dragoons), 39
Sierra Leone Battalion, 274

Sierra Leone Company, Royal Garrison Artillery, 46
Signal Corps, Canada, Militia, 95
Sikh Pioneers, 23rd., *167,* 225
Sikh Pioneers, 32nd., *168,* 227
Sikh Pioneers, 34th., *169,* 228
Sikhs, 35th., *169,* 228
Sikhs, 36th., *169,* 228
Sikhs, 47th., *170,* 231
Sikhs (Frontier Force), 51st., *171,* 232
Sikhs (Frontier Force), 52nd., *171,* 232
Sikhs (Frontier Force), 53rd., *171,* 232
Sikhs (Frontier Force), 54th., *171,* 233
Simcoe Foresters, 130
Simla Volunteer Rifles, 269
Simur Sappers and Miners, *189,* 265
Sind Volunteer Rifles, 269
Singapore Volunteer Corps, 278
(Sirmoor Regiment, The) King Edward's Own Gurkha Rifles, *179,* 253
Skinner's Horse, Duke of York's Own Lancers, *125,* 203
Skinner's Horse, 3rd., *125,* 203
Somaliland Camel Corps, *191,* 275
(Somerset Light Infantry), Prince Albert's, 53, *110*
Somerset Militia, 53
Soo Rifles, 131
South African Medical Corps, 198
South African Mounted Riflemen, Permanent Force, *123,* 160, 193
South African Ordnance Department, 198
South African Service Corps, 198
South Andaman Volunteer Rifles, 270
South Australian Mounted Rifles, 142
South Australian Scottish Regiment, 147, Note 149
South Battalion, 82
South Canterbury Mounted Rifles, 154
South Canterbury Regiment, 155
South Cork Militia, 76
South Indian Railway Volunteer Rifles, 270
South Irish Horse, 44
(South Lancashire Regiment), Prince of Wales's Volunteers, 64, *113*
South Nottinghamshire Hussars, 40
South Otago Rifles, 156
South Staffordshire Regiment, 63, *113*
South Wales Borderers, 57, *111*
South Waziristan Militia, 270
Southern Mounted Rifles, 194
Southern Provinces Mounted Rifles, 267
Southern Rhodesia Volunteers, 278
Southern Rifles, 1st., 195
Southern Rifles, 2nd., 195
Southland Mounted Rifles, 154
Southland Rifles, 156
Staffordshire Yeomanry, (Queen's Own Royal Regiment), 39
Stanstead Dragoons, 94
Steyn's Bereden Schutters, 194
Stormont and Glengarry Regiment, 132
Sudanese units—see Egypt-Egyptian Army
Suffolk Regiment, 53, *109*
Suket Infantry, 272
Supply and Transport Corps, *181,* 256
Surma Valley Light Horse, 266
Surrey Yeomanry (Queen Mary's Regiment), 43
Sussex Yeomanry, 43
Sutherland and Caithness Highland Battalion, 73
Sydney University Scouts, 146

Taranaki Rifles, 156
Tasmanian Mounted Infantry, 142
Tasmanian Rangers, 148
Tehri-Garhwal Sappers and Miners, *189*, 266
Tembuland Light Horse, 194
Temiscouata and Soulanges Hussars, 134
Thal Scouts, 270
Tiwana Lancers, 208
Tochi Scouts, 270
Torrens Infantry, 148
Transkei Mounted Rifles (1909), 194
Transkei Mounted Rifles (1913), 195
Transvaal Cycle and Motor Corps, 198
Transvaal Cycle Corps, 198
Transvaal Horse Artillery, 196
Transvaal Medical Volunteers, 198
Transvaal Scottish, 197
Travancore Infantry, 1st., 272
Travancore Infantry, 2nd., 272
Trinidad Battery of Garrison Artillery, 278
Trinidad Light Horse (Yeomanry), 278
Trinidad Light Infantry (Volunteers), 278

Udaipur Lancers, *189*, 266
Uganda Rifles, 275
Umvoti Mounted Rifles, 194
United Provinces Horse, 1st., 266
United Provinces Horse, 2nd., 266
Upper Burma Volunteer Rifles, 270

Vaudrevil and Soulanges Hussars, 94
Vaughn's Rifles (Frontier Force), *171*, 234
Victoria Fusiliers, 134
Victoria Regiment (Argyll Highlanders), 134
Victoria Regiment, 45th., 131
Victoria Rifles of Canada, 95
Victorian Mounted Rifles, 141
Victorian Rangers, 147
Victorian Scottish Regiment, 146, *Note* 149
Voltigeurs de Quebec, 96
Volunteer Automobile Corps, 143
Volunteer Forces, India, 266-270

Waikato Mounted Rifles, 153
Waikato Regiment, 157
Wakefield Infantry, 148
Wallajahbad Light Infantry, *174*, 240
Wanganui Highland Rifle Volunteers, *Note* 157
Warwickshire Militia, 1st., 51
Warwickshire Militia, 2nd., 51
Warwickshire Yeomanry, 39
Waterloo Regiment, 130
Watson's Horse, 127, 206
Weald of Kent Battalion, 50
Wellesley's Rifles, *176*, 245
Wellington East Coast Mounted Rifles, 154
Wellington Highland Volunteers, *Note* 157
Wellington Rifles (Canada), 130
Wellington Rifles, (New Zealand), 156
Wellington West Coast Mounted Rifles, 153
Wellington West Coast Rifles, 156
Welsh Guards, *Note* 48
Welsh Regiment, 64, *113*
Wentworth Regiment, 133
Werriwa Infantry, 146
West Africa Regiment, *190*, 274
West African Frontier Force, Infantry, *190*, 274
West African Frontier Force, Artillery, *190*, 274
West African Frontier Force, Engineers, *191*, 274
West Battalion, 82
West India Regiment, *190*, 274
West Kent Militia, 68
(West Riding Regiment), Duke of Wellington's, 61, *112*
West Somerset Yeomanry (Hussars), 42
West Suffolk Militia, 53
West York Militia, 1st., 68
West York Militia, 2nd., 53
West York Militia, 3rd., 71
West York Militia, 4th., 53
West York Militia, 5th., 55
West York Militia, 6th., 61

(West Yorkshire Regiment), Prince of Wales's, 53, *110*
Western Australian Mounted Infantry, 142
Western Australian Rifles, 148
Western Province Mounted Rifles, 194
Western Province Rifles, 1st., 195
Western Province Rifles, 2nd., 195
Western Province Rifles, 3rd., 195
Westminster Dragoons, 2nd County of London Yeomanry, 43
Westminster Fusiliers of Canada, 135
Westmorland and Cumberland Yeomanry, 41
Wide Bay Infantry, 143
Wilde's Rifles (Frontier Force), *171*, 233
(Wiltshire Regiment), Duke of Edinburgh's, 70, *115*
Winnipeg Grenadiers, 135
Winnipeg Light Infantry, 135
Winnipeg Rifles, 134
Witwatersrand Rifles, 198
Woollahra Infantry, 144
Worcester Militia, 59
Worcestershire Regiment, 59, *112*

Yarra Borderers, 146
Yarrowee Light Horse, 142
Yeomanry regiments of the Territorial Force, Great Britain, 39-44
Yercaud Rifle Volunteers, 270
York and Lancaster Regiment, 71, *115*
York Militia, 1st., 68
York Rangers, 96
York Regiment, 133
Yorkshire Hussars (Alexandra, Princess of Wales's Own), 39
(Yorkshire Light Infantry), King's Own, 68, *114*
(Yorkshire Regiment), Alexandra, Princess of Wales's Own, 55, *110*

Zhob Militia, 270
Zululand Mounted Rifles, 194